Hill Economies and Sustainable Development in India

About the Editors

Sushanta Kumar Nayak is a Professor of Economics at Rajiv Gandhi University, Itanagar. He is the Head of Department of Economics of the University and is having a number of prestigious publications in refereed and peer review Journals. He has coordinated many major projects of the government such as Arunachal Pradesh State Development Report, Evaluation of Flagship Programmes and Evaluation of State Finances of Arunachal Pradesh.

Lijum Nochi is an Assistant Professor of Economics at Rajiv Gandhi University. Itanagar and is having a good number of publications in refereed, peer review Journals and edited volumes. He has presented more that 20 papers in National and International Seminars and has coordinated two workshops. He has contributed chapters in major studies like Evaluation of Flagship Programmes and Evaluation of State Finances of Arunachal Pradesh.

Maila Lama is an Assistant Professor of Economics at Rajiv Gandhi University. Itanagar and is having a good number of publications in refereed, peer review Journals and edited volumes. He has presented about 20 papers in National and International Seminars and has contributed chapters in major studies like Evaluation of Flagship Programmes, Evaluation of State Finances of Arunachal Pradesh. He has completed one major project sponsored by ICSSR, New Delhi and also completed two minor projects.

Hill Economies and Sustainable Development in India

Emerging Realities

Edited by

Sushanta Kumar Nayak
Lijum Nochi
Maila Lama

CONCEPT PUBLISHING COMPANY PVT. LTD.
NEW DELHI-110059

ISBN-13: 978-93-88937-25-2

First Published 2019

Published and Printed by

Concept Since 1974

Concept Publishing Company Pvt. Ltd.
A/15-16, Commercial Block, Mohan Garden,
New Delhi-110059 (INDIA)
T: 91 11 25351460, 91 11 25351794
E: publishing@conceptpub.com; *W*: www.conceptpub.com

Cataloging in Publication Data--Courtesy: D.K. Agencies (P) Ltd. <docinfo@dkagencies.com>

National Seminar on 'Hill Economies and Sustainable Development in India: Challenges and Prospects' (2018 : Itanagar, India)
Hill economies and sustainable development in India : emerging realities / edited by Sushanta Kumar Nayak, Lijum Nochi, Maila Lama.
pages cm
"This book is based on the papers presented in the National Seminar on 'Hill Economies and Sustainable Development in India: Challenges and Prospects' organised by the Centre for Development Studies (CDS), Department of Economics, Rajiv Gandhi University, Itanagar, Arunachal Pradesh from 5th to 6th February, 2018"—Acknowledgements.
Includes bibliographical references and index.
ISBN 9789388937252

1. Sustainable development—India, Northeastern—Congresses. 2. Sustainable development—India—Congresses. 3. India, Northeastern—Economic conditions—Congresses. I. Nayak, Sushanta Kumar, editor. II. Nochi, Lijum, editor. III. Lama, Maila, editor. IV. Rajiv Gandhi University. Department of Economics. Centre for Development Studies, organizer. V. Title.

LCC HC440.E5N38 2018 | DDC 338.92709541 23

Foreword

The hill regions of India have diverse resource base, potentialities and socio-cultural differentiations. The mountains play a pivotal role in the delivery of ecosystem services such as regulation of climate, water and air quality, tourism, recreation and spiritual experiences which are essential for sustaining the well-being of the people. However, the industrial base is generally weak in the hills and services sector largely consists of government aided activities. Therefore, the hill economies have to depend on Central fund transfers for promoting development. The development in these economies is largely driven by the exogenous factors rather than endogenous momentum of growth.

Although the hill economies are rich in natural resources, yet many of the hill States have not been able to harness their rich resources for economic progress. Some hill states like Himachal Pradesh, Uttarakhand and Sikkim have achieved high economic progress but the North Eastern hill states are lagging far behind. There are many challenges of development being faced by the hill states such as scarcity of both physical and human resources, high cost of infrastructure development, limited arable land. The industrialization is the primary mover of development but there is a need to establish that type of industry which is suitable for the region given the geographical conditions. Every hill state has its own comparative advantage in resource base and potentials. The policy should be designed to create sufficient amount of incentives so as to translate potentials into reality. The emphasis should be laid on such activities which would put them on the path of sustainable development.

In this direction, the efforts of the editors in compilation of this book by highlighting the issues and challenges of sustainable development in the hills economies of India entitled '*Hill Economies and Sustainable*

Development in India: Emerging Realities' are appreciable and note-worthy. The book will be useful to the researchers as well as policy planners in designing the policies for sustainable development in the hill states.

Prof. N.C. Roy
Department of Economics
Rajiv Gandhi University
Itanagar, Arunachal Pradesh

Acknowledgements

This book is based on the papers presented in the National Seminar on '*Hill Economies and Sustainable Development in India: Challenges and Prospects*' organised by the Centre for Development Studies (CDS), Department of Economics, Rajiv Gandhi University, Itanagar, Arunachal Pradesh from 5th to 6th February, 2018. We are thankful to the Centre for Development Studies (CDS), Department of Economics, Rajiv Gandhi University for providing financial support in organising the National Seminar and also for financially supporting the publication of this edited volume. Our heartiest thank also goes to all the faculty members of the Department of Economics, Rajiv Gandhi University for their cooperation and help during the seminar. We are also thankful to research scholars and Post Graduate students of the Department of Economics, Rajiv Gandhi University for extending help in various capacities during the seminar. Last but not the least, we are grateful to all the paper contributors without whom this edited volume would not have seen light of the day.

Editors

Contents

List of Contributors

Abdus Samad, Department of Forestry, North Eastern Regional Institute of Science and Technology, Nirjuli, Arunachal Pradesh. **Email:** *asamad969@gmail.com*

Anup Kr. Das, Department of Economics, Rajiv Gandhi University, Arunachal Pradesh-791112, **Email:** *anupdas97@gmail.com*

Apilang Apum, Department of Economics, Jomin Tayeng Government Model Degree College, Roing, Arunachal Pradesh.

Bhabesh Hazarika, National Institute of Public Finance and Policy, New Delhi.

B. Singh, Department of Forestry, North Eastern Regional Institute of Science and Technology, Nirjuli, Arunachal Pradesh.

Dhanraj Rai, Department of Political Science, Sikkim Government College, Gyalshing, Sikkim. **Email:** *dhanraj15pols@gmail.com*

Dil B. Gurung, Department of Economics, Rajiv Gandhi University, Arunachal Pradesh-791112. **Email:** *gurung_dil@rediffmail.com*

Dol Bahadur Thapa, Department of Economics, Rajiv Gandhi University, Arunachal Pradesh-791112.

Gebi Basar, Department of Humanities and Social Sciences, North Eastern Regional Institute of Science and Technology, Arunachal Pradesh.

Gibji Nimasow, Department of Geography, Rajiv Gandhi University, Arunachal Pradesh. **Email:** *gibji.nimasow@rgu.ac.in*

Gulshan Chaddha, Principal, National Institute of Mountaineering and Allied Sports, Dirang, Arunachal Pradesh.

K.J. Joseph, St. Joseph College, Darjeeling, West Bengal.

Kul Bahadur Chettri, Department of Economics, Sikkim University, Sikkim.

Lakpa Doma Sherpa, Department of Economics, Sikkim University, Sikkim.

Lilika K. Zhimomi, Department of Rural Development, University of Science and Technology Meghalaya, **Email:** *Lilikazhimomi@gmail.com*

Maila Lama, Department of Economics, Rajiv Gandhi University, Arunachal Pradesh. **Email:** *mlamargu@gmail.com*

Manash Roy, Department of Economics, Assam University, Silchar, Assam. **Email:** *manash.roy015@gmail.com*

Manoj Shukla, Department of Economics, Aggarwal College, Ballabgarh, Faridabad, Haryana. **Email:** *drmanojshukla1963@gmail.com*

M. Nagentran, Department of Economics, Thiru. Vi. Ka. Government Arts College, Thiruvarur, Tamil Nadu.

Mridul Dutta, Department of Business Administration, Tezpur University, Assam.

Mudang Tagiya, Department of Humanities and Social Sciences, North Eastern Regional Institute of Science and Technology, Arunachal Pradesh. **Email:** *mudangtagiyamanagement@gmail.com*

Niranjan Debnath, Department of Economics, Tripura University, Tripura. **Email:** *n2n.nath@gmail.com*

N. Kumar, M.S. Swaminathan Research Foundation, Chennai, Tamil Nadu.

Pallabi Dhar, Department of Economics, Assam University, Silchar, Assam.

Paranan Konwar, Department of Economics, Sonari College, Charaideo, Assam. **Email:** *ppkkpkonwar@gmail.com*

P.R. Gajurel, Department of Forestry, North Eastern Regional Institute of Science and Technology, Nirjuli, Arunachal Pradesh.

Papiya Dutta, Head, Department of Rural Development, University of Science and Technology Meghalaya.

Raju Mandal, Department of Economics, Assam University, Silchar, Assam. **Email:** *rajum06@gmail.com*

Rimjim Bordoloi, Department of Economics, Rajiv Gandhi University, Arunachal Pradesh.

R. Rajendran, P.G. and Research Department of Economics, Periyar E.V.R. College (Autonomous), Tiruchirappalli, Tamil Nadu.

Ruma Kundu, Department of Economics, Sikkim University, Sikkim.

R. Vadivelu, P.G. and Research Department of Economics, Periyar E.V.R. College (Autonomous), Tiruchirappalli, Tamil Nadu. **Email:** *vadivelu1978@gmail.com*

Salim Shah, Department of Economics, Tripura University, Tripura. **Email:** *salimshah.tu@gmail.com*

S. Sinha, Department of Humanities and Social Sciences, North Eastern Regional Institute of Science and Technology, Arunachal Pradesh.

Subrata Dutta, Sardar Patel Institute of Economic and Social Research, Ahmedabad, Gujarat. **Email:** *subratacalcutta@hotmail.com*

Surendra Rai, Department of Political Science, Sikkim Government College, Gyalshing, Sikkim. **Email:** *surendrarai210@yahoo.in*

Tashi Dorjee Bapu, Department of Geography, Rajiv Gandhi University, Arunachal Pradesh. **Email:** *tashi.bapu@rgu.ac.in*

Tridib R. Sarma, Department of Business Administration, Tezpur University, Assam.

Introduction

The present volume is the outcome of efforts put in by the Centre for Development Studies (CDS), Department of Economics, Rajiv Gandhi University. The Centre's quest is to unravel pragmatic parallels which are often either over or under looked upon. While theoretical rhetoric survives generality of principles, case studies in developmental researches reveal many contextual divergences from generality. Indeed theories, at best, are ideal realms and how far reality differs makes the quest of research. Developmental paradigms and dimensions, therefore, require decoding and deciphering such undercurrents and dynamics. In other words, the case by case differential at the backdrop of theoretical generality has to be put into context—be it historicity, social, economic or polity. In fact, the case study output or ground realities may differ either across time within a given context and across board on the socio-spatial and locational dimensions. Decoding such particular specificities in addition to the generality, not only deciphers the variations, instead, helps in creating tailored ecosystem for intervening agencies for policy and programmed interventions. Unless, such an exercise is undertaken before hand, any interventions with all good intent will be either conflicting or unsustainable which is but worse than interventions with the best of evil intentions.

Positive interventions are but the reality for the welfare state and it calls forth not only policy perspectives and its execution but also attitudinal and outlook make ups of the aspiring constituents. The diversity along the hills economy is often in diametric contrast to its plain counterparts, more so economically. Plains *per se* too are diverse, say, costal, flood plains and mainland, but are not as susceptible economically as the hills due to their peculiar characteristics. This peculiar sub-set of characteristics even within a confined spatial-location, changes with altitudinal ascend, and so does it with latitudinal shifts. The rugged topography with crisscross rivulets, rivers, gorge, valleys etc. are an ecosystem in itself sustaining varied life forms. History is witness as to how the culture, and need for subsistence and extraneous forces regulated or threatened these ecosystems. While the economic dependence cannot be put to hold for long, the sustainable symbiosis of know how is required as an approach.

With relatively lesser proportion of suitable plain lands, the challenges like food security, human settlement, urbanisation, trade off between alternative uses of resources has become an enigmatic puzzle. Even utilisation of rugged landscapes for industrious livelihood and settlement purposes escalates the cost of its utilisation, be it economic or social, making even enterprising industrious individuals to end up pondering upon competitive feasibility.

The future, however, becomes reliably predictable if the present is contextualised analytically in the projection of future. Nonetheless, the present itself has evolved upon series of past instances. Unless the relevant past or history and its impact on present day are evaluated, contextualising present for future may be often futile, rather, will not be sustained. In this regard, Joseph articulates and analyzes the historicity of the imperial interest and the Raja of Sikkim (Chapter 13). The chapter diagnostically evaluates and reveals the impact on the ecology of Darjeeling hills during the intervening period of two World Wars in serving the British imperial interest.

In the similar line, Raj and Rai, analyzes the political economy of development in Sikkim (Chapter 14). In pursuance of the neo-liberal ideas, they argue, the pertinent question of development for whom are either discarded or often disregarded. Authors have tried to build the political economy arguments as to how the shift towards neo-liberation economy without consideration to human face has backfired into conflict and threats. It tries to establish the casualty between politics and economy leading to policy execution and the welfare deprivation of the indigenous populace.

Of many pursuits in the hills agriculture is one challenging task. Samad, Singh and Gajurel have tried to contextualize the issues related to advantages that the hills of North Eastern Region posses (Chapter 1). They further advances the ideation of sustainable inroads to supply chain and the diversification through creation of various chains of value addition processes. In fact, a diversified horticultural sector backed with supply chain and value addition at various stages indeed proved sustainable for many economies. They posit this as the alternative to employment oriented livelihood options as seen in various developing and developed world.

In the similar line, Lama and Bordoloi, makes a comparative study of hills and plains with regard to production and productivity of potato (Chapter 7). Their study revealed that potato cultivation significantly contributed to both income and employment avenues in both hills and plains. It has been underpinned in the study that the productivity is higher in plains due to improved technique of cultivation. Their analysis yielded a significant positive influence by modern input on productivity. Henceforth, the need to improvise the technique of cultivation and making available the modern input becomes imperative.

Rajendran and Kumar dealt about the dynamics of agricultural developments in Kolli Hills of Tamil Nadu at backdrop of liberation period, particularly during the post liberal era (Chapter 8). Focusing on the tribal households, their study, especially emphasized on how, consequent upon liberalisation, the land use pattern changed during preceding two and a half decades which had influenced cropping pattern, diversification, post-harvest management and its sustainability. In yet another study, Nagentran and Vadivelu, briefs the narrative of animal husbandry and agricultural sustainability of the same tribal areas of Kolli Hills (Chapter 9). They examined the income and employment generation through animal husbandry and tried to map the linkages to crop sector for a better and more sustainable tribal development. It was revealed that the regularity of income generation through livestock was usually more pronounced, but less in quantum. Nonetheless, the regularity did cushion the income of the households. As is evident from the study the liberalisation of the economy did had significant impact not only upon the advanced sector and populace but also upon the laggard ones like agricultural sector and upon the Tribal's residing up in the hills in a significant and a diverse way. Lilika (Chapter 22) highlighted the importance of farming in sustaining the livelihood of tribal people in the Naga hills where the dominant form of farming is the shifting *(Jhum)* cultivation. The system is guided by the indigenous knowledge and practices that people acquired as a result of continuous exposure and rigorous experimentation with the nature that has overtime become the base of their culture and tradition. The article also discusses the role of folklores in influencing farming activities in the hills and assesses their scientific rationale.

Another force and dimension of development is that of migration and urbanization. This, however, potentially have preverse effect in hilly states. Development interventions and the ever growing governmental activities do induce related non-governmental activities. Thus, there emerges a conglomeration of populace giving rise to urban centres calling forth the need for various amenities and related engineered public health. As such, urbanization and supply of portable drinking water and sanitation not only becomes a priority but is an issue of significant importance. This issue has been addressed by Sherpa in backdrop of Sikkim (Chapter 12). The study suggests a plan need to regulate and direct the creation of required infrastructures for sustainable growth of towns in the state. In the same line, of sustainability, the issues and challenges of migration is dealt by Shukla (Chapter 15). The attempts are to elucidate the socio-economic factors responsible for migration of populace from the hills towards plains. The chapter systematically puts forth the pull factor, i.e. better livelihood options in the plains which happen to be the predominant factor of the migrants' gradual permanent settlement. Unlike the popular notion of migrant population being of lower socio-economic stratum, Shukla underlines the case of Uttarakhand where the migrant populace constitutes skilled human capital of various knowledge domains. Consequently, the trend hampers the growth and development of the origin of migration more than the contribution to the destination which is unsustainable. The footloose theory provides proof that population tends to move in towards incentivising destinations due to its prosperous spillovers.

The pull and push factors are usually due to poverty and insecure livelihood options available in the hilly states. Poverty breeds inequality and which itself further leads to dampening of development initiatives. Poverty is reflected not only in command over resources but also in skills and knowledge, physical and mental well-being and on livelihood alternatives which give rise to deprivation and therefore, differential impact on morality, outlook, thereof, growth and development. A thorough investigation of poverty in multidimensional direction is undertaken by Debnath and Shah for the North Eastern Region of India (Chapter 4). Taking a wide variety of variables such as health, education, employment, living conditions it formulated inter as well as intra-disparity in terms of multidimensional poverty index. The determinants of multidimensional poverty index revealed dependency ratio, household size, nature of employment, level of education of head of household, and cast were yielder as major non-monetary poverty determinants. A similar attempt to comparatively study the poverty, inequality and sectoral development of the hills and planes of North East India was attempted by Konwar (Chapter 3). This chapter traces the sectoral trends of poverty and inequality based on monthly per capita consumption expenditure. While underlining the poverty and inequality amongst the North Eastern States of India, it revealed that agriculture and allied sector contributed least in comparison to other sector of the economy. Hence, it is indicative that the rural sector is either progressing inadequately or the rural pursuits are changing. With this backdrop, the chapter suggests and calls for a balanced approach to development in terms of capacity expansion, infrastructural improvements and diversification of agricultural and allied activities.

Unless poverty and inequality along with issue of livelihood diversification are addressed properly, there exists the issue of households' consumption shock. In fact, one common issue either for hills or plain concerning the poor rural populace is that of households' food insecurity. The insecurity is more in the hills economy than plains, partly due to limited option of land to grow major staple, and partly due to higher transaction cost involved in the production; in dissemination of know-how and input, transportation as well as costs arising out of bottlenecks peculiar to the hills economies. This factor has been commonly perceived as the basic of food security differential between hills and plains. In this regard, Raju and Dhar (Chapter 5) attempted to identify the determinants of food insecurity with a special focus on the difference between hills and plains. Using the nationally representative household level data set of the second round of India Human Development Survey (IHDS-II) they found large scale disparities of food insecurity among the states and various socio-religious groups, and also between hilly and plain regions. Per capita income, female adult education, remittances and cultivation as the main occupation reduce the probability of food insecurity. Finally, given other factors food insecurity is found to be higher in the hills compared to the plains. Roy also addresses the issue of food security in the hilly region of North East India by constructing a composite food security index for two time periods (Chapter 6). Unlike the common perception, the study found that food security is moderate with no significant difference between the hilly States and the plains. Interestingly, the determining factor concerning the hills from plains was found to be diametrically opposed. It was availability rather than affordability and absorption instead of commonly perceived basic notion of food insecurity difference. The chapter suggests that over the period of time, the food insecurity along the hilly States has increased with slight decline at interstate level. This has become trigger for the search of alternative livelihood concerns. As such, in the line of alternative livelihood concern Bapu and Nimasow elaborately discussed how the livelihood of the rural people could be enhanced through the proper exploitation of the medicinal plants (Chapter 10). While suggesting and paving way forward, they maintain a balance approach towards the sustainable best practices and emphasises the need for conversation as well as regeneration.

While the case of livelihood has become as loose as it can be due to its attachment to wide range of activities that individuals and households undertake while managing their income-consumption shocks. It is not only extended to one dimension of managing income-consumption shocks but have of late even been attached to adventure and sports. Interestingly, what began as conservation activity of aquatic life, especially fishery, has but turned into an adventure sport and tourist attraction in Sikkim. This has been dealt in detail by Chetri and Kundu (Chapter 2). This chapter begins by recognising the fact that fisheries, in addition to supplementing the protein needs, has also turned into livelihood earnings activity of the rural populace. Of late, the activity is also proactively attracting and involving the rural youth towards setting up fishery based adventure sports enterprises attracting huge numbers of tourists. On the whole, it gives account of how fisheries can play crucial role in the hilly state and what could be done so that the activity becomes a sustainable livelihood avenue. Nonetheless, while tourism generates employment and livelihood avenues, it also brings into the scenario various impacts that have certain environmental and social implications. While significant amount of literature are found in case of environmental consequences due to tourism, it is not in case of social conflicts and are usually undermined. This is true either at policy or administration level or both simultaneously. Addressing these issues, Dutta, Chaddha and Sarma have evaluated comparatively, at length, the various dimensions upon which responsible tourism can be developed in Arunachal Pradesh (Chapter 11). They hypothesised as to how capacity building based on community model of tourism will go a long way to develop the industry without any social and ecological conflict.

One common suggestion that ran across all the chapters was the required intervention of governing dispensation. While suggestions itself are subject to discretion of those in the helm of affair, there is no denying that the existence of numbers of positive intervention schemes are indicative of the welfare intentions of the dispensation. It is needless to say that the intervention even if positive with the best of intention succeeds depending upon the public perception about it. Even entitled provisions as rights under law may not be claimed by individuals for asymmetry in information. This has perverse impact upon the public perception, thereby, rendering the interventions itself to be perceived with all negativity. Thapa attempts to understand the ground realities and the prevailing context, especially in terms of the public perception of intervention programme (MGNREGA), thereof, its working (Chapter 19). The study pertained to sample drawn from the hill state of Arunachal Pradesh reveals that there information lag. As such, despite the programme being a right in itself, the demand side claims over it are poor.

Public funding or financing has a normative dimension, even though principles of finance lie in the positive domain. While norms and normative consideration may call for greater amount of positive interventions, hence financing, the dispensation but needs also to consider the feasibility as well as its sustainable limits. In other words, it must adhere to certain principles for responsible fiscal operations. In this regard, Dutta, deals with the issue of fiscal governance of the hilly states of India (Chapter 16). The chapter, in the backdrop of FRBM (Financial Responsibility and Budget Management) Act, examines the fiscal situations and evaluates, whether or not, the revenue and capital consolidation have improved around the hilly states. In the similar line of analysis but pertaining to Arunachal Pradesh, Das and Hazarika, ascertains the areas where the state needs to concentrate to improve efficiency and revenue productivity along with compression of unproductive expenditures (Chapter 17). Specifically, the study focuses on the fact that the fiscal health of the state has improved a little after adoption of the FRBM guidelines despite its own fiscal performances being poor.

Change is a motion and motions are the laws of life. As such constant development is but fact of national life. The world after the revolutionary advent of Information Technology (IT) has become more locally accessible with almost near about symmetric information flow. In this changing IT world, the nation as a whole is also changing fast. In this context, Mudang, Sinha and Basar have tried to locate the state of Arunachal Pradesh (Chapter 18). Their chapter tries to take stock of prevailing ground realities and yields into the digital preparedness, extent of penetration and its relevance in relation to entrepreneurship in Arunachal Pradesh. The IT revolution has brought about not only dynamism but also change in outlook altogether to a higher level of plateau. Achieving commanding heights without commensuration of the benefits to all sections of society is but yield without distributive consonance. Concern arises about special attention required in this dimensions pertaining towards women and children. This is true to a developing world and specially if it has the laggard regions, late starters of development initiatives, and disadvantaged regions as hilly states. Gurung deals elaborately with the work and time utilisation of women in rural Arunachal Pradesh (Chapter 20). Dwelling upon the field data the study reveals that women folks contribute ninety per cent of their weekly time but on the activities that are either under SNA primary or SNA extended which goes unremunerated. Nonetheless, it is not only the womenfolk who undergoes unremunerated. It is also the progeny who undertakes the daily unpaid household chores. In an attempt to decipher these syntax, Apum, identifies the agrarian nature of rural set up in the hills of Arunachal Pradesh (Chapter 21). Her analysis reveals that consequent upon the lack of avenues of alternative employment, the majority of the households engage themselves in agricultural activities leaving many of the household chores and affairs to their progeny. As such, the analysis reveals that children are at drudgery with no luxury for leisure and education.

It is, therefore, important that in designing policy initiatives not only the stock of generality is underlined. Instead, while not denying the holistic approach, the peculiarities of the context upon which the initiatives are to be operationalised has to be underpinned. This will not only call forth proactive people's participation but will also endure them to self-motivate in reaching the very zeal enshrined as development. This volume with all its limitations has, therefore, attempted in bringing forth the dynamics, emerging realities, and undercurrents for further streamlining the developmental ideals and will act as major policy input to practitioners and executioners at various levels pertaining to hill economies.

26th October, 2018 **Lijum Nochi**

1
Potential of Horticulture Diversification for Enhancing Livelihood in North Eastern Region of India

Abdus Samad, B. Singh and *P.R. Gajurel*

Introduction

The North Eastern Region (NER) of India comprises of eight states, viz. Assam, Arunachal Pradesh, Manipur, Meghalaya, Mizoram, Nagaland, Sikkim and Tripura. The region covers about 8 per cent of the total geographical area of the country. The economy of the NER is primarily agro-based with 77 per cent of the working population engaged in agricultural and allied activities (Gautam and Handa, 2012). However, agriculture of the region is characterized by traditional subsistence farming techniques, low level of modern input use, lack of farm mechanisation, low level of productivity, huge post-harvest loss of perishable products, lack of processing and value addition, poor marketing system, poor infrastructure etc. among others.

There are several factors contributing to the present state of agriculture in the region. One of the important reasons is lack of adequate market and value additions to agricultural and allied produce, which makes it a less attractive and low remunerative occupation. In such situations, there arises the need for diversification and commercialisation, such as value addition and marketing to ensure economic sustainability of small and marginal farmers. In addition to unsustainable land holdings and low productivity, post-harvest loss to the extent of about 25 per cent due to inadequate processing and storage facilities is the major constraint in the overall development of horticulture in the region.

Despite various constraints, the region is endowed with diverse and congenial agro-climatic conditions, varied soil types and abundance rainfall offer immense potential for production of different types of horticultural crops including fruits, vegetables, flowers, plantation crops, spices, medicinal and aromatic plants as well as other economically valuable agro-forestry crops. According to Shadeque (1989), the North Eastern Region of India with a mixed terrain of hills and plains, intercepted by large number of small and big rivers, streams is nature's unique gift for production of number of horticultural crops. Weinberger and Lumpkin (2007) viewed that horticulture production can be highly profitable, increase employment opportunities and bring about increasing commercialisation of rural sector. Moreover, growing population and rise in income level will lead to increase in demand for high-value agricultural produce like fruits, vegetables, flowers, spices etc. as well as processed value-added products.

Considering the above facts in view, the relevant secondary data were collected from the official sources of Department of Agriculture and Cooperation (DAC), Government of India (GOI), National Horticulture Board (NHB), Small Farmers' Agribusiness Consortium (SFAC), various government departments etc. and an attempt has been made to analyse the potentials of horticulture diversification in the region for sustainable livelihood opportunities.

Horticulture Diversification

Diversification refers to intensification of cropping both in time and space dimensions. Since, there is rapid increase in population and the target is to meet their demand from the limited cultivated area. Therefore, only way is to replace inefficient crops by different efficient high yielding and high value low volume horticultural crops, so as to increase the total production and productivity of the region. The economic growth of the region, particularly in the hilly areas, greatly depends on proper land use planning, which involves covering the areas with different horticultural crops like fruits, vegetables, flowers, spices, plantation crops and medicinal and aromatic plants. Moreover, from the soil conservation and ecological point of view also it may be desirable to cover the region with perennial vegetation (Shadeque, 1989). There is immense potential for both vertical and horizontal diversification of horticulture sector in the region. Vertical diversification is possible through induction of innovative production technologies, use of quality planting materials, proper land use, and reduction of post-harvest loss of perishables by processing and value addition etc. while horizontal diversification can be done through area expansion under different horticultural crops. Horticultural crops grown in the region are presented in the Table 1.1. They are considered important for improving land use, promoting crop diversification, generating employment as well as providing nutritional security to the people. In hilly areas, horticultural crops are also considered economically viable and ecologically sustainable alternative to *jhum* or shifting cultivation. Thus, the opportunities for horticultural diversification in the region have been analysed from perspectives of Area and production, Post-harvest processing and value addition, Organic horticulture, Marketing and supply chain and Impact on economy and livelihood generation.

Area and Production

The horizontal diversification of horticulture can be done through expansion of area. The state-wise total area and production of horticultural crops in the region for the period 2011-12 to 2015-16 is furnished in Table 1.2. According to the Table 1.2, the highest area under the horticultural crops is in Assam followed by Mizoram, Tripura, Meghalaya, Arunachal Pradesh, Manipur and Sikkim, respectively. During 2001-02 to 2014-15 Area under various horticultural crops in the region has been increased by 698.69 thousand hectares under the Horticulture Mission for North East and Himalayan States (HMNEH) a sub-scheme of Mission for Integrated Development of Horticulture (MIDH) (Table 1.3).

It has been observed that during the period, Mizoram has reported expansion of an area of 99.64 thousand hectares followed by Assam (99.45 thousand hectares), Tripura (97.80 thousand hectares), Meghalaya (88.51 thousand hectares), Arunachal Pradesh (80.31 thousand hectares), Manipur (79.31 thousand hectares) and Sikkim (78.20 thousand hectares), respectively as depicted in Table 1.3. The area expanded under horticultural crops under the HMNEH are highly encouraging. In case of production also, an increasing trend was observed during the period (Figure 1.1). Increase in production has been achieved mainly because of area expansion rather than increase in productivity. The productivity of horticultural crops in the region could be increased by adoption of improved production technology and management practices.

Table 1.1: Horticultural Crops of NER

Major Fruits	Tropical and Subtropical fruits—Banana, Pineapple, Papaya, Lemon, Orange, Litchi, Guava, Mango, Sapota, Jackfruit etc. Temperate fruits—Apple, Kiwi, Pear, Plum, Passion fruits etc. Minor indigenous fruits—Aonla, Carambola, Leteku, Paniyal, Thekera, Pumelo, Ber, Dillenia etc.
Vegetable crops	Potato, Brinjal, Tomato, Broccoli, Cabbage, Capsicum, Carrot, Cauliflower, Gourds, Chow-chow, Cowpea, Cucumber, Knolkhol, Okra, Pea, Pointed Gourd, Pumpkin, Radish, Spinach, Musk Melon, Water Melon, Sweet Potato, Tapioca, Colocasia, Yam etc.
Spices and condiments	Ginger, Chilli, Turmeric, Onion, Garlic, Black Pepper, Cardamom, Coriander, Cumin, Black Cumin, Mint, Fennel, Fenugreek, Bay leaf, Curry Leaf, Cinnamon, Vanilla etc.
Flowers and ornamental plants	Orchids, Roses, Marigold, Tuberose, Gladioli, Gerbera, Bougainvillea, Mussaenda, Chrysanthemum, Dahlia, Antirrhinum, Aster, Balsam, Calendula, Carnation, Petunia, Portulaca, Salvia, Zinnia etc.
Medicinal and Aromatic plants	Tulsi, Aloevera, Amlakhi, Silikha, Bhomora, Bael, Brahmi, Maha Brhringaraj, Sarpagandha, Kalmegh, Neem, Safed Musli, Agar, Citronella, Lemongrass, Vetiver, Patchouli, Sugandha-mantri etc.
Plantation crops	Tea, Coffee, Arecanut, Coconut, Cashewnut, Betelvine, Rubber etc.

Source: Prepared by Authors.

Post-harvest Processing and Value Addition

The highly perishable fruits and vegetables need very careful handling at every stage from pre-harvest to post-harvest, sorting, grading, packaging, storage and marketing. Despite being a major producer of many horticultural crops, there is very little attention in value addition to the horticultural produces leading to lower market values and low returns. The present infrastructure for value addition are quite meagre and far below the desired level. There is a vast scope for value addition.

Table 1.2: Statewise Area and Production of Horticultural Crops in NER

(Area: in Lakh hectares; Production in Lakh MT)

States	2011-12		2012-13		2013-14		2014-15		2015-16	
	Area	Prod.	Area	Prod.	Area	Prod.	Area	Prod.	Area	Prod.
Arunachal Pradesh	1.02	4.54	1.04	5.23	1.07	5.30	1.07	5.46	1.25	6.18
Assam	5.96	54.27	6.26	59.71	6.24	55.14	6.94	72.14	6.80	67.24
Manipur	0.81	6.30	0.84	6.85	0.91	8.13	0.95	8.48	0.98	7.88
Meghalaya	1.12	7.89	1.14	8.24	1.22	9.77	1.24	10.23	1.29	10.48
Mizoram	1.02	6.12	1.20	7.61	1.30	8.35	1.43	9.16	1.49	6.73
Nagaland	0.77	6.10	0.75	5.33	0.91	9.54	0.91	9.54	0.97	9.71
Sikkim	0.63	2.31	0.67	2.43	0.74	2.30	0.76	2.17	0.78	2.31
Tripura	1.04	12.38	1.26	15.03	1.37	16.17	1.24	12.17	1.48	17.66
NER Total	**12.37**	**99.91**	**12.16**	**110.33**	**13.76**	**114.70**	**14.53**	**129.35**	**15.04**	**128.19**

Sources: 1. Area and Production 2011-12: Indian Horticulture Database, 2014, NHB, DAC, GOI.
2. Area and Production 2012-13 to 2014-15: Horticultural Statistics at a glance, 2015, DAC, GOI.
3. Area and Production 2015-16: Agricultural Statistics at a glance, 2016, DAC, GOI.
4. Compiled and computed by A. Samad.

Table 1.3: Area Expansion under Horticultural Crops in NER During 2001-02 to 2014-15

State	Total Area Expansion ('000 Ha)
Arunachal Pradesh	80.31
Assam	99.45
Manipur	79.31
Meghalaya	88.51
Mizoram	99.64
Nagaland	75.46
Sikkim	78.20
Tripura	97.80
NER Total	**698.69**

Source: www.midh.gov.in

Due to lack of proper infrastructure facilities post-harvest losses range from 25 per cent to 40 per cent, depending upon the produce. According Patil (2007) major causes of these losses of fruits and vegetables are their fragile nature and prone to damage by virtue of improper harvesting, non conducive conditions, manual handling, and biological process of

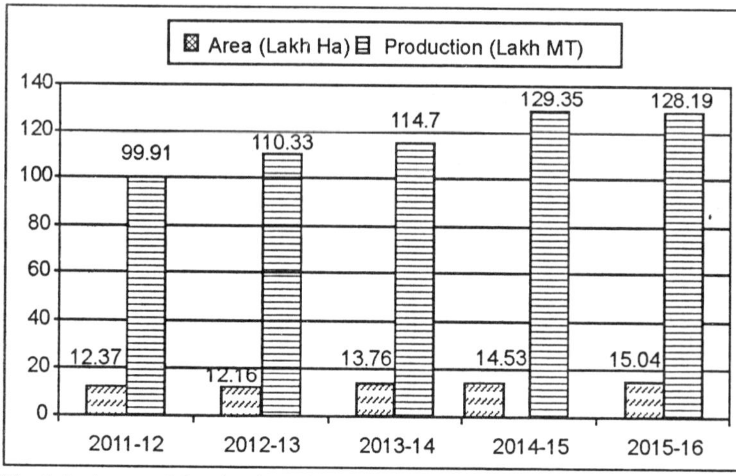

Fig. 1.1: Area and Production of Horticulture in NER

ripening and very low level of processing. Only about 2 per cent of the total horticultural produce is converted to value added products of long shelf life in India. Potential horticultural crops of the NER for value addition are presented in Table 1.4.

According to Ministry of Food Processing Industries (MOFPI), the food processing sector employs about 13 million people directly and about 35 million people indirectly. In 2004-05, food processing sector contributed about 14 per cent of manufacturing GDP with a share of Rs. 2,80,000 crores. Of this the unorganised sector accounted for more than 70 per cent of production in terms of volume and 50 per cent in terms of value. Changing age profile, increase in income, social changes (Increasing number of working women), life style factors, organized retail outlets etc. are all factors favouring the growth of the food processing sector. Food processing sector generates significant employment. The multiplier effect of investment in food processing industry on employment generation is 2.5 times than in other industrial sectors, higher than any other sector. Diversification of horticulture may be achieved through value addition and processing, which would increase production, offer higher return, open new markets, create recognition for farm as well as would expand the seasonal availability of the products.

Organic Horticulture

The organic farming is emerging as another way of horticultural

Table 1.4: Potential Horticultural Crops and Their Value-added Products

Potential crops	*Value-added products*
Fruits	
Mango	Pulp, juice, slice, squash, jam, jelly, pickles, powder etc.
Pineapple	Squash, jam, jelly, canned slices, juice, concentrates, RTS etc.
Jackfruit	Brine cured products, juice, pickles, chips, osmo-dried bulks etc.
Banana	Banana pulp, juice, concentrate, fruit bar, powder, chips etc.
Cashew nut	Processed nuts, clarified juice etc.
Papaya	Tutti-fruity, papain, pulp, jam etc
Oranges	Juice, concentrate, squash, cordials, jam, preserve from peels etc.
Passion fruit	Squash, syrup, juice, RTS beverages etc.
Guava	Jam, jelly, juice, pulp, concentrate, powder etc.
Amla	Candy, preserve, pickle, juice, powder etc.
Bael	Squash, juice, pulp, concentrate etc.
Vegetables	
Potato	Dehydration, drying, chips, frying etc.
Mushrooms	Dehydrated, soup mix, pickles, sauce etc.
Tomato	Pickle, ketchup, sauces, juice, puree, powder, canning etc.
Bamboo	Dehydrated products, pickles, preserves, brine cured products etc.
Mix vegetables	Canning, minimally processed products, pickles, dehydration etc.
Spices	
Ginger	Preserve, candy, paste, powder, oil and oleoresin etc.
Turmeric	Curing, drying, polishing, powder, curcumin, oleoresin etc.
Pepper	Black pepper, white pepper, powder, oil and oleoresin etc.
Chilli	Dried red chilli, dehydrated green chilli, powder, oil and oleoresin etc.
Garlic	Flakes, powder, paste etc.
Mix spices	Mix spices powder, graded spices, cleaned and packed spices etc.
Flowers	Dry flowers, potpourris, essential oils, flavours, pigments, dyes, *gulkand*, rose water, vanilla products etc.

Source: Prepared by A. Samad.

diversification due to environmental concerns and booming market for organically produced agricultural produces. Organic farming is a production system that avoids or excludes the use of chemical fertilizers and pesticides. The main aim of organic farming is to ensure sustained productivity, environmental protection and raising crops without chemicals of any kind. North Eastern States have natural advantages for organic farming due to their geographical locations and the least utilisation of chemical inputs like chemical fertilizers, chemical pesticides including fungicides and weedicides. With the sizeable acreage under naturally organic or by default organic cultivation, the region has tremendous potential to grow various high value horticultural crops organically. Sikkim and Mizoram have already become organic agriculture states of the region. Organic products fetch premium price of 10 per cent to 50 per cent over the conventional horticultural products. Market of organic products is also growing at the rate of 20 per cent to 22 per cent as compared to traditional ones (Rana, 2011). The prospects of organic agribusiness trade increasing, because of increasing demand for safe food and an approach to sustainable development of farming based rural livelihoods (Planning Commission, 2007).

Organic horticulture is based on the principles of (1) On farm waste recycling, (2) Biological weeds and pests control, (3) Integrated nutrient management (INM), (4) Integrated pest management (IPM), (5) Improve and maintain the natural landscape and agro-ecosystem etc. among others, which promotes establishment of employment intensive subsidiary enterprises like vermin compost units, bio-fertilizer units, bio-pesticides units, organic product outlets etc.

Marketing and Supply Chain

With an increasing working population, rising disposable income and greater international exposure, the fast-growing Indian market is witnessing paradigm shift in its aspirations and lifestyle. It is observed that food products capture about 53 per cent of private consumption expenditure and their demand rises consistently at almost 8 per cent, the consumer basket is continuously undergoing change in favour of perishables such as fruits, vegetables, etc. and healthy processed products. In order to harness the potential of emerging consumer demand both domestic and international, a professionally managed marketing system that provides multiple choices to farmers for sale of their produce is necessary (DAC, 2006).

Marketing system and supply chain of horticultural produce in the NER is very complex. The present marketing system is characterized by a long, fragmented supply chain, high wastages, low share of producers in consumer's price, is inadequately equipped to meet the growing needs of the consumers for quality and safe products. There is involvement of many stakeholders between farmers and consumers in the existing market channels, which is the main cause of price rise and cost build-up. According to MOFPI (2006), a study conducted by National Institute of Agricultural Marketing (NIAM) found that while the consumer pays an amount of Rs. 11.60 for a kg of fruit, the price realized by the farmer is only Rs. 3.30 (28%), the trader at village takes Rs. 4.1 (35%), the wholesaler takes Rs. 1.70 (15%) and the retailer takes Rs. 2.50 (22%). All these margins are without any value addition to the product (Figure 1.3). The studies also reported that there are 6-7 intermediaries in the supply chain for fruits and vegetables in India as against 2-3 in developed countries. This reduces the farm gate price and income levels of farmers. Appropriate institutional development at grassroots level, with the involvement of farmers is essential for addressing the constraints of marketing and enhancing remunerative farm gate price and the income levels of the small and marginal growers.

Employment and Livelihoods Generation

The production of horticultural products offers opportunities for poverty alleviation because it is usually more labour intensive than the production of staple food crops (Weinberger and Lumpkin, 2007). Shifting from production of cereal crops to the production of horticultural crops generates additional employment. Growing of different kinds of horticultural crops can provide gainful employment to a larger majority of farmers and agricultural labour throughout the year. According to Gogoi and Borah (2013), one hectare of fruit production generates 860 man-days per annum as against 143 man-days for cereal crops. Further, average labour required for growing horticultural crops is about 450 to 2500 man-days as compared to only 150 to 200 man-days for field crops (MOFPI, 1993).

Table 1.5: Employment Generation in Fruits and Vegetable Processing Sector

	Organized Sector	*Unorganised Sector*
Fixed investment	Rs. 10 million	Rs. 0.2 million
Output per year	500 tonnes	120 tonnes
Total Employment	140	21
Total employment for Investment of Rs. 10 million	140	1050

Source: Eleventh Five Year Plan, Report of the Working Group on Food Processing Sector 2006, MOFPI, GOI.

Food processing sector generates significant employment. The multiplier effect of investment in food processing industry on employment generation is 2.5 times than in other industrial sectors, higher than any other sector. At present the food processing sector employs about 13 million people directly and about 35 million people indirectly (MOFPI, 2006). It is revealed that the employment intensity within food processing industry is significantly higher in the unorganised sector as compared to the organized sector for the same level of investment (Table 1.5). Total number of employment created for the investment of Rs. 10 million is 140 in the organised processing sector, whereas 7.5 times higher employment created in the unorganized processing sector to the tune of 1050 for the same amount of capital investment. It can be attributed from the above facts that at the various stages of diversification of horticulture from farm to fork have significant impact on enhancing employments and livelihoods in the region.

Conclusion

Horticulture sector is considered as the main axis of sustainable economic development in the region. Diversification of horticulture can play a pivotal role in enhancing livelihoods generation in terms of increasing production, value addition to perishables, providing food and nutrition, besides income and employment. Despite several constraints, horticulture sector possesses significant multifarious diversification potential for improving land-use, generating ample livelihoods opportunities as well as proving nutritional security coupled with augmenting income. It also produces increased biomass per unit area, conserve biodiversity as well as helps in maintaining ecological balance and aesthetic value of landscape. This region of the country is an untapped reservoir of potential for sustainable horticulture development. Hence, for realizing this huge untapped potential of horticulture as an industry, the areas like crop diversification, technological intervention, post-harvest and value-addition, will need adequate attention coupled with equal importance on infrastructure development, hassle free credit flow and proper market linkage.

References

DAC (2006). *Modified Concept Note on Modern Terminal Market for Fruits, Vegetables and other Perishables*, Department of Agric and Coop, Ministry of Agriculture, Government of India, New Delhi.

Gautam, H.R. and Handa, A. (2012). "Horticulture can be fortune turner for North East", *Kurukshetra*, 61(1):8-10.

Gogoi, M. and Borah, D. (2013). *Baseline Data on Area, Production and Productivity of Horticulture Crops in North-East and Himalayan States—A Study in Assam*, AERC for NE India, AAU, Jorhat.

MOFPI (1993). *Food Processing Industries in India*, Ministry of Food Processing Industries, Government of India, New Delhi.

MOFPI (2006). *Eleventh Five Year Plan, Report of the Working Group on Food Processing Sector 2006*, Ministry of Food Processing Industries, Government of India, New Delhi.

Patil, R.T. (2007). *Means and Ways of Post-harvest Management in Arunachal Pradesh*, ICAR (RC) for NEH Region AP Centre Basar Souvenir, 2007, pp. 4-8.

Planning Commission (2007). *Report of the Working Group on Horticulture, Plantation Crops and Organic Farming for the XI Five Year Plan (2007-12)*, Government of India, New Delhi.

Rana, S.S. (2011). *Organic Farming*, Dept. of Agronomy, CSK Himachal Pradesh Krishi Vishvavidyalaya, Palampur.

Shadeque, A. (1989). "Impact of fruits plantation on economy and ecosystem of N.E. India", In: P.C. Goswami (ed.) *Agriculture in Assam,* Assam Institute of Development Studies, Guwahati, pp. 98-110.

Weinberger, K. and T.A. Lumpkin (2007). "Diversification into Horticulture and Poverty Reduction: A Research Agenda", *World Development*, 35(8):1464-1480.

2
Role of Fisheries in Economic Growth of Sikkim

Kul Bahadur Chettri and *Ruma Kundu*

Introduction

Sikkim is a tiny state situated in the lap of Eastern Himalayan Region. The nature has endowed it with distinct advantage of abundance water bodies and varied aquatic life. The State has various water resources in the form of rivers, lakes, streams and perennial springs which provide immense scope for the development of inland fisheries. The State has a huge potential in the fishery sector both for capture and culture fisheries due to the abundance of coldwater resources. Fish farming has become an important source of livelihood for the rural people in the upland areas due to the hilly terrain, agriculture and other allied activities is not only sufficient for the rural development. Initially, development programme of fisheries in the State was mainly on conservation of aquatic life and encouraged sport fisheries. But now fisheries activities has been expanded for the promotion of sustainable fish culture as an income generating activities in the rural areas, augmenting nutritious food production, generating supplementary source of income to fish farmers and fishermen, promoting fishery for tourism and conservation of riverine fish germplasm. The fisheries activity is linked with tourism and the educated unemployed youth are motivated towards fish culture practices which help them to lift up the economic condition of the people in the rural area. It has been an important enterprise for livelihood security to the rural people of Sikkim.

Review of Literature

The fisheries sector occupies a very important place in the socio-economic development of the country and it is a source of livelihood for a large sections of economically backward rural population (Ayyapan and Krishnan, 2004; Jana, 2007). It ensures food security as well as tackles unemployment in these regions, which are predominately inhabited by rural populace. It has become an important activity and is recognized as a rich source of cheap nutritious food (Kumar *et al.*, 2007; Sundararaj, 2007, Kumar, 2007). This sector contributes rural development, more effective administration of natural resources and conservation of biological diversity (Dagtekin *et al.*, 2007).

Gopalan (1976) reveals that fisheries play a significant role in developing countries like India. It contributes fish protein to a large population that suffers from malnutrition. It is unlike the cereal protein. Fish contains amino acids such as lysine and this serves as an efficient supplement to the low protein, high carbohydrate diet of developing nations like India. From the above study it is a fact that fisheries play an important role for the development of nation having immense water resources.

The most important indigenous cold water fish species are sahar (*Tor* spp), katle (*Neolissocheilus hexagonolepis*) and snow trout (*Schizothoraichthys* spp and *Schizothorax* spp). They are excellent from the economic and sport fishery point of view, but many other species are fished for subsistence. Cold water fisheries offer a great opportunity for self-employment and income generation among poor people living along rivers, lakes and other natural waters (Shrestha, 1995; Subba and Ghosh, 1996; Shrestha, 1999).

Singh *et al.* (2017) pointed out that Rainbow trout (*Oncorhynchus mykiss*) has established itself as prime cultivable coldwater species in the Indian Himalayan regions and now farmed on commercial scale. Its production has increased markedly in last ten years (2004-2014) from 147.0 to 834.0 tonnes, with a growth rate of 31 per cent per annum. Availability of technical know-how of trout farming, breeding and artificial diets has immensely helped in promoting aquaculture of trout in the country. Himalayan region of India is the major producer of rainbow trout (81.2%) while contribution from other regions of the country is meagre.

Macharia *et al.* (2015) stated that Rainbow trout aquaculture is a lucrative venture having it to be the second most expensive fish in Kenya after Nile perch (*Lates niloticus*) in both fresh water fish and marine fish. Investment in this area has a very high potential of improving the livelihoods of the rural people in areas where trout fish aquaculture is feasible.

Mahaseer (*Tor putitora*), one of the well-known large fresh water game fish of mountain rivers and lakes of most Trans-Himalayan countries, is reported to be declining in their natural habitats due to pollution, overfishing, industrialisation, urbanization and agricultural development causing ecological alterations and physical changes in natural environment in lakes and rivers of mid-hills (Das and Joshi, 1994; Shrestha, 1994). Attempts to culture and conserve *Tor* spp have been initiated in most Trans-Himalayan countries (Joshi, 1994; Shrestha, 1997). To replenish the declining populations of mahseer in its natural habitats, attempts are being made to breed and develop culture techniques of the *Tor* species.

Tunde *et al.* (2015) analysed that the Inland fish production is found to be a highly feasible and profitable venture and also a way to use effectively the water resources of all kinds, which are locally available. Sonawane *et al.* (2005) stated that more attention is required for the development of fishery resources through better understanding of ecological principles, production and exploitation techniques. He further says that the co-operative sector has to be organized in such a way that it should become more competitive and better managed. Ele *et al.* (2013), Olaoye *et al.* (2013) found that feed (kg), years of farming experience and stocking density have significant effect on output levels. Their study recommends among others, that fish hatcheries and feed mill should be established in the study area and government should provide credit facilities with small interest rate to fish farmers.

Objectives of the Study

The objectives of this study are as follows:

1. To know the present status of fisheries resources and role of fisheries in the hill economy of Sikkim.
2. To analyse the trends of fish production in Sikkim and other Himalayan states of India.
3. To address the major issues and strategies for fisheries and aquaculture development in hilly state of Sikkim.

Data and Methodology

The study is solely based on secondary sources. The secondary data and information were collected from the different secondary sources such as Department of Animal Husbandry, Dairying and Fisheries, Government of India and Government of Sikkim, Fishery Survey of India, National Fisheries Development Board, Central Coldwater Research Institute etc. Along with these various published books, hand books, annual reports released by both Central and State governments, statistical abstracts, and reports studied by various research organizations were also referred in the study. Data on numbers of fish farmers in all the four districts of Sikkim from 2009-10 to 2013-14, fish production from the Himalayan states for the period 2003-04 and 2013-14, and fish production of Sikkim from 2006-2015 were collected. Both qualitative and quantitative analyses were carried out. The results were analysed by using the simple graphical analysis.

Results and Discussions

Fishery Resources and Fish Diversity in Sikkim

The estimated total inland water bodies of the State is 0.03 lakh hector, length of rivers is 900 km and area of ponds and lakes is 0.1 and 3.2 thousand ha, respectively. Teesta and Rangeet are the main river system with their numerous tributaries which support the major riverine fisheries resources of the State. The total length of riverine system including the stream, steep or gradual from an altitude of 300 m to 8580 m is about 900 km. The water resources of Sikkim contain 48 fish species belonging to 9 families under 23 genera. Most of the species belong to Cyprinidac family. The most important fish species are Mahaseer (*Sahar*), Snow trout (*Asla*), Cat fish (*Ther, Gandi*), some carps (*Budana, Nak Kauta*) etc. are found in rivers and streams. The fish cultivated area is categorized into two parts. The area which falls above 1500 m sea level is identified as cold water zone and cold water fishes like trout are encouraged for stocking in the streams and lakes for angling purposes and culture in raceway in the private sector specially the rainbow trout and brown trout. Below 1500 m from the sea level is identified as carp zone and cultivation of carp fishes like grass carp, silver carp, common carp and other species are suitable for cultural purposes in the lower belt of Sikkim. The total annual fish yield from the riverine resources is 120-150 tonnes annually and about 1500-2000 villagers living close to the river banks are engaged in part-time fishing. This serves as a source of additional income and nutrients to fisher folk.

Trout Fishery

Earlier, in Sikkim, trout fishery was confined to production and stocking of brown trout fish seed in the coldwater streams and lakes for promoting angling and latter it was extended to rainbow trout farming as an economy activity in the private sector due to the growing population and demand of trout fish in the State. Farming rainbow trout is a profitable alternative to conventional agriculture that can be practiced within very limited land. Due to its taste and medical value this fish is highly preferred over other locally available fishes; hence the total demand of trout is very high. Realizing the benefits of this farming system the government is promoting trout farming among the rural masses as an income generating activity. The government is providing financial as well as technical assistance for trout farming under the scheme named "Trout culture in raceways". There are total five trout farms along with hatcheries set up in Sikkim for brown and rainbow trout seed production. The seed production capacity of the individual hatchery is given in Table 2.1.

Table 2.1: Trout Farm in Sikkim

Sl. No.	*Name of the Trout Farm*	*Location*	*District*	*Hatchery Capacity*
1.	Yuksom Trout Farm	Yuksom	West	5 lakh
2.	Uttarey Trout Farm	Uttarey	West	2 lakh
3.	Men-Moi-Tso Trout Farm (Brown Trout)	Kupup	East	5 lakh
4.	Sharchok Trout Farm	Lachung	North	1 lakh
5.	Lachen Trout Hatchery	Lachen	North	0.50 lakh

Source: Directorate of Fisheries, Government of Sikkim.

These trout farms were established for seed production and demonstration purposes. The fingerlings are distributed to the fish farmers in order to encourage them for aquaculture.

Carp Fishery

With the objective to utilize the water resources of mid-altitude level carp fishery is initiated under various beneficiary schemes in the private water bodies for carp fish production and in the public water bodies for carp seed production for availing to the farmers. The major carp species that has been cultivating are common carp, grass carp and silver carp. Recently, a Hungarian strain of common carp and mirror carp has been introduced in the State which is said to have 47 per cent higher growth rate than existing strain of carp available in the state. There are six carp seed production farms set-up in Sikkim for the production of quality carp seed for distribution to the beneficiaries and to stock in village ponds and other different resources of State. The district-wise farm and location is shown in Table 2.2 below.

Table 2.2: Carp Farm in Sikkim

Sl. No.	*Name of the Carp Farm*	*Location*	*District*
1.	Gayzing Carp Farm	Gyaba	West
2.	Rothok Carp Farm	Rothok	West
3.	Rangpo Carp Farm	Rangpo	East
4.	Rorathang Carp Farm	Rorathang	East
5.	Kabi Carp Farm	Kabi	North
6.	Makha Carp Farm	Makha	East

Source: Directorate of Fisheries, Government of Sikkim.

Mahaseer Fishery

Mahaseer is one of the very important game fish species which is available in the foothills of the Himalayan river system. It is also called the King of Game Fish locally known as Sahar is available in the lower belt of the river Teesta and Rangit. It is observed that population of Mahaseer has been decreasing in the river system due to habitat destruction by man-made activities across the river and diversion of river water and natural calamities. This species is declared as endangered fish species which is under the threat of becoming rare. The artificial stocking of mahaseer seed in necessary to sustain mahaseer population in the river system and therefore, one small mahaseer farm has been constructed at Baguwa in South Sikkim.

Farmers Engaged in Fish Farming

Fig. 2.1 shows the number of farmers practicing fish farming in the hilly state of Sikkim. The aquaculture or fish farming has been an additional source of income, employment and protein in the rural and remote parts of Sikkim. Fish farming can be practiced in the limited areas of land with other farming activities. In the hilly areas due to fragile and small holding of agricultural land, agriculture and farming is done in small scale which is based on seasonal. A particular farming cannot support the economy of the household unlike in plain farming. So, in the hilly area, fish farming has been an additional economic activity which supports livelihood in the rural areas.

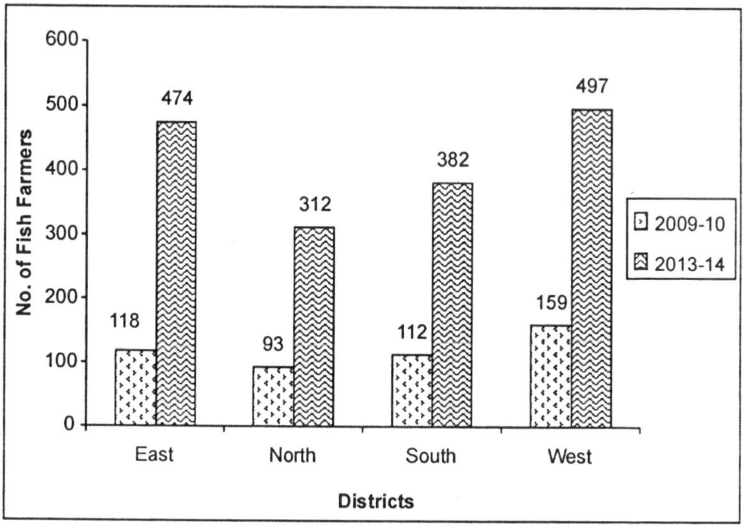

Fig. 2.1: Farmers engaged in Fish farming

From Fig. 2.1, it is clear that fish farmers in all the districts of Sikkim have increased. There is a positive growth of farmers in the State of about 245.44 per cent during 2009-10 to 2013-14. West district of Sikkim has the largest fish farmer of about 497 as on 2013-14. West Sikkim has more potential of fish farming having the availability of fresh and cold water that support rainbow trout farming and in lower belt carp farming. In 2009-10, there were only 159 farmers. Within this period of five years there is a 212.58 per cent increase in farmers. Similarly, East Sikkim has the second largest number of fish farmers in the state. During 2009-10, there were only 118 farmers which are increased to 474 in 2013-14 and the percentage increase is about 301.69 per cent. In east Sikkim also more land is suitable for aquaculture. North Sikkim has the least number of fish farmers in the state because north Sikkim has very fragile land and less land is suitable for farming and habitation in fact the total area is highest amongst all the district. The slope of the land is very steep and population is less as a result farming activities is less as compared to other districts of Sikkim. During 2009-10 the reported farmers were about 93 and it is increased to 312. Southern parts of Sikkim have the scarcity of water and are not suitable for trout culture. In some parts of it people are rearing carb fishery, because of this problem farmers are less in South. In 2009-10, the number of people engaged in fish farming was 112 and it was increased to 382. At present, there are more than 1500 fisher folk who are actively engaged in catching the fishes from the rivers and streams in Sikkim.

Fish Production from Himalayan States

The Himalayan States of India consist of Jammu & Kashmir, Himachal Pradesh, Uttarakhand, Sikkim and Arunachal Pradesh which are suitable for the cultivation of coldwater fishes. The potential coldwater fisheries resources of India include the long stretch of Himalayas of around 2500 km from Jammu & Kashmir in the West to Arunachal Pradesh in the East and 200-400 km from North to South comprising an area of 5,33,604 km^2 (FAO, 2003). There are around 10,000 km long streams and rivers, 20,500 ha high and low altitudinal lakes and 50,000 ha of reservoirs both natural and man-made and 2500 ha brackish water lakes in the high altitudes. These varied water resources in the uplands harbour are rich ichthyofaunal diversity comprising large population of indigenous and exotic, cultivable and non-cultivable coldwater fish species which have potential for aquaculture practices as well as capture fisheries. These

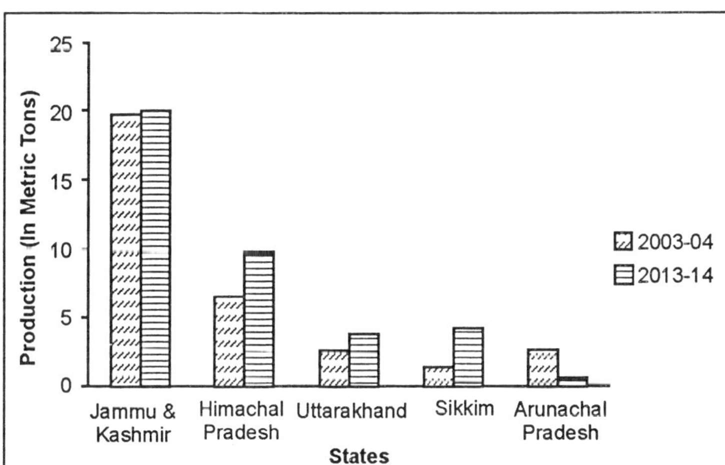

Fig. 2.2: Fish production in Himalayan States

coldwater resources are suitable for the cultivation of coldwater fishes like trout and exotic carp species (Bora *et al.*). The aquatic resources available are quite valuable for the development of fishery both for food and sport. The mountain areas are mostly landlocked; fish in ponds, lakes, streams, rivers and reservoirs play an important role in providing food, income to people and source of animal protein (Kumar *et al.*, 2012). The following Fig. 2.2 gives the brief view of production of fishes from these five Himalayan States of India.

Fish production status of a decade is taken for all these five Himalayan States. This figure illustrates that there is not much increased of fish production from Jammu & Kashmir but the production is highest among these states. In 2003-04 the production was 19.75Mt and increased to only 19.98 Mt in 2013-14. Himachal Pradesh is the second largest cultivator and producer of coldwater fisheries in India. Its production increased from 6.53Mt to 9.83 Mt in 2013-14. The production of fish is increased in both the states of Uttarakhand and Sikkim but percentage increase is higher in case of Sikkim. Sikkim being a small states of Himalaya performing well in terms of fish farming with a growth of 200 per cent during this decade. Arunachal Pradesh is the only state which recorded decline in the production of fish. Its production greatly declined from 2.65 Mt to 0.61 Mt from 2003-04 to 2012-13.

Fish Production in Sikkim from 2006-07 to 2014-15

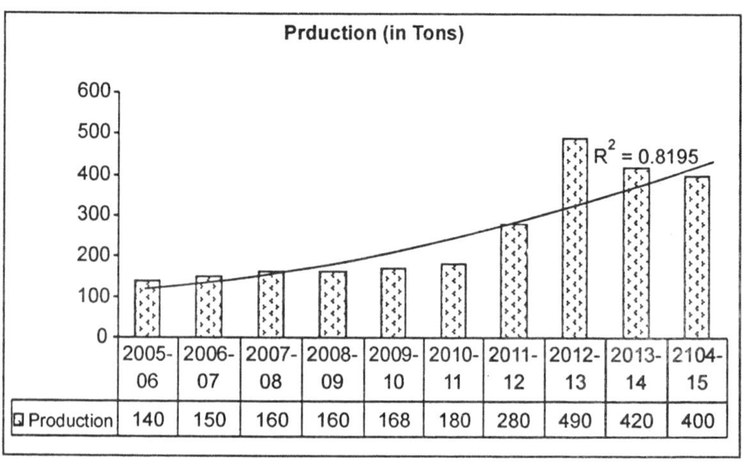

Fig. 2.3: Fish production in Sikkim (2006-07 to 2014-15)

The production of fish in Sikkim was gradually increasing making the highest production in the State in 2012 of about 490 tons. But its performance is decreased from 2012 onwards and during 2014 to 2015, its shows the zero growth rates. If we see the overall trend within this ten years period, it is observed that on an average fish production is moving on the positive trend.

Issues and Strategies for Fisheries and Aquaculture Development in the Hills

There are vast water resources in the State which are virgin and unutilised. The perennial springs and streams in the State are flowing from the uplands to low lands which are ultimately going into wasted. In the hill fisheries sector is facing the problems like poor accessibility, difficult hilly terrain, lack of transportation and proper market, lack of infrastructure for aquaculture etc. as a results this sector could not foster to the extended level. Even though the above problems exist in the hill state, following are the some of the strategies that could be done in order to increase the level of production and to bring resources in proper utilization.

1. The water resources of the state could be brought into fish farming and aquaculture development by bringing these resources in an efficient and proper way rather than going into wasted.
2. Awareness on the importance and role of fisheries and aquaculture in the rural development and nutritional value can motivate the younger generations as a result more people can get opportunities in fish farming.
3. Fish is a highly perishable product, so accessibility, cold storage, proper transportation and marketing linkage facilities can foster this sector so that local fish can be easily sold in the market.
4. Use of modern technology and training of farmers can increase the level of production.
5. Local fish market centre in the market area could encourage the farmers for extensive farming and supply surplus production in urban areas.

Concluding Observations

The study found that fish farming has been a source of livelihood, additional source of income, earning, employment and nutrition in the rural parts of Sikkim. In the rural areas, people do not buy fishes from the market, they produce and consume and sell surplus in the village itself. Fish farming is helping the village economy to grow and sustain. The Government of Sikkim has been focusing to increase the level of production by encouraging rural people, giving them financial assistance and technical knowhow and by providing various Central and State schemes. From the above study it is known that in Sikkim trout such as rainbow trout and brown trout; carps such as grass carp, common carps and silver carps have been culturing for the purpose of food and sport. Mahaseer is the important game fish available in the foothill rivers—Teesta and Rangit. In Sikkim, fish farmers in the entire district have been increasing. There is a growth of 245.44 per cent during 2009-10 to 2013-14 in the State. Sikkim is showing a positive trend in terms of fish production amongst the five Himalayan states of India, even though production is less as compared to some other states. There are some of the problems such as poor accessibility, poor transportation and absence of marketing facilities etc. for local fish farmers in Sikkim. As a consequence of these, the fisheries sector could not foster to the extended level. So, proper planning, methodologies and implementation are required in order to solve these problems.

References

Ayyappan and Krishna, M. (2007). "Changing consumption pattern", *The Survey of Indian Agriculture,* 6(6).

Bora, D.C., Sharma, S. and Sharma, D. (2015). "Coldwater fish diversity and abundance of upper reaches of Sonkosh River, Kokrajhar, Assam", *Science Vision*, 15(1), 8-18.

Ele, E.I., Ibok, O.W., Obong, E.A., Okon, I.E. and Udoh, E.S (2013). "Economic analysis of fish farming in Calabar, cross river state, Nigeria", *Greener. Journal of Agricultural Sciences*, 3(7): 542-549.

Gopalan, C. (1976). *Nutritive Values of Indian Foods*, NIN, ICMR, Hyderabad.

Government of India (2014). *Handbook on Fisheries Statistics*, Agriculture Ministry of India, Department of Animal Husbandry, Dairying and Fisheries, Government of India.

Government of Sikkim (2010). *Annual Report 2009-10*. Department of Animal Husbandry Livestock, Fisheries and Veterinary Services, Government of Sikkim, Gangtok.

Kumar, R., Umesh, K.B., and Rajesh, E. (2007). "Economics of inland fish production Karnataka", *Journal of Rural Development*, 26(1).

Olaoye, O.J., Ashley-Dejo, S.S., Fakoya, E.O., Ikeweinwe, N.B., Alegbeleye, W.O., Ashaolu, F.O. and Adelaja, O.A. (2013). "Assessment of socio-economic analysis of fish farming in Oyo State, Nigeria", *Double Blind Peer Reviewed International Research Journal*, Global Journals Inc. (USA) 13 (9).

Shrestha, J. (1999). "Coldwater fish and fisheries in Nepal", *FAO Fisheries Technical Paper. No. 385*: 13-40. Rome, FAO.

Singh, N.D., Krishnan, M., Sivaramane, N., Ananthan, P.S., and Satyasi, K.J.S. (2015). "Determination of efficiency of fish farms in North-East India using data envelopment approach". *Agricultural Economics Research Review*, 28(2): 329-337.

Sonewane, S. and Ambhure, S. (2005). "Evolution and impact of selected fisheries management practices of co-operative and non-cooperative fisheries sector in Aurangabad district of Maharashtra India", *Journal of Fisheries Economics and Development*, 6(1).

Tunde, A.B., Kuton, M.P., Ayegbokiki Adedayo Oladipo, A.A. and Olasunkanmi, L.H. (2015). "Economic analyze of costs and return of fish farming in Saki-East Local Government Area of Oyo State, Nigeria". *Aquaculture Research and Development*. 6:306. doi: 10.4172/21559546.1000306

3
Poverty, Inequality and Sectoral Development in the Hill and Plain States of North East India

Paranan Konwar

Introduction

The saying "South East Asia begins where North East India ends" indicates the socio-cultural, genealogical, geographical and psychological bond or linkage of ethnic tribes of "North East India" with "South East Asia". This North-Eastern region of India consisting of Arunachal Pradesh, Assam, Manipur, Meghalaya, Mizoram, Nagaland, Sikkim, and Tripura occupies 7.98 per cent of India's geographical area with 3.76 per cent of India's total population. The North East India constitutes 34 per cent of the country's water resources and 40 per cent of India's hydro power potential covering nearly 90 per cent India's international boundaries. As per Census 2011, Dibang valley district of Arunachal Pradesh has the lowest population (7,948) in the country. Serchhip district in Mizoram records at highest literacy rate of 98.76 per cent among all India districts. Aizawl (Mizoram) is with highest literacy rate of 98.80 per cent among the Indian cities. Among the NE States, shares of services to Gross State Domestic Product (GSDP) are high. Next are industry and agriculture and allied sector.

The level of per capita income and expenditure of rural sectors signifies the rural development of a state. As poverty and inequality are calculated based on per capita income and expenditure; so, poverty ratio and economic inequality reflect the level of rural development of that concerned state. Similarly, growth rate of agriculture and its share in GSDP shows another side of rural development.

Objective

The study is planned to examine the trends of poverty and inequality in the hill and plain states of north-eastern region of India. Attempts have been made to analyse the sectoral development in the region.

Data and Methodology

The study is based on secondary sources of data collected from different departments and ministries of India. Head-count ratio has been used to measure uni-dimensional poverty or absolute poverty, Multidimensional Poverty Index (MPI) to estimate multi-dimensional poverty, and Lorenz ratio and Gini coefficient to measure relative poverty or inequality.

Results and Discussions

Overview of North East India

Average rural population in the North Eastern (NE) states was recorded at 72.67 per cent with highest rural people in Assam (85.92%) and lowest in Mizoram (48.49%). Except Nagaland where growth of population (-0.58%) was negative, growth rate of population in remaining NE States was above 12 per cent. Among the North Eastern (NE) states percentage of population living in rural area is highest in Assam (85.92) and lowest in Mizoram (48.49) as per 2011 Census. As compared to other states of North East India, *only in Mizoram, rural population (48.49%) was lower than the national level (68.84%) and urban population (51.51%) was higher than that the national level (31.16%).* Sex ratio is highest in Manipur (992) followed by Meghalaya (989) and Mizoram (976) and lowest in Sikkim (890). As per Census 2011, population density in Assam (398 persons per sq. km) is close to that of Tripura (350); but about three times higher than the density of Manipur (115), Meghalaya (132) and Nagaland (119). Density of population is the lowest in Arunachal Pradesh (17) followed by Mizoram (52) (see Table 3.1).

Poverty and Inequality

Incidence of poverty is measured by headcount ratio (HC). In some cases, high incidence of poverty (HC) is found with low depth of poverty (poverty gap index or PGI) and in certain cases low incidence of poverty (HC) is

Table 3.1: Area, Population, Density, Sex ratio and Literacy of North East India

States	Area Sq. km	Population			Growth rate of population (%)	Density	Sex ratio	Literacy
		Rural (%)	Urban (%)	Total				
Arunachal Pradesh	83743	77.33	22.67	1,383,727	26.03	17	938	65.38
Assam	78438	85.92	14.08	31,205,576	17.07	398	958	72.19
Manipur	22327	69.79	30.21	2,570,390	12.05	115	992	79.21
Meghalaya	22429	79.92	20.08	2,966,889	27.95	132	989	74.43
Mizoram	21081	48.49	51.51	1,097,206	23.48	52	976	91.33
Nagaland	16579	71.03	28.97	1,978,502	-0.58	119	931	79.55
Sikkim	7096	75.03	24.97	610,577	12.89	86	890	81.42
Tripura	10486	73.82	26.18	3,673,917	14.84	350	960	87.22
Total	**262179**			**45,486,784**				
India	3287240	83,30,87,662 (68.84)	37,71,05,760 (31.16)	1,210,193,422	17.64	382	940	74.04

Source: Government of India, 2011.

found with high depth of poverty (PGI). The following Table 3.2 exhibits percentage of population below poverty line by states in 2011-12 in NE India. Here, Tendulkar Methodology for the Poverty Line has been expressed in terms of MPCE based on Mixed Reference Period (MRP), while Rangarajan Methodology for the Poverty Line is based on Modified Mixed Reference Period (MMRP). In 2011-12, below poverty line (BPL) population (as per Rangarajan Methodology) was estimated at highest in

Table 3.2. Percentage of Population Below Poverty Line by States, 2011-12

Sl. No.	States	As per Tendulkar Methodology based on MRP *			As per Rangarajan Methodology based on MMRP #			Rank
		Rural	Urban	Total	Rural	Urban	Total	
1.	Arunachal Pradesh	38.93	20.33	34.67	39.3	30.9	37.4	3
2.	Assam	33.89	20.49	31.98	42.0	34.2	40.9	2
3.	Manipur	38.80	32.59	36.89	34.9	73.4	46.7	1
4.	Meghalaya	12.53	9.26	11.87	26.3	16.7	24.4	6
5.	Mizoram	35.43	6.36	20.40	33.7	21.5	27.4	4
6.	Nagaland	19.93	16.48	18.88	6.1	32.1	14.0	7
7.	Sikkim	9.85	3.66	8.19	20.0	11.7	17.8	8
8	Tripura	16.53	7.42	14.05	22.5	31.3	24.9	5
	All India	**25.70**	**13.70**	**21.92**	**30.9**	**26.4**	**29.5**	**–**

Source: *Planning Commission, 2013; #Planning Commission, 2014.

Note: Population as on 1st March 2012 has been used for estimating number of persons below poverty line. (2011 Census population extrapolated).

Assam (42.0%) followed by Arunachal Pradesh (39.3%) and Manipur (34.9%) and exceeding the all India level (30.9%) in rural sector. But, it was estimated to be higher in Manipur (73.4%) followed by Assam (34.2%) and Nagaland (32.1%). *Poverty ratio was higher in Manipur (46.7%) followed by Assam (40.9%) and Arunachal Pradesh (37.4%) exceeding the all India level (29.5%) during 2011-12 as per Rangarajan Methodology. Exceptionally, urban poverty was higher in Manipur (73.4 per cent in urban > 34.9 per cent in rural), Nagaland (32.1% > 6.1%), and Tripura (31.3% > 22.5%) than the rural poverty in respective States.*

Multi-dimensional Poverty Index (MPI) value is highest in Assam (0.316) followed by Meghalaya (0.307) exceeding the all India level (0.283) and lowest in Mizoram (0.094). Inequality among the MPI Poor is high in Meghalaya (0.248) followed by Arunachal Pradesh (0.237) overcoming the all India level of inequality (0.234). In 2011-12, BPL population (as per Rangarajan Methodology) was estimated at highest in Manipur (46.7%) followed by Assam (40.9%) and Arunachal Pradesh (37.4%) exceeding the all India level (29.5%).

Table 3.3. Multi-dimensional Poverty Index and Population Below Poverty Line by States-2011-12.

Region	*MPI (H x A)*	*H (Incidence) $k \geq 33.3\%$*	*A (Intensity)*	*Inequality Among the MPI Poor*	*Population Share*
India	**0.283**	**53.7%**	**52.7%**	**0.234**	**100%**
Urban	0.116	24.6%	47.2%	–	30.6%
Rural	0.357	66.6%	53.6%	–	69.4%
Arunachal Pradesh	0.274	53.0%	51.7%	0.237	0.1%
Assam	0.316	60.1%	52.6%	0.213	2.7%
Manipur	0.191	40.8%	46.7%	0.154	0.2%
Meghalaya	0.307	56.6%	54.3%	0.248	0.3%
Mizoram	0.094	21.0%	44.7%	0.113	0.1%
Nagaland	0.264	51.7%	51.1%	0.201	0.1%
Sikkim	0.150	31.8%	47.0%	0.167	0.1%
Tripura	0.269	54.6%	49.3%	0.188	0.3%

Source: OPHI, 2015:5. All India estimate includes all States/UTs. Population as on 1st March, 2012 has been used for estimating number of persons below poverty line. (2011 Census population extrapolated).

From Table 3.4, we observe four types of association between MPCE (monthly per capita consumption expenditure) and inequality among the NE States: lower MPCE with higher inequality, lower MPCE with lower inequality, higher MPCE with lower inequality and higher MPCE with higher inequality. For example, in rural area, it was evident that MPCE was lower in Assam (1218.57). But, inequality in consumption expenditure measured by Lorenz ratio was higher in Assam (0.221). But Meghalaya was a state with lower MPCE with lower inequality. Contrary to that, MPCE was higher in Nagaland (2058.58) with rank 1 among the NE States along with low level of inequality (0.192) with rank 2 among the NE States. On the other hand, Arunachal Pradesh was a state with higher level of expenditure (1781.74) with rank 2 in NE States with higher level of inequality (0.346) with rank 8 in NE States. Almost same trends happen in case of urban areas also. If we observe the inequality in all India level, it is found that in rural India, Meghalaya, Nagaland, Sikkim, Manipur and Tripura were among the seven states with lowest Lorenz ratios. For urban India, Manipur, Meghalaya, Nagaland and Mizoram were the first four states with lowest Lorenz ratios.

Table 3.4: $MPCE_{MMRP}$ in 2011-12

States	*Rural sector*			*Urban Sector*		
	MPCE (All India Rank)	*Lorenz ratio (All India Rank)*	*NE Rank in MPCE (Lorenz ratio)*	*MPCE*	*Lorenz ratio*	*NE Rank in MPCE (Lorenz ratio)*
Arunachal Pradesh	1781.74 (6)	0.346 (26)	2(8)	2654.17 (9)	0.365 (22)	1(8)
Assam	1218.57 (21)	0.221 (8)	8(6)	2189.15 (19)	0.326 (15)	5(7)
Manipur	1501.89 (17)	0.211 (6)	5(4)	1482.63 (27)	0.209 (1)	7(1)
Meghalaya	1474.78 (18)	0.190 (1)	6(1)	2435.66 (16)	0.226 (2)	4(3)
Mizoram	1643.69 (11)	0.240 (13)	3(7)	2567.72 (13)	0.233 (4)	3(5)
Nagaland	2058.58 (4)	0.192 (2)	1(2)	2284.43 (18)	0.232 (3)	4(4)
Sikkim	1564.91 (14)	0.197 (3)	4(3)	2607.87 (N.A)	0.213 (NA)	2(2)
Tripura	1334.39 (19)	0.219 (7)	7(5)	2144.45 (20)	0.297 (8)	6(6)
India	**1429.96**	**0.283**		**2629.65**	**0.363**	

Source: Government of India, 2014.
Note: Lowest Lorenz ratio shows rank 1 and highest average $MPCE_{MMRP}$ indicates rank 1.

Table 3.5 depicts the trends of poverty ratios from 2004-05 to 2011-12. Rural poverty in 2004-05 was estimated to be highest in Tripura

Table 3.5. Trends of Poverty Ratio from 2004-05 to 2011-12

States	*Rural*				*Urban*				*Total*			
	2004-05	*2011-12*	*Change*	*Growth*	*2004-05*	*2011-12*	*Change*	*Growth*	*2004-05*	*2011-12*	*Change*	*Growth*
Arunachal Pradesh	33.6	39.3	5.7	16.96	23.5	30.9	7.4	31.49	31.1	37.4	6.3	20.26
Assam	36.4	42.0	5.6	15.38	21.8	34.2	12.4	56.88	34.4	40.9	6.5	18.90
Manipur	39.3	34.9	–4.4	–11.20	34.5	73.4	38.9	112.75	38.0	46.7	8.7	22.89
Meghalaya	14.0	26.3	12.3	87.86	24.7	16.7	–8	–32.39	16.1	24.4	8.3	51.55
Mizoram	23.0	33.7	10.7	46.52	7.9	21.5	13.6	172.15	15.3	27.4	12.1	79.08
Nagaland	10.0	6.1	–3.9	–39.00	4.3	32.1	27.8	646.51	9.0	14.0	5	55.56
Sikkim	31.8	20.0	–11.8	–37.11	25.9	11.7	–14.2	–54.83	31.1	17.8	–13.3	–42.77
Tripura	44.5	22.5	–22	–49.44	22.5	31.3	8.8	39.11	40.6	24.9	–15.7	–38.67
India	**41.8**	**30.9**	**–10.9**	**–26.08**	**25.7**	**26.4**	**0.7**	**2.72**	**37.2**	**29.5**	**–7.7**	**–20.70**

Source: Planning Commission, 2014.

(44.5%) followed by Manipur (39.3%) and Assam (36.4%). The figures had changed in 2011-12. During that period, rural poverty was higher in Assam (42.0%) followed by Arunachal Pradesh (39.3%) and Manipur (34.9%). It means rural poverty was continuing at higher level in Manipur and Assam. It is feel good factor that growth rate poverty had decreased in Manipur, Nagaland, Sikkim and Tripura. But, growth of poverty during 2004-05 to 2011-12 was recorded at highest in Meghalaya (87.86%) and Mizoram (46.52%). During 2004-05, poverty ratio (rural and urban) was higher in Tripura (40.60%) followed by Manipur (38.0) and Assam (34.4). In 2011-12, poverty ratio (total) was higher in Manipur (46.7%) followed by Assam (40.9) and Arunachal Pradesh (37.4). Assam was remaining as second highest state with higher poverty ratios among the NE States. During 2004-05 to 2011-12, poverty ratios were increasing in all states of NE India except Sikkim and Tripura with negative growths. For instance, growth of poverty ratio was higher in Mizoram (79.08) followed by Nagaland (55.56) and Meghalaya (51.55) from 2004-05 to 2011-12.

Table 3.6: Trends of $MPCE_{MMRP}$ from 2004-05 to 2011-12

States	*Rural*			*Urban*		
	2004-05	*2011-12*	*Growth*	*204-05*	*2011-12*	*Growth*
Arunachal Pradesh	771.53	1781.74	130.94	881.10	2654.17	201.23
Assam	543.18	1218.57	124.34	1057.99	2189.15	106.92
Manipur	614.20	1501.89	144.53	726.38	1482.63	104.11
Meghalaya	655.30	1474.78	125.05	1190.09	2435.66	104.66
Mizoram	778.35	1643.69	111.18	1200.51	2567.72	113.89
Nagaland	1010.81	2058.58	103.66	1498.47	2284.43	52.45
Sikkim	688.53	1564.91	127.28	1106.79	2607.87	135.62
Tripura	487.63	1334.39	173.65	1000.54	2144.45	114.33
India	**558.78**	**1429.96**	**155.91**	**1052.36**	**2629.65**	**149.88**

Source: Government of India, 2006; Government of India, 2014.

Note: The MPCE based on the uniform reference period of "last 30 days" for all items is referred to as "MPCE (U30)", or simply "MPCE."

Table 3.6 shows the trends of MPCE from 2004-05 to 2011-12. From 2004-05 to 2011-12, growth rate of MPCE in rural areas was estimated to be highest in Nagaland (96.47%) followed by Mizoram (89.95) and Assam (80.42) exceeding the all India level (64.14). Similarly, in urban areas, growth rate of MPCE was highest in Nagaland (190.65%) followed by Manipur (96.05) and Meghalaya (95.55) exceeding the all India level (66.72). Of course, in rural areas, poverty ratios had decreased in Manipur, Nagaland, Sikkim and Tripura as a result of higher growth of MPCE. On the other hand, poverty ratios had decreased in comparing the growth rate of MPCE and growth rate of poverty ratios among the NE States, three things were observed: (i) growth rate of MPCE was higher than that of poverty ratios; (ii) In spite of higher growth of MPCE, poverty ratio did not decrease. Rather poverty ratios had also increased, and (iii) growth rate of MPCE and growth rate of poverty ratios in urban areas were higher than that in rural areas in NE India.

Table 3.7: Trends of Lorenz Ratio from 2004-05 to 2011-12

States	*Rural*			*Urban*		
	2004-05	*2011-12*	*Change*	*2004-05*	*2011-12*	*Change*
Arunachal Pradesh	0.272	0.346	0.074	0.243	0.365	0.122
Assam	0.197	0.221	0.024	0.314	0.326	0.012
Manipur	0.158	0.211	0.053	0.175	0.209	0.034
Meghalaya	0.155	0.190	0.035	0.258	0.226	–0.032
Mizoram	0.194	0.240	0.046	0.244	0.233	–0.011
Nagaland	0.209	0.192	–0.017	0.233	0.232	–0.001
Sikkim	0.263	0.197	–0.066	0.257	0.213	–0.044
Tripura	0.215	0.219	0.004	0.338	0.297	–0.041
India	**0.297**	**0.283**	**–0.014**	**0.373**	**0.363**	**–0.01**

Source: Government of India, 2006; Government of India, 2014.

The trend of inequality measured by Lorenz ratio of 2004-05 and 2011-12 has been shown in Table 3.7. It was found that economic inequality in rural areas in 2011-12 was estimated to be the highest in Arunachal Pradesh (Lorenz ratio 0.346) and the lowest in Meghalaya (0.190). From 2004-05 to 2011-12, inequality had decreased only in two states, such as Nagaland and Sikkim. During 2011-12, inequality in rural and urban sectors, was higher in Arunachal Pradesh (with Lorenz ratios 0.346 and 0.365 respectively) followed by Mizoram (0.240 and 0.233) and Assam (0.221 and 0.326). During 2004-05 to 2011-12, inequality in rural areas had increased in all states of India except Nagaland and Sikkim. On the other hand, inequality in urban areas has decreased in all states of NE India except Arunachal Pradesh, Assam and Manipur.

Sectoral Development

Table 3.8 shows Average annual growth rate over the period 2005-06 to 2011-12 (in %). Average annual growth rate of agriculture was highest in Mizoram (10.4%) and lowest in Meghalaya (2.6%). In most of the NE States annual growth rate in agriculture was lower than those in industry, manufacturing and services sector. It signifies the slow development in rural sector. Average annual growth rates of Industry and Manufacturing over the period 2005-06 to 2011-12 in Assam were 2.5 per cent and 1.8 per cent respectively which were lower among all States of North East India. The average annual growth rate of agriculture in Assam (3.4%) was lower than those figures of Arunachal Pradesh (8.3%), Manipur (7.6%), Mizoram (10.4%), Sikkim (4.2%) and Tripura (4.8%). Average annual growth rate in services of Assam (8.9%) is lower that the growth rates of Arunachal Pradesh (10.5%), Mizoram (9.6%) and Sikkim (9.4%).

Table 3.8: Average annual Growth Rate over the Period 2005-06 to 2011-12

(in per cent)

States	*Agriculture*	*Industry*	*Manufacturing*	*Services*
Arunachal Pradesh	8.3	8.0	8.6	10.5
Assam	3.4	2.5	1.8	8.9
Manipur	7.6	4.4	6.9	6.6
Meghalaya	2.6	10.1	25.6	8.8
Mizoram	10.4	12.7	8.3	9.6
Nagaland	3.3	11.2	15.5	8.0
Sikkim	4.2	37.1	190.0	9.4
Tripura	4.8	9.4	5.3	8.3
Total	**4.0**	**6.0**	**6.9**	**8.7**

Source: Central Statistics Office (CSO), 2014; Ministry of Agriculture, Ministry of Industry, Government of India.

It is an important input to the production process and raises the productivity of other sectors. Infrastructure connects goods to the markets, workers to industry, people to services and the poor in rural areas to urban growth centres. Infrastructure lowers costs, enlarges markets and facilitates trade. Thus, infrastructure provides services that support economic growth by increasing the productivity of labour and capital thereby reducing the costs of production and raising profitability, production, income and employment (CSO, 2014:28). Table 3.9 portrays the share of agriculture and allied sector in GSDP (Gross State Domestic Product) at current prices 2011-12. It was apparent from data that share of agriculture and allied sector in GSDP was lower as compared to that of industry and services sector.

Conclusion

The North Eastern Region of India is still lagging behind as compared to many States of India in spite of huge natural and human resources. The

Table 3.9: Sectoral Shares in GSDP at Current Prices: 2011-12 (%)

India/States	*Share of Agriculture & Allied Sector in GSDP at current prices: 2011-12 (% of GSDP)*	*Share of Industry in GSDP at current prices: 2011-12 (% of GSDP)*	*Share of Services Sector in GSDP at current prices: 2011-12 (% of GSDP)*
Arunachal Pradesh	31.6	34.6	33.8
Assam	27.9	23.3	48.8
Manipur	24.7	29.7	45.6
Meghalaya	17.4	34.1	48.6
Mizoram	18.8	21.4	59.8
Nagaland	23.8	20.3	56.0
Sikkim	10.8	38.4	50.7
Tripura	18.1	30.1	51.8
India	**17.2**	**26.4**	**56.4**

Source: Central Statistics Office (CSO), 2014.

region is still deprived in various socio-economic developments. In North-Eastern States, except Mizoram still a vast majority of people live in rural areas. The percentage of rural population varies from as high as 85.92 per cent in Assam, 79.92 per cent in Meghalaya and 77.33 per cent in Arunachal Pradesh. The poverty ratio the region is also very high. In 2011-12 rural poverty varied from 46.7 per cent in Manipur followed by Assam (40.9%) and Arunachal Pradesh (37.4%) exceeding the all India level (29.5%). Exceptionally, urban poverty as compared to the rural poverty was higher in Manipur (73.4% > 34.9%), Nagaland (32.1% > 6.1%), and Tripura (31.3% > 22.5%). The ratio and growth of poverty has increased both in rural and urban areas. It was found that Multidimensional Poverty Index (MPI) value is higher in Assam but inequality among the MPI Poor is higher in Meghalaya. The magnitude of poverty among the NE States measured by Multidimensional poverty index differs from the population below poverty line measured by Tendulkar or Rangarajan methodology. Rate of poverty reduction or growth of poverty ratio is too lower as compared to the growth of monthly per capita consumption expenditure (MPCE).

Four types of correlation between MPCE and inequality are found among the NE States: lower MPCE with higher inequality, lower MPCE with lower inequality, higher MPCE with lower inequality and higher MPCE with higher inequality. During 2004-05 to 2011-12, poverty ratios were increasing in all states of NE India except Sikkim and Tripura. During 2004-05 to 2011-12, inequality in rural areas had increased in all States of India except Nagaland and Sikkim, while, inequality in urban areas has decreased in all states of NE India except Arunachal Pradesh, Assam and Manipur. On the other hand, inequality in rural areas measured by Lorenz ratio from 2004-05 to 2011-12 had increased in all States of NE India except Nagaland and Sikkim.

In most of the NE States annual growth rate in agriculture was lower than those in industry, manufacturing and services sector. It was apparent from data that share of agriculture and allied sector in GSDP was lower as compared to that of industry and services sector. All these factors indicate the slow progress in rural sector or agriculture in NE region. Thus, it is recommended for consistent and balanced development approach, expansion of capability, improvement in infrastructure and diversification of agriculture across the eight States of North East India. In addition, Multi-dimensional Poverty Index would be better measure of poverty as compared to unidimensional poverty measure.

References

Government of India (2001). *Census of India 2001*, Office of the Registrar General and Census Commissioner, New Delhi: Ministry of Home Affairs.

Government of India (2005). *Household Consumption Expenditure*, National Sample Survey Office, New Delhi: Ministry of Statistics and Programme Implementation.

Government of India (2006). *Level and Pattern of Consumer Expenditure, 2004-05*, NSS 61st Round, *Report No. 555. New Delhi, NSSO: Ministry of Statistics and Programme Implementation.*

Government of India (2008 and 1993). *Housing Condition and Amenities in India, 49th & 65th Round, NSSO Report Nos. 429 & 535*, New Delhi: Ministry of Statistics and Programme Implementation.

Government of India (2011). *Census of India 2011*. New Delhi, Office of the Registrar General and Census Commissioner.

Government of India (2014). *Level and Pattern of Consumer Expenditure, 2011-12, NSS 68th Round, Report No. 555, New Delhi, NSSO: Ministry of Statistics and Programme Implementation.*

Haughton, Jonathan and Khander, S.R. (2010). *Handbook on Poverty and Inequality*. New Delhi: Rawat Publications.

OPHI (2015). OPHI Country Briefing January 2015. India: University of Oxford.

Planning Commission (July 2014). *Press Note on Poverty Estimates, 2011-12*. Planning Commission: Government of India.

Planning Commission (June 2014). *Report of the Expert Group to Review the Methodology for Measurement of Poverty*. Planning Commission: Government of India.

4

Multidimensional Poverty in North Eastern Region of India

An Empirical Study

Niranjan Debnath and *Salim Shah*

Introduction

There has been a conceptual revolution in measuring poverty during the last few decades focusing towards more comprehensive multidimensional framework due to lot of criticism regarding the measurement of poverty based on monetary attribute such as consumption or income. The critics claim that monetary poverty measures are not sufficient to explain multifaceted deprivation of well-being. Poverty measures should contain basic human needs, such as education and health (Tsui, 2002). Poverty is characterised by multidimensional deprivations and therefore be explained by a multidimensional approach (Bourguignon & Chakravarty, 2003). There are a number of possible methodologies for identifying who are multidimensionally poor, namely counting approaches, multiple correspondence analysis, latent variable techniques, and fuzzy set theory. Many of the researchers proposed different multidimensional poverty measures based on the capability approach with a normative framework. The Alkire and Foster (2007) methodology of multidimensional poverty measurement is one of them based on the counting approach (Atkinson, 2003) along with the axiomatic approach following the FGT's (Foster-Greer-Thorbecke) class of unidimensional measures. So that, the axioms of *subgroup decomposability* and *dimensional break down* are allowed to decompose the aggregate value into different population subgroups such as social and religion groups to identify the major drivers of poverty

(Alkire & Foster, 2011). Decomposability of poverty measure appears to be an important component to the policy maker to take effective multi-sectoral planning across different states and districts.

Traditionally, poverty measurement in India revolved around the ability to spend on goods and services that were measured from the consumption side (monetary attribute only) rather than the capability to being and functioning in society (Sen, 1985). Though there has been methodological revisions and debates on multifaceted nature of poverty and need for inclusive growth (GoI, 2009, 2014; Sen and Himanshu, 2004; Deaton and Dre'ze, 2009; Subramanian, 2011, Ahluwalia, 2011). Many of the empirical studies have shown that a significant percentage of multidimensionally poor are not income poor and *viceversa* (Laderchi, Saith and Strewart, 2003; Wang, Feng, Xia and Alkire, 2016). However, the Government of India has moved from an income approach to a multidimensional approach to identify the poor families targeting a better government service provisions since the year 2002. Construction of a new 'index of multiple deprivations' in India has been started in 2008. There has been a wide range of empirical studies on multidimensional poverty measures in India, those are mainly confined to the major states of India.

Recently various studies on multidimensional poverty in India have demonstrated that poverty has fallen between the 1990s and early 2000s (Jayaraj and Subramanian, 2009; Alkire and Seth, 2008, 2013; Mishra and Ray, 2013). Both Jayaraj and Subramanian (2009) and Misha and Ray (2013) using the measure proposed by Chakravarty and D. Ambrosio (2006) found that the reduction in multidimensional poverty at the national level, has not been followed uniform reductions across different population subgroups. Alkire and Seth (2013) found that the population subgroups (by state, caste or religion) that were poorest in 1999 could reduce poverty the least in the next seven years period. Alkire and Seth (2014) show the importance of inequality measures to improve the Alkire-Foster class of poverty measures. Two rounds of Demographic Health Surveys (DHS) with representative years 1998-99 and 2005-06 have been used for inter-temporal analysis of poverty in India and DHS for the year 2005-06 has also been used to compute the global MPI for India by Alkire and Santos (2010). Their study reveals that poverty in terms of MPI as well as the intensity of poverty has fallen between 1999 and 2006. The national MPI has declined at 0.251 in 2006 from 0.300 in 1999; whereas, the intensity has reduced to 51.7 per cent in 2006 from 52.9 per cent in 1999. Although the MPI and its components have been reduced for each of the caste-group, i.e. Scheduled Castes (SC), Scheduled Tribes (ST), Other Backward Classes (OBC), and General, the inequality among the poor appears to be higher for the poorest subgroup, i.e. STs. There has been reduction in inequality across the poor from 0.100 to 0.097 in India as whole, but no such reduction is noticed for each of the subgroups in this regard. The inequality across the poor has fallen within Scheduled Castes and OBCs, but not within Scheduled Tribes and the general category. It is also observed that inequality across the poor within the poorest subgroup has risen though inequality has been reduced in both the overall intra-group and the between-group.

This is fact that there has been a wide range of literature pertaining to poverty measurements in the context of India as a whole or in the context of the major states of India. But, there is dearth of literature related to poverty measurements with a focus to the NER States, neither in terms of monetary nor in terms of non-monetary approaches. Most of the available studies are descriptive in nature mainly focusing on the states as a unit of analysis (Nayyar, 2005; Kurian, 2000; Roy and Haldar, 2008). One recent comprehensive study on the subject of poverty measurement in terms of multidimensional approach related to non-monetary variables by Aklire and Seth (2013) has covered the NER to examine the changes in multidimensional poverty for the period from 1999 to 2006. Moreover, the whole region of the North East is the adobe of diversity with numerous ethnic groups, varied languages and diverse religions, varied forms of governance, varied topography and natural climate, uneven economic development. The whole region is recognised as economically backward characterised by poor educational performances, lack of adequate health service facilities, insufficient road connectivity between and within states and lack of basic amenities. So, uni-dimensional measure of poverty is unable to capture all the dimensions of deprivations as well as the actual causes of backwardness of the region. Only a multidimensional measurement of poverty based on capability approach is expected to reveal the actual problems of the north-eastern region and its states. In spite of the provision for Non-Lapsable Central Pool of Resources (NLCPR) and many other development initiatives, there have been enormous variations among the states within the region of North-East in terms of poverty reduction, curbing inequality, growth rate of per capita NSDP etc. (Shah and Debnath, 2015; Debnath & Shah, 2015; Dehury and Mohanty, 2015; Radhakrishna, 2015; Alkire and Seth, 2013). Thus, there is a need for multidimensional poverty measurement to track the region's poverty levels, to monitor the variation between and within states, across social groups, religions and dimensions that are non-monetary in nature.

Objectives of the Study

For an in-depth understanding of multidimensional deprivations of the NER States and to formulate some pragmatic policy directions for the development of the North Eastern region, the present study mainly focuses on the following research objectives:

(i) To investigate the social and religion group-wise disparity in case of the NER States in terms of multidimensional poverty index (MPI).
(ii) To estimate the relative contribution of each of the indicators to the overall MPI for each of the States across the social and religion groups.

Methodological Issues

The present section of the chapter exemplifies an outline of the methods and materials used to explain the state of multidimensional poverty for the NER States across social and religion groups. This section specifically outlines the data sources, methods of constructing the composite (multidimensional) poverty index and the idea of its decomposition across social and religion groups.

Alkire-Foster Methodology

It has been mentioned earlier that the present assessment of multidimensional poverty is based on the counting approach developed by Alkire and Foster (2007, 2011) owing to its advantages of dual off, joint distribution and decomposability. The present study concentrates on the general form of the social indicators with their ordinal meaning. The in-depth explanation of the methods is available in Alkire and Foster (2011). UNDP has been using the Alkire-Foster methodology to calculate Multidimensional Poverty Index (MPI) for several countries since the year 2010.

Let us consider a group of individuals from which the poor are needed to be identified by using dual cut-off in terms of deprivation cut-off and poverty cut-off in a multidimensional space of achievement. Suppose $d \geq 2$ be the number of dimensions and $X = [x_{ij}]$ be the $n \times d$ matrix of achievements, where x_{ij} is the achievement of individual $i(= 1, 2, 3, \ldots, n)$ in dimension $j(= 1, 2, 3, \ldots, d)$. Let Z be a row vector of dimension-specific deprivation cut-offs z_j. Suppose the deprivation matrix $X^0 = [x_{ij}^0]$ is derived from achievement matrix X as $x_{ij}^0 = 1$ if $(x_{ij} < z_j)$ means that individual i is deprived in dimension j and $x_{ij}^0 = 0$ if $(x_{ij}\ ^3\ z_j)$ implies individual i is not deprived. Let k $(0 < k < 1)$ be the threshold to define an individual as poor. Let C be a column vector of weighted deprivation scores obtained from X^0 deprivation matrix. Column vector C contains sum of weighted derivation scores of each individual counts by each row of x_{ij}^0. An individual i will be considered as poor if $c_i \geq k$. Let $p_i(k)$ be the multidimensionally poor defined as $p_i(k) = 1$ if $c_i\ ^3 \geq k$ and if $p_i(k) = 0$ otherwise. Now the multidimensional headcount ratio H (*incidence of poverty)* is defined as the ratio of total number of multidimensionally poor q_k to the total population (n), that is, H = (q_k/n) where, $q_k = \sum_{i=1}^{n} p_i(k)$. The share of possible deprivations suffered by a poor individual i is obtained by $\overline{c}_i(k) = (1/d)\cdot[c_i p_i(k)]$ and the average deprivation share across the poor *(intensity of poverty)* obtained by $A = [1/(q_k \cdot d)]\cdot \sum_{i=1}^{n} c_i \cdot p_i(k)$. Therefore, the Multidimensional Poverty Index (MPI) defined as the product of *incidence* and *intensity* of poverty. So the value of MPI of a society obtained by $MPI = H \times A$.

However, the major advantage of this measure is of decomposability across population subgroups and across indicators. Thus, MPI is decomposable by the population subgroups because the measure is expressible as the weighted sum of individual poverty and also decomposable by its indicators, because the measure is expressible as the weighted sum of the censored deprivations by indicators to obtain the contribution of each of the indicators to the overall MPI.

Description of Data

The study uses houschold level information from the District Level Household and Facility Survey (DLHS-4), 2013-14 to analyse the multidimensional poverty for the NER States of India. These data were collected for the whole country and covers both rural and urban populations of different states and union territories. DLHS-4 covers 3,91,774 households comprising 17,34,213 individuals and collects the information relating to maternal and child health (MCH) indicators along with demographic and socio-economic characteristics of households etc. However, the present study focuses only on the north-eastern states of

India, namely Arunachal Pradesh, Manipur, Meghalaya, Mizoram, Nagaland, Sikkim, and Tripura and also on the districts of each of these States. The study excludes the state of Assam as it is not covered in the DLHS-4 for household survey. All these seven states together cover about 15 per cent of the surveyed households and 16 per cent of the population covered.

In total 60,227 households were surveyed from 2,237 primary sampling units (PSU), in which rural areas cover 45,868 households from 1696 PSUs and urban areas cover 13,560 households from 541 PSUs for the NER states. The fundamental rationale behind the choice of a household as a unit of analysis is the assumption of sharing of resources among the households. The study uses health, educational information of each individual and information regarding household amenities, housing type, sources of water, lighting and cooking fuel to measure multidimensional poverty.

Selection of Dimensions, Indicators and Cut-offs

The selection of dimensions, indicators and cut-offs for each of the indicators is one of the complex matters that involve methodological decisions and socio-political considerations to measure multidimensional poverty. The present study deals with the problem by following exhaustive literature survey and availability of data. The present study selects three dimensions, viz. health, education, and standard of living. Following Alkire and Seth (2013), the present study has considered *ten* indicators and set the deprivation cut-offs with equal weight to each of the dimensions (*Table A1, Appendix*). The study chooses $k = 0.33$ to identify the multidimensionally poor households to make similarity with the poverty cut-offs set by UNDP to measure Global MPI.

Results and Discussion

Keeping in consideration the diversified developmental experiences of the NER States, the present section of the chapter tries to explore the state of multidimensional poverty across the social and religion groups in each of the states of NER using *ten* indicators of the dimensions of health, education and standard of living in the line of international MPI.

Multidimensional Poverty in the NER States

This section focuses on the intra-state and inter-state disparity in the NER

States in terms of multidimensional poverty across social and religion groups. Regarding values of Multidimensional Poverty Index (MPI), there are observable differences among the North-eastern States of India (Table 4.1). MPI value for the state of Tripura is 0.146, which is two times more than that of the state of Sikkim (0.072). It should be noted that MPI is a product of *incidence* of multidimensional poverty and *intensity* of poverty. Incidence of poverty represents proportion of people who are multidimensionally poor, using the poverty cut-off [$c_i \geq k (= 0.33)$], whereas intensity of poverty indicates the average deprivation among the poor. From Table 4.1, it is observed that intensity of poverty is almost same for all the states, but the incidence of multidimensional poverty varied across the states. In the state of Tripura, 35.8 per cent people are multidimensionally poor which is again almost twice of that of Sikkim.

The total population of each of the states of NER has been divided into different social groups, such as, Scheduled Tribes (STs), Scheduled Castes (SCs), and General (Table 4.1). NER as a whole excluding Assam consists of nearly 75 per cent of ST households, 19.1 per cent of General/UR households including OBC and 6.3 per cent of SC households in case of the present sample. It is worthy to note that for the present sample, the ST population coverage are 80.2 per cent in Arunachal Pradesh, 90.4 per cent in Meghalaya, 93.1 per cent in Nagaland, 96.3 per cent in Mizoram, 43.9 per cent on Manipur, 43.6 per cent in Sikkim and 26.2 per cent in Tripura. Now, it is evident that the values of MPI do not differ widely across the social groups for the states of Manipur and Sikkim. However, poverty in terms of MPI and incidence is highest among STs (MPI: 0.209; Incidence: 0.490) for the state of Tripura followed by SCs (MPI: 0.143; Incidence: 0.359), and General (MPI: 0.114; Incidence: 0.287). Poverty in terms of MPI and incidence is highest among General (MPI: 0.239; Incidence: 0.511) for the state of Mizoram followed by STs (MPI: 0.084; Incidence: 0.198) and SCs (MPI: 0.062; Incidence: 0.167). Poverty in terms of MPI and incidence is highest among SCs (MPI: 0.158; Incidence: 0.360) for the state of Meghalaya followed by STs (MPI: 0.136; Incidence: 0.320) and General (MPI. 0.070; Incidence: 0.175). Poverty in terms of MPI and incidence is highest among SCs (MPI: 0.127; Incidence: 0.283) for the state of Nagaland followed by General (MPI: 0.095; Incidence: 0.225) and STs (MPI: 0.077; Incidence: 0.196). Poverty in terms of MPI and incidence is highest among General (MPI: 0.179; Incidence: 0.370) for the state of Arunachal Pradesh followed by STs (MPI: 0.125; Incidence: 0.296) and SCs (MPI: 0.109; Incidence: 0.256). This is also clear from the above (Table 4.1) that intensity of poverty

Table 4.1: State of Multidimensional Poverty: Across Social Groups

States	*Incidence*				*Intensity*				*MPI*			
	SC	*ST*	*General*	*Overall*	*SC*	*ST*	*General*	*Overall*	*SC*	*ST*	*General*	*Overall*
Arunachal Pradesh	0.256	0.296	0.370	0.305	0.426	0.421	0.483	0.432	0.109	0.125	0.179	0.132
Manipur	0.295	0.285	0.276	0.282	0.404	0.401	0.415	0.408	0.119	0.114	0.115	0.115
Maghalaya	0.360	0.320	0.175	0.316	0.438	0.427	0.403	0.427	0.125	0.136	0.070	0.135
Mizoram	0.167	0.198	0.511	0.206	0.371	0.423	0.467	0.425	0.062	0.084	0.239	0.088
Nagaland	0.283	0.196	0.225	0.200	0.450	0.392	0.420	0.396	0.127	0.077	0.095	0.079
Sikkim	0.186	0.179	0.189	0.185	0.400	0.392	0.385	0.390	0.074	0.070	0.073	0.072
Tripura	0.359	0.490	0.287	0.358	0.399	0.426	0.396	0.407	0.143	0.209	0.114	0.146

Source: Authors' Estimation, 2018.

does not have much variation across the social groups of the states but incidence of poverty varies widely across the social groups. Therefore, more policy focus would be on favourable distribution of facilities among the social groups in each of the States.

Regarding religious distribution, the total population of the NER (excluding Assam) may be divided into five major religious groups, namely Hindu, Muslims, Christian, Buddhist and Others (*Table A2, Appendix*). All the religious groups excluding Hindu, Muslims, Christian, and Buddhist are combined in one population subgroup as 'Others'. In the present sample, about 56 per cent of the Christian and nearly 25 per cent of the Hindu households of the NER have been covered. For state specific distribution of households, the states of Mizoram, Nagaland and Meghalaya have about 85 per cent Christian, the state of Tripura has about 80 per cent Hindu, the states of Arunachal Pradesh and Manipur have a combination of Hindu and Christian majority and the state of Sikkim has a majority combination of Hindu and Buddhist. This is also evident that Muslim has highest value of MPI along with higher proportion of multidimensionally poor household in the states of Nagaland, Meghalaya, and Arunachal Pradesh among the different religious groups. On the other hand, both the MPI value and incidence of multidimensional poverty are highest for the Buddhist for the state of Mizoram and Manipur. Further, the Muslim population has the second highest MPI value and incidence of poverty for the state of Manipur. The Christian in Mizoram and Hindus in Manipur have the lowest incidence of poverty as well as MPI values. In case of Sikkim, Buddhist population has the lowest incidence of poverty as well as lowest value of MPI followed by Hindus (the two dominant population subgroups). However, the Muslims of Sikkim has the highest incidence as well as MPI value excepting the 'Others' (whose representation is negligible in sample population). For the state of Tripura, both the MPI values and incidence of poverty are highest for the Buddhists and Muslims, excepting the 'Others' whose sample population representation is negligible.

To summarise, there is a significant variation in the state of poverty among the social groups as well as among the religious groups across the states of north eastern region of India. This is largely due to their variations in incidence of multidimensional poverty. However, there has been little variation in intensity of poverty among the social groups as well as among the religious groups across the states of NER.

Dimensional Decomposition of Poverty

Breaking down of multidimensional poverty allows us to have a clear picture of the composition of different dimensions and indicators and their relative contribution to overall poverty as the MPI can be expressed as an average of censored head count ratios of indicators weighed by their relative weight.

Censored Headcount Ratio: Across Social and Religious Groups

The decomposition of multidimensional poverty has been carried out to the composition of different indicators to multidimensional poverty in the NER States. Censored Headcount Ratio of any indicator indicates the proportion of population, who are multidimensionally poor as well as deprived in that indicator. The censored headcount ratios make a clear picture of disparity in the composition of poverty across the social and religious groups. For example, the censored headcount ratio for malnutrition is 0.298 for the social group SC in Tripura, which indicates that 29.8 per cent of SC households are multidimensionally poor as well as deprived in malnutrition (*Table A3, Appendix*). It also appears that censored headcount ratios for education and standard of living dimensions are higher among the multidimensionally poor, who belong to the General category in the states of Arunachal Pradesh and Mizoram. On the other side, SC households are relatively more deprived in standard of living dimension in the states of Manipur, Meghalaya, Nagaland and Sikkim. Deprivation in health and standard of living dimensions appears to be more among the SC households in Tripura. ST households are more deprived in health dimension in the states of Mizoram, Nagaland and Sikkim. However, the censored headcount ratios are higher in malnutrition indicator for health dimension and cooking fuel, housing type and asset holding indicators for the standard of living dimension among the social groups across the NER States. Therefore, target specific policies are essential to reduce the disparity among social groups across the states of NER in terms of multidimensional non-monetary poverty.

The censored headcount ratios for each indicator of multidimensional poverty are given in *Table A4, Appendix* corresponding to the religious groups for each of the states of NER. Censored headcount ratios appear to be relatively higher for the Muslims in each of the indicators of health, education and standard of living dimension for the states of Manipur and Nagaland. Deprivation in school attendance and years of schooling indicators of education dimension; malnutrition indicator of health dimension; safe drinking water, cooking fuel, housing type and asset holding indicators of standard of living dimension are in more vulnerable condition for the Muslims in Nagaland, whereas, malnutrition indicator of health dimension and all six indicators of standard of living dimension are in susceptible situation for the Muslims in Manipur. Deprivation in health, education and standard of living dimensions are relatively more in vulnerable condition for the Buddhist in the state of Mizoram and Tripura. The Muslims are also in relatively susceptible condition in Arunachal Pradesh and Sikkim in the indicator of health and education dimension as well as some indicators of standard of living dimension.

Indicator-wise Contribution to MPI Across the Groups

The dimensional contribution to MPI across the social and religious groups for each of the states of NER is represented by the sum of the contribution of each of the indicators to MPI. The contribution of each of the indicators to the overall MPI for each of the subgroups is given in *Table A5* and *Table A6* in the *Appendix*. From *Table A5*, it is clear that the states of Sikkim, Nagaland and Mizoram have almost equal level of multidimensional poverty among the Scheduled Tribes (STs) but the contribution of each of the dimensions and indicators to poverty of the STs varies across the states. For example, health dimension alone contributes 46.2 per cent of deprivation whereas its indicators, namely mortality and malnutrition separately contribute 14.2 per cent and 32.0 per cent to deprivation respectively for the STs for the state of Mizoram. For Nagaland, health dimension contributes 33.1 per cent of deprivation for STs whereas its indicators mortality and malnutrition respectively contribute 6.4 per cent and 26.7 per cent for the STs (*Table A5, Appendix*). Similarly, deprivation in standard of living dimension contributes 39.1 per cent to overall poverty of which cooking fuel contributes 10.8 per cent followed by asset holding (8.5%), housing type (8.4%), safe drinking water (4.9%), sanitation facility (4.9%) and electricity (1.6%) for STs of the state of Mizoram. However, deprivation in standard of living dimension contributes 48.3 per cent to overall poverty of which cooking fuel contributes 13.8 per cent followed by housing type (12.0%), asset holding (11.6%), safe drinking water (6.6%), sanitation facility (3.6%) and electricity (0.6%) for STs of the state of Nagaland. Taking the NER as a whole, standard of living dimension is the highest contributor to the MPI, followed by health and education dimension among the Schedule

Tribes (STs) and this is true for all the States. In a nutshell, malnutrition indicator of health dimension, years of schooling indicator of education dimension, and cooking fuel, housing type and asset holding indicators of standard of living dimension appear to be the most important indicators for the people belong to the social group STs in each of the states of NER. The states of Tripura and Meghalaya have almost the equal value of MPI. However, the health dimension contributes 45.0 per cent to the MPI of which 10.5 per cent arises from mortality indicator and 34.5 per cent from malnutrition for the Schedule Castes (SCs) in case of Tripura. For Meghalaya, the health dimension contributes 29.2 per cent and the whole is owing to the malnutrition indicator. The standard of living dimension contributes nearly 46 per cent for the both states of Tripura and Meghalaya. Where cooking fuel, asset holding, housing type and sanitation indicators contribute nearly 43 per cent to the MPI for SCs in Meghalaya but only three indicators—cooking fuel, housing type and asset holding contributes more than 37 per cent for the SCs in Tripura. Education dimension contributes more or less 20 per cent to the MPI for the social group SCs in case of all of the states of NER, except Tripura and Manipur. Standard of living dimension contributes more than 40 per cent to the MPI for SCs for each of the states of NER, except Mizoram. In case of standard of living dimension, major contributors are cooking fuel, housing type and asset holding. Deprivation in education dimension contributes more or less 20 per cent to the MPI for the General category in case of all of the states of NER, except Sikkim, Tripura and Manipur. In education dimension, years of schooling contributes highest to poverty. Malnutrition contributes highest to poverty for health dimension as well as among the other indicators of all dimensions for General category. Standard of living dimension contributes, nearly 40 per cent to the MPI for General category in each of the states of NER of which major contributors are cooking fuel, housing type and asset holding.

The contribution of each of the indicators to MPI across the religious groups for each of the states of NER is shown in *Table A6* in the *Appendix*. The states of Manipur and Meghalaya have equal value of MPI for the Hindus but there is a clear variation in dimensional and indicator wise contribution to multidimensional poverty. For example, deprivation in standard of living dimension and health dimension contribute 51.9 per cent and 43.1 per cent respectively in Manipur where the contributions are respectively 49.7 per cent and 34.4 per cent for the state of Meghalaya for the Hindus. Again, for the Hindu's, years of schooling contributes more than three times to poverty in Meghalaya than that of Manipur and on other hand, mortality contributes more than five times to poverty in Manipur than that of Meghalaya (*Table A6, Appendix*). This is also evident that the contribution of different dimensions or indicators to the multidimensional poverty varies for Muslims in the states of Manipur and Tripura, though the value of MPI reveals to be the same. Deprivation in the health and standard of living dimension is higher for the religious group Muslims in Manipur than that of Tripura. However, years of schooling, malnutrition, cooking fuel, housing type and asset holding are indicator wise relatively major contributor to poverty Tripura than that of Manipur for the Muslims. The variation in contributions all the dimensions to multidimensional poverty is also noticed for the Christian in the states of Arunachal Pradesh, Meghalaya and Tripura in spite of almost equal value of MPI.

Conclusion

The present study systematically exemplifies that huge disparity is there regarding the state of multidimensional poverty across the States, social groups and religious groups in the North East Region of India. The variation is mainly due to the differences in incidence of multidimensional poverty across the entities. However, there is marked average deprivations (intensity of poverty) among the poor with more or less uniform spread. For the social groups, the dominant social groups (majority people) are in relatively better position than the minority groups in majority of the states. The censored headcount ratios and decomposition of multidimensional poverty indicate that some of the indicators are more crucial for the purpose of developmental policy formulation. Malnutrition appears to be the robust indicator for majority of the north-eastern states with a higher contribution to overall MPI values. Censored headcount ratios and decomposition reveal that deprivation in the health and standard of living dimension is higher for the social and religious groups in general and years of schooling, malnutrition, cooking fuel, housing type and asset holding are indicator-wise relatively major contributor to poverty.

Appendix

Table A1: Dimensions, Indicator, Drivation Cut-offs and Weights for the MPI

Dimension (Weight)	*Indicator (Weight)*	*Deprivation Cut-off*
Education (1/3)	Years of Schooling (1/6)	Deprived if at least any adults member of household has not completed primary level of education
	Child Enrolment (1/6)	Deprived if any school-aged child (6-14 years) in the household is not attending school in the academic years
Health (1/3)	Mortality (1/6)	Deprived if any member of the household including children has died in the family since 2008
	Nutrition (1/6)	Deprived if any adult or child for whom there is nutritional information is mal-nourished
Standard of Living (1/3)	Electricity (1/18)	Deprived if the household has no electricity
	Drinking water (1/18)	Deprived if the household does not have access to clean drinking water
	Sanitation (1/18)	Deprived if they do not have an improved toilet or if their toilet is shared
	Flooring (1/18)	Deprived if the household has *kachha* House or other
	Cooking Fuel (1/18)	Deprived if they cook with fire wood, crop-residue, kerosene or cow-dung-cake
	Assets (1/18)	Deprived if the household owns any of the following assets: television, radio, telephone or mobile, Watch Clock, By-cycle, cart driven by animal or other cart. At the same time, does not own any of the following assets: a refrigerator, a motorbike, a car, a computer, washing machine, sewing machine. Air Conditioner, water pump, a thresher, or a tractor

Table A2: State of Multidimensional Poverty: Across Religious Groups

State	*Poverty*	*Hindu*	*Muslim*	*Christian*	*Buddhism*	*Others*
Arunachal Pradesh	Population Share	25.8%	1.6%	34.1%	11.7%	26.7%
	Incidence	0.305	0.360	0.330	0.318	0.263
	Intensity	0.451	0.462	0.438	0.428	0.401
	MPI	0.138	0.166	0.145	0.136	0.105
Manipur	Population Share	43.5%	5.1%	44.6%	0.3%	6.5%
	Incidence	0.252	0.466	0.289	0.596	0.270
	Intensity	0.411	0.423	0.402	0.465	0.407
	MPI	0.104	0.197	0.116	0.277	0.110
Meghalaya	Population Share	7.1%	3.1%	85.7%	0.1%	4.0%
	Incidence	0.254	0.518	0.310	0.000	0.401
	Intensity	0.419	0.447	0.425	0.000	0.445
	MPI	0.106	0.232	0.132	0.000	0.179
Mizoram	Population Share	1.2%	0.4%	89.0%	9.1%	0.3%
	Incidence	0.189	0.274	0.159	0.663	0.260
	Intensity	0.430	0.355	0.402	0.481	0.373
	MPI	0.082	0.097	0.064	0.319	0.097
Nagaland	Population Share	3.6%	1.6%	94.7%	0.1%	0.1%
	Incidence	0.201	0.516	0.194	0.292	0.148
	Intensity	0.400	0.480	0.392	0.389	0.359
	MPI	0.080	0.248	0.076	0.114	0.053
Sikkim	Population Share	53.7%	2.1%	8.8%	34.6%	0.8%
	Incidence	0.188	0.325	0.226	0.157	0.387
	Intensity	0.391	0.388	0.390	0.389	0.345
	MPI	0.073	0.126	0.088	0.061	0.133
Tripura	Population Share	83.9%	7.9%	4.9%	3.2%	0.1%
	Incidence	0.339	0.479	0.375	0.536	0.607
	Intensity	0.404	0.411	0.427	0.439	0.500
	MPI	0.137	0.197	0.160	0.235	0.303

Source: Author's Estimation.

Table A3: Censored Head Count Ratio Across the Social Groups of NER States

States	*Caste Category*	*Education*		*Health*			*Standard of Living*				
		D_{11}	D_{12}	D_{21}	D_{22}	D_{31}	D_{32}	D_{33}	D_{34}	D_{35}	D_{36}
Arunachal Pradesh	SC	3.9	12.2	3.1	17.1	3.5	12.7	20.9	22.0	8.1	19.8
	ST	7.0	16.2	9.9	20.8	2.4	S.6	12.4	10.8	2.6	9.3
	GN	9.4	21.1	6.2	23.8	8.6	19.2	35.1	33.4	15.9	28.1
Manipur	SC	1.8	3.6	5.6	23.9	19.1	10.6	27.3	23.1	5.2	24.5
	ST	1.6	6.9	7.6	29.5	8.9	5.1	13.5	11.7	3.5	11.6
	GN	1.1	2.9	6.9	21.6	19.8	9.3	25.2	21.0	11.9	21.7
Meghalaya	SC	7.2	15.3	0.1	27.7	2.8	25.3	35.5	27.9	8.6	33.1
	ST	6.9	19.4	3.9	23.6	4.8	6.8	12.8	8.9	2.8	10.2
	GN	2.3	5.8	2.1	14.4	2.9	7.4	15.9	11.4	4.9	10.6
Mizoram	SC	3.4	3.5	0.4	16.1	2.1	2.4	12.1	11.1	2.0	11.6
	ST	3.3	11.5	14.2	32.0	4.9	4.9	10.8	8.4	1.6	8.5
	GN	12.1	30.4	5.3	26.0	32.5	31.2	49.1	43.1	9.5	43.3
Nagaland	SC	6.0	14.5	5.5	19.9	12.3	4.6	24.3	24.0	1.5	25.1
	ST	3.3	15.4	6.4	26.7	6.6	3.6	13.8	12.0	0.6	11.6
	GN	3.4	9.4	2.7	18.1	6.2	3.8	20.8	18.4	0.3	20.0
Sikkim	SC	0.5	8.3	3.0	13.0	6.5	2.2	17.6	15.7	1.3	16.4
	ST	2.4	16.3	14.9	23.8	6.9	1.6	13.0	8.1	0.9	12.2
	GN	0.8	5.8	5.6	14.4	6.8	1.9	15.8	11.0	0.9	15.2
Tripura	SC	1.7	6.2	9.0	29.8	8.1	9.3	34.8	33.3	4.8	27.8
	ST	3.1	13.1	3.6	26.9	7.1	7.5	13.0	12.7	3.4	9.7
	GN	0.7	4.5	7.8	24.8	5.8	7.7	27.0	25.8	3.8	21.0

Source: Authors' Estimation, 2018.

Notes: D_{11} denotes Currently School Attendence; D_{12} denotes Highest Years of Schooling, D_{21} denotes Motality, D_{22} denotes Malnutrition, D_{31} denotes Safe Drinking Water, D_{32} denotes Sanitation, D_{33} denotes Cooking Fuel, D_{34} denotes Housing Type, D_{35} denotes Electricity; D_{36} denotes Assets.

Table A4: Censored Head Count Ratio Across the Religious Groups of NER States

States	Religious Group	Education		Health		Standard of Living					
		D_{11}	D_{12}	D_{21}	D_{22}	D_{31}	D_{32}	D_{33}	D_{34}	D_{35}	D_{36}
Arunachal Pradesh	Hindu	6.4	15.3	6.2	18.2	4.8	17.2	28.4	26.5	9.2	23.2
	Muslim	9.6	22.3	4.1	21.3	8.1	19.7	30.8	32.2	6.9	29.9
	Christian	7.0	12.9	7.4	18.6	8.9	21.2	31.0	29.7	9.2	22.3
	Buddhist	4.8	18.9	6.2	14.5	6.0	21.9	30.0	18.9	10.0	24.6
	Others	3.7	9.4	1.1	13.7	2.1	16.6	24.4	21.7	2.6	18.6
Manipur	Hindu	0.6	2.5	6.7	20.1	17.2	8.2	22.8	19.3	9.0	20.2
	Muslim	5.4	6.7	7.5	34.3	36.0	17.2	44.7	35.0	25.0	35.3
	Christian	1.2	4.8	5.4	20.5	18.8	10.7	28.2	24.5	7.1	24.1
	Buddhist	0.0	9.9	5.1	45.6	59.6	54.7	54.5	59.6	37.2	51.3
	Others	1.2	2.6	5.7	21.3	19.4	8.4	25.1	19.1	12.7	21.1
Meghalaya	Hindu	2.2	8.0	1.4	20.5	9.9	16.4	23.6	19.1	5.8	20.4
	Muslim	11.3	23.5	0.0	39.7	1.7	39.2	51.3	40.0	14.0	47.1
	Christian	5.5	15.3	3.3	18.7	11.3	15.6	30.6	21.0	6.4	24.1
	Buddhist	0.0	0.0	0.0	0.0	0.0	0.0	0.0	0.0	0.0	0.0
	Others	9.3	26.2	1.8	19.6	13.7	27.6	39.7	26.9	10.7	32.1
Mizoram	Hindu	2.9	8.6	1.6	13.9	3.0	6.4	17.2	17.3	2.8	18.9
	Muslim	4.4	1 3	3.6	21.1	9.6	j.6	18.4	11.3	0.0	23.0
	Christian	1.0	3.2	7.0	13.8	4.6	4.3	12.3	8.5	1.0	9.5
	Buddhist	11.2	37.5	7.2	40.3	42.9	44.7	65.5	62.3	17.3	52.5
	Others	0.0	5.9	20.1	26.0	1.1	0.0	5.9	5.9	0.0	3.3
Nagaland	Hindu	1.5	7.6	3.6	16.0	7.6	2.5	15.0	15.4	0.8	17.2
	Muslim	15.7	32.8	8.5	35.1	17.6	9.1	49.7	44.4	1.6	47.4
	Christian	1.5	7.0	2.9	12.2	9.1	4.9	19.0	16.5	0.9	16.0
	Buddhist	0.0	0.0	0.0	29.2	29.2	0.0	29.2	29.2	0.0	29.2
	Others	0.0	2.3	0.0	14.8	2.3	0.0	14.8	14.8	0.0	12.6
Sikkim	Hindu	0.8	6.0	5.6	13.5	7.6	2.0	16.4	12.0	1.0	15.4
	Muslim	6.0	16.0	6.1	30.1	2.8	4.3	14.0	7.9	0.0	22.7
	Christian	1.0	7.6	4.8	15.9	9.1	3.6	21.8	15.8	1.2	19.2
	Buddhist	0.6	6.5	6.0	8.1	7.2	1.5	14.3	8.4	1.3	13.6
	Others	0.0	7.4	2.4	33.1	14.9	0.0	36.3	23.8	0.0	36.3
Tripura	Hindu	1.5	6.5	7.6	27.6	10.6	11.7	32.6	31.4	5.4	25.0
	Muslim	3.4	13.9	6.6	38.5	11.0	17.0	47.1	45.2	7.3	33.7
	Christian	1.7	15.4	4.0	23.5	22.0	22.2	37.5	36.3	9.6	27.1
	Buddhist	4.8	21.5	4.7	30.0	31.6	35.5	53.6	52.1	25.6	41.8
	Others	0.0	60.7	0.0	60.7	0.0	0.0	60.7	60.7	0.0	60.7

Source: Authors' Estimation, 2018.

Notes: D_{11} denotes Currently School Attendence; D_{12} denotes Highest Years of Schooling, D_{21} denotes Mortality, D_{22} denotes Malnutrition, D_{31} denotes Soft Drinking Water, D_{32} denotes Sanitation, D_{33} denotes Cooking Fuel, D_{34} denotes Housing Type, D_{35} denotes Electricity; D_{36} denotes Assets.

Table A5: Indicator-wise Contribution to the MPI: Across the Social Groups

States	*Caste Category*	*Education*		*Health*			*Standard of Living*				
		D_{11}	D_{12}	D_{21}	D_{22}	D_{31}	D_{32}	D_{33}	D_{34}	D_{35}	D_{36}
Arunachal Pradesh	SC	5.9	18.7	4.8	26.1	1.8	6.5	10.7	11.2	4.2	10.1
	ST	7.0	16.2	9.9	20.8	2.4	8.6	12.4	10.8	2.6	9.3
	GN	8.8	19.7	5.7	22.2	2.7	6.0	10.9	10.4	4.9	8.7
Manipur	SC	2.5	5.1	7.8	33.5	8.9	4.9	12.7	10.8	2.4	11.4
	ST	1.6	6.9	7.6	29.5	8.9	5.1	13.5	11.7	3.5	11.6
	GN	1.6	4.2	10.1	31.4	9.6	4.5	12.2	10.2	5.8	10.5
Meghalaya	SC	7.6	16.2	0.0	29.2	1.0	8.9	12.5	9.8	3.0	11.7
	ST	6.9	19.4	3.9	23.6	4.8	6.8	12.8	8.9	2.8	10.2
	GN	5.3	13.8	4.9	34.1	2.3	5.8	12.5	9.0	3.8	8.4
Mizoram	SC	9.2	9.4	1.0	43.4	1.9	2.2	10.8	10.0	1.7	10.4
	ST	3.3	11.5	14.2	32.0	4.9	4.9	10.8	8.4	1.6	8.5
	GN	8.5	21.2	3.7	18.1	7.6	7.3	11.4	10.0	2.2	10.1
Nagaland	SC	7.8	18.9	7.2	26.0	5.4	2.0	10.6	10.5	0.6	11.0
	ST	3.3	15.4	6.4	26.7	6.6	3.6	13.8	12.0	0.6	11.6
	GN	5.9	16.6	4.7	31.9	3.7	2.2	12.2	10.8	0.2	11.8
Sikkim	SC	1.1	18.5	6.7	29.1	4.9	1.6	13.2	11.8	1.0	12.3
	ST	2.4	16.3	14.9	23.8	6.9	1.6	13.0	8.1	0.9	12.2
	GN	1.9	13.2	12.8	32.9	5.1	1.5	12.0	8.4	0.7	11.6
Tripura	SC	2.0	7.2	10.5	34.6	3.1	3.6	13.5	12.9	1.9	10.8
	ST	3.1	13.1	3.6	26.9	7.1	7.5	13.0	12.7	3.4	9.7
	GN	1.0	6.6	11.4	36.4	2.8	3.8	13.2	12.6	1.9	10.2

Notes: D_{11} denotes Currently School Attendence; D_{12} denotes Highest Years of Schooling, D_{21} denotes Morality, D_{22} denotes Malnutrition, D_{31} denotes Soft Drinking Water, D_{32} denotes Sanitation, D_{33} denotes Cooking fuel, D_{34} denotes Housing Type, D_{35} denotes Electricity; D_{36} denotes Assets.

Source: Authors' Estimation, 2018.

Table A6: Indicator-wise Contribution to the MPI Across the Religious Groups

States	Religious Group	Education		Health		Standard of Living					
		D_{11}	D_{12}	D_{21}	D_{22}	D_{31}	D_{32}	D_{33}	D_{34}	D_{35}	D_{36}
Arunachal Pradesh	Hindu	7.7	18.6	7.5	22.1	1.9	6.9	11.5	10.7	3.7	9.4
	Muslim	9.6	22.3	4.1	21.4	2.7	6.6	10.3	10.8	2.3	10.0
	Christian	8.1	14.9	8.6	21.5	3.4	8.1	11.9	11.4	3.5	8.5
	Buddhist	5.9	23.1	7.6	17.8	2.5	9.0	12.2	7.7	4.1	10.1
	Others	5.8	14.9	12.1	21.8	1.1	8.7	12.9	11.4	1.4	9.9
Manipur	Hindu	1.0	4.0	10.8	32.3	9.2	4.4	12.2	10.4	4.8	10.9
	Muslim	4.6	5.6	6.4	29.0	10.1	4.9	12.6	9.9	7.0	9.9
	Christian	1.7	6.9	7.7	29.5	9.0	5.1	13.5	11.7	3.4	11.5
	Buddhist	0.0	5.9	3.1	27.4	12.0	11.0	10.9	12.0	7.5	10.3
	Others	1.8	3.9	8.6	32.3	9.8	4.3	12.7	9.6	6.4	10.6
Mizoram	Hindu	6.0	17.7	3.2	28.4	2.1	4.3	11.8	11.8	1.9	12.9
	Muslim	7.5	12.5	6.1	36.2	5.5	2.0	10.5	6.5	0.0	13.1
	Christian	2.5	8.4	18.3	36.0	3.9	3.7	10.6	7.3	0.9	8.2
	Buddhist	5.9	19.6	3.7	21.1	7.5	7.8	11.4	10.9	3.0	9.1
	Others	0.0	10.1	34.6	44.7	1.9	0.0	3.4	3.4	0.0	1.9
Meghalaya	Hindu	3.4	12.5	2.2	32.2	5.2	8.6	12.3	10.0	3.0	10.7
	Muslim	8.1	16.9	0.0	28.6	0.4	9.4	12.3	9.6	3.4	11.3
	Christian	6.9	19.3	4.1	23.7	4.8	6.6	12.9	8.8	2.7	10.2
	Buddhist	0.0	0.0	0.0	0.0	0.0	0.0	0.0	0.0	0.0	0.0
	Others	8.6	24.4	1.7	18.3	4.3	8.6	12.4	8.4	3.3	10.0
Nagaland	Hindu	3.1	15.8	7.4	33.2	5.3	1.7	10.4	10.6	0.6	11.9
	Muslim	10.6	22.0	5.7	23.6	4.0	2.0	11.1	9.9	0.4	10.6
	Christian	3.3	15.3	6.4	26.8	6.6	3.6	13.8	12.0	0.6	11.6
	Buddhist	0.0	0.0	0.0	42.9	14.3	0.0	14.3	14.3	0.0	14.3
	Others	0.0	7.1	0.0	46.5	2.4	0.0	15.5	15.5	0.0	13.1
Sikkim	Hindu	1.9	13.6	12.6	30.7	5.8	1.5	12.4	9.1	0.7	11.7
	Muslim	8.0	21.1	8.1	39.8	1.2	1.9	6.5	3.5	0.0	10.0
	Christian	2.0	14.4	9.2	30.0	5.7	2.3	13.7	9.9	0.7	12.1
	Buddhist	1.6	17.7	16.5	22.2	6.6	1.3	13.0	7.7	1.2	12.3
	Others	0.0	9.2	3.0	41.4	6.2	0.0	15.1	9.9	0.0	15.1
Tripura	Hindu	1.8	7.9	9.2	33.6	4.3	4.8	13.2	12.7	2.2	10.1
	Muslim	2.9	11.8	5.6	32.7	3.1	4.8	13.3	12.8	2.1	11.0
	Christian	1.8	16.0	4.1	24.5	7.6	7.7	13.0	12.6	3.3	9.4
	Buddhist	3.4	15.2	3.3	21.3	7.5	8.4	12.7	12.3	6.0	9.9
	Others	0.0	33.3	0.0	33.3	0.0	0.0	11.1	11.1	0.0	11.1

Notes: D_{11} denotes Currently School Attendence; D_{12} denotes Highest Years of Schooling, D_{21} denotes Morality, D_{22} denotes Malnutrition, D_{31} denotes Soft Drinking Water, D_{32} denotes Sanitation, D_{33} denotes Cooking Fuel, D_{34} denotes Housing Type, D_{35} denotes Electricity; D_{36} denotes Assets.

Source: Authors Estimation, 2018.

References

Ahluwalia, M.S. (2011). "Prospects and policy challenges in the twelfth plan", *Economic and Political Weekly*, 46(21): 88-105.

Alkire, S. and Foster, J.E. (2007). *Counting and Multidimensional Poverty Measures*, Oxford: University of Oxford, OPHI Working Paper 07.

Alkire, S. and Foster, J.E. (2011). "Counting and multidimensional poverty measurement", *Journal of Public Economics*, 95(7): 476-487.

Alkire, S. and Santos, M.E. (2010). *Acute Multidimensional Poverty: A New Index for Developing Countries*, Oxford: University of Oxford, OPHI Working Paper 38.

Alkire, S. and Seth, S. (2008). Measuring Multidimensional Poverty in India: A New Proposal. *Working Paper 15.* Oxford University, United Kingdom: Oxford Poverty and Human Development Initiative.

Alkire, S. and Seth, S. (2013). Multidimensional Poverty Reduction in India between 1999 and 2006: Where and How? *OPHI Working Paper No. 60.* United Kingdom: Oxford Poverty and Human Development Initiative, University of Oxford.

Atkinson, A.B. (2003). "Multidimensional deprivation: Contrasting social welfare and counting approaches", *Journal of Economic Inequality*, Vol. 1, pp. 51-65.

Bourguignon, F. and Chakravarty, S.R. (2003). "The measurement of multidimensional poverty", *Journal of Economic Inequality*, 1(1): 25-49.

Deaton, A. and Dreze, J. (February 2009). "Food and nutrition in India: Facts and interpretations", *Economic and Political Weekly*, XLIV(7): -42-65.

Debnath, N. and Shah, S. (March 2015). "Regional disparity in terms of economic well-being using multidimensional poverty index: A case study in Tripura", *Vidyasagar University Journal of Commerce*, Vol. 20, pp. 136-150.

Dehury, B. and Mohanty, K.S. (November, 2015). "Regional estimates of multidimensional poverty in India", *Economics: The Open-Access, Open-Assessment E-Journal*, Vol. 9, pp. 1-35. http://dx.doi.org/10.5018/economics-ejournal.ja.2015-36.

Government of India (November 2009). *Report of the Expert Group to Review the Methodology for Estimation of Poverty.* New Delhi: Planning Commission.

Government of India (June 2014). *Report of the Expert Group to Review the Methodology for Measurement of Poverty.* New Delhi: Planning Commission.

Jayaraj, D., Subramanian, S. and Chakravarty, D. (2010). "Ambrosio view of multidimensional deprivation: Some estimates for India", *Economic and Political Weekly*, 45(6): 53-65.

Kurian, N.J. (2000). "Widening regional disparities in India: Some indicators", *Economic and Political Weekly*, 35(7): 538-550.

Laderchi, C.R., Saith, R. and Stewart, F. (2003). "Does it matter that we do not agree on the definition of poverty? A comparison of four approaches", *Oxford Development Studies*, 31(3): 243-274.

Mishra, A. and Ray, R. (2013). "Multi-dimensional deprivation in India during and after the reforms: Do the household expenditure and the family health surveys present consistent evidence?" *Social Indicators Research,* 110(2): 791-818.

Nayyar, G. (2005). "Growth and poverty in rural India: An analysis of inter-state differences", *Economic and Political Weekly,* 40(16): 1631-1639.

Radhakrishna, R. (2015). "Well-being, inequality, poverty and pathways out of poverty in India", *Economic and Political Weekly,* Vol. L (41): 59-71.

Roy, K. and Haldar, S.K. (2008). "Multidimensional poverty in India: A state-level study from 1981 to 2001", *Indian Journal of Regional Science,* Vol. XXXX (2): 7-20.

Sen, A. and Himanshu (September, 2004). "Poverty and inequality in India-II widening disparities during the 1990s", *Economic and Political Weekly,* pp. 4361-4375.

Sen, A.K. (1985). *Commodities and Capabilities,* Oxford University Press.

Seth, S. and Alkire, S. (2014). Measuring and Decomposing Inequality among the Multidimensionally Poor Using Ordinal Data: A Counting Approach. OPHI Working Papers 68, University of Oxford.

Shah, S. and Debnath, N. (2015). *Regional and Social Disparity A Special Focus on Tripura,* Kolkata: Progressive Publishers.

Subramanian, S. (November 2011). "The Poverty line: Getting it wrong again", *Economic and Political Weekly,* 46(48): 37-42.

Tsui, K. (2002). "Multidimensional poverty indices", *Social Choice and Welfare,* 19(69-93).

UNDP (2010). *Human Development Report 2010: The Real Wealth of Nations: Pathways to Human Development.* New York: Oxford University Press.

Wang, X.; Feng, H.; Xia, Q. and Alkire, S. (2016). "On the relationship between income poverty and multidimensional poverty in China", *OPHI Working Paper 101,* University of Oxford.

5
Food Insecurity in India
A Comparative Study of Hills and Plains

Raju Mandal and *Pallabi Dhar*

Introduction

Achieving and maintaining food security for the growing populations is a major challenge faced by the countries today. This has become more challenging because of the fact that food security requires not only availability of a sufficient physical quantity of food but it has to be accessible to people, nutritious in contents and stable over time. According to FAO (2009), food security is said to exist when all people at all times have physical, social and economic access to sufficient, safe and nutritious food that meets their dietary needs for an active and healthy life.

Technological improvements have led to enormous increase in the production of food items in a country like India over the years. This, along with trade liberalization, has enabled the country to increase availability of physical quantity of food. Nonetheless, it has not been accessible to millions of households which is quite evident from the fact that more than a third of its population is estimated to be absolutely poor, and as many as half of its children have suffered from malnourishment over the last three decades (Upadhyay and Palanivel, 2011). According to Radhakrishna (2005), the achievement of macro foodgrain security at the national level did not percolate down to households as a result of which the level of chronic food insecurity in India is still high. On the other hand, use of excessive chemicals in cultivation and adulteration of food items have severely damaged their nutritional contents. In the process of intensive use of both natural and chemical factors for producing rice and wheat the Green Revolution has led to serious environmental problems such as reduction in soil fertility, imbalance in nutrient contents of soil, depletion of groundwater etc. (Bhushan, 2018), which has the potential to adversely affect not only production but also their nutritional quality. Besides, the stability of food supply is under serious threat due to the already evident and anticipated adverse impact of climate changes on food production (Sarma and Mandal, 2018). All this coupled with a huge and growing population, and changes in land use pattern across the country pose enormous risk of food insecurity in the India in the days to come.

The objective of this chapter is to measure the incidence and depth of food insecurity, and also its inequality among the households of India with a special focus on its hill *vis-à-vis* plain States and union territories using suitable aggregated measures. It also examines the differentials in the incidence of food insecurity between the hills and plains. It further tries to identify the factors that affect household level food insecurity in the said area. The available literature in this regard has mainly focused on food security in India (Dev and Sharma, 2010; Kumar *et al.*, 2012; Brahmanand *et al.*, 2013; Ittyerah, 2013; Singh, 2014), and a few others have studied food insecurity on a regional basis (Agarwal *et al.*, 2009; Chinnakali *et al.*, 2014; Mukherjee, 2016). To the best of our knowledge Sarma and Mandal (2018) have studied the extent of food insecurity at the household level. However, any study on the incidence, depth and inequality of food insecurity at the household level and with a special focus on hills *vs.* plains of India is yet to comeby. This study has been taken up to fill this gap to some extent. This will provide important insights about the status of food insecurity in the hills and plains of the country. Given the fact that the geographical and socio-economic factors in the hills are quite distinct from the plains, it calls for special attention as far as the policy actions with regard to food insecurity in these areas are concerned.

The chapter is organized in six sections. Section two outlines data and methodology used. Section three discusses the status of food insecurity in the hills and plains of India. Section four outlines the regression model. Section five covers analysis of regression results and their discussion whereas section six deals with concluding remarks.

Data and Methodology

Study Area and Data Source

This study is based on secondary data compiled from the second round of India Human Development Survey (IHDS-II) for the year 2011-12. The IHDS is a nationally representative survey conducted jointly by the University of Maryland and the National Council of Applied Economic research. The data set covers a sample of 42,152 households spread across

33 States and union territories, 384 districts, 1420 villages and 1042 urban blocks. The IHDS-II provides data on a large number of dimensions and variables. The data were thoroughly cleaned and a few variables relevant for the present chapter were taken into account while a few others were created from the data set. This way we end up with total observations of 39,644 for our analysis. To make a comparative study of hills and plain we have considered 11 States as hills following Pandey and Dasgupta (2014). They are Jammu and Kashmir, Himachal Pradesh, Uttarakhand, Sikkim, Arunachal Pradesh, Nagaland, Manipur, Mizoram, Tripura, Meghalaya and Assam.

Methodology

Identification of Food Insecure Households

To measure the magnitude of food insecurity we have used some aggregated measures of food insecurity[1]. The first step towards obtaining an aggregated measure of food insecurity is to identify the households that are food insecure. For this we have defined indicator of food insecurity and food insecurity lines as follows.

It is not only the quantity of food available and accessible but also its quality in the form of nutritional contents that are important from food security point of view. Hence, as argued by Nanda Kumar *et al.* (2010) the issue of food security is not so much about availability of food grains but the composition of the overall food basket[2]. Therefore, keeping in view nutritional requirements the food insecure households are identified as follows. The report of the Expert Group (Rangarajan) to the Planning Commission (Government of India, 2014) has outlined the normative requirements of expenditures on food comprising calories, proteins and fats.[3] We have taken this recommended expenditure (per capita per month) on calories, proteins and fats as the cut-off for separating the food insecure households from others. Thus, following Government of India (2014) the national food insecurity lines have been defined as monthly per capita food expenditure (calorie + protein + fat) of Rs. 554 in rural areas and Rs. 656 in urban areas. These food insecurity lines are then adjusted by price indices to estimate State specific food insecurity lines (separately for rural and urban areas) so as to capture spatial differentials in the price level (see Appendix-I). A household whose per capita monthly expenditures on calories, proteins and fats are below this benchmark are considered to be food insecure. The national and State specific food insecurity lines are shown in Table 5.1.

Table 5.1: National and State Specific Food Insecurity Lines

States/UTs	*Food Insecurity Line (Rs.)*	
	Rural	*Urban*
Andhra Pradesh	588.05	639.14
Arunachal Pradesh	656.03	691.41
Assam	573.75	662.12
Bihar	553.59	573.15
Chhattisgarh	519.69	573.34
Delhi	850.64	717.12
Goa	684.29	685.41
Gujarat	628.57	702.65
Haryana	642.81	712.56
Himachal Pradesh	607.92	658.14
Jammu & Kashmir	595.31	654.25
Jharkhand	515.25	593.09
Karnataka	555.95	640.28
Kerala	600.75	631.14
Madhya Pradesh	536.73	624.89
Maharashtra	614.61	727.51
Manipur	675.51	728.16
Meghalaya	633.04	710.72
Mizoram	701.64	794.44
Nagaland	700.95	753.34
Odisha	499.52	561.99
Punjab	642.62	689.70
Rajasthan	590.46	655.60
Sikkim	641.92	719.25
Tamil Nadu	616.66	643.58
Tripura	533.21	641.80
Uttar Pradesh	507.16	619.89
Uttarakhand	578.48	656.52
West Bengal	532.40	640.00
Puducherry	644.11	644.49
Andaman & Nicobar Islands	749.48	838.16
Chandigarh	742.75	690.60
Dadra & Nagar Haveli	574.74	718.39
Daman & Diu	684.29	669.02
Lakshadweep	756.77	680.10
All India	554.00	656.00

Source: Authors' Calculation from IHDS-II, 2011-12.

Measuring Food Insecurity

Once the food insecure households are identified aggregated measures of food insecurity have been obtained using three different indices, viz., head count ratio (HCR), food insecurity gap index (FIGI) and squared food insecurity gap index (SFIGI)[4]. They are calculated as follows:

$$HCR = \frac{N_{FI}}{N} \times 100 \quad \ldots (1)$$

$$FIGI = \frac{1}{N} \times \sum_{i=1}^{N} \left(\frac{G_i}{L} \right) \quad \ldots (2)$$

$$SFIGI = \frac{1}{N} \times \sum_{i=1}^{N} \left(\frac{G_i}{L} \right)^2 \quad \ldots (3)$$

Where, N refers to total population, N_{FI} stands for number of food insecure households, L for food insecurity line, and G for food insecurity gap which is the gap between L and actual per capita monthly expenditure on calorie, proteins and fats as mentioned in section II.2.1. Moreover, the food insecurity gaps G for the food secure households are assumed to be 0.

The HCR measures the incidence of food insecurity. While it is easy to calculate and interpret it cannot capture depth and inequality among the households as far as food insecurity is concerned. On the other hand, although FIGI is sensitive to the depth of food insecurity meaning it captures how far the food insecure households are from the food insecurity line, it does not take care of inequality among these households with respect to the same. However, the SFIGI is sensitive to inequality among the food insecure households which implies that if the distribution of the per capita monthly expenditure on food is changed by transferring some amount from one food insecure household to another then the value of the index changes[5]. Hence, these three measures of food insecurity have been used to examine the incidence and depth of food insecurity and its inequality among the households.

Food Insecurity in India: Hills *vs.* Plains

The extent of food insecurity in the hills and plains of India are presented in Table 5.2 and Table 5.3 respectively. As seen from Table 5.2, among the hill States the incidence, depth and inequality of food insecurity is highest in Meghalaya. On the other hand, the same is lowest in Tripura. As seen from the table there is large scale variations in these measures among the states. Similarly, there is large scale variations in the incidence, depth and inequality of food insecurity among the plain states and union territories of India with Goa having the lowest and Chhattisgarh highest figures (Table 5.3).

Table 5.2: Extent of Food Insecurity in the Hills of India

States	*HCR (in %)*	*FIGI*	*SFIGI*
Jammu & Kashmir	4.59	0.009	0.095
Himachal Pradesh	22.10	0.049	0.220
Uttarakhand	43.21	0.123	0.351
Sikkim	8.33	0.001	0.038
Arunachal Pradesh	19.30	0.036	0.189
Nagaland	5.56	0.008	0.092
Manipur	26.19	0.025	0.158
Mizoram	21.43	0.030	0.173
Tripura	0.00	0.000	0.000
Meghalaya	63.21	0.201	0.448
Assam	33.02	0.069	0.262

Source: Authors' Calculation from IHDS-II, 2011-12.

Table 5.3: Extent of Food Insecurity in the Plains of India

States/UTs	*HCR*	*FIGI*	*SFIGI*
Punjab	13.63	0.022	0.148
Haryana	23.11	0.050	0.223
Rajasthan	24.26	0.059	0.242
Uttar Pradesh	31.51	0.080	0.282
Bihar	45.44	0.114	0.337
Jharkhand	44.51	0.124	0.353
Odisha	54.25	0.144	0.379
Chhattisgarh	67.72	0.226	0.476
Madhya Pradesh	39.30	0.112	0.335
Gujarat	20.39	0.044	0.210
Daman & Diu	10.17	0.012	0.108
Dadra & Nagar Haveli	38.46	0.115	0.340
Andhra Pradesh	20.75	0.041	0.204
Goa	0.00	0.000	0.000
West Bengal	26.67	0.057	0.238
Maharastra	38.60	0.096	0.309
Karnataka	21.41	0.045	0.213
Kerala	21.85	0.051	0.225
Tamil Nadu	41.92	0.125	0.354
Puducherry	4.92	0.007	0.081

Source: Authors' Calculation from IHDS-II, 2011-12.

We further examine whether the incidence of food insecurity in the hills is statistically different from that in the plains. For this we have used proportion-test. The test results are shown in Table 5.4. The null hypothesis (H_0) that there is no difference in the proportion of food insecure households between the hills and plains has been rejected and the alternative hypothesis (H_a) that the former has a lower proportion of food insecure households than the later has been accepted at 1 per cent level of significance. Thus, we can say that food insecurity is lower in the hills than in the plains of India.

Table 5.4: Two-sample Test of Proportions (of food insecure households)

Variable	*Mean*	*Std. Err.*	*z*	*P>|z|*
Plains	.2870668	.002333		
Hills	.1920457	.0058391		
Proportion difference (Plains-Hills)	.0950211	.0062879		
	under Ho:	.0070222	13.53	0.000
Ha: diff < 0			Ha: diff > 0	
Pr (Z < z) = 1.0000			Pr (Z > z) = 0.0000	

The Model

To examine the determinants of food insecurity, a binary logistic regression model is used. The model is—

$$FI_i = \frac{1}{1+e^{-(\beta' X_i' + u_i)}} = \frac{1}{1+e^{-Z}} \qquad \ldots (1)$$

Where,

$$Z = \beta_0 + \beta_1 Hill_i + \beta_2 Urban_i + \beta_3 Poor_i + \beta_4 HS_i + \beta_5 Remit_i + \beta_6 Cultivation_i + \beta_7 PCI_i + \beta_8 DR_i + \beta_9 EAF + \beta_{10} OBC_i + \beta_{11} SC_i + \beta_{12} ST_i + \beta_{13} OC_i + u_i \qquad \ldots (2)$$

Here the dependent variable FI_i indicates food insecurity status of the ith household which takes value 1 if a household is food insecure and 0 otherwise. The definitions, measurement and summary statistics of the explanatory variables are shown in Table 5.5.

Results and Discussion

The results of the binary logistic regression of food insecurity are shown in Table 5.6. It is to be noted that the odds ratio are reported here rather than the coefficient, and the results are interpreted accordingly.[6]

Table 5.5: Definition and Summary Statistics of the Explanatory Variables

Non-categorical Variables	*Definition*	*Unit*	*Mean*	*Std. Dev.*	*Min.*	*Max.*
HS	No. of household members	Number	4.85	2.32	1	33
PCI	Per capita income	Rupees	29,402	53,996	–2,89,008	41,61,000
DR	Dependency ratio	%	76.10	74.42	0	80
EAF	Highest education of adult female member	Years	5.65	5.27	0	16

Categorical Variables	*Definition*	*% age*
Hill	= 1 if a household belongs to a hill state, 0 otherwise	11%
Remit	= 1 if a household receives remittance, 0 otherwise	13.28%
Poor	= 1 for poor households, 0 otherwise	16.42%
Urban	= 1 for households living in urban areas, 0 otherwise	34.57%
OBC	= 1 for households belonging to OBC category, 0 otherwise	40.46%
SC	= 1 for households belonging to SC category, 0 otherwise	21.21%
ST	= 1 for households belonging to ST category, 0 otherwise	8.64%
OC	= 1 for households belonging to other category (excluding general caste), 0 otherwise	1.35%
Cultivation	= 1 if the main occupation of a household is cultivation, 0 otherwise	24.40%

Source: Authors' Calculation from IHDS-II, 2011-12.

Table 5.6: Results of the Binary Logistic Regression

Explanatory Variables	*Odds Ratio*	*Std. Err.*	*z*	*P>z*
Hill	0.74	0.04	–6.00	0.00
Urban	1.04	0.04	1.16	0.25
Poor	12.66	0.47	68.03	0.00
HS	1.20	0.01	29.03	0.00
Remit	0.92	0.04	–1.99	0.05
Cultivation	0.80	0.03	–6.45	0.00
PCI	0.99	0.00	–27.00	0.00
DR	1.16	0.02	8.09	0.00
EAF	0.99	0.00	–3.21	0.00
OBC	1.47	0.05	10.37	0.00
SC	1.65	0.07	11.85	0.00
ST	2.13	0.12	13.77	0.00
OC	1.10	0.14	0.73	0.46
Constant	0.11	0.01	–40.03	0.00
Pseudo R squared	0.2887			
LR $\chi^2(15)$	13625.85			
Prob > χ^2	0.00			
Observations	39644			

The odds ratio of *Hill* has turned out to be less than one. This implies that the probability of being food insecure is less in the hill areas than the plains. More precisely, the probability of being food insecure in the hilly areas is 26 per cent lower than the plains.

The odds ratio of *Urban* has turned out to be greater than one. This implies that the probability of being food insecure is more in the urban areas than in the rural areas. The odds of food insecurity for an urban household are 1.04 times that of his rural counterpart. The reason for rural households being less food insecure is that they are mostly engaged in cultivation as subsistence farmers, and hence they have better availability of food items in the villages.

The odds ratio of *Poor* is found to be as high as 12.66. This implies that the probability of food insecurity for the poor households is higher than others. Food insecurity of a poor household is 12.66 times of a non-poor household. This is quite intuitive. The poor do not have enough resources to purchase the required amount of food items for their household which raises their probability of being food insecure.

HS is found to have a positive impact on food insecurity. This implies that the probability of food insecurity increases with increase in the size of households. Larger sized households have more mouths to feed and hence have lesser availability of food consumption per capita. An increase in household size by one member causes the probability of food insecurity to increase by 20 per cent.

The odds ratio for *Remit* has turned out to be 0.92. This implies that remittances into a household reduce its likelihood to be food insecure. More precisely, the households receiving remittances are 8 per cent less likely to be food insecure than others. This is because receipt of remittances enhances liquidity and hence the household can spend more on food.

The odds ratio of *Cultivation* is found to be 0.80. This implies that the households whose main occupation is cultivation are less likely to be food insecure than others. This is quite intuitive. The cultivator households in India are primarily subsistence farmers, and hence allocate a considerable amount of farm produce on household consumption.

PCI is found to have a negative impact on the probability of household level food insecurity. This implies that an increase in per capita income of the households by one rupee reduces its probability of food insecurity by 99 per cent. This is quite expected because an increase in per capita income capacitates a household to access a higher amount of food items for its members.

DR, showing the number of young and adult dependents as a percentage of number of economically active members in the households, is found to increase the probability of food insecurity. The odds ratio of this variable is 1.16 which implies that an increase in dependency ratio by 1 per cent increases the probability of food insecurity by 16 per cent.

EAF is found to have a negative impact on food insecurity with odds ratio of 0.99. This means an increase in the years of schooling of adult female members reduces the probability of food insecurity by 1 per cent. The female adult household members in India take the responsibility of preparing and distributing food in the household. Hence, as their level of education increases they become more aware about the importance of nutritious contents of food. Thus, with improvements in their education expenditure by the households on food items containing calorie, proteins and fats also increases, thereby reducing food insecurity.

As far as the differences in food insecurity among social groups are concerned it is found that compared to general caste, food insecurity is more among Other Backward Classes (*OBC*), Scheduled Castes (*SC*) and Schedule Tribes (*ST*). Moreover, the differences in the magnitudes of odd ratios for *OBC*, *SC* and *ST* indicate existence of sharp differences in the probability of food insecurity among them.

Conclusion

This chapter examined the incidence, depth and inequality of food insecurity at the household level in the hills and plains of India. The study reveals that around 29 per cent of the households in the plains of India are food insecure compared to around 19 per cent in the hills and this difference is found to be statistically significant. Further, there is prevalence of large scale disparity in food insecurity within the hill and plain areas of the country.

This chapter further identifies the factors affecting household level food insecurity in India.

Food insecurity in India is found to be affected, among other things, by poverty, per capita income, and education of female adults and main occupation of the household. While per capita income and education of female adults reduce the probability of being food insecure, poverty has the reverse impact. The households with cultivation as the main occupation are relatively less food insecure. Similarly, as far as the major social groups are concerned people belonging to general caste are less food insecure followed by OBC, SC and ST. While government policy needs to make concerted efforts to ensure food security across the country, special focus may be given on the regions and communities suffering from higher incidence of food insecurity, which may help reduce regional and inter-community disparities in this regard.

Appendix-I

Estimation of national and State-specific Food Insecurity Lines

The report of the Expert Group (Rangarajan) to the Planning Commission (Government of India, 2014) has outlined the normative requirements of expenditures on food comprising calories, proteins and fats. This recommended expenditures (per capita per month) amount on calories, proteins and fats are used as the benchmark for measuring food insecurity in this chapter. Thus, the national food insecurity lines have been defined as the monthly per capita food expenditure (calorie+protein+fat) of Rs. 554 in rural areas and Rs. 656 in urban areas. These national food insecurity lines are then adjusted as follows to estimate state specific food insecurity lines (separately for rural and urban areas) so as to capture spatial variations in the price level.

The ratio of price index of a state to the national average is worked out as follows. Suppose, the price index of Assam is P_A and that of India is P_I. The poverty line of Assam (PL_A) can be thought of as the national poverty line (PL_I) adjusted by the ratio of price index of Assam to price index of India. Thus,

$$PL_A = PL_I . \frac{P_A}{P_I} \quad \text{... (A.1)}$$

$$\frac{P_A}{P_I} = \frac{PL_A}{PL_I} \quad \text{... (A.2)}$$

Thus the ratics of state-specific poverty lines to the national poverty line give the price ratios for different states. From equation A.1 it is seen that multiplication of the national poverty line by the state specific price ratio yields the state specific poverty lines. The same way, state-specific food insecurity line is calculated by multiplying the national food insecurity line by the respective state specific price ratio, where the price ratio is obtained by dividing the state specific poverty line by the national poverty line, as shown by equation A.2.

Notes

1. Here we have taken the idea from the literature on poverty measurement.
2. A change in the consumption patterns from cereals to high value food is observed in both rural and urban areas of India.
3. This Expert Group was constituted in June 2012 by the Planning Commission under the Chairmanship of Dr. C. Rangarajan to suggest a methodology for measurement of poverty in India. It has re-computed the average requirements of calories, fats and proteins on the basis of the 2010, Indian Council of Medical Research norms (Government of India, 2014).
4. These are analogous to head count ratio, poverty gap index and squared poverty gap index in the literature on poverty measurement.
5. In the context of poverty measurement this is known as 'Pigou-Dalton Transfer Principle'. According to this principle, if some income is transferred from a not-so poor to a relatively poorer individual then social welfare must increase and *vice versa*.
6. This is because there is a direct relationship between the two. Odds ratios greater than 1 and less than 1 imply positive and negative coefficients respectively. Therefore, our analysis is carried out in terms of odds ratio as it is easier to interpret the impact of the explanatory variables in terms of odds ratio.

References

Agarwal, S., Sethi, V., Gupta, P., Jha, M., Agnihotri, A. and Nord, M. (2009). "Experiential household food insecurity in an urban underserved slum of North India", *Food Security*, 1(3): 239-250.

Bhushan, S. (2018). "Environmental consequences of the green revolution in India", In: Goswami, B., Bezbaruah, M.P. and Mandal, R. (ed.), *Indian Agriculture after the Green Revolution: Changes and Challenges*, Routledge, London and New York, pp. 183-197.

Brahmanand, P.S., Kumar, A., Ghosh, S., Chowdhury, S.R., Singandhupe, R.B., Singh, R. and Behera, M.S. (2013). "Challenges to food security in India", *Current Science*, 841-846.

Chinnakali, P., Upadhyay, R.P., Shokeen, D., Singh, K., Kaur, M., Singh, A.K., Goswami, A., Yadav, K. and Pandav, C.S. (2014). "Prevalence of household-level food insecurity and its determinants in an urban resettlement colony in north India", *Journal of Health, Population and Nutrition*, *32*(2): 227-236.

Dev, S.M. and Sharma, A.N. (2010). "Food security in India: Performance, challenges and policies", *Oxfam India Working Paper Series*, OIWPS-VII.

FAO (2009). *The State of Food Insecurity in the World*, Food and Agriculture Organization of the United Nations, Rome.

Government of India (2014). *Report of the Expert Group to Review the Methodology for Measurement of Poverty*, Planning Commission.

Ittyerah, A.C. (2013). "Food security in India: Issues and suggestions for effectiveness", In: *Theme paper for the 57th Members' Annual Conference,* Indian Institute of Public Administration, New Delhi.

Kumar, A., Bantilan, M.C.S., Kumar, P., Kumar, S. and Jee, S. (2012). "Food security in India: Trends, patterns and determinants", *Indian Journal of Agricultural Economics*, *67*(3): 445-463.

Mukherjee, Protap (2016). "Levels, Patterns and Determinants of Food Insecurity in Urban India", Downloaded from http://siteresources.worldbank. org/INTURBANDEVELOPMENT/Resources/336387-1272506514747/Mukherjee.pdf, Accessed on 18th November, 2016.

Nandakumar, T., Ganguly, K., Sharma, P. and Gulati, A. (2010). "Food and Nutrition Security Status in India: Opportunities for Investment Partnerships," *ADB Sustainable Development Working Paper Series*, No. 16.

Pandey, R. and Dasgupta P. (2014). "Developmental Disability Index for Hill States in India", *Working Paper No. 2014-134*, National Institute of Public Finance and Policy, New Delhi.

Radhakrishna, R. (2005). "Food and nutritional security of the poor: Emerging perspectives and policy issues", *Economic and Political Weekly*, 40(18): 1817 1821.

Sarma, M. and Mandal, R. (2018). "Food insecurity in India: Extent, variations and determinants", *Assam Economic Review*, Vol. 11.

Singh, J.S. (2014). "Challenges to food security in India", *IOSR Journal of Humanities and Social Science,* 19(4): 93-100.

Upadhyay, R.P. and Palanivel, C. (2011). "Challenges in achieving food security in India", *Iranian Journal of Public Health, 40*(4): 31.

6
Food Security in the Hills and the Plains of India
An Empirical Analysis

Manash Roy

Introduction

Indian states are characterised by diverse ecosystems in terms of varied topography and other biophysical characteristics. This feature has created locational advantages as well as disadvantages for the hill and plain area dominated states. The states in the hill are relatively more blessed with natural ecosystem services that are important for local, regional, national and international well-being in the context of sustainability. The hill areas, therefore, face unique challenges in addressing their developmental needs in a manner that takes care of conservation concerns for sustainable development. However, the hill states in India also seem to be at a disadvantage in terms of multiple social and economic indicators as compared to the rest of India. They face the dual challenge of maintaining their natural resource base and simultaneously striving for a development process which requires creation of jobs and income generation, sustaining local resource based livelihoods and ensuring a quality of life at par with other states in the economy (Rao, 2007).

In view of the hill-plain disparities in developmental status, as evidenced by socio-economic indicators, the present chapter attempts to address the issue of food security within the hills and also between the hills and the plains empirically. The prime motto behind this empirical exercise is to assess the nature of food security across the hill states and also to make a relative comparison between the hills and the plains in respect of food security. It is to be noted that this analysis has been carried out for two cross-sections, viz. 2001-04 and 2011-14.

This chapter is organised into nine sections. Section 1 is an introductory one representing background of the study. Conceptualisation of hill economy and food security is presented in Section 2 and Section 3 respectively. Section 4 and 5 take care of objectives and research questions. Section 6 discusses about the data base and data source while Section 7 throws light on the methodology of the study. Section 8 provides the results and finally, in section 9, the summary of the findings and concluding remarks of the study are presented.

Hill States: Conceptualisation

The hills of India are comprised sixteen states, viz. Arunachal Pradesh, part of Assam, Manipur, Meghalaya, Mizoram, Nagaland, Tripura, Sikkim, Himachal Pradesh, Jammu and Kashmir, Uttarakhand, part of Karnataka, Kerala, Maharashtra, part of Tamil Nadu and part of West Bengal. This classification is based on what percentage of land of the states is under hilly terrain using data from the India State of Forests Report, 2013. It may be noted that this classification of hill states follows from the definition of a hill district as a district with more than 50 per cent of its area under 'hill talukas' based on critieria adopted by the Planning Commission for Hill Area and Western Ghats Development Programme (State of Forests Report, 2013).

Food Security: Conceptualisation

In the 1970s, food security was understood as the 'availability at all times of adequate supply of basic foodstuffs' (UN, 1975). However, the concept of food security has undergone considerable modifications in recent years. Amartya Sen (1981) added a new dimension to food security and emphasized 'access' to food through what he called 'entitlements'—a combination of what one can produce and exchange in the market, along with the state or other socially provided supplies. Subsequently, Sen and other scholars put much stress on the aspects of adequate nourishment and adequate healthiness in achieving food security. Accordingly, there has been a substantial shift in the understanding of food security, and WFS in 1995 declared, 'Food security at the individual, household, national, regional, and global level exists when all people, at all times, have physical and economic access to sufficient, safe and nutritious food to meet their dietary needs and food preferences for an active and healthy life' (FAO, 1996). This definition essentially covers three dimensions of food security, viz. availability, accessibility and absorption of food.

Food Availability: The availability of food essentially encompasses domestic agricultural production and food imports. However, due to lack of reliable data on food imports, in the present study we have focused only on the domestic agricultural production (Sharma, 2010).

Food Accessibility: Access to food has two dimensions, viz. physical and economic, of which the latter is more important. Economic access to food is largely determined by the households' purchasing power and food subsidies (Sharma, 2010).

Utilisation of Food: The utilization dimension of food security is concerned with the nutritional requirements of household members, based on their age and sex. The pattern of food utilization at the household level generally depends on cultural factors, (diet preferences, nutritional knowledge and caring practices), distributional factors (intra-household distribution of food and other reasons), and absorption possibilities (depending upon quality of water and sanitation, health, and the quality of food itself) (Sharma, 2010).

The indicators chosen for analysing various dimensions of food security is done in line with the methodology of Roy and Deb (2017) and these are shown in Table 6.1:

Table 6.1: Dimensional Indicators of Food Security

Dimensions of Food Security	*Variables/Indicators*
Food Availability	Per Capita Food Grain Production
Food Accessibility	Per Capita Income
Food Absorption	Percentage of Households Having Access to Safe Drinking Water

Source: Roy and Deb (2017).

Objectives

1. To make an inter-state analysis of food security within the hills of India.
2. To look into the food security status of the hills *vis-à-vis* to the plains of India.

Research Questions

1. What is the state of food security across the hill states of India?
2. What is the state of food security of the hills in relation to the plains of India?

Data Base and Data Source

The present study is based on secondary data. The data sources of various dimensional indicators of food security are shown in Table 6.2.

Table 6.2: Data Sources of Dimensional Indicators of Food Security

Indicators/Variables	*Sources*	*Reference Year*
(1) Food Availability		
• Per capita production of food grains[1]	Hand Book of Statistics on Indian Economy (RBI, 2016)	2001-02 to 2003-04 and 2011-12 to 2013-14
(2) Food Accessibility		
• Per capita NSDP (at constant prices)	Hand Book of Statistics on Indian Economy (RBI, 2016)	2001-02 to 2003-04 and 2011-12 to 2013-14
(3) Food Absorption		
• Percentage of households having access to safe drinking water	Census of India	2001 and 2011

Methodology

Analysis of food security in the present study is made by constructing a composite Food Security Index (FSI) as developed by Roy and Deb (2017). This composite index is a summary measure of average achievement of a country/state on the front of three dimensions of food security, viz. availability, accessibility and absorption. This FSI is constructed for the states within the hills and also for the state across the hills and plains for two cross-sections, viz. 2001-04 and 2011-14 with a view to assess the inter-temporal status of food security.

Apart from the construction of the composite FSI, some statistical measures like mean, standard deviation, Spearman's correlation coefficient, Student's t test, paired t-test are also calculated for throwing further light on the situation of food security in the hills and across the hills and the plains.

The method of constructing FSI in line with the methodology developed by Roy and Deb (2017) involves the following two steps.

Step I. Construction of Dimensional Index for Food Security:

$$\text{Dimensional Index} = \frac{X_{ij} - X_{\min}}{X_{\max} - X_{\min}}; \; 0 \leq \text{Dimensional Index} \leq 1$$

Where X_{ij} = Actual value of the jth dimensional indicator for the ith state

X_{min} = Minimum value[2] of the jth dimensional indicator for the ith state

X_{max} = Maximum value[3] of the jth dimensional indicator for the ith state

Step II. Finally, the Food Security Index (FSI) has been constructed by taking the simple average of dimensional indices, i.e.

$$FSI = \frac{\text{Availability Index} + \text{Accessibility Index} + \text{Absorption Index}}{3}; \quad 0 \leq \text{FSI} \leq 1$$

Table 6.3: Categorisation of the Level of Food Security using FSI

FSI	*Level of Food Security*
0 ≤ FSI ≤ 0.20	Very Low
0.21 ≤ FSI ≤ 0.40	Low
0.41 ≤ FSI ≤ 0.60	Moderate
0.61 ≤ FSI ≤ 0.80	High
0.81 ≤ FSI ≤ 1	Very High

Source: Roy and Deb (2017).

Results and Discussions

The results of the study are incorporated in two sub-sections. Section 8.1 represents the food security status of the hill states while Section 8.2 provides the findings related to hill-plain comparison.

1. Inter-state Status of Food Security in the Hills

Table 6.4 shows that in terms of FSI value, Himachal Pradesh is the most food secure state in 2001-04 while Sikkim is the most food secure state

Table 6.4: Values of Dimensional Indices and FSI of Hill States

Hill States	*Food Availability Index*		*Food Accessibility Index*		*Food Absorption Index*		*Food Security Index (FSI)*	
	2001-04	*2011-14*	*2001-04*	*2011-14*	*2001-04*	*2011-14*	*2001-04*	*2011-14*
Arunachal Pradesh	0.938	1.000	0.361	0.226	0.830	0.749	0.709	0.658
Assam	0.622	0.521	0.029	0.000	0.543	0.605	0.398	0.375
Himachal Pradesh	1.000	0.729	0.987	0.523	1.000	1.000	0.996	0.751
Jammu & Kashmir	0.562	0.464	0.144	0.136	0.641	0.719	0.449	0.440
Karnataka	0.572	0.641	0.478	0.377	0.939	0.897	0.663	0.638
Kerala	0.000	0.000	0.851	0.594	0.000	0.000	0.284	0.198
Maharashtra	0.436	0.333	1.000	0.761	0.865	0.829	0.767	0.641
Manipur	0.749	0.662	0.000	0.012	0.209	0.198	0.319	0.291
Meghalaya	0.377	0.318	0.301	0.230	0.239	0.186	0.306	0.245
Mizoram	0.619	0.158	0.493	0.303	0.193	0.447	0.435	0.303
Nagaland	0.838	0.879	0.404	0.458	0.354	0.337	0.532	0.558
Sikkim	0.783	0.542	0.398	1.000	0.725	0.860	0.636	0.801
Tamil Nadu	0.333	0.376	0.676	0.656	0.954	0.980	0.654	0.671
Tripura	0.780	0.653	0.463	0.375	0.446	0.565	0.563	0.531
Uttarakhand	0.844	0.586	0.344	0.593	0.971	0.975	0.720	0.718
West Bengal	0.870	0.598	0.460	0.209	0.998	0.975	0.776	0.594
Statistical Measures								
Mean	0.645	0.529	0.462	0.414	0.619	0.645	0.575	0.526
t statistic (paired)	t = 3.103*		t = 0.982		t = 1.210		t = 2.117***	
Standard Deviation	0.254	0.246	0.288	0.266	0.329	0.315	0.194	0.186

Source: Calculated by the Author, * and *** mean significant at 1 and 10 per cent level of significance.

in 2011-14. Kerala has emerged as the least food secure state in both the time points under consideration. An individual look at each dimensional index indicates that in case of food availability, Himachal Pradesh has attained the highest position in 2001-04 while Arunachal Pradesh has topped the list in 2011-14. Kerala has done most badly in respect of food availability in both the cross-sections. Maharashtra has emerged as the highest performer with regard to food accessibility in 2001-04 while Sikkim has received this reward in 2011-14. Two north-eastern states, viz. Manipur and Assam are found as the worst performers in case of food accessibility in 2001-04 and 2011-14 respectively. So far as food absorption is concerned, Himachal Pradesh tops the list while Kerala sits at the bottom in both the time points under consideration. Comparison between the FSI values of each hill state and the mean FSI value reveals that Arunachal Pradesh, Himachal Pradesh, Karnataka, Maharashtra, Nagaland, Sikkim, Tamil Nadu, Tripura, Uttarakhand and West Bengal have performed better than the hill average in 2011-14. The remaining states fall under the group of performing lower than the hill average. It is to be noted that Nagaland and Tripura have performed lower than the hill average in 2001-04. Thus these two north-eastern states have done well in terms of food security in 2011-14.

Based on the mean values of FSI from Table 6.4, it can be concluded that on the average, the Hill region of India is moderately food secure with a sharp decline in the level of food security over time. The value of the t statistic also shows that this decline is statistically significant. The mean values of food availability index exerts that the hill region faces a higher level of food availability in the beginning of the study period but slips down to a moderate level by a handsome margin during the end. This decline of food availability is found statistically highly significant as reflected by the t value in Table 6.4. Food accessibility is found moderate with a statistically insignificant rise in its level over time. Food absorption in the hill region is found high in both the time points with a bit of increase in its level, though this increase is not statistically significant. These findings from Table 6.4 indicate that the hill region is slightly stepping down in terms of food security in course of time and it is mainly caused by a significant decline in the level of food grain production.

The values of standard deviation indicate that disparities among the hill states on the matter of food security and its dimensions have declined. Disparities are found relatively higher in case of food absorption and relatively lower in case of overall food security.

Table 6.5 depicts the ranking of hill states in respect of food security. It is seen from Table 6.5 that Himachal Pradesh tops the list in 2001-04 while Sikkim gets first position in 2011-14. Kerala sits at the bottom in both the cross-sections. Sikkim's splendid performance on the food security front is mainly contributed by her magnificent rise in per capita income and thus enhancing the level of food accessibility. Due to this reason, in spite of experiencing a fall in per capita food grain production, Sikkim has emerged as the most prominent food secure state within the hills in 2011-14. This result implies that food security at a higher level can be achieved by a state even in the absence of sufficient amount of domestically produced food stuff if it can import food grains by possessing a strong accessibility to food. Kerala's poor performance on the matter of food security in both time points is mainly due to her vulnerable

Table 6.5: Ranking of the Hill States in terms of FSI values

Hill States	*Food Security Ranking*		*Comparison of Ranks*	*Spearman's Rank Correlation Coefficient*
	2001-04	*2011-14*		
Arunachal Pradesh	5	5	No change	
Assam	13	12	Slight improvement	
Himachal Pradesh	1	2	Slight deterioration	
Jammu & Kashmir	11	11	No change	
Karnataka	6	7	Slight deterioration	
Kerala	16	16	No change	
Maharashtra	3	6	Major Improvement	
Manipur	14	14	No change	
Meghalaya	15	15	No change	R = 0.84*
Mizoram	12	13	Slight deterioration	
Nagaland	10	9	Slight improvement	
Sikkim	8	1	Major Improvement	
Tamil Nadu	7	4	Major Improvement	
Tripura	9	10	Slight deterioration	
Uttarakhand	4	3	Slight improvement	
West Bengal	2	8	Major deterioration	

* means significant at 1 per cent level of significance.

Source: Calculated by the Author on the basis of FSI values of the hill states shown in Table 6.4.

positions in terms of availability and absorption of food. States like Arunachal Pradesh, Jammu & Kashmir, Kerala, Manipur and Meghalaya have not seen any change in the level of food security. Maharashtra, Sikkim and Tamil Nadu are faced with major improvement in the food security rankings. The rankings of Assam, Nagaland and Uttarakhand have slightly improved in course of time. West Bengal has experienced major deterioration while the food security ranking of the other states has slightly deteriorated as visible from Table 6.5. The value of Spearman's rank correlation coefficient is strong and positive and also statistically significant showing that difference in food security rankings of the hill states over two points of time is significant and these rank differences are not due to the fluctuations of sampling.

2. The State of Food Security in India in 2001-04: Hills vs. Plains

Table 6.6 depicts the combined picture of food security for the hill and plain with respect to the cross-section 2001-04. All together 27 states are taken into consideration out of which 16 fall under hill region while the rest 11 comes under the group of plain region. In consultation with the

Table 6.6: Values of Dimensional Indices and FSI: Hills *vs*. Plains in 2001-04

Hill States	*Food Availability Index*	*Food Accessibility Index*	*Food Absorption Index*	*FSI*	*Plain States*	*Food Availability Index*	*Food Accessibility Index*	*Food Absorption Index*	*FSI*
Arunachal Pradesh	0.197	0.500	0.729	0.475	Andhra Pradesh	0.154	0.554	0.764	0.491
Assam	0.131	0.329	0.477	0.312	Bihar	0.116	0.000	0.852	0.323
Himachal Pradesh	0.210	0.823	0.879	0.637	Chhattisgarh	0.230	0.301	0.635	0.389
Jammu & Kashmir	0.118	0.388	0.563	0.356	Gujarat	0.079	0.662	0.818	0.520
Karnataka	0.120	0.560	0.825	0.502	Haryana	0.596	1.000	0.845	0.814
Kerala	0.000	0.753	0.000	0.251	Jharkhand	0.067	0.215	0.259	0.180
Maharashtra	0.092	0.830	0.760	0.560	Madhya Pradesh	0.203	0.251	0.606	0.354
Manipur	0.157	0.314	0.183	0.218	Odisha	0.148	0.230	0.550	0.309
Meghalaya	0.079	0.469	0.210	0.253	Punjab	1.000	0.965	1.000	0.988
Mizoram	0.130	0.568	0.170	0.289	Rajasthan	0.213	0.365	0.604	0.394
Nagaland	0.176	0.522	0.311	0.336	Uttar Pradesh	0.234	0.173	0.868	0.425
Sikkim	0.165	0.519	0.637	0.440					
Tamil Nadu	0.070	0.662	0.838	0.524					
Tripura	0.164	0.552	0.392	0.369					
Uttarakhand	0.177	0.491	0.853	0.507					
West Bengal	0.183	0.551	0.877	0.537					
Statistical Measures									
Mean	0.135	0.552	0.544	0.411		0.276	0.429	0.709	0.471
Student's t statistic	t = 1.980 ***		t = 1.088		t =1.59			t = 0.743	
Standard Deviation	0.053	0.148	0.289	0.124		0.266	0.311	0.195	0.223

*** means significant at 10 per cent level of significance

Source: Calculated by the Author.

results of Table 6.6 and categorization of the levels of food security in Table 6.3 (page 73), it is seen that in 2001-04 two plain states, viz. Punjab and Haryana have secured very high level of food security while only Himachal Pradesh in the hills has attained the same status. 50 per cent of the states in the hills have achieved low level of food security and 43.71 per cent of the states are found moderately food secure. 45.45 per cent of the states are found with low level of food security in the plain region while 33.33 per cent of the states are associated with moderate level. In the plains, one state, viz. Jharkhand has even attained a very low level of food security. Thus, overall in terms of categorization of food security levels, hill region have little edge over the plain area though the later is blessed with two very highly food secure states in the form of Punjab and Haryana. On this very finding it could be rather concluded that the picture of food security would be more dismal if Punjab and Haryana are left out from the analysis.

Comparison of the mean values of dimensional indices and FSI from Table 6.6 reveals that apart from food accessibility dimension, hill region is lagging behind the plains in respect of all other fronts. However, besides food availability, all other mean differences between the dimensional indices and that between respective FSI of the hill and the plain have not turned out to be statistically significant. This is reflected in terms of the t values incorporated in Table 6.6. Thus statistical analysis shows that in 2001-04 there is no significant difference in the level of food security between the states of hills and plains but availability of food in the plains is significantly higher than that of the hills. The values of standard deviation in Table 6.6 indicate that inter-state disparities in the hill region in comparison to the plains is relatively lower in case of food availability, food accessibility and overall food security while it is relatively higher in case of food absorption.

Thus from the analysis of the results in Table 6.6, no significant line of demarcation regarding food security is found to exist between the hills and the plains, though the former is associated with a relatively better position of food availability in the form of a good per capita production of food grain. However, in respect of inter-state disparities with regard to food security, the hill region has performed better than the plains.

Table 6.7 represents the combined picture of food security for the hill and plain with respect to the cross-section 2011-14. In line with the categorization of the levels of food security given in Table 6.3 (page 73), it is found from Table 6.6 that among the states under hill area, Sikkim has achieved high level of food security while Punjab and Haryana have

Table 6.7: Values of Dimensional Indices and FSI: Hills vs Plains in 2011-14

Hill States	*Food Availability Index*	*Food Accessibility Index*	*Food Absorption Index*	*FSI*	*Plain States*	*Food Availability Index*	*Food Accessibility Index*	*Food Absorption Index*	*FSI*
Arunachal Pradesh	0.277	0.324	0.704	0.435	Andhra Pradesh	0.203	0.402	0.889	0.498
Assam	0.144	0.127	0.568	0.280	Bihar	0.127	0.000	0.944	0.357
Himachal Pradesh	0.202	0.584	0.939	0.575	Chhattisgarh	0.280	0.211	0.824	0.438
Jammu & Kashmir	0.129	0.245	0.676	0.350	Gujarat	0.123	0.706	0.886	0.571
Karnataka	0.178	0.456	0.842	0.492	Haryana	0.632	0.779	0.941	0.784
Kerala	0.000	0.646	0.000	0.215	Jharkhand	0.119	0.198	0.415	0.244
Maharashtra	0.092	0.791	0.778	0.554	Madhya Pradesh	0.284	0.166	0.694	0.381
Manipur	0.134	0.137	0.186	0.169	Odisha	0.167	0.164	0.652	0.328
Meghalaya	0.038	0.327	0.175	0.197	Punjab	1.000	0.523	1.000	0.841
Mizoram	0.044	0.391	0.420	0.285	Rajasthan	0.250	0.256	0.696	0.400
Nagaland	0.243	0.526	0.317	0.362	Uttar Pradesh	0.226	0.067	0.961	0.418
Sikkim	0.150	1.000	0.808	0.653					
Tamil Nadu	0.104	0.700	0.920	0.575					
Tripura	0.181	0.454	0.530	0.388					
Uttarakhand	0.162	0.644	0.916	0.574					
West Bengal	0.166	0.309	0.916	0.464					
Statistical Measures									
Mean	0.146	0.479	0.606	0.410		0.310	0.315	0.809	0.478
Student's t statistic		t = 2.330**	t = 1.691		t =1.984***			t = 0.908	
Standard Deviation	0.068	0.233	0.296	0.148		0.257	0.243	0.169	0.178

** and *** mean significant at 5 per cent and 10 per cent level of significance.

Source: Calculated by the Author.

attained the same status in the Plains. 43.71 per cent of the states are found moderately food secure in the hills while 18.75 per cent of the states fall under the category of low level of food security. Manipur and Meghalaya are placed with very dismal position as their food security status is very low. 45.45 per cent of the states in plains are moderately food secure while 36.36 per cent of the states are found with low level of food security. Thus overall again the plain region has done better in relation to the hill.

The mean values in Table 6.7 shows that in 2011-14, the hill region is relatively doing well in terms of food accessibility but in respect of the other two dimensions and overall food security she has outperformed by the plain area. This is exactly the repetition of the picture in 2001-04. The values of Student's t statistic show that food availability and food absorption are significantly higher in the plain in relation to the hill in 2011-14. This means that in course of time the relative performance of the plain region in terms of some dimensional indices has got bettered while that of the hill region has got worsened. However, no significant difference in the level of overall food security is found between the hill and the plain. The values of standard deviation in Table 6.7 indicate that inter-state disparities in the hill region in comparison to the plains is relatively lower in case of food availability, food accessibility and overall food security while it is relatively higher in case of food absorption. This is exactly the repetition of the picture in 2001-04 so far as the hill-plain comparison of inter-state disparities in respect of food security is concerned.

Summary of the Study and Concluding Remarks

The study analysed the status of food security from two angles. First, it makes an inter-state analysis of food security across the hill states and then it tries to make a hill-plain comparison in respect of food security. The empirical findings show that Himachal Pradesh is the most food secure hill state in 2001-04. But in 2011-14 Sikkim attained the position of the most food secure hill state. Kerala has emerged as the least food secure hill state in both the time points under consideration. On the average, the hill States of India are found moderately food secure with a significant decline in the level of food security over time. They faced a higher level of food availability in the beginning of the study period but slips down to a moderate level by a handsome margin during the end.

There is no significant difference in the level of food security between the hills and the plains. However, availability of food is found significantly higher in the plain in relation to the hill in 2001-04 and 2011-14 and the same situation is found in case of food absorption for the time point 2011-14. In respect of inter-state disparities with regard to food security, the hill region has performed better than the plains both in 2001-04 and 2011-14. Hence steps should be undertaken to raise the level of food grain production in the hills so that a higher level of food security can be ensured in this region. For the plains the utmost need of the hour is to address the inter-state inequality in the level of food security. In this connection it is worth mentioning that two states under the plains, viz. Punjab and Haryana are performing tremendously well in terms of food security but the achievement of other states in this regard is not up to the mark. Hence, the disparity gap among the plain states has become wider and wider. Thus it is important to take up the issue of food security for the other plain states seriously so that they can catch up the speed of the progress of Punjab and Haryana in the level of food security faster.

Notes

1. Per capita food grain production is found by dividing total food grain production of a state by its total projected population. In order to take into account the cyclical nature of food grain production, we have used an average of three years food grain production from 2001-02 to 2003-04 and another one from 2011-12 to 2013.
2. In case of inter-state analysis of food security within the hills, the maximum value of the jth dimensional indicator refers to that of a hill state while in case hill-plain analysis of food security, the value of the jth dimensional indicator refers to that of a state (hill/plain) after combining all the hill and plain states together.
3. *Ibid.*

References

Census (2001). Government of India, Ministry of Home Affairs, Office of the Registrar General, India

—— (2011). Government of India, Ministry of Home Affairs, Office of the Registrar General, India.

FAO (1996). *Report of the World Food Summit, Rome,* www.fao.org.

RBI (2016). *Hand Book of Statistics on Indian Economy*, Reserve Bank of India.

Rao, Govind (2007). *Report on North Eastern Region Vision 2020*, NIPFP.

Roy, Manash and Deb, Arnab (2017). "Status of food security across major states of India: An empirical analysis", In: Maumita Ghosh (ed.), *Dimensions of Science Research: A Methodological Perspective*, Levant Books, Kolkata, India.

State Forest Report (2013). available in fsi.nic.in

Sharma, N. Alakh (2010). "Food and Nutrition Security in India", In: Asian Development Bank (Ed.) *Agriculture, Food Security and Rural Development*, Oxford University Press.

Sen, Amartya (1981). *Poverty and famines: An essay on entitlement and deprivation*, Oxford: Clarendon Press.

United Nations (UN) (1975). Report of the World Food Conference, 1975 (Rome), New York: United Nations.

7
Potato Productivity in North East India

A Comparative Study of the Hills and Plains

Maila Lama and *Rimjim Bordoloi*

Introduction

Potato *(Solanumtuberosum L.)* is one of the important crops which contribute to food and nutritional security in the world. Potato is a tuber crop and has multiple uses. It is used as food for both humans and animals. It also has industrial and medicinal use. In developing countries like India, potato cultivation plays a very important role in generating employment and income to the rural people.

Potato which is regarded as the 'king of all vegetables' has emerged as the foremost important crop in India after rice, wheat and maize. India is the second largest producer of potato in the world. In 2010-11, potato accounted for 0.79 per cent of the gross cropped area in the country (Economic Survey 2011-12). Potato is an important crop in the North Eastern Region of India. The region is highly suitable for the cultivation of *tuber crops* (potato, sweet potato, carrot etc.). The tuber crops provide food and nutritional security to many people of the region. In fact, the tribal people of the region are already in the habit of growing these crops. These crops are cultivated both in the hilly and the plain areas of the region. These crops do not require much attention or care and no serious disease or insect damages are observed. Therefore, they get preference as risk aversion crops in this difficult region. Among the tuber crops, potato is extensively grown in all the states of the region. The crop is grown throughout the year in one or the other part of the region contributing about 10 per cent of the total area under potato cultivation in the country.

However, the productivity of potato is in the region is found to be relatively low. There is a need to improve its productivity in the region. In fact, Niti Ayog also identified increasing agricultural productivity as one of the issues in order to improve the livelihood of farmer households (Chandrasekhar and Mehrotra, 2016). At the same time, difference in productivity of potato is found between hills and plains of the region. An overview of literature revealed that there is a dearth of empirical studies on comparative analysis of potato productivity in the hills and plains of the region. Hence, the present study is an attempt to fill the gap in knowledge. The study aims to examine the productivity of potato in the hills and plains and to find out the factors responsible for such difference. It also tries to identify the challenges faced by potato growers and make policy suggestions. The study is expected to have significant policy implications for improving potato productivity and livelihood of the farmers.

Area of Study

The study was undertaken in Sonitpur district (undivided) of Assam and West Kameng district of Arunachal Pradesh. Sonitpur district is one of the potato bowls of Assam. It is situated in Brahmaputra valley covering a vast tract of plain land. The soil type of the district is alluvial which is highly suitable for agricultural production. This district with an area of 5,324 sq. km. is the second largest district of Assam. It accounts for 6.79 per cent of the State's total area. The district with population of 19,24,110 persons is the third most populous district of Assam (Census of India, 2011). The literacy rate of the district was 69.96 per cent which was lower than the State average of 73.18 per cent. The district is divided into fourteen development blocks. It is inhabited by heterogeneous group of people.

West Kameng district is a hilly and mountainous one as it falls in the Eastern Himalayan ranges. This district is spread over an area of 7422 sq. km accounting for 8.86 per cent of the total geographical area of the State. The topography of the district is predominantly hilly and mountainous. The total population of this district is 87013 persons (6.30 per cent of the total population of the State) with a population density of only 12 persons per sq. km (Provisional Census 2011). It is inhabited by six tribes, namely *Monpas, Sherdukpen, Mijis, Sartangs, Akas* and *Buguns*. In this district, 80 per cent of the people live in rural area and agriculture is the mainstay of majority of the people. The temperate climatic condition of the area favours cultivation of potato, off-season vegetables and temperate fruits.

Objectives

The study was conducted with the following objectives:

1. To analyse and compare the potato productivity in the hills and plains of North-East India.
2. To identify various inputs used in hills and plains in potato production.
3. To measure potato productivity and to find out the factors responsible for difference in productivity in hills and plains.

Sample Design and Methodology

The study is based on both primary and secondary data. The secondary data were collected from various sources such as Statistical Handbook of Assam, Economic Survey of Assam, Statistical Abstract of Arunachal Pradesh and Agriculture Census 2010-11. The primary data were collected by conducting survey of the farmers. The survey was conducted with the aid of well framed pre-tested questionnaire. The questionnaire was designed to collect information relating to area sown, output, inputs used, cost of inputs, quantity sold and prices. It also contained questions to gather data on socio-economic profile of the farm households. The survey was based on multi-staged random sampling technique. From Sonitpur district, four blocks namely, Sakomotha, Baghmara, Biswanath and Naduar were selected on the basis of distance from the district headquarter and from West Kameng two blocks were selected, namely Kalaktang and Dirang. From each block two villages were selected. The villages were selected on the basis of distance from the block headquarter. One village located near the block headquarters and other village located far from the block headquarter were selected to make the sample representative. Finally, from each village around 15-20 farmers were randomly selected and interviewed for collection of necessary data. The size of the sample was 200 farm households.

The data were tabulated in a systematic manner and analysed using descriptive statistical methods, regression analysis, graphs etc. The Cobb-Douglas type production function was applied to find out the factors influencing productivity.

The Cobb-Douglas type production function is given as:

$$Y = A.X_1^{b1}.X_2^{b2}.X_3^{b3}.X_4^{b4}...........$$

Taking log to both sides, the function becomes

$$\text{Log } Y = a + b_1 \log X_1 + b_2 \log X_2 + b_3 \log X_3 + b_4 \log X_4 + \mu$$

Where,
Y stands for output per hectare
A stands for technological parameter
b_1, b_2, b_3, b_4 are regression coefficient representing output elasticity.

The data were processed using the statistical package *Ms Excel* and *SPSS*.

Growth of Area, Production and Yield of Potato

In this section an attempt has been made to analyse the trend and growth in area, production and productivity of potato in Assam and Arunachal Pradesh.

Table 7.1: Growth of Area, Production and Yield of Potato in Assam and Arunachal Pradesh

(Area in '000 Hectare, Production in '000 Tonnes and Yield in quintals/Hectare)

Year	*Assam*			*Arunachal Pradesh*		
	Area	*Production*	*Yield*	*Area*	*Production*	*Yield*
2003-04	78	543	69.72	4.02	29.57	73.52
2004-05	73	589	80.58	4.22	27.52	65.30
2005-06	70	354	50.79	3.96	29.84	75.29
2006-07	78	505	64.93	3.97	31.69	79.92
2007-08	75	521	69.26	3.84	29.17	75.91
2008-09	78	516	65.85	4.06	33.41	84.50
2009-10	83	600	72.63	4.24	36.65	86.10
2010-11	85	658	77.35	4.33	35.83	82.67
2011-12	98	683	69.78	4.60	40.00	86.95
2012-13	105	806	76.75	4.82	38.87	80.70
2013-14	97	700	71.5	4.93	40.66	82.40
2014-15	99	706	72.0	5.09	42.00	82.50
2015-16	104	1037	98.9	5.98	43.09	72.00
CARG	**3.66**	**5.13**	**1.41**	**1.80**	**4.00**	**2.00**

Source: Handbook of Statistics.

The analysis showed that the area under potato cultivation in Assam has increased from 78 thousand hectares in 2003-04 to 105 thousand hectares in 2012-13. The compound annual rate of growth of area was 3.66 per cent during this period. During the same period the area under potato in Arunachal Pradesh increased from 4.02 thousand hectares to 4.82 thousand hectares with CARG of 1.80 per cent (Table 7.1). It is found the area under potato is expanding at a faster rate in the plains than in the hills. This may be due to limited cultivable land in the hills. During the same period the production of potato in Assam grew at CARG of 5.13 per cent. This was mainly on account of area expansion as the productivity grew at CARG of only 1.41 per cent. While in Arunachal Pradesh the production of potato grew at CARG of 4 per cent which was contributed both by area expansion and productivity growth. But the contribution of productivity growth was more. While the area under potato in Arunachal Pradesh increased at CARG of 1.80 per cent, the productivity improved at CARG of 2 per cent which a positive development.

The comparison of productivity of potato in the hills and plains shows that it is slightly high in hills than the plains. For example, in 2003-04 potato yield in Assam was 69.72 quintal per hectare which was lower than the 73.53 quintal per hectare in Arunachal Pradesh. The potato productivity in Assam rose over the years to 76.75 quintals per hectare in 2012-13. In Arunachal Pradesh it rose to 80.70 quintals per hectare. The CARG of potato productivity during 2003-04 to 2012-13 was 1.8 per cent in Assam and 2 per cent in Arunachal Pradesh which is marginally high.

The analysis shows that during the period 2003-04 to 2012-13 productivity of potato in the both the states has grown but at a slower rate. In fact there were some fluctuations in productivity in both the States. But in the recent period 2009-10 to 2012-13, potato productivity has shown upward trend in Assam.

The low and fluctuating productivity of potato is a cause of concern and calls for attention of the policy makers. There is a need to make necessary intervention to improve productivity of potato in both the state for well-being of cultivators.

Level of Input Use, Costs and Returns

The study also made an attempt to measure the level of various inputs used in production of potato in the hills and plains and also estimate the costs and returns from potato production. The principle inputs used in potato production in the area were: seed (HYV and local variety), fertilizers, chemicals, manure (cow dung and oil cake), labour, machinery (tractor and sprayer) and irrigation (pump irrigation). The farmers were applying both High Yielding Variety (HYV) seeds (*Panjab Pokhraj, Punjab Jyoti, Mohendra Jyoti, Super S1)* and local seed. But due to high cost of HYV seed, most of the farmers were using local variety of seed. Regarding fertilizer farmers were found to be using mainly Di Amino Phosphate (DAP). Along with DAP they were using Urea, Potash and Super in limited quantity. Farmers were found to use manure too. They were applying mainly cow dung and oil cake. The quantity of seed, fertilizer and manure used per hectare in hills and plains is given below:

Table 7.2: Level and Pattern of Input Use in Hills and Plains

Inputs	*Sonitpur*	*West Kameng*
Seed (in kg/hect)	2035	1520
Fertilizer (in kg./hect)	315	125
Manure (in kg/hect)	1767	453
Chemical (in kg/hect)	6.43	NA
Labour (in days/hectare)	151	240
Machinery (days/hect)	11	NA
Irrigation (in hours/hect)	18.88	NA

Source: Field Survey, 2015.

The Table 7.2 shows a significant difference between hills and plains in level and pattern of inputs used in potato cultivation. The inputs used in plains were: seed (HYV and local variety), fertilizer, manure, chemical, labour, machinery (tractor) and irrigation. But in the hills only seed, fertiliser, manure and labour were used as the main inputs in potato cultivation.

At the same time, considerable difference was observed in the level of inputs used in potato cultivation between the hills and plains. For example, quantity of seed used per hectare was 2035 kg per hectare in Sonitpur while in West Kameng district it was only 1520 kg per hectare. The use of fertilizer was also less in the hills. It was only 125 kg per hectare in West Kameng district which was much lower than 315 kg in Sonitpur district. The use of manure was also very high is plains as compared to the hills. The comparatively low level of inputs used in the hills was mainly due to non-availability of inputs as well as high price of inputs. Hence, there is a need to improve supply of inputs at subsidised rate to farmers in the hills so that they may also be able to apply inputs in good quantity to enhance production and productivity of potato.

Productivity of Potato and its Determinants

Improving productivity of a crop is essential to increase production and enhance farm income. Since, the objective of the government is to increase farm income, there is a need to focus on ways and means to improve crop as this will help to realise higher output without area expansion and enhance farm income. However, there are several factors which determine the productivity of a crop in a region or area. In this section, an attempt has been made to measure the productivity of potato and difference in productivity in hills and plains of the North-East India and to find out the determinants of productivity. The table below shows the productivity of potato in Sonitpur and West Kameng districts.

Table 7.3: Productivity of Potato in Sonitpur and West Kameng Districts

Size of holdings (in Hectares)	*Yield (in quintal/hectare)*	
	Sonitpur	*West Kameng*
Small (1-2 hectares)	198	78.3
Semi-medium (2-4 hectares)	201.13	98.64
Medium (4-10 hectares)	207.81	92.65
Large (10 and above hectares)	210.53	90.5
All total	**204.36**	**90.4**

Source: Field Data, 2015.

The above table shows that the productivity of potato is much higher in Sonitpur than the West Kameng district. The yield of potato per hectare in Sonitpur district was measured as 204 quintals while in West Kameng district it was 90.40 quintals. This shows that the productivity of potato in the hills is low as compared to plains. This may be attributed to difference in natural soil nutrients as plains soil is alluvial type and is rich in various nutrients while the mountain soil lacks such nutrients. At the same time the level of various inputs used in hills were found to be low except labour.

The size-wise analysis of productivity revealed that in plains the productivity of potato is the highest in large holdings (210.5 quintals per hectare) followed by medium holdings (207.8 quintals per hectare), while in the hills productivity was found to be the highest in semi-medium holdings (98.64 quintals per hectare) followed by medium holdings (92.65 quintals per hectare). This is because most of the holdings in the hills were semi-medium and small which is mainly due to hilly and mountainous topography. In both the plains and hills, productivity was found to be the lowest in small sized holdings. Hence, the policy should focus on creating medium and large holdings in the plains and semi-medium and medium holdings in the hills to enhance potato productivity.

The study also made an attempt to examine the net return per hectare from potato production and farm efficiency in the hills and plains. The net income per hectare was measured by taking the difference of total revenue and total cost per hectare. It is one of the measures of farm efficiency. The estimated net return per hectare from potato production in Sonitpur and West Kameng district is shown in the table below:

Table 7.4: Net Return Per Hectare in Potato Production in Hills and Plains

District	*Total revenue per hectare (in Rs.)*	*Total cost per hectare (in Rs.)*	*Net revenue per hectare (in Rs.)*
Sonitpur	165438	120763	44675
West Kameng	117520	63656	53864

Source: Field Survey, 2015.

Above table shows that although the total revenue per hectare is higher in the Sonitpur district, net return per hectare is lower compared to West Kameng district. This is mainly due high cost of production as in Sonitpur district high cost inputs like fertiliser, chemical and tractor are used while in West Kameng district cost of production is low as the use of these inputs is limited. The net return per hectare was estimated to be Rs. 44,675 per hectare in Sonitpur district and Rs. 53,864 per hectare in West Kameng district. Another reason for difference in net return between hills and plains is price difference. In the hills (West Kameng) potato is grown as off-season vegetables. So the farmers are able to get higher price while in the plains the price is low due to plenty supply from all across the country. The average price received by the farmers in West Kameng was Rs. 15/kg while in Sonitpur it was Rs. 7/kg.

Determinants of Potato Productivity

An analysis of determinants of potato productivity is important as it explains the relative importance of various inputs. It can help in formulation of appropriate policy for improving productivity and farm income. There are many inputs which are used in production of potato such as seed manure, fertilizers, chemical, labour, machinery days, irrigation and so on. The available literature indicated that some inputs such as fertilizer, manure, irrigation, machinery use as important determinants of productivity of crops. Hence, these factors were considered in regression model to ascertain the relationship between inputs and output of potato. But this analysis does not give insight in judging the relative efficiency of the various inputs used in the production of output. To neutralise the impact of area, values of all the inputs and output were converted into per hectare. To identify the impact of each and every input on farm output; Cobb-Douglas type specifications of production functions were estimated for potato production.

Determinants of Potato Productivity in Sonitpur

Initially, the regression was run with seven variables. But correlation between the variables labour and machinery was found to be positive and significant. Similarly, there was a positive correlation between chemical cost and fertilizers. Hence, to avoid multicollinearity, variables labour and chemical cost were removed and finally, five explanatory variables as specified above were considered for the analysis. The result of the regression analysis is presented in Table 7.5.

Table 7.5: Regression Result for Determinants of Potato Productivity (Sonitpur)

[Dependent Variable: Log of output (Y) per hectare]

Independent Variables	*Co-efficient*	*SE*	*t-value*	*p-value*
Log Fertilizer (F)	0.35	0.122	2.905***	0.004
Log Manure (M)	0.23	0.038	6.059***	0.00
Log Machinery Use (MU)	0.29	0.124	2.405**	0.018
Log Seed Cost (SC)	0.076	0.051	1.503	0.136
Log Farm Size (FS)	0.037	0.039	0.952	0.343
Constant	3.89	1.134	3.434	0.001
R-Square	0.35			
Adjusted R Square	0.32			

Note: *** and ** indicate significant at 1 and 5 per cent level respectively.

The result in Table 7.5 shows that the coefficients of manure and fertilizer and positive and significant at 1 per cent level. However, the output was found to be more elastic to fertilizer than manure. The coefficient of machinery was also positive and significant at 5 per cent level. The coefficients of Seed cost and area were positive but were not statistically significant at any critical level. Thus, it is seen that, among the five explanatory variables output was more elastic to fertilizer followed by manure and machinery use. The relationship between farm size (FS) and productivity in case of potato was positive but not significant. Hence, positive relationship between farm size and productivity could not be confirmed. The sum of the coefficients in Cobb-Douglas production function indicates returns to scale. The sum of the coefficient was found to be 0.98 which indicated decreasing returns to scale in potato production. The R-square and adjusted R-square were 0.35 and 0.32 respectively. The F-Statistic was found to be statistically significant at 1 per cent level indicating good fit of the model.

Determinants of Potato Productivity in West Kameng

Potato is one of the major cash crops grown in the district. The most important inputs used in potato production were found to be fertiliser, manure and labour. The results of the regression analysis for determinants of potato output showed that the coefficient of fertiliser was positive and significant at 1 per cent level (Table 7.6).

Table 7.6: Production Function Estimates for Potato (Per Bigha Analysis)

Variable	*Coefficient*	*Std. Error*	*t-value*	*Sig.*
Constant	5.091	0.232	21.949	0.000
Log of fertiliser	0.394***	0.038	10.308	0.000
Log of manure	0.091***	0.035	2.560	0.012
Log of labour	0.033	0.064	0.517	0.606
R^2	0.690			
F-Statistic	41.51***			

Dependent Variable: Log of Output
Note: *** indicates significant at 1 per cent level.

The coefficient of manure was also positive and significant at 1 per cent level. This implied that output of potato is highly elastic to fertilizer and manure. The coefficient of labour was positive but it was not significant. The high R-square value of 0.69 with highly significant F-Statistic indicated good fit of the model. The sum of the regression coefficients which represents returns to scale was found to be 0.518 (less than one). This implied that output of potato was subjected to decreasing returns to scale.

Thus, it can be concluded that potato production is elastic to modern inputs like fertilizer, machinery and HYV seed both in hills and plains. Fertilizer and machinery had positive and significant impact on potato production. It can be suggested to encourage judicious use of modern inputs such as HYV seed to raise productivity of potato.

Policy Implications

The above findings and discussion emanate the following policy implications:

- Quality seed is one of the most important elements in potato cultivation. Therefore, government should take major initiatives for providing quality planting material in adequate quantities to the farmers particularly in the hills.
- Access to credit was limited. Since, potato production requires a number of inputs, farmers need affordable credit facilities. Hence, special scheme of loan should be given to the potato growers.
- Post-harvest losses are found to be high due to lack of appropriate storage facilities and unsatisfactory handling and packaging systems. Hence, appropriate training on post-harvest handling techniques and storage facilities should be provided.
- Indiscriminate use of chemicals and pesticides may result in elimination of beneficial micro-organisms and insects. It may also create water pollution and human health hazards. Therefore, for sustainability of the potato crop yield, these biotic stresses need to be managed through eco-friendly measures supported by need-based and judicious use of chemicals.
- Steps should also be taken for establishing a direct link between farmers and markets so that they get remunerative price.

Conclusion

From the above discussion and findings, it can be concluded that potato cultivation occupies an important place in both the hills and plains of North-East India. The study shows how income and employment can be generated in the rural areas of North-East India through the cultivation of potato. The productivity was found to be high in the plains but net income per hectare was found to be higher in the hills. It varied positively with productivity and price indicating importance of improving agricultural productivity in raising farm income. The productivity of potato was found to be positively influenced by modern inputs such as HYV seeds, and fertilizers. It was also influenced positively by manure. Hence, judicious use of modern inputs may be promoted along with the use of traditional eco-friendly inputs. But there are certain issues like, inadequate availability and high cost of HYV seeds, lack of cold storage and irrigation, inadequate access to credit, improper marketing channel etc. which need to be addressed. This will go a long way in improving the livelihood of potato growers both in the hills and plains. At the same time, the policy makers should design location specific policy as a policy for plains may not be suitable for hills given the difference in climatic condition, topography and nature of soil.

References

Bara, B.C. (2006). *Agricultural Development in North-East India: Challenges and Opportunities*, National Centre for Agricultural Economics and Policy Research, New Delhi.

Chandrasekhar, S. and N. Mehrotra (2016). "Doubling farmers' incomes by 2022: What would it take?"*Economic and Political Weekly*, Vol. LI, No. 18, pp. 10-13.

Deka, K.C., S.B. Mukhopadhaya and S. Kumar (2014). "Constraints in potato cultivation in Assam: Farmers' experiences", *International Journal of Agricultural Sciences*, 10: 488-492.

Dutta, K.B. (2003): *Theories of Share Cropping: Evidence from North-East India*, New Delhi: Mittal Publications Pvt. Ltd.

Government of Assam (2013-14). *Economic Survey of Assam*, Directorate of Economics and Statistics, Planning and Development Department.

Government of Assam (2014). *Statistical Hand Book*, Directorate of Economics and Statistics, Government of Assam.

Government of India (2016). *Economic Survey of India 2015-16*, Ministry of Finance, Government of India.

Government of India (2015). *Basic Statistics of North Eastern Region 2015*, North Eastern Council, Shillong.

Kumar, P. and S. Mittal, (2006). "Agricultural productivity trends in India: sustainability issues", *Agricultural Economics Research Review*, 19: 71-88.

Kumar, S., Uma Sah and N.K. Pandey (2006). "SWOT analysis of potato cultivation in East Khasi hills district of Meghalaya: Farmers' perception", *Potato Journal*, 33(3-4): 144-148.

Lal, H. and K.D. Sharma (2006). "Economics of potato production in Lahaul Valley of Himachal Pradesh", *Potato Journal*, 33 (3-4): 139-143.

Pandey, S.K. and D. Sarkar (2005). "Potato in India: Emerging trends and challenges in the new millenium", *Potato Journal*, 32(3-4): 93-104.

Sah, Uma, S.K. Dubey and J.P. Sharma, (2011). "Potato marketing in North

East region of India: A diagnostic study", *Community Mobilization and Sustainable Development,* 6(2): 194-201.

Saikia, M., R. Helin, K.C. Thakur and P.S. Naik (2007). "Evaluation of potato-based crop sequences for upland cultivation in Assam", *Potato Journal,* 34(1-2): 113-114.

Saxena, Rani and P. Mathur (2013). "Analysis of potato production performance and yield variability in India", *Potato Journal,* 40 (1): 38-44.

8
Agricultural Development in Kolli Hills of Tamil Nadu

R. Rajendran and *N. Kumar*

Introduction

According to 2011 Census the size of tribal population is 10.42 million. It accounts to 8.6 per cent of the total population (104 million) and accounts to 11.3 per cent in the total rural population of India. Ninety per cent of the tribal population live in rural areas and 10 per cent in urban areas. The decadal population growth of the tribal population from 2001 to 2011 is 23.7 per cent against the 17.7 per cent in the previous decade. Proportion of Scheduled Tribes in total population of the country has continuously increased from 5.3 in 1951 to 8.6 in 2011. India has the largest tribal population in the world. As per the Census of India 2011, the number of individual groups notified as Scheduled Tribes is 705 (Government of India, 2013). The tribal population thickly concentrated in the states of Assam, Meghalaya, Tripura, Arunachal Pradesh, Mizoram, Manipur, Nagaland, Jammu and Kashmir, Himachal Pradesh, and Uttar Pradesh; they are also concentrated in the hilly tracts in Madhya Pradesh and Odisha; and thinly concentrated in Andhra Pradesh, Bihar and West Bengal. There are smaller numbers of tribal groups in Karnataka, Tamil Nadu, and Kerala, Gujarat and Rajasthan. A sizeable proportion of tribals are living in the union territories of Lakshadweep and the Andaman and Nicobar Islands. The extent of tribal population varies considerably across the Indian states. In the North-eastern states of Arunachal Pradesh, Meghalaya, Mizoram, and Nagaland, upward of 90 per cent of the population are tribal. However, in the remaining North Eastern states of Assam, Manipur, Sikkim, and Tripura, tribal people form between 20 and 30 per cent of the population. The largest tribes are found in central India, although the tribal population accounts for only around 10 per cent of the region's total population. Majority of tribal people live in Maharashtra, Orissa, and West Bengal. In the south, about 1 per cent of the population of Kerala and Tamil Nadu are tribal, whereas about 6 per cent in Andhra Pradesh and Karnataka are members of tribes.

Liberalization-Privatization-Globalization along with other natural forces brings many changes in economic activities of tribals as in the case of general people. After the policy changes, social and economic infrastructure is slowly reaching the tribal people. Chances for integrating economic activities of tribes into others have increased in the LPG era. Many internal and external tribal forces paved ways for inclusive growth of tribal in nation building. Main economic activities of tribals are cropping, livestock rearing, and collection of forest produce for their livelihood. A lot of changes are expected in these economic activities. Proper observation and time-to-time evaluation of such changes help in directing them in a sustainable path. With this aim, present study is conducted among tribal households in Kolli Hills of Tamil Nadu, South India. Tribal people living in these hills are called as *Malayalis*.

Objectives of the Study

The main objectives of the study are: to observe the changes in land use pattern in Kolli Hills during last 25 years and associate them with the changes in social, economic and tribal development policies; to examine the changes in cropping pattern and factors determining it; to measure the diversification in agriculture in terms changes in cropping pattern, livestock rearing, method of marketing of agricultural and allied products, non-farm employment, changes in income of the tribal households; and to analyse the effects of changes in cropping pattern and diversification on sustainability of agricultural development in this tribal area. Expected results from the present study would help to compare the changes happened in agriculture of tribal communities in the North-Eastern States of India, and help to make further necessary changes in tribal policies of India.

Materials and Methods of the Study

The Kolli Hills belong to Namakkal district of Tamil Nadu. It is inhabited tribal population which accounts for 68.34 per cent of total tribal population (57,059) in the district. These tribal people are spread in 14 village *panchayats* and revenue villages across the Kolli Hills. Name of the villages are Alathur Nadu, Ariyur Nadu, Bail Nadu, Cithoor Nadu, Devanur Nadu, Edapuli Nadu, Gundur Nadu, Kolli Hills, Kunduni Nadu, Perakarai Nadu, Selur Nadu, Thinnanur Nadu, Thirupuli Nadu, Valappur Nadu and Valavanthi Nadu. Both primary and secondary data are used for the study. Secondary data have been collected from the published reports of Government of India, reports of Directorate of Economics and Statistics of Government of Tamil Nadu, State Revenue Authorities at district, *taluk* and village level. For the collection of primary data, the study adopted a multi-stage random sampling method for the selection of sample villages and households. Size of the sample for study is 340 tribal households. Survey schedule method was employed to collect primary data from the tribal households. Collected data were analysed with appropriate statistical tools like averages, percentage, cross tabulation and diagrammatical representation.

Location of the Kolli Hills

The Kolli Hills, located in Tamil Nadu, South India in Namakkal District (78° 17′05″E to 78° 27′45″E and 11° 55′05″N to 11° 21′10″N), are low ranging hills spread over an area of 441.41 km^2. It is situated an altitude ranging from 1000 to 1300 m above mean sea level. Some part of the eastern portion of the hill lies in the Perambalur district. It stretches eastward of the hill lies in *Pachamalai*. The Kolli Hills and *Pachamalai* are divided by a broad valley. The Kolli Hills on the western, eastern and southern sides rises abruptly from the plains and on the northern side ascends to the plain by numerous long and gently sloping spurs. The Kolli Hills contains high rising peaks and ravines. It enjoys a salubrious climate throughout the year. It is a fertile pocket in Namakal district. The place is inhabited by a group of tribals known as the *Malayalis* who are supposed to have migrated from the plains of Kanchipuram and settled in various hill ranges of the Eastern Ghats including the Kolli Hills (Vedavalli *et al.*, 2002) about five centuries ago (Thurston and Rangachari, 1975). During settlement, they cleared forests and utilized land for cultivation of food crops, notably millets. Kolli Hills is located in the extreme eastern part of Namakkal district of Tamil Nadu. It is bounded on the north by Namagiripet Block, on the east by Uppiliapuram Block (Tiruchirappalli District), on the west by Sendamangalam and Erumaipatty Blocks and on the south by Erumaipatty Block.

The Semmedu, headquarter of Kolli Hills block is located about 60 km away from the district headquarters. The Kolli Hills consists of 14 village panchayats. This block has 16 inhabited revenue villages comprise 273 settlements. As per 2011 Census, total population in Kolli Hills is about 40,479. Of this, 95.55 per cent (38,678) belongs to Scheduled Tribes. Kolli Hills constitutes about 68.34 per cent of the total tribal population in the district.

Historical Background of the Kolli Hills

The Kolli Hills are featured in several works of classical Tamil literature such as Silappathigaram, Manimekalai, Purananuru and Ainkurnuru. The region was ruled by Valvil Ori around 200 A.D., who is praised as one of the seven great philanthropists of ancient Tamil Nadu. The hills are said to be guarded by *Kollipavai*, the local deity. The mountains have several mythological legends associated with them, and often come across as an eerie place in contemporary tales due to the unexplored and less travelled terrain. Apart from known abode of the Saints, the Buddhists, the Jains set up a number of retreats, those fell prey to time. A stone image of Theerthangar reminds the existence of the earlier Jain influence. The famous Shiva Temple called Arappalleeswarar Temple dating back to Twelfth century situates at Periakoviloor near the famous waterfalls Akasa Gangai. It attracts large pilgrims on new moon days originally a Jain retreat.

Table 8.1: Population in Kolli Hills Block and Study Villages: 2011

Particulars	*Study Area*				
	Total in Kolli Hills	*Thiruppuli Nadu*	*Alathur Nadu*	*Gundani Nadu*	*Gundur Nadu*
Total Geographical Area (in Hectares)	26600	1300	1080	2300	3376
Total Households	10910	642	375	380	992
Total Population	40479	2399	1348	1412	3810
Total Male Population	20862	1215	697	736	1961
Total Female Population	19617	1184	651	676	1849
Total Scheduled Castes Population	668	20	–	–	4
Total Scheduled Castes Male Population	337	10	–	–	3
Total Scheduled Castes Female Population	331	10	–	–	1
Total Scheduled Tribes Population	38678	2339	1344	1376	3737
Total Scheduled Tribes Male Population	19963	1188	695	715	1932
Total Scheduled Tribes Female Population	18715	1151	649	661	1805

Source: Census 2011, Directorate of Census, Government of India.

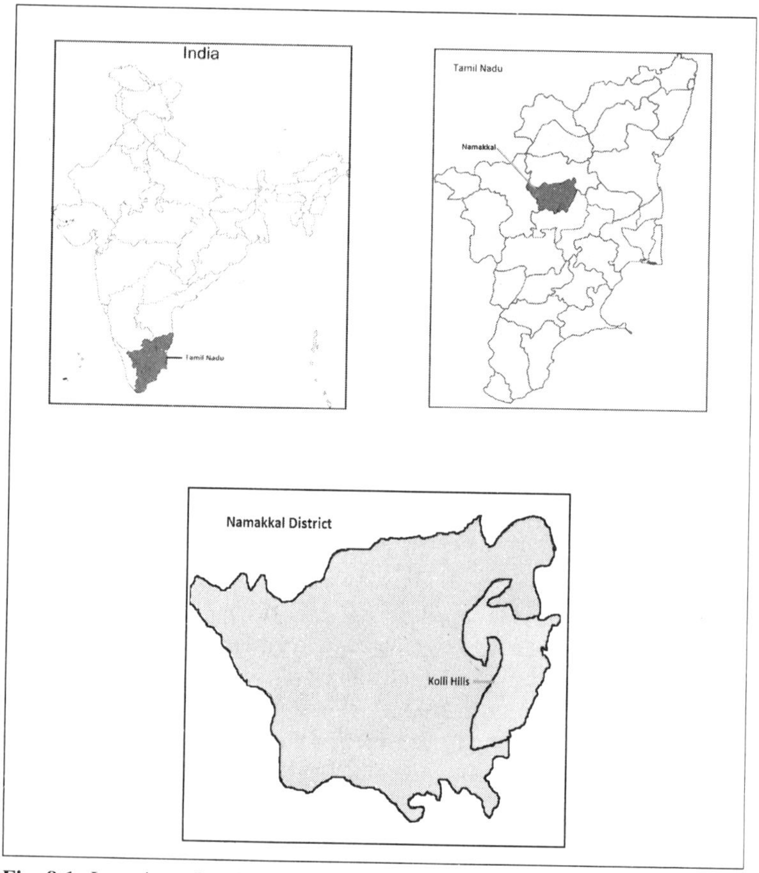

Fig. 8.1: Location of Kolli Hills

Land Use and Cropping Pattern

The Kolli Hills is a mountainous area with a temperate climate located on the eastern border of the Namakkal district in Tamil Nadu. Forests occupy 44 per cent of the total area of 28,293 ha, while agricultural activities take place on 52 per cent of the total area, leaving 4 per cent for other activities (Kumaran, 2004). Agricultural land-use in the Kolli Hills can be classified into three types: first spring-fed valley lands, mainly under paddy; second, rain-fed lands, allocated for millets and cassava, and three, land on the valley fringes, under pineapple, coffee, pepper and other crops (Gruere *et al.*, 2009; Kumaran 2004). The Kolli Hills region is characterized by significant *in-situ* crop genetic diversity of minor millets (Jayakumar *et al.*, 2002; King *et al.*, 2008).

Over the last three decades, land use changes induced by the introduction and cultivation of cash crops like cassava, coffee and pepper, expansion of roads and provision of subsidized food supplies by the state, have affected the use these mullents in Kolli Hills. Low economic profitability of millets compared to cassava, weakening of traditional seed system, the drudgery involved in processing, and poor market opportunities have all contributed to relegating these highly nutritious and resilient millets to increasingly smaller areas (King and Padulos 2017). Forest area is shrinking considerably during the study period. At the same time land put into non-agricultural uses has increased nearly four-times within a period of 10 years between 2000-01and 2010-11. Net area sown varies within a limited band. But, lands are cultivated intensively.

Table 8.2: Land Utilization in the Kolli Hills from 2001 to 2011 (Area in Hectare)

Sl. No.	*Details*	*2000-01*	*2008-09*	*2010-11*
1.	Forests	15869	15571	14965
2.	Barren and uncultivable lands	1517	743	945
3.	Land put to non-agricultural uses	1091	4468	4176
4.	Cultivable wastes	1371	1314	1405
5.	Permanent pastures and other grazing land	219	717	680
6.	Land under miscellaneous tree crops and groves	421	622	603
7.	Current fallow	1453	1722	1923
8.	Other fallow	4771	1146	2031
9.	Net area sown	9685	10094	9669
10.	**Total area**	**36397**	**36397**	**36397**

Source: Block Development Office, Kolli Hills.

Agriculture Economy of the Kolli Hills

Land is broadly classified as *vayal* (wet land), *mettukadu* (dry land) and *kollukadu* (rocky land). *Vayal* is irrigated land, mostly by streams in the case of the Kolli Hills. *Mettukadu* (dry lands) is mostly used to cultivate minor millets such as *ragi*, *samai* and *thinai* and over the last few years cash crops. *Kollakadu* has been mostly home to minor millets or left for grazing purposes. Lands which are not cultivated, moreover, are usually considered to be *dhirasu* (fallow).

Agriculture happens to be the major occupation for the Malayalis. Some people get honey from the forest and make an extra living. Beehive honey collection is also another source of additional income. They rear goats, hens and pigs for their food. As there are no suitable animals for them to hunt in the forest, the habit of hunting is not found. They grow rice in wet areas and dry crops in dry regions. As their habit of consumption has changed they do not show much interest now in the traditional cultivation of crops. They buy rice from the plains as the areas suitable for rice cultivation is very less. The ration rice provided by the government comes handy to them. In most of the areas they grow tapioca.

They consider tapioco as a cash crop. Other cash crops are: plantain guava, lemon and pineapple. From the growth of such cash crops they get some material comfort. Though the soil and geographical condition are suitable to grow pepper and coffee, few of them are ready to grow these cash crops. It is because of the fear that these crops would give them late yield. But, it is common to see people who come from plains involving themselves in growing pepper and coffee. The pepper and coffee are cultivated only in limited places by the Malayalis. Still this takes place below 1 per cent per cent in the total cultivable land. The practice of felling trees was one of the main occupations for about 10 to 30 years. The region, known for its heavy rain, becomes a dry region on account of felling trees. This has caused hazardous change in the ecological system.

Growing silver oak to facilitate the growth of pepper creepers is very much effective for the past 10 years among the rich Malayalis. The benefit from pepper growth comes to them after waiting for 6 to 7 long years. Many are not ready to cultivate pepper because of this delayed yield.

On contract basis, farmers get money from the agents of tapioca merchants. As a result, the farmers do not get any desirable profit. Further the fluctuations found in the market also affect the farmers. But now many farmers show great interest in growing traditional crops like millets and fruits.

As mentioned previously, the total area of the Kolli Hills is 28,293 ha. Of this, the cultivated land is of 14,609 ha. (52%). Long-term averages show that the net sown area is 12,009 ha (42% of the total area). Cultivable waste is 1,223 ha, fallow is of the order of 2,669 ha while land put to other uses is 3,830 ha. Forest occupies 12,454 ha (44%). Grassland is of the order of 985 ha. Tapioca 4,453 ha, millets 1,727 ha, paddy 1,502 ha, ragi 1,337 ha, pine apple 1,000 ha, *mochai* 599 ha, guava 381 ha, banana 300 ha, soybeans 279 ha, coffee 234 ha, pepper 100 ha, silver oak 332 ha and mangoes 107 ha. Crops such as cardamom, clover and turmeric are grown in areas less than 100 ha. Thus millets including ragi and pine apple have greater proportion of area under them, with plantation crops and tree crops occupying considerable area under cultivation.

Table 8.3(a): Trend of Millet Cultivation (Food crop) in Kolli Hills from 1970 to 2015

Sl. No.	*Year*	*Area in Hectare*
1.	1970-1971	1799
2.	2000-2001	1570
3.	2003-2004	1311
4.	2012-2013	404
5.	2014-2015	288

Table 8.3(b): Tapioca and Pepper Cultivation in Kolli Hill from 1999 to 2013

(Area in Hectare)

Sl. No.	*Year*	*Cassava*	*Pepper*
1.	1999-2000	6255	255
2.	2000-2001	5460	441
3.	2001-2002	7540	553
4.	2003-2004	5848	581
5.	2014-2015	4885	760

Note: There is no tapioca, coffee and pepper cultivation prior to 1970 in Kolli Hills.

Source: 1. Directorate of Economics and Statistics, Chennai.
2. Assistant Director of Agriculture, Kolli Hills block.

Table 8.3(c): Coffee Cultivation in the Kolli Hills from 1970 to 2015

Sl. No	*Year*	*Area in Acre*
1.	1970	2.0
2.	1980-1989	223
3.	1990-1999	1453
4.	2000-2007	1977
5.	2014-2015	2053

Source: 1. Directorate of Economics and Statistics, Chennai.
2. Assistant Director of Agriculture, Kolli Hills block.

A Micro Level Analysis

Following section provides details on present condition of agriculture in Kolli Hills through primary data collected among select sample households.

Socio-economic Conditions

For the research, four village panchayats have been chosen among 14 village panchayats in the Kolli Hills block of Namakkal district and names of the villages are: Thiruppuli Nadu, Gundur Nadu, Alathur Nadu and Gundani Nadu. As mentioned in the introductory chapter, in the first stage, these four villages are selected based on random sampling method and in the next stage, sample household are selected and classified into four categories namely Landless (LL), Marginal Farmers (MF), Small Farmers (SF) and Large Farmers (LF). Total sample households of the study are 340, which belong to various categories of tribal farmers from these four villages of the Kolli Hills.

Out of the 340 sample households, nearly 65 per cent comes from upper elevated village panchayats, viz. Gundur Nadu and Thiruppuli Nadu and the remaining 35 per cent of sample households comes from lower elevated village panchayats, viz. Alathur Nadu and Gundani Nadu. Analysis also shows that large amount of sample households are from marginal farm category (48%) and least amount of households are represented under landless category (13%).

The data show that more than 80 per cent of the respondents are male (81.0%) and nearly 19 per cent of the respondents are female respondents. Out of 340 respondents, 163 respondents (129 male and 34 female) come under marginal farmers and this analysis indicates that highest number of respondents come under marginal farmers when compared to other category of farmers.

Table 8.4: Distribution of Sample Households According to Villages and Categories

(in numbers)

Name of village	*Landless (LL)*	*Marginal Farmers (MF)*	*Small Farmers (SF)*	*Large Farmers (LF)*	*Total*
Thiruppuli Nadu	12	41	22	13	88 (26)
Gundur Nadu	16	69	31	15	131 (38)
Alathur Nadu	9	33	17	11	70 (21)
Gundani Nadu	7	20	15	9	51 (15)
Total	**44**	**163**	**85**	**48**	**340 (100)**

Note: 1. Figures in parentheses indicates percentage to column total
2. The source and note is common to all the tables in the present and next chapters

Source: Field survey.

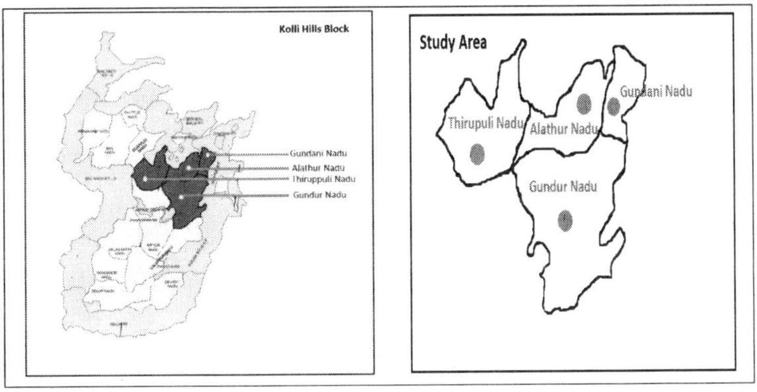

Fig. 8.2: Location of Study Villages

Occupation of the Households

The study indicates that respondents avail three types of primary occupation, namely agriculture, livestock and non-farm activities. Table 8.5 furnishes details on the occupation of sample households. For the analytical convenience, the households' occupations are classified into four categories as livestock rearing, livestock-agriculture, livestock-non-farm, and livestock-agriculture-non-farm.

Table 8.5: Occupation of the Households

(in numbers)

Particulars	*LL*	*MF*	*SF*	*LF*	*Total*
Livestock farm alone	8	–	–	–	8 (2)
Livestock+Agriculture	–	135	75	40	250 (74)
Livestock+Non-farm	36	–	–	–	36 (11)
Livestock+Agriculture+ Non-farm	–	28	10	8	46 (13)
Total	**44**	**163**	**85**	**48**	**340 (100)**

Source: Field Survey.

The occupational structures of the tribal households give some interesting picture. Nearly three-fourth of the households simultaneously carry out livestock and agriculture, and another (nearly) one-fourth of the households have the occupation of both 'livestock and non-farm' or 'livestock-agriculture-non-farm' combination. Thus, most of the tribal households opted 'livestock-agriculture' as the best occupational combination for them. This is true in all land owning categories. However, 'livestock-non-farm' is a most preferable occupation in the case of landless labour households.

Average Household Income from Different Sources

This part of the study provides the details on primary income sources of tribal farmers in the study area. It is classified into three categories and they are as follows: agriculture, livestock and non-farm activities. Agriculture income is through cultivation of paddy, tapioca, coffee, pepper, pulses, millets and fruits. Livestock income is through sale of milk, plough, manure, eggs and sales of animals. Non-farm income is wage earning through government employment schemes like MGNEGP, construction work, running petty shops and so on (*see* Table 8.6).

Agriculture (Crop Cultivation): Landless respondents do not earn any income from farming sector as they do not have any farm land. Tapioca cultivation is carried out by most of the land owning groups and 80 per cent of agriculture income is got from tapioca cultivation. Households receive relatively lesser income from millet crop because millet is cultivated mainly for household consumption.

Livestock Farming: Households earn 42-45 per cent of income from milk production and it is higher than the income received from plough (19%), manure (14%), egg (6%) and sale of animal (18%).

Non-Farm Activities: Landless households are getting more income from MGNREGP (51%). Small and large farm households do not obtain any from this source. Marginal and landless households are receiving more or less 40 per cent of revenue from labour supply to constructions works.

Hence, it is concluded that agriculture sector provides more income (52%) for landholding households. Livestock farming activities contribute about 30 per cent to the total income for all the respondents. Non-farm activities is a major income source for landless farmers (more than 60%) and this is least source of income for other landholding categories (*see* Table 8.7).

Employment Opportunities from Different Enterprises

Except landless category of households, all other receive employment opportunities from all three sources like crop enterprise, livestock enterprise and other activities. Average number of employment received

Table 8.6: Average Household Income from Different Sources

(in Rs.)

Sources of income	*LL*	*MF*	*SF*	*LF*	*Overall Average*
I. Crop					
Paddy	–	2,571	4,235	5,067	2,968 (13)
Tapioca	–	17,589	24,357	35,159	19,276 (82)
Coffee and Pepper	–	773	1,552	1,975	1075 (4)
Other (Millets)	–	218	414	538	293 (1)
A. Total	–	21,151	30,558	42,739	23,612 (100)
II. Livestock					
Milk	4,447	6,331	4,976	8,282	6,009 (43)
Plough	2,062	3,154	2,233	3,131	2,645 (19)
Manure	1,253	2,262	1,473	2,689	1,919 (14)
Egg	477	883	738	942	760 (6)
Sale of animals (calf, goat, pig etc.)	1,724	2,627	2,479	3407	2,559 (18)
B. Total	9,963	15,257	11,899	18,451	13,892 (100)
III. Non-Farm Activities					
MGNREGP	7,957	3,048	–	–	2,751 (35)
Building Works	5,998	3,242	988	–	2,558 (32)
Petty Shop	791	903	2,969	–	1,166 (15)
Others	756	912	1,012	2,965	1,411 (18)
C. Total	15,502	8,105	4,969	2,965	7,885 (100.0)
Total (A+B+C)	25,465	44,513	47,426	64,155	45,389
Percentage of Share from Different Sources of Income					
Agriculture	–	48	64	67	52
Livestock	39	34	25	29	31
Non-farm activities	61	18	11	4	17

Source: Field Survey.

by the households worked out is 879 man-days, and it ranges significantly between 700 man-days for landless category and 960 man-days for large farm category. It reveals that there is a positive relationship between size of landholding and size of employment generation.

When the employment opportunities are classified on the basis of types of enterprise, the households receive highest number of man-days from livestock enterprise (404 man-days), followed by crop enterprises (345 man-days), and other enterprises give more employment opportunities for the tribal households.

Table 8.7: Employment Opportunities from Different Enterprises

(in man-days, per household and per annum)

Category of farmers	Crop Enterprise			Livestock Enterprise			Non-Farm Enterprises			Total
	Male	Female	Total	Male	Female	Total	Male	Female	Total	
Landless	–	–	–	252 (60.02)[b]	167.85 (39.98)[b]	419.85 (59.95)[a] (100.00)[b]	150 (53.48)[b]	130.50 (46.52)[b]	280.50 (40.05)[a] (100.00)[b]	700.35 (100.00)[a]
Marginal	105 (45.16)[b]	127.50 (54.84)[b]	232.50 (29.84)[a] (100.00)[b]	336 (82.96)[b]	69 (17.04)[b]	405 (51.97)[a] 100.00)[b]	86.33 (60.94)[b]	55.33 (39.06)[b]	141.66 (18.19)[a] (100.00)[b]	779.16 (100.00)[a]
Small	109.17 (39.34)[b]	168.33 (60.66)[b]	277.50 (34.44)[a] (100.00)[b]	360 (88.24)[b]	48 (11.76)[b]	408 (50.63)[a] (100.00)[b]	75 (62.33)[b]	45.33 (37.67)[b]	120.33 (14.93)[a] (100.00)[b]	805.83 (100.00)[a]
Large	205.50 (39.14)[b]	319.50 (60.86)[b]	525 (54.71)[a] (100.00)[b]	273 (71.09)[b]	111 (28.91)[b]	384 (40.02)[a] (100.00)[b]	28.80 (57.03)[b]	21.70 (42.97)[b]	50.50 (5.27)[a] (100.00)[b]	959.50 (100.00)[a]
Overall	139.89 (40.55)[b]	205.11 (59.45)[b]	345 (38.44)[a] (100.00)[b]	305.25 (75.52)[b]	98.96 (24.48)[b]	404.21 (45.04)[a] (100.00)[b]	85.03 (57.36)[b]	63.22 (42.64)[b]	148.25 (16.52)[a] (100.00)[b]	897.46 (100.00)[a]

Notes: (a) Figures in parentheses indicate percentages to total.
(b) Figures in parentheses indicate percentages to total of respective enterprises.

Source: Field Survey.

It is quite interesting to note that a clear difference is observed between employment opportunity for male and female household members. Female members get higher employment opportunities in crops enterprise (205 man-days) when compared to other enterprises (99 days from livestock enterprise and 63 man-day from other activities). But, male members get higher employment opportunities from both livestock enterprise (305 man-days) and other activities (85 man-days) than the crop enterprises (140 man-days).

Scope for Sustainability and Agricultural Production

Organic markets for pineapple and minor millets in the Kolli hills, five villages with a large area under pineapple production were identified. The pineapple farmers were mobilized into self-help groups (three women, one man and one mixed groups). Their capacity to negotiate was developed through group discussions and training programmes with external agencies. MSSRF brought together the pineapple farmers and the Ion Exchange Enviro-Farms Pvt. Ltd. (IEEFL), a marketing agency. ECOCERT International, a Germany-based organic certifying agency, was approached for certification. A group of multidisciplinary experts inspected the site and certified the entire area as an organic production zone for pineapple cultivation (232 acres). Men and women members of the self-help groups pooled the produce coming from the various localities to ensure quality while marketing it at the collection centres. The process instilled a feeling of collective ownership and enhanced the business skills of the self-help members. The collection was done under the supervision of IEEFL. Nearly 40 tonnes have been marketed, out of an estimated potential of 400 tonnes. The increase in profit through organic marketing is estimated at about 40 per cent. The International Life and Food Association, a Japan-based NGO working primarily to revive the millet diet in Japan, is negotiating with the self-help groups of the Kolli Hills to procure minor millet (MSSRF 2003) (*see* Table 8.8).

About 90 per cent of respondents are aware of the service of M.S. Swaminathan Research Foundation (MSSRF) in the study area. MSSRF has been involving in about 2 decades for better livelihood of poor tribal farmers through development of agriculture, livestock and natural resource management in the study area. There are many number of training and awareness programmes conducted on improvement of agriculture and livestock farming activities and almost 90 per cent of households have received them. Remaining 11.8 per cent of households are associated

Table 8.8: Association of Tribal Households with NGOs

(in numbers)

Particulars	LL	MF	SF	LF	Total
MSSRF	39	143	76	42	300 (88)
Other NGOs	5	20	9	6	40 (12)
Total	**44**	**163**	**85**	**48**	**340 (100)**

Source: Field Survey

with other local non-governmental organizations (NGOs) for their financial needs through formation of Self Help Groups (SHGs) and Farmers Clubs (FCs).

Suggestions

The study provides following suggestions to improve the status of the tribal people in the Kolli Hills and similar to it.

Revival of millet cultivation by reducing cash crops like tapioca and pepper will be helpful to maintain the ecological balance and food security status of the region concerned. From the literature and from the opinions of the tribal households it is understood that the tapioca has entered the region in large scale during the past three decades. It occupies approximately 70 per cent of the cropped area of this region. Market for tapioca is highly volatile. There is no tapioca processing units in the hill area and the farmers depend on agents and millers coming from the plain area. If the there is bumper harvest in plain regions, there is lack of demand for the tapioca of this region. Price volatility is high for the tapioca crop. Further, farmers started to use synthetic inputs for this crop. Introduction of this crop also affected the ecological balance of the region. Another cash crop, pepper also hinders the ecological balance and landscape of the region. Government, research organization like M.S. Swaminathan Research Foundation and some of the non-governmental organizations are working for enhancing millet cultivation, setting up of millet processing units, providing training for production value added commodities from the millets, and arranging marketing facilities. However, these efforts reached the tribal farmers partially. Continuous and widespread efforts are needed to increase the millet cultivation, maintaining ecological balance and food security. Expanding the market beyond the district is the need of the hour.

Conclusion

A collective action from government, research organizations, non-governmental organizations, and tribal farm household has significant role in establishing a successful promotional strategy for traditional millet crops in the region. Intensive training for the farmers in production, processing, value addition and successful marketing are needed. Modern marketing technologies including web based techniques are essential to get wider market for the produce of tribal households. All these will help to maintain ecological balance, food security and sustainable development of the hill regions.

References

Esparcia, Javier (2014). "Innovation and networks in rural areas". *An analysis from European innovative projects*, 34:1-14.

Felzensztein, Christian (2014). "Do strategic marketing and social capital really matter in regional clusters? Lessons from an emerging economy of Latin America", *Journal of Business Research*, 67(4):498-507.

Government of India (Ministry of Tribal Affairs) (2014). Report of High Level Committee on Socio-Economic, Health and Educational Status of Tribal Communities of India.

Gruere, G. (2008): "The role of collective action in the marketing of underutilized plant species." *Food Policy*, 2008 (doi:10.1016/j. foodpol.2008.10.006 http://www.thehindu.com/todayspaper/ article1796907. Ece).

Gruere G., Nagarajan L., King, EDIO (2009). "The role of collective action in the marketing of underutilized plant species: Lessons From a case study on minor millets in South India", *Food Policy*, 34, 39-45.

Jayakumar, S.; Arockiasamy, D.I. and Britto, S.J. (2002). "Conserving forests in the Eastern Ghats through remote sensing and GIS: A case study in Kolli Hills", *Current Science*, 82(10): 1259-1267.

Kenneth, M. Weiss (1976). *The Demographic stability of small human populations*, 5(6): 59-73

King, E.D.I.O., Nambi, V.A. and Nagarajan, L. (2008). Integrated approaches in small millet conservation: a case from Kolli Hills, India, in: Jaenicke H., Ganry J., Hoeschle-Zeledon, I., Kahane, R. (Eds.), *Proceedings of the International Symposium on Underutilized Plants for Food Safety, Nutrition, Income and Sustainability Development*, Vol. 1: *International Society for Horticultural Sciences.*

King, E.D.I.O. and Padulos, Steafano (2017). *Agricultural biodiversity and women's empowerment: a successful story from Kolli Hills, India.* (http://59.160.153.185/library/ node/625. Date of access 31.12.2017).

Kumaran, M. (2004). *Assessment of development interventions of M.S. Swaminathan Research Foundation in Kolli Hills using Geographical Information Systems*, Unpublished: MS Thesis in Geoinformatics, Gandhigram Rural Institute Deemed University, Gandhigram, Tamil Nadu, India,

MSSRF (2004). *Mouth-Watering Gourmets from Traditional Foods of Kolli Hills. Published Booklet from the Field station (MSSRF),* Kolli Hills and Namakkal.

MSSRF and FAO (2002). *Rural and Tribal Women in Agrobiodiversity Conservation*, M.S. Swaminathan Research Foundation at Chennai, India and Food and Agriculture Organization for Asia and Pacific at Bangkok, Thailand.

Mutoke, M.C. (2014). "Farm diversity, resource use efficiency and sustainable land management in the western highlands of Kenya", *Journal of Rural Studies*, 36:108-120.

Narayanasamy, P. (2006). "Traditional knowledge of tribals in crop protection," *Indian Journal of Traditional Knowledge*, 5(1): 64-70.

Pradeep, V. and Rajasekeran, J. (2006). *Classification and Characterization of Self Help Groups (SHG's) Enterprises in Kolli Hills Developed by MSSRF*. Unpublished: MA Report in Social Works, American College, Madurai, India.

Zhang, Qian (2015). "Farmers' attitudes towards the introduction of agri-environmental measures in agricultural infrastructure projects in China: Evidence from Beijing and Changsha", *Land Use Policy*, 49:92-103.

Sofia Karina Trommlerov (2015). "Determinants of empowerment in a capability-based poverty approach: Evidence from the Gambia", *World Development*, 66:1-15.

Veloutsou, Cleopatra (2009). "Brand relationships through brand reputation and brand tribalism", *Journal of Business Research*, 62(3):314-322.

Ward, R.H. (1976). "The demographic evolution of human populations", *Journal of Human Evolution*, 5(1):1-23.

9
Animal Husbandry and Agricultural Sustainability in Kolli Hills of Tamil Nadu

M. Nagentran and *R. Vadivelu*

Introduction

Livestock, an integral component of agriculture, makes multifaceted contributions to the growth and development of agricultural sector in India. They help to improve food security by providing nutrient-rich food products, generating income and employment in rural areas, and acting as a cushion against crop failure. They also provide draught power and manure inputs to the cropping sub-sector, and contribute to foreign exchange through exports of dairy products and meat. India is one of the largest countries in livestock population in the world and it is accounting for 57 per cent of world's buffalo and 16 per cent of world's cattle and ranks first in respect of cattle and buffalo, third in sheep and second in goat population in the world. Livestock population in India has a positive growth trend over the years and as per 2012 Livestock Census in India, cattle is accounted 190.9 million, buffalo is 108.7 million, sheep is 65.07 million, goat is 135.17 million and pig is 10.29 million (FAOSTAT 2012; Indian livestock Census 2012).

Due to poor productivity of the crop sector, decreasing availability of per capita arable land and lack of other income generating avenues, there is heavy dependence of tribal households on animal husbandry activities. It is expected that the livestock rearing offers substantial income to tribal people particularly during non-agricultural seasons, which can create an impact within the shortest period on the tribal economy. The livestock keeping generates a continuous stream of income and employment, which is an inevitable component of tribal development. The crop enterprise alone cannot help the tribal farmers for sustained survival and to increase their income and employment. A considerable scope exists to improve the economic status of the tribal through livestock enterprise, which provides a sufficient year round employment and income opportunities. In this background, the study is conducted among tribal households of the Kolli Hills in Tamil Nadu.

The study is an attempt to understand the nature of crop husbandry and animal husbandry of the tribal households; to examine the income and employment generation through livestock farming in tribal areas; and assess the linkage effects of animal husbandry and crop husbandry towards sustainable tribal development.

Scope of the Study

The study focuses on the income pattern of tribal farmers, the employment potential of livestock farming, contribution of livestock rearing to the income of the tribal households, the factors influencing the livestock production and linkage effect between crop and animal husbandry in the study area. These will be useful for the planners and policy makers to suggest suitable recommendations for improving the living standard of tribal farmers through livestock farming. As this study also attempts to explore the constraints in livestock production, it will be helpful to suggest measures to overcome them in future and to improve the income and employment of tribal people through livestock farming.

Materials and Methods

For the research, four village Panchayats have been chosen among 14 village Panchayats in Kolli Hills block of Namakkal district and name of the villages are: Thiruppuli Nadu, Gundur Nadu, Alathur Nadu and Gundani Nadu. In the first stage, these four villages are selected on the basis of random sampling method and in the next stage, sample household are selected and classified into four categories, namely Landless (LL), Marginal Farmers (MF), Small Farmers (SF) and Large Farmers (LF). Total sample households of the study are 340, which belong to various categories of tribal farmers from these four villages of Kolli Hills.

Table 9.1: Distribution of Sample Households According to Villages and Categories

(In numbers)

Name of Village	Landless (LL)	Marginal Farmers (MF)	Small Farmers (SF)	Large Farmers (LF)	Total
Thiruppuli Nadu	6	21	11	6	44 (26)
Gundur Nadu	8	35	16	7	66 (38)
Alathur Nadu	5	17	8	5	35 (21)
Gundani Nadu	4	10	7	4	25 (15)
Total	**23 (13)**	**83 (49)**	**42 (25)**	**22 (13)**	**170 (100)**

Notes: 1. Figures in parentheses indicate percentage to column total.
2. The source and note is common to all the tables in the present and follow up sections.

Source: Field survey.

Sample Design

Out of the 170 sample households, nearly 65 per cent come from upper elevated village Panchayats, viz. Gundur Nadu and Thiruppuli Nadu and the remaining 35 per cent of sample households come from lower elevated village Panchayats, viz. Alathur Nadu and Gundani Nadu. Analysis also shows that large number of sample households are from marginal farm category (49%) and least number of households are represented under landless category (13%).

Data for the Study

The data for the study were collected by both primary and secondary methods with the help of a well-structured and pre-tested schedule, specially designed for the objectives specified in the study. The information regarding the size of the family, educational status, pattern of household employment, land holding details, cropping pattern, size and kind of livestock holding, system of rearing, management practices, production costs, risk management, income from livestock, agriculture and non-farm activities, household consumption, status of marketing, credit for livestock, animal health, linkage between livestock and crop husbandry and saving details were collected from each farmer. The farmers were also made to identify the constraints in livestock production faced by them.

Besides the data collected from the selected farmers, secondary data relating to human population, literacy rate, agro-climate conditions, rainfall, soil type, livestock population, veterinary institutions, crops and cropping pattern etc. for the study area were collected from the local bodies, Block Development Offices, Census Reports, Assistant Director's Office of Animal Husbandry, Assistant Director's Office of Statistics, District Collectorate, Directorate of Economics and Statistics of Chennai, journals, electronic sources, and reports of research and non-governmental organizations. The secondary data collected from different sources are cross-checked with adequate care.

Tools of Analysis

The data collected from primary and secondary sources were analyzed with the help of relevant techniques like bi-variate tabulation, percentages, averages (Conventional analysis), multiple linear regression analysis, forward and backward linkage technique and Garett's Ranking technique. Tools were selected and used after assessing the nature of the primary data collected from the respondents.

Analysis and Discussion

Management of Livestock Farming

Management of livestock is carried out in three different means: head of the household; head of the household and spouse of the head of the household; and head of the household and other household members. It is evident from the primary data that one-fifth of the households manage the livestock enterprise only through the head of the household. And in majority of the households (48%), livestock enterprise is managed by both head of the household and their spouse jointly. In the remaining households (34%), the livestock management is done by all the household members including head of the households. The data also reveals that a significant proportion of households from landless and marginal farm households manage the livestock through head of the households from small farm. At the same time the large farm households manage the livestock enterprise with all the members of the households.

Table 9.2 gives details on employment opportunity of household members from various economic activities.

Table 9.2: Employment Opportunities from Different Enterprises

(In man-days, per household per annum)

Category of farmers	Crop Enterprise			Livestock Enterprise		
	Male	Female	Total	Male	Female	Total
Landless	–	–	–	252	170	420
Marginal	105	127	233	336	69	405
Small	109	168	278	360	48	408
Large	205	319	525	273	111	384

Source: Field Survey.

Credit Facilities and Extension Activities in the Study Area

Financial assistance is one of the important livelihood capital to start and expand any enterprise. Landless, small and marginal farmers are very poor in financial asset and that is why, most of the small and marginal farmers could not expand their livelihood activities into next level. The current part of the study examines the credit facilities and extension activities availed by the households.

Households receive loans from various financial institutions like Indian Bank, Large scale Multi-Purpose Society (LAMPs) and other private sources. Nearly 80 per cent of the households received financial assistance from one of the public sector banks, namely Indian Bank, followed by cooperative banks (LAMPs) (15%) and other private sources (6%). There are some degrees of variations that have been observed among households of different categories with respect to sources from which they receive financial assistance. The proportion of households which depend on nationalised bank varies negatively with farm size and it ranges between 68 per cent for large farm category and 84 per cent for landless category. At the same time, the proportion of households that depend on cooperative society varies directly with farm size of the households. It varies between zero per cent for landless households and 27 per cent for large farm households. There is no systematic relationship that has been observed between size of farm of the households and number of households obtained loans in the case of private sources. In short, a large proportion of the tribal household depends on nationalised banks for their financial needs. The national bank provides loans at a reasonable rate of interest, which varies between 4 per cent (for subsidised jewel loans) and 13 per cent (with collateral security for any purpose). The cooperative credit society provides loan at the rate of interest from zero per cent (for conditioned subsidized crop loan) to 18 per cent (for other non-subsidized loans). However, only a few households accessed the loan from the cooperative society, because loan is the target based as well as issued only for a limited period of time in a year.

Survey data show that majority of the households receive jewel loan (59%) followed by agricultural loan from the financial institutions (34%) and other type of loans (7%) from non-institutional sources. Aggregate average loan amount received from all sources varies largely between Rs. 2,000 for landless households and Rs. 35,476 for large farm households. Jewel loan is a major type of loan for landless and marginal farm households, whereas agricultural loan is a major type of loan for small and large farm households.

Most of the households receive loan for cropping (30%) and educational (28%) purposes. Other important purposes for which loans are received is family expenses (13%), livestock purchase (11%) and medical expenses (9%). Loans are received for the purposes such as repayment of old debt. The inter-group variations exist among households on the purpose for which loans are received. A negative association appears between the size of land holding and the number of households who receive loan for family expenses; a similar kind of relationship exists for educational purpose also. But, a positive association appears between the number of households who receive loan for cropping and size land holding.

Willingness to Stay in Livestock Farming

Fifty four per cent of the households are willing to continue the livestock enterprises in the future also. At the same time, different categories of households show differential levels of willingness to stay on this field. Most landless (57%) and marginal farm households (66%) show willingness to continue the livestock enterprise even though they have many hurdles in it. This is mainly because the livestock enterprise provides a reasonable size of income and continuous employment for these two categories of the households.

Reasons for Continuation of Livestock Farming

Reasons for the continuation of the livestock farming by the tribal households are analysed in this section. The main reasons reported by them are easy to manage the livestock in tribal area; it provides additional income for the households; it enhances the employment opportunity for the household members; it gives livestock products to households like meat, milk and manure; and it helps to receive subsidized loans. To collect data especially for this item, first the reasons have been listed to the respondents, and asked to converse on each reason for a minute or two. From their responses the level or degree of the reasons [measured with five-point scale as strongly agree, agree (really reason for the continuation), neutral (undecided), disagree, and strongly disagree (really not a reason for the continuation) are measured with utmost care.

According to the households (without categorization), livestock enterprises are run continuously by them for the strong reasons like provision of additional income for the households (91%), provision of continuous employment to the household members (91%), convenient form of occupation for the tribal households (79%) and provision of low-cost products for the households (77%). However, getting subsidised loan for livestock enterprises is not a reason for continuous running of livestock enterprises.

Opinion on the Functioning of Veterinary Dispensary Officials

The government of Tamil Nadu provides medical, reproductive, advisory, awareness creation and other services like exposure visits, for the livestock development, through its Animal Husbandry Department. For these purposes, the government runs Veterinary Hospitals at district level and Veterinary Dispensaries at (major) villages. There are two such dispensaries functioning in Kolli Hills. Treatment and medicines for livestock are given at free of cost. These dispensaries are functioning with a doctor, a livestock inspector and an assistant. It is the routine duty of the doctor, livestock inspector and assistant to provide necessary services to needy households with livestock. Since the villages in the study area are located in hilly region, according to some of the households, these officials are reluctant to visit hospital and discharge their duty.

Twenty-one per cent of the households with livestock enterprise have made such complaints. But, majority of the households (79%) have satisfaction over the functioning of the officials in veterinary dispensaries in this area.

Awareness on Livestock Insurance

The livestock insurance scheme has emerged as a saviour over the years for landless, marginal, small and large farmers, and for those whose major occupation is domestic animal rearing. Purchase of livestock is very expensive, and thus carries higher risk exposure. Any disease, accident or theft leads to significant loss to the households. In this reason, livestock insurance was initiated in India through the Small Farmers' Development Agency (SFDA) in year 1971.

From the data it is understood that only 5 per cent of households have awareness on livestock insurance and have brought their livestock under the insurance scheme. The other households are not aware on such insurance to mitigate the risk and uncertainty in the livestock rearing.

Source of Buying of Livestock

All the households do not get livestock from their own breeding (except poultry). Most of the households get livestock from other sources like buying from local markets (Kolli Hills and surrounding areas), friends and relatives and nearby towns (mainly from Namakkal and Puthan Santhai).

India's animal wealth is quite large in terms of its populations. The source of information provides facilities of sale/purchase information on all kinds of animals, such as, cattle, buffalo, sheep, goat, pigs, poultry, horse, camel, pet animals like dog, cat and other exotic animals. It enables the seller and buyers to have a wider choice so that it enables to eliminate the middlemen who actually make major profit in such dealings. It may also offer an opportunity to new livestock entrepreneurs to select quality animals from trusted sources. The following table portrays the information of purchase of livestock in the study area.

Field data show that households make intermittent sales of animals mainly to meet the family expenditure (42%), aging of livestock (35%), manpower shortage in relation to increase in size of livestock enterprise in due course (27%) and diseased animals (16%). It is also observed there are inter-group differences among the households with respect to reasons for sale of livestock. Family expenditure is the major reason (55 per cent altogether) for landless and marginal farm households for sale of livestock, because they largely rely on this enterprise for their source of income. Manpower shortage and aging livestock are the major reason for small and large farm households (60 per cent altogether). Manpower shortage is not at all the reason for intermittent sale of livestock for the landless households.

Linkage between Livestock and Crop Husbandry

Crop and livestock farming complement each other. Half of the world's food comes from farms that raise both. Animals pull ploughs and carts, and their manure fertilizes crops, which supply post-harvest residues to livestock. The quest for 'intensification' in livestock farming has thundered ahead with little regard for sustainability and overall efficiency. With animal protein set to remain part of the food supply, we must pursue sustainable intensification and figure out how to keep livestock in ways that work best for individuals, communities and the planet. The following table enlightens about households' opinion on use of inputs from animal husbandry and crop husbandry.

Table 9.3: Opinion on Transaction of Inputs between Animal Husbandry and Crop Husbandry

(In numbers)

Opinion	*MF*	*SF*	*LF*	*Total*
Yes	82 (100.0)	42 (100.0)	24 (100.0)	148 (100.00)

All the land-owning households are of the opinion that output of livestock enterprise is input of crop enterprise and *vice versa*. Livestock enterprise outputs like manure and drought power are used as input in crop enterprise; similarly, output of crop enterprise like crop residues and green fodder are used as input in livestock enterprise.

Mutual Inter-Dependence

Table 9.4 presents the mutual inter-dependence of livestock and crop husbandry. It includes plough, manure and crop harvesting and process; manure and drought power; and green fodder and paddy straw.

Table 9.4: Mutual Inter-Dependence of Livestock and Crop Husbandry

(In numbers)

Mutual Usage	*MF*	*SF*	*LF*	*Total*
Livestock Husbandry to Crop Husbandry—**Backward Linkage**				
Plough + Manure + Harvesting process	82	42	24	148
Manure + Drought power	82	42	24	148
Crop Husbandry to Livestock Husbandry—**Forward Linkage**				
Green fodder + Paddy straw	82	42	24	148
Total	**82**	**42**	**24**	**148**

Entire land owning households are using output of one enterprise as input in the other enterprise. Farmers use livestock for ploughing, manure and harvesting activities. At the same time, they use crop enterprise's output such as green fodder, dry fodder and paddy straw to the livestock enterprise.

Cost and Return from Livestock Farming

The following are the main findings arrived with regard to cost returns from livestock farming among the sample farmers of the Kolli Hills.

1. Costs of livestock are categorised into two; Fixed Cost [that conveys depreciation on building (10%) and interest on investment (10%) on animal purchase, and variable cost (that includes dry fodder, concentrate, medicine cost and miscellaneous cost). Finally, returns of livestock farming comprise sale of animals and eggs (calf, goat, pig, and bird), value of milk, value of draught power and manure of all animals and birds.

2. The analysis shows that marginal and large farmers have invested a huge amount in livestock rearing (Rs. 47,736 and Rs. 44,894 respectively) than landless and small farmers (Rs. 30,523 and Rs. 37,329 respectively). The fixed cost worked out for large farmers (Rs. 6,597) is higher than that of marginal farmers (Rs. 6,179), small farmers (Rs. 4,966) and landless households (Rs. 4,005). The study indicates that in the case of variable cost, same pattern prevail as in the case of fixed cost. Large farmers spend more (Rs. 3,963) than marginal farmers (Rs. 3,220) and small farmers (Rs. 2,770) and landless households (Rs. 2,168). Landless households earn poor net returns (Rs. 3,790) than other households. Large farmers net income (Rs. 7,891) was relatively higher than marginal (Rs. 5,858) and small farmers (Rs. 4,163). Overall Cost benefit ratio from livestock farming is 1.64. It clearly indicates that livestock farming is economically viable for the tribal households.

3. The bottom 55 per cent of the landless households earns about 40 per cent of their income from livestock farming, while the top 14 per cent of these households earns 21 per cent of the income from same farming system. In case of marginal farm households, bottom 51 per cent the farm households earns 31 per cent of the income, while the top two per cent of these households earns three per cent of the income. It indicates that there is a smooth sharing of income among this category of households. It indicates that the bottom 53 per cent of the small farm households earns 33 per cent of the income, while the top four per cent of

these households earns ten per cent of the income. It is concluded that income distribution for is such that higher income group of these households earn almost ten per cent of the income. About 47 per cent of the respondents come under the middle income group and they receive 57 per cent of the income. In case of large farm households, the bottom 65 per cent of the farm households earns 51 per cent of the income, while the top 10 per cent of these households earn eighteen per cent of the income. It is concluded that income distribution is very close to equality curve. Higher income group of these respondents are earning more than one-fifth of the income.

4. Multiple regression analysis helps to understand the factors influencing milk production of dairy farming. The co-efficient of multiple determinations (R^2) is 0.637, which indicates that the variables included in the analysis shows roughly 64 per cent variation in total milk production. Among the variables, number of cow is significant at 1 per cent level and dry fodder cost and medicine cost are significant at 5 per cent level. This study also illustrates that the number of cows is one important factor which determines the milk production. This finding coincides with the result obtained by Sharma and Singh (1993), Singh *et al.* (1998) and Singh (2000). The variables like depreciation on livestock shed, interest on investment, miscellaneous cost, and educational qualification of the respondents are not significant in influencing milk production.

Linkage between Livestock and Crop Husbandry

1. Crop and livestock farming complement each other. Half of the world's food comes from farms that raise both. Animals pull ploughs and carts, and their manure fertilizes crops, which supply post-harvest residues to livestock. The quest for 'intensification' in livestock farming has thundered ahead with little regard for sustainability and overall efficiency.
2. All the land-owning households have the opinion that output of livestock enterprise is input of crop enterprise and *vice versa.* Livestock enterprise's outputs like manure and drought power are used as input in the crop enterprise; similarly, output of crop enterprise like crop residues and green fodder are used as input of livestock enterprise.
3. *Mutual Inter-dependence:* It includes plough, manure and crop harvesting and process; manure and drought power; and green fodder and paddy straw. Entire land owning households are using

output of one enterprise as input for other enterprise. Farmers use livestock for ploughing, manure and harvesting activities. At the same time, they use output of crop enterprise such as green fodder, dry fodder and paddy straw for the livestock enterprise. It shows that there is a strong forward and backward linkage between crop husbandry and animal husbandry.

4. *Method of Land Preparation for Crop Cultivation:* Fifty to 70 per cent of the lands owning households utilize cattle alone for the land preparation; and remaining 46 per cent of the households use both cattle and machine power like tractor. This shows that cattle (bull and bullock) are the most important resources for land preparation in the study area.
5. *Forms of Manure:* Farmers of developing countries traditionally use organic inputs for agriculture. Even after the introduction of modern agriculture, most of the marginal and small land holders of these countries use a sizeable amount of organic inputs like farm yard manure, many natural pesticides and weedicides derived from livestock enterprises. It is evident from the study that all the households use fully composted manure for their crop cultivation. None of the households use any other form of manure.

Policy Implications

The above analysis and discussion leads to the following policy implications:

The study indicates that cattle and goat provide more income; priority may be given on these farming practices. To boost up their production, policy makers should take efforts to ensure the availability of high performing local and improved breeds of animals, so as to ensure viable livestock farming to poor tribal farm families.

In case of fodder production in the tribal area, tribal farm families should be encouraged to allocate land for suitable fodder cultivation, besides initiating concerted efforts to improve the productivity of such livestock.

As lack of marketing facilities is felt as the main constraint in the case of dairy by the tribal farmers in the study area, the concerned authorities may be suggested to establish more milk co-operative societies with genuine quality checking instruments, cooling storage for procuring the milk produced by tribal farmers.

Lack of adequate credit facilities is the foremost problem in livestock farming in the study area. Hence concerned efforts may be taken by financial/co-operative institutions to provide loans for buying animals and construction of proper sheds to the needy farmers.

Since, inadequate knowledge about the improved techniques of livestock farming is also the problem in tribal households, it is important to make them aware and motivate them about scientific feeding of concentrates effectively through intensive extension programmes on animal husbandry, by means of demonstration and field trips.

Since the livestock sector provides a stable income and year round employment compared to non-farm and agriculture, measures may be initiated to involve this weaker group more actively in livestock farming, while framing the policies and strategies for any tribal development programme in the state.

In order to ameliorate the productivity level of the existing livestock resources of the tribal households, steps should be initiated to provide the facilities such as health care, provision of technical helps and facilities for improving the breed of the animals at a reasonable cost.

Lack of transport facilities is another important problem in livestock and agriculture farming in the study area. Concerned authorities should establish proper and adequate transport facilities for easy marketing of livestock and farm produces.

The study indicates that tribal households get additional income from milk production; the concerned authorities may be suggested to organize Farmers Producer Company for dairy farming. This may enable farmers to get substantial income without any struggles.

Finally, the study clearly shows that as livestock farming is an available enterprise that provides income and employment for tribal farm families, which implies the need for the Central and State Governments to establish the research and extension centres like Krishi Vigyan Kendra (KVK), livestock based research and demonstrations centres in the study area that is required to motivate the tribal farmers to take up livestock farming as a primary occupation.

Conclusion

The study found that livestock, agriculture and non-farm have a significant contribution to the income and employment of the tribal households. The income analysis shows that crop income formed the major proportion of the household income followed by livestock and non-farming activities.

Though crop sector contributes more income, but it is the livestock sector that contributes continuous and moderate income to the tribal farm families. Livestock safeguards the tribal families, even at the time of any crop failures. Livestock enterprise offers adequate and continues employment opportunities when compared to agriculture and non-farming sectors. There is a good forward and backward linkage between agriculture and livestock sectors that ensure the traditional organic farming, reducing external inputs and fewer amounts spent on feed for livestock. Thus, the livestock enterprise makes a substantial contribution to the tribal economy by improving standard of living and it plays a major role in alleviation of poverty in tribal areas. Strengthening of forward and backward linkages is essential to achieve alternative models of agriculture like integrated farming, organic farming, sustainable farming, and precision farming. To minimize the problems of livestock enterprises, immediate attention is needed in the areas of improved sheltering for animals, allotment of pasture lands, provision of relevant and reliable credit facilities, improved marketing and transport practices, good level of health and extension services for livestock through government and non-government agencies.

References

Food and Agricultural Organizations (2012). *FAOSTAT*. http://www.fao.org/faostat/en/#data, date of access: 31.12.2017.

Government of India, Ministry of Agriculture, Department of Animal Husbandry (2012). 19th Livestock Census-2012—All India Reportdahd.nic.in/sites/default/files/Livestock%20% 205, pdf, date of access 31.12.2017.

Sharma, V.P. and Singh, R.V. (1993). "Resource productivity and associated efficiency in milk production in Himachal Pradesh", Indian Journal of Agricultural Economics, 48(2): 201-205.

Singh, N.K.; Singh, R.V. and Singh, R.P. (1998). "Livestock status and potentialities of increasing income and employment under mixed farming system", *The Bihar Journal of Agricultural Marketing*, 6(4): 417-424.

Singh, R.P. (2000). "Contribution of livestock and crop enterprises to the economy of tribal farmers", *Livestock in different farming systems*, VIII Annual Conference, TANUVAS, Chennai. p. 38.

10

Medicinal Plants as a Source of Livelihood in Arunachal Pradesh

Tashi Dorjee Bapu and *Gibji Nimasow*

Introduction

Arunachal Pradesh is a tribal inhabited area where the way of living is directly or indirectly based on the natural vegetation or environment. The mountainous region of Arunachal Pradesh is endowed with rich variety of medicinal and aromatic plants of IUCN listed species. The forests of Arunachal Pradesh harbours over 5000 species of plants, over 500 birds, about 85 terrestrial mammals, and a large number of butterflies, insects and reptiles (http://arunachalpradesh.gov.in/forest.htm). Medicinal plants are an important source of raw material for traditional medicines and a large number of people derive employment and income from the collection, processing and trade of these plants (Sarma and Sharma, 2014). Almost 80 per cent of world population relies upon plant based traditional medicines for primary health care (Gopal *et al.*, 2014). Besides, the medicinal plants are also used in modern drug discoveries across the world. Fifty plant species belonging to 29 families have been reported from West Kameng district of Arunachal Pradesh that are used for treating 22 human and 3 veterinary ailments (Namsa *et al.*, 2011). Despite tremendous progress in human medicines, infectious diseases caused by bacteria, fungi, viruses and parasites are still a major threat to public health (Arya, *et al.*, 2010). With the increase in market demand for modern drug manufacturing, the medicinal plants are exploited without any concern for regeneration and conservation. Due to over-exploitation coupled with poor regeneration and pressure from adverse natural factors, certain medicinal plants have become endangered (Hussain and Hore, 2008). The tribal communities of the study area largely depend on wild plants for rituals to medicine. Besides, the rural communities also gather substantial amount of market demanding medicinal plants to meet their cash needs (Bapu and Nimasow, 2017).

A livelihood refers to a set of activities to acquire the basic necessities of life. The environment factors like climate, soil and relief not only impose certain constraints and limitations but also provide opportunities upon the range of livelihood activities. The livelihood pattern is determined by the people's appraisal of the potentialities bestowed by the existing physical and socio-economic environment. These are also shaped by the political system within which they operate (Hoeck, 2001).

During the last two decades, various studies have been carried out in West Kameng district in relation to the status, traditional use and conservation of the medicinal plants. This chapter is an attempt to suggest for sustainable livelihood in the region. The present work focuses on the assessment of extraction of medicinal plants especially endemic and endangered species from the study area and the income generated from these plants for the rural communities of the district. It tries to explore the relationship between livelihood adaptation and strategies among rural communities in West Kameng district for the sustainable co-existence.

Methodology

Data Collection

Various existing works on medicinal plants have been consulted for understanding and relating the present work. The information on medicinal plants extraction and trade were collected through open-ended participatory discussions with local informants (Joshi and Edington, 2010) residing in the study area. Besides, a primary survey was conducted by filling up questionnaires, personal contacts, self-observation and audio-visual tools in the field. In total 60 (sixty) questionnaires were filled up from the local people of Kalaktang, Balemu, Shergaon and Dirang circles of West Kameng district comprising 15 (fifteen) each from the surveyed circles between October 2017 and November 2017. The questionnaires were filled up from the rural people who were actively involved in the extraction and trade of medicinal plants in the study area like nomadic herders, hunters and villagers involved in extraction. The information collected from the field has been analyzed and interpreted.

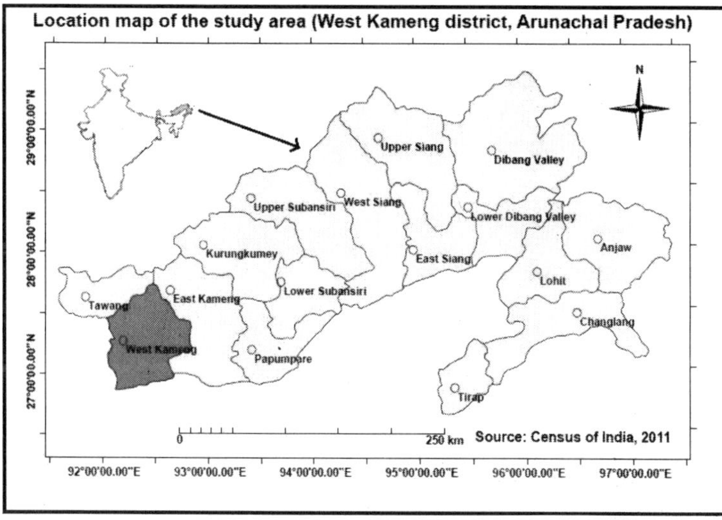

The Study Area

The present work was carried out in the West Kameng district of Arunachal Pradesh. The West Kameng district occupies an area of 7, 422 km^2 and is located between 26° 54′N to 28° 01′N latitudes and 91° 30′E to 92° 40′ E longitudes. The district shares an international boundary with Bhutan in the west and is bordered by Sonitpur and Darrang district of Assam in the south, East Kameng district in the east and Tawang districts in the north. The study area has been selected based on the available records of high rate of medicinal plants extraction from the district.

Results and Discussion

The study is based on three selected medicinal plants, i.e. *Paris polyphylla, Taxus baccata* and *Illicium griffithii*. These plants have both medicinal and economic values and are presently vulnerable due to over-exploitation, poor regeneration and lack of conservation strategies. The local communities practice agricultural farming for their sustenance and the extraction of medicinal plants and its trade aids in managing their daily financial needs. The priorities of rural dwellers have been studied based on 3 (three) important parameters, such as Income per kg, its demand and its availability of two time periods. The income from the agriculture and other allied activities have not considered for the present study.

Table 10.1: Priority based on certain parameters

Medicinal plants	2000s				2010s			
	Income per kg (in Rs.)	*Demand*	*Availa-bility in study area*	*Per annum collection (kg)*	*Income per kg (in Rs.)*	*Demand*	*Availa-bility in study area*	*Per annum collection (kg)*
Paris polyphylla	80-100	National	Available nearby	2	3500-4500	Interna-tional	Rare	10
Illicium griffithii	100-150	National	Available nearby	100	30-80	National	Available nearby	20
Taxus baccata	350-450	National	Rare	2	350-450	National	Rare	1

Source: Primary survey, October, November 2017.

Paris polyphylla

Paris polyphylla is an important medicinal plant that is considered vulnerable in many parts of the world (Deb *et al.*, 2015). In Arunachal Pradesh it is reported from West Kameng, Lower Dibang Valley, Upper Siang and Lower Subansiri districts. It is a traditional Chinese medical herb that has been used in treating cancer for thousands of years (Lee *et al.*, 2005). It is also used in several pharmacological activities, namely anti-inflammatory, spermicidal, hemostatic, anti-bacterial, sedative and analgesic (Lee and Lin, 1988). The local people reported that the paste of the rhizome of *Paris* is used against snake bites during the past. Earlier the plant was abundantly found in the wild, however, owing to high demand in the international market, the mass exploitation of its rhizome for the commercial purposes started by the year 2005 (Paul *et al.*, 2015) and subsequently became rare. Basar (2014) reported illegal exporting of rhizomes of *Paris polyphylla* from Arunachal Pradesh to China *via* Myanmar. The collection of *Paris polyphylla* has increased by 5 times over a decade from 2 kg per annum to 10 kg per annum (Table 10.1). During 2000s, the amount per kg of rhizomes was about Rs. 80-100, which has increased considerably to around Rs. 3500-4500 at present. This may be the result of its rareness in the jungle, illegal marketing and growing demand at international market. The rural communities fetch about Rs. 40000 from the trade of *Paris polyphylla* in a year at present which was only 200 during 2000s (Table 10.2).

Table 10.2: Average annual income from medicinal plants

(*in Rupees*)

Medicinal plants	*2000s*	*2010s*
Paris pollyphylla (dry)	200	40000
Illicium griffithii	13000	800
Taxus baccatta	700	350
Total	**13860**	**41150**

Source: Primary survey, October, November 2017.

Illicium griffithii

Illicium is enlisted as endangered species by International Union for Conservation of Nature and Natural Resources (IUCN) in its Red data book (Saha *et al.*, 2015) and it is found in Tawang, West Kameng, Lower Subansiri, West Siang and Lower Dibang Valley districts of Arunachal Pradesh (Paul *et al.*, 2013). The fruits are used to treat cough, sinusitis, toothache, regurgitating, dyspepsia, abdominal pain, and food poisoning and are considered carminative, stomachic, and galactagogic (Hung *et al.*, 2016). Scientists have found a shikimic acid in the fruits of *Illicium griffithii* which are used for the manufacturing of anti-influenza drug called 'Tamiflu'. These carpels are used for curing cough, toothache, flavouring tea, to increase the potency of *ara* (local wine), incense in Bhutan (Mukhia, 2006) and in Arunachal Pradesh (Bapu and Nimasow, 2017).

Due to its high demand in spice and pharmaceutical industry, local communities harvest huge quantity of fruits from different parts of Arunachal Pradesh (Paul *et al.*, 2013). Table 10.1 reflects that the preferences of the rural communities for the extraction of medicinal plants have changed in last 1 (one) decade. During 2000s, *Illicium griffithii* is found to be the most preferred medicinal plant for the extraction by the local people, as it was available nearby the rural dwellers and it provided around Rs. 10000-15000 per annum to a household. The local people collect around 100 kg of *Illicium griffithii* in a year, which they sell to the middlemen, mostly from Tezpur, Udalguri (Assam) at around Rs. 100-150. Bapu and Nimasow in 2017 reported large scale extraction during 2002-2007 and one middleman was reported of collecting around 500 kg of dry fruits of *Illicium* from the local communities of the districts. They reported that there were around 15-20 middlemen in West Kameng and Tawang districts. The rural people reported that the regeneration of *Illicium* was very negligible during 2000s due to huge extraction of its fruits before the exact time compromising the natural regeneration.

However, the plant started regenerating rapidly in the wild from 2009-10 onwards, as the collection of fruits of this plant has declined significantly. At present, the rural dwellers collect about 10 kg of its fruits per annum, which may be due to its fall in price or market demand.

Taxus baccata

Taxus baccata (Himalayan Yew) is a small to medium sized tree, valuable for taxol or paclitaxel extraction (Phillips *et al.*, 1998) used in the manufacturing of anti-cancer drugs, especially breast and ovarian cancer. Table 10.1 suggests that the extraction of *Taxus baccata* from the district

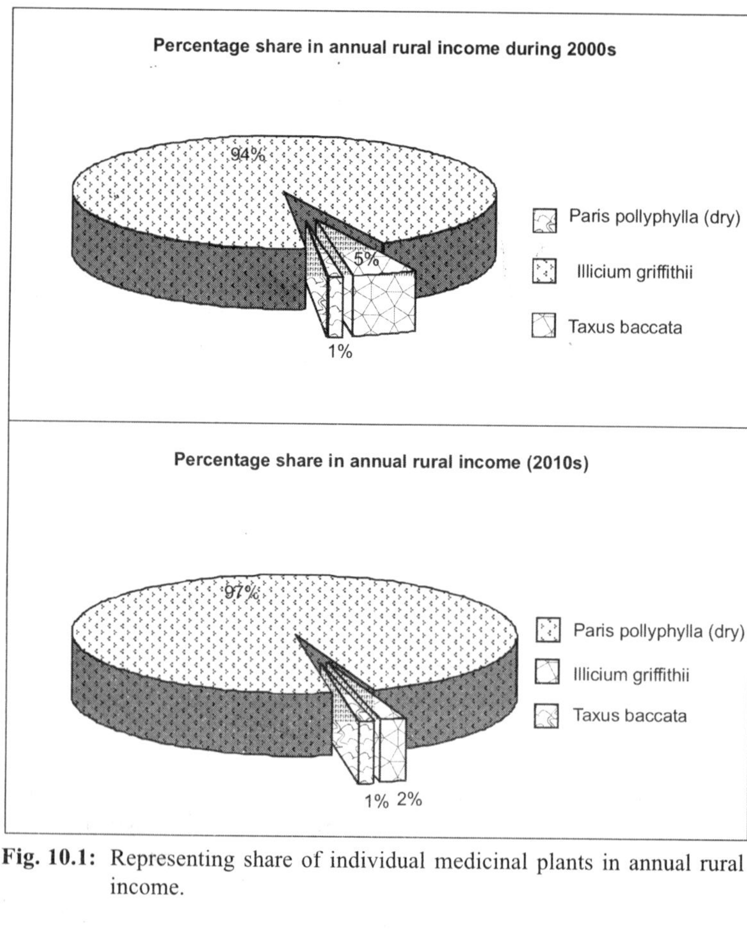

Fig. 10.1: Representing share of individual medicinal plants in annual rural income.

is very negligible during 2000s and at present as well. This may be the result of huge exploitation of *Taxus* from the district in 1990s as reported by villagers and various researchers. Nimachow *et al.* in 2010 reported that *Taxus* is not found in the 8-10 km radius from the villages in West Kameng district of Arunachal Pradesh due to the large-scale exploitation of *Taxus* plants during 1990s. Rawat *et al.*, in 2011 reported that about 70 to 80 trucks of the *Taxus* leaves were supplied from Morshing, Domkho, Sanglem and Khelang villages of West Kameng district, where one truck would need 30 fully grown trees to be completely pruned. It has been observed that the rampant extraction of leaves without standard lopping method has resulted in the death of *Taxus* plants in the area.

The above results (Fig. 10.1) reveal that the extraction and trade of *Paris polyphylla* contributes a lot in the rural economy at present. However, it has become rare in the forest due to the rapid extraction and high demand. The share of *Paris polyphylla* to the rural income has risen from only 1 per cent during 2000s to 97 per cent during 2010s. On the other hand, share of *Illicium griffithii* in rural income has declined from 94 per cent during 2000s to only 2 per cent at present. And the share of *Taxus* was very negligible in both the periods.

(A) *Paris polyphylla* (B) ***Illicium griffithii***

(C) Rhizome of *Paris polyphylla* (D) ***Taxus baccata***

Conclusion and Suggestions

The study shows that the extraction of medicinal plants in the study area has shifted from *Taxus baccata* during 1990s to *Illicium griffithii* during 2000s and at present, the rural people are mostly involved in extraction of *Paris polyphylla.* All these medicinal plants have contributed largely to the rural economy from time to time. The availability of plants plays a significant role in determining the price of the plant. The price rises as it becomes rare. The extraction of medicinal plants from the forest has become an integral part of rural livelihood as it contributes a major share of the economy. Besides, the villagers also depend on agriculture and its allied sector.

The findings show that the adverse effects of exploitation, very poor natural regeneration of plant, localized natural growth and no tangible efforts to regenerate the plants have pushed these important resources to extreme limit of extinction. Thus, its conservation is the need of the hour. At the same time, the study also reflects that the cultivation of medicinal plants can play an important role in the livelihood strategies of the villagers in the study area. The villagers may be encouraged for cultivation of these plants in religious places, kitchen gardens and farm land for sustainable utilization. Further, such efforts would contribute directly in conservation of biodiversity and can meet the future demand of these medicinal plants. Thus, Government should facilitate the rural dwellers of the study area to opt for the cultivation of important medicinal plants for sustainable livelihood. Data of the present study confirms that cultivation of medicinal plants is a potential option to improve the livelihoods of poor farmers and thereby curtail the incentives to collect from the wild (Alam and Peppelenbos, 2009).

The ban should be lifted partially for the extraction of medicinal plants as these plants fetches high income to the rural people. And the execution of policies for its conservation should be tasked to the Village Councils, as the villagers in the district are very submissive to the rule of the Village Council. On the other hand, Government must develop suitable strategies to conserve medicinal plants from the area by providing subsidies in horticulture sector as an alternative livelihood. It is also essential to carry out deep research on these plants, its distribution, so that the value, importance and protection measures could be mitigated and disseminated down to the rural people.

References

Alam, G. and Peppelenbos, L. (2009). "Cultivation of medicinal plants in Uttarakhand", *Economic and Political Weekly*, 99-104.

Arya, V.; Yadav, S.; Kumar, S. and Yadav, J.P. (2010). "Antimicrobial activity of *Cassia occidentalis* L. (leaf) against various human pathogenic microbes", *Life Sciences and Medicine Research*, 9, 1-11.

Bapu, T.D. and Nimasow, G. (2017). "Extraction of important medicinal plants and the need for conservation strategies in Eastern Himalayan Region", In: Kaur, K. and Khan, S.A. (Ed.), *Development of Nations: An Interplay of Economics, Politics and Society* (pp. 177-181). Patiala, India: Madaan Publishing House.

Basar, E. (2014). *The Arunachal Times* (www.arunachaltimes.com/26.08.2014).

Bhattarai, D.R. (2016): *Livelihood Pattern and Adaptation Strategies: Sustaining Development Interventions in Western Mid-Hills of Nepal* (Doctoral dissertation, Singhania University).

Deb, C.R.; Jamir, S.L. and Jamir, N.S. (2015). "Studies on vegetative and reproductive ecology of Paris Polyphylla Smith: A vulnerable medicinal plant", *American Journal of Plant Sciences*, *6*(16): 2561.

Gopal, N.M.; Tejaswini, J., Mantry, S. and Kumar, S.A. (2014). "International standards of medicinal plants", *International Journal of Innovative Pharmaceutical Sciences and Research*, *2*, 2498-2532.

Hung, N.V.; Dai, D.N.; Thanh, B.V. and Ogunwande, I.A. (2016). "Constituents of essential oils from *Illicium micranthum* Dunn and *Illicium griffithii* Hook. f. & Thoms." *Journal of Medicinal Plants*, *4*(6), 80-84.

Hussain, S. and Hore, D.K. (2008). "Collection and conservation of major medicinal plants of Arunachal Pradesh", *Indian Forester*, *12*, 1663-1679.

Lee, H. and Lin, J.Y. (1988). "Antimutagenic activity of extracts from anticancer drugs in Chinese medicine", *Mutation Research/Genetic Toxicology*, *204*(2), 229-234.

Lee, M.S.; Chan, J.Y.W.; Kong, S.K.; Yu, B.; Eng-Choon, V.O.; Nai-Ching, H.W. and Fung, K.P. (2005). "Effects of polyphyllin D, a steroidal saponin in Paris polyphylla, in growth inhibition of human breast cancer cells and in xenograft", *Cancer biology and therapy*, *4*(11), 1248-1254.

Mukhia, P.K. (2006). Management Guidelines for *Illicium griffithii* for Community forests of Bhutan, Participatory Forest Management Project Report 32, Social Forestry Division, Department of Forests, Ministry of Agriculture, Thimbu, Bhutan.

Namsa, N.D.; Mandal, M.; Tangjang, S. and Mandal, S.C. (2011). "Ethnobotany of the Monpa ethnic group at Arunachal Pradesh, India", *Journal of Ethnobiology and Ethnomedicine*, *7*(1), 31.

Nimachow, G.; Rawat, J.S. and Dai, O. (2010). "Status of Himalayan yews in West Kameng district of Arunachal Pradesh", *Current Science*, *98*(11): 1434-1437.

Paul, A.; Kalita, J.; Khan, M.L. and Tripathi, O.P. (2013). "*Illicium griffithii* Hook. f. and Thoms.: A potential source of natural off-farm income to the rural people of Arunachal Himalaya, India", *Indian Journal of Natural Products and Resources*, *4(*2): 131-137.

Phillips, D. and Dwyer, D.B. (1998). Dabur Research Foundation, "Sustainable harvesting of Himalayan yews," *Medicinal plant trade in Europe: conservation and supply, Traffic Europe, Eds. Cambridge: Europe*, 147-154.

Rawat, J.S.; Nimachow, G.; Dai, O.; Norbu, L. and Loder, T.O. (2011). "Cancer of illegal trade threatens the anti-cancer Yews", *Science and Culture*, *77*, 46-51.

Saha, D.; Ved, D.; Ravikumar, K. and Haridasan, K. (2015). *Illicium griffithii*. The IUCN Red List of Threatened Species 2015: e.T50126617A50131370. Accessed on 20 December, 2017.

11
Promoting Responsible Tourism in Western Arunachal Pradesh

Mridul Dutta, Gulshan Chaddha and *Tridib R. Sarma*

Introduction

Community based tourism (CBT) holds long term sustainable benefits for host community, local business intermediaries, residents, divergent needs, potential of the primary stakeholder, its inhabitants (Brohman, 1996) and provides satisfying experience to tourists (Dutta, 2014) with benefit sharing models (WWF, 2001) leading the destination as a regional tourism brand (Sproule, 1996). The business practices in responsible tourism has holistic objectives through homestay operations, guiding and leisure activities, home-based ethnic cuisines, food and beverages, souvenir, craft sales (Cohen, 2002; Sarma, 2004 Dutta, 2014), dance performances as content (The Mountain Institute, 2000) aligned with endogenous leisure attractions (Ashley & Garland, 1994) in collaborations of enterprises engaging in the Tourism Value Chain (Dutta & Barua, 2016) with handholding institutional support (NEDFI, 2000). There is a contrasting command of tourism intermediaries which consume about one-third in the tourism value chain by disseminating information in the distribution management (Dyson, Hendricks & Grant, 2007). Collaborative planning with grassroots level participation can have combination of niche attractions in eco-tourism, community-based tourism and heritage tourism having lower environmental impact may reduce leakages (Porter, 1985; Dutta, 2014). Among few success stories from 36 Endogenous Tourist Project sites promoted by Ministry of Tourism, the Gondhmow Endogenous Tourist Project, Sualkuchi of Assam (Dutta, 2014) and the annual Hornbill Festival of Nagaland representing tribes and communities, in spite of troubled political past (Deka & Baishya, 2009), of North Eastern India (NEI) are a few. The operational aspects of developing sustainable tourism initiatives (Cooper, 2004) and the strategy of benefits sharing (Gyamtsho, 1996) will extend further from sustainable development goals. At operational level, satisfaction parameters such as miscommunication of service quality perception, unjustified homestay prices, tariff plan1 (Dhan, Gurung & Seeland, 2008), hygiene, safety and privacy, and utilities related with Accommodation and Food and Beverages of the home based restaurants and kitchens of homestay is of primary importance in leisure capacity of the host community. Thought leadership in improving the capacity in community based tourism operations are the micro-finance model for renovation of homes in Nanda Devi Campaign (Equations, 2008) and positive impact on social development indexes, and social safety programme (Berranger & Raufflet, 2008). Segmentation strategy in profiling of tourists to CBT destination suggests a significantly higher proportion of leisure motivation as compared to business travelers (Foo, McGuiggan & Yiannakis, 2004) and relevance of tourist roles (Gibson & Yiannakis, 1992; 2002). Therefore, a discussion is required in the preparing tourism roadmap preparation in context of leisure capacity and tourism content of the supply side with suitable match with low impact high value demand side.

Attractions of Western Arunachal Pradesh

Tawang District

Tawang Monastery of Tawang was founded by the Merak Lama Lodre Gyatso in 1681 in accordance with the wishes of the 5th Dalai Lama, Ngawang Lobsang Gyatso. The word 'Tawang' means "Chosen by Horse". The 6th Dalai Lama, Tsangyang Gyatso, was born on 1st of March, 1683 in Tawang. The Tawang sub-division is sub-divided into 10 administrative circles in which Zemithang is one of them. This place is connected through a two lane pristine view of 242 km from Assam to Bumla area of Tawang. The nearest Railway station head is Dekargaon Railway Station and Airport is at Salonibari, Tezpur.

Zemithang Circle: Zemithang Circle comprises 12 Census villages. Among these villages, Muchat (also known as Kharakpu), Lumpo, and Gorsam have significant tourism attractions. There is a tourist lodge in Zemithang Circle comprising 8-10 rooms, but not in good hospitable condition. The Muchat village has the Gorsam Chorten, but it also lacks accommodation facility. The community in Zemithang belongs to Monpa ethnicity.

Wildlife, forest and natural landscape Zemithang: The villagers of Muchat and Lumpo claim to have sizeable numbers of Red Panda, Barking Deer, Wild Boar, Himalayan Langur, Snow Leopard, Black Deer, Snakes, Black Necked Crane, Blood Pigeon, Kite and Mountain Goats.

Festivals, fairs and rituals: The dates for the festivals are arranged by the Rimpoche of Tawang monastery. Some important festivals and rituals are Chotpa, Choskar, Losar, Gorsam Mela, Dunchang, marriage ceremony, christening, and funeral.

Ser-Tsang Gompa: The Ser Tsang Gompa is in Lumpo village about the 100 years old. It has the Chamba statue or Maitreya Buddha (Buddha-to-come in future). During 1962 Chinese aggression into Tawang, the People's Liberation Army's soldiers captured this Gompa. In 2013, the statue was again renovated and brought into original format.

Gorsam Chorten: Gorsam Chorten or Gonsum Chotëm is about two kilometres before reaching Zemithang. It is believed that this Chorten is about 300 years old and the largest Stupa in India. The Chorten's architecture is based on the Boudhnath Stupa of Nepal. The construction of the Chorten involved extensive use of traditional skills, consistency in architecture and use of locally available raw materials.

Pangchen Lumpo Muchat Community Conservation Management Area: The village councils (panchayats), with institutional support from World Wide Fund for Nature (India) and Sir Dorabji Tata Trust, initiated conservation activities under their customary legal rights by institutionalising Community Conserved Areas (CCA) in 98 square km area of community forest in Lumpo and Muchat village. Indigenous and community conserved area is defined as natural or modified ecosystem containing significant biodiversity values and ecological services, voluntarily conserved by indigenous and local communities, through customary laws or other institutional/effective means (IUCN, World Parks Congress of 2003). WWF-India has helped in awareness creation and capacity building for Pangchen Lumpo Muchat Community Conservation Management Area with few homestays in these two villages. Village entrepreneurs accept tourists for overnight stay in their homes. Accordingly, few residents have renovated and made modification/ improvement in their house and toilets and kitchen get the feel of Monpa community homestay accommodation. Accordingly, CBT guidelines and rules are framed and economic opportunities arising from tourism is shared among the tourism entrepreneurs. The overall tourist arrival is limited to two seasons, i.e. September, October and November serves as the peak season with significantly high percentage of inbound tourist arriving and the March, April and May is the second season with tourist interested in adventure and culture attractions.

Thembang, West Kameng District

The Thembang Circle is subdivided into 12 census villages of which Thembang Village is important benchmark for responsible tourism. The old name of Thembang village is Yuchho-pema-chen. The villages in the nearby area are Semnak, Cherong, Panchavati, Lagam, Gonthung, Pangma, Chander and Lachong. Tourists can see the traditional life style of the Monpa household, trekking in temperate climate, view the beautiful peaks 'Gorichen, Kangto, Nyegi Kangsang in Himalayas and experience folk dance by residents.

Thembang Bapu Community Conserved Area Management Committee: WWF-India (Western Arunachal Landscape) started conservation of environment in traditional sustainable system in 2004 with the village councils. The model was successful in linking conservation with economic opportunities. As on 2011, 312 square km area of community forest is protected under Thembang Bapu Community Conservation Area as extension of their customary law under the registered society Thembang Bapu CCA Management Committee. However, the model is losing its interest among stakeholders.

Dirang: Dirang is a pleasant weather town about 40 km from Bomdila towards Tawang. Dirang has a tourist lodge and number private hotels and a government operated PWD inspection bungalow as accommodation facilities. This town serves as halting place for tourists travelling from Guwahati/Tezpur to Tawang. Attractions of Dhirang are *Monpa* villages of Namshu, Kalachakra Gompa, hot springs, Dhirang Dzong, National Yak Research and Breeding Centre, Sheep breeding farms, kiwi and apple orchards.

Dirang Dzong: The Dirang Dzongused to be administrative headquarters, or garrison fort office and residential quarter of the Governor. It was believed to be built in 1831. However, after the lapse of the Tibetan Government, this *Dzong*lost it's importance, become purposeless with little care initiated in conservation, documentation, and relocation of the settlements from the garrison fort. There are about 42 households in the fort area which is also called as *Dirang Basti.*

Sangti Valley: The picturesque Sangti valley is sparsely populated and named after the river Sangti, the lifeline of the valley. It is located about 7 km away from Dirang town. The millet and paddy fields in Sangti valley attracts the rare Tibetan migratory bird *black-necked crane* during their breeding period from November to late February.

Endemic attractions: The trekking route includes *Thembang* village, *Pangma* village (about 7500 feet above MSL, Monpa settlement), *Chander* village, *Namshu* (7100 feet above MSL, Monpa village) *Sangti* valley (5000 feet above MSL). The Community Based Tourism under Thembang Bapu Community Conserved Area Management Committee provides trained cook, trekking guides, porters and mules for transportation. Traditional cultural programme and folk dance are other attractions. The point *Chander,* 9200 feet above MSL, is a barren ridge and provides a panoramic view of *Gorichen* Peak of Himalayan range. The next trekking destination is *Namshu* (Monpa village), located at 7100 feet above MSL and finally, at *Sangti* valley with an altitude of 5000 feet above MSL.

National Institute of Mountaineering and Allied Sports, Dirang: NIMAS is a state-of-the-art campus serving base camp for different professional adventure activities, adventure sports programmes, rafting and aero sports. NIMAS operates under the Ministry of Defence, Government of India in collaboration with Government of Arunachal Pradesh. Since 2013, NIMAS is providing *in situ* training for numerous batches of adventure enthusiast along with accommodation.

Livelihood and Organic cultivation: Farming and livestock is the two primary livelihoods. Other professions are logging, carpentry, road repairing, petty shops, porters, and guiding personals for Indian Army troops. The agriculture produce is entirely organic and based on traditional knowledge of the indigenous population. But, very little certification or acknowledgement has been received for the farming practices with no insecticides, pesticides, growth enhancing hormones and inorganic fertilizers. The local farm produce is *Khrye* (finger millet locally called *Maruwa), Nasphey* (sweet wheat), spinach (*lai patta*), cabbage, cauliflower, beans, chilly vegetable (similar to capsicum), cucumber, *Chong* (local onion), *Braing* (local garlic), Vicsi (coriander), *Khe* (potato), *Mula* (radish). The orchards are of fruits producing varieties of apple, kiwi, plum, peach, oranges and walnut.

Way side attractions: The potential locations for way side amenities on route from Dirang to Tawang are Dirang Hot spring, Sela pass, Jung village, Jaswantgarh War Memorial, Nuranang Waterfall, Tawang War Memorial, Bap Teng Kang Waterfall and Taktsang Monastery. Though there are few utilities based wayside available, the amenities may not qualify in terms of hygiene aspects and quality of services.

What is to be Done to Achieve "High Value, Low Impact Tourism" for Next 10 Years

Tawang and West Kameng districts have significant potential for nature, adventure and cultural tourism. CBT is in forefront for promotion of sustainable development in this region in practice for last few years, though with substantial scope for improvement. The authors argue for sustainable strategy based on three core competencies, i.e. rich bio-diversity content of the region, less dilution of cultural diversity and responsible tourism business model in practice. This region has the capacity for upgradation and incorporation into Wildlife Sanctuary. The Bumdeling Wildlife Sanctuary of in North Eastern Bhutan of Trashiyangtse District and Sakteng Wildlife Sanctuary in Trashigang District of Bhutan are potential runner for UNESCO inclusion. These sanctuaries were planned some 20 years and located adjacent to this region and can be role model for Thembang and Zemithang. The cultural lineage of indigenous communities, the historical patronage of Tawang Monastery, Gorsam Stupa etc. are living heritage of the region. The conservation of CCA efforts need alternate backup livelihood opportunity for the ethnic communities through community based tourism (Dorjee, Dutta & Wange, 2012). The competencies and desirable actions are given below.

Traditional ownership and Customary laws: Remote and ecologically sensitive sites in the tourism destinations of India are either within protected areas or in areas under the jurisdiction of the state Forest Departments. But in Western Arunachal Pradesh, a significant number of potential tourism sites are managed by indigenous communities with traditional ownership and customary laws. It is being argued to have inclusive policy bestowing exhaustive participation in tourism related activities with the host community and stakeholders.

Change Management and Learning cycle stages: Responsible Tourism contributes to mobilise local community for conservation and preservation of environment, but that cannot happen over a short period of one five-year plan. Entrepreneurs and host community engaged in responsible tourism will have economic expectations in short-run. This is because of switching cost of maintain low carbon footprint business, minimize use of non-degradable waste, as well as allowing participation of tourist in the rituals and their heritage sites. With the initial resistance to change management, and in the growth stage of the project learning stage, some of the responsible tourism best practices may be transformed into norm and regulatory mechanism.

Capacity development guidelines and marketing roadmap: Based on existing leisure delivery capacity, it is argued to have gap analysis of the destination. The roadmap for high value low impact tourism is proposed on internal selling with the cognizance of Ministry of Defence and Ministry of Development of North Eastern Region. The consumption pattern of arrival of tourists to be stretched into entire business season cycle and reduce underutilization of assets during off-season. Marketing and branding of host communities with distributers of Common Wealth Countries and A-tiers Cities of India and adopt low cost promotion channels is also required to achieve sustainable results. Packaging the leisure product from weekend plan to family plan and avoiding repetitive entry formalities of Protected Area Permit/Inner Line Permit (Barua & Choudhary, 1998), transportation, wayside amenities, accommodation with host communities, recreation activities with folk/cultural/nature content. At operational level, the room-capacity with the centralised reservation system of wholesale tour operators through mobile app based business needs to be augmented. The segmentation strategy should capture niche of culture, wildlife and nature based attractions. People's skill to be included in the interpretation capacity with identifying existing village level escorts to upgrade themselves to Regional Expert Guide or even to Linguistic Guides. Public opinion and leveraging international links with organisations likes of IATA, WWF and National Geographical Society.

Communication Strategy: Unique selling proposition (USP) for next 5-year's timeline is to be built on the perspectives of the community's way of life. The message will convince the premium responsible tourist that "*this is what to experience in Thembang and Zemithang*". Reflection of royal treatment should not need to be communicated for the objectives of advocacy and volunteering. Suggestions about communication strategy should tell about *"Do's and Don'ts"*, avoid exaggeration of facts beyond proportion, and discourage menace of social imbalances like trafficking, substance abuse and mass market. Practices of USP design should include assessing crafting festivals and fairs as cultural and anthropological content, Traditional Knowledge Digital Library, offload pressure on biodiversity (Das, Dutta, Sundriyal & Dutta, 2013) and heritage, adventure content and self-drive segments, reliability of souvenir, ethnicity in Food and Beverages, hygiene conditions of wayside amenities, village and accommodation and the host community's attitude towards tourists.

Conclusion

The study highlights the need to have a strategic approach to boost the responsible tourism practice of Western Arunachal Pradesh. Like other Himalayan destinations (ECOSS, 2006-2007), Western Arunachal Pradesh landscape is no exception of interdependency of host community in economic and social activity (Murphy, 1985). Aesthetic appeal, ecological and cultural parameters, life support system and fragile biological diversity (Dhyani, Gupta & Gupta, 2006) cannot be compromised otherwise the fundamental strength of this region will be lost. Community conserved areas (CCA) or indigenous and community conserved areas (Kothari, 2006) are the forest governed by ethnic communities of the region and therefore, a single pro-poor tourism strategy (Nadkarni, 2008) of endogenous tourism policy will not serve the purpose as it is seen that 'one size fits all' has numerous limitations in destination with diverse cultural background and heterogeneous environment. This thought leadership will provide the best practice framework to other projects in emerging tourism destinations and research inputs for sustainable livelihood practices of Himalayan region of North Eastern India emanating from leisure and high value tourism products of Western Arunachal Pradesh. Tourism revenue and income distribution (Arbache, Blake, Sinclair & Teles, 2008) may eventually increase the disposable income for the host community but a check and balance needs to be administered by village governance institutions like *Khel*[2], Village Council or *Gaonburah* host community level about the undesirable civic and social nuances. This chapter will provide references to future studies on responsible leisure models.

The authors understand that taking host community into confidence is the one big step to reduce resistance and conflicting ideas in a region with customary laws. There is a need to understand and research the change management aspects while mobilizing resources for responsible tourism model.

Notes

1. Also called *Demi-Pension* plan. The room tariff includes guest stay, continental breakfast and either a lunch of dinner in the price of the room.
2. *Khel* is an institution in village governance among indigenous communities of North Eastern India. This institution brings together several clans within

the village community. Membership of a *khel* is either decided by birth or heredity. There are very few instances of village decision taken without the consensus of the *khel* of the village.

References

Arbache, J.S.; Blake, A.; Sinclair, M.T. and Teles, V. (2008). "Tourism and poverty relief", *Annals of Tourism Research,* 35(1): 107-126.

Ashley, C. and Garland, E. (1994). *Promoting Community-Based Tourism Development: Why, What and How?* Directorate of Environmental Affairs, Ministry of Environment and Tourism, Namibia.

Barua, N. and Choudhary, A.J. (1998). *Tourism in Assam: Paradigm of a Thriving Industry, Tourism Towards 21st Century,* New Delhi: Deep & Deep Publications Pvt. Ltd.

Berranger, A. and Raufflet, E. (2008). "Innovation in business-community partnerships: Evaluating the impact of local enterprise and global investment models on poverty, bio-diversity and development", *Corporate Governance.* Emerald Group Publishing Limited, ISSN: 1472-0701, Vol. 8, No. 4.

Brohman, J. (1996). "New directions in tourism for the third world", *Annals of Tourism Research,* 23(1):48-70.

Cooper, G. (2004). "Community Based Tourism-Experiences in the Caribbean: Lessons and key considerations, 6th Annual Caribbean Conference on Sustainable Tourism Development: Keeping the right Balance—Land and Sea Encounters. Caribbean Natural Resources Institute at the Caribbean Tourism Organisation, Havana, Cuba.

Cohen, E. (2002). "A Phenomenology of Tourist Experiences", In: Y. Apostolopoulos, S. Leivadi and A. Yiannakis (eds.) *The Sociology of Tourism: Theoretical and Empirical Investigations.* London: Routledge.

Das, A.K.; Dutta, P.K.; Dutta, B.K. and Sundriyal, R.C. (2013). "Diversity, representativeness and biotic pressure on plant species along alpine timberline of western Arunachal Pradesh in the Eastern Himalaya, India", *Current Science.* 105(5): 701-708.

Deka, P.K. and Baishya, P. (2009). "Economy of Nagaland: Its strengths and potential", *Journal of Economics and Commerce,* Nagaland, India, 1(1): 54-60.

Dhan, B.; Gurung and Seeland, K. (2008). "Ecotourism in Bhutan-Extending its benefits to rural communities", *Annals of Tourism Research,* 35(2):489-508.

Dhyani, S.; Gupta, P. and Gupta, S.K. (2006). "Community based tourism management in protected areas of Garhwal: Key issues and challenges". *Tourism Department Journal,* 4 (1): 84-94.

Dorjee, D., Dutta, P.K. and Wange, P. (2012). "Community based tourism for environmental conservation: Experiences from Western Arunachal Landscape,

India", *Land Management in Marginal Mountain Regions: Adaptation and Vulnerability to Global Change*. United Nations University. Bishen Singh Mahendra Pal Singh, Dehradun, India. pp. 285-292.

Dyson, L.E.; Hendriks, M. and Grant, S. (2007). *Chapter 15: E-Community Based Tourism for Asia's Indigenous People-Information Technology and Indigenous People: Issues and Perspectives*, New Delhi: IGI Publishing, India.

Dutta, M. (2014). *Community Based Tourism: A study of select destinations*, Ph.D. thesis, Gauhati University, India.

Dutta, M. (2014). "Craft as a pull factor for tourism: A case of few select villages in North East India", *Tourism and Handicrafts: Challenges and opportunities for local economic development:* 44-47.

Dutta, M. and Barua, N. (2016). "Impact of healthcare utilities and law and order conditions on tourism: A study on community-based tourism in North East India". *International Journal of Tourism and Travel*. IX(Nos. 1 and 2): 8-20. ISSN: 0974-2603.

Ecotourism and Conservation Society of Sikkim. (2007). Available at http://www.sikkiminfo.net/ecoss/Dzongu.htm (Accessed on 23 February, 2010).

Ecotourism and Conservation Society of Sikkim. (2008). Available at http://www.sikkiminfo.net/ecoss/kbr.htm, (Accessed on 23 February, 2010).

EQUATIONS, (2008). *Can Tourism Transform? Community-based Tourism Initiatives in India*, Bengaluru, India. Available at www.equitabletourism.org (Accessed on 20 February, 2011).

Foo, J.; McGuiggan, R. and Yiannakis, A. (2004). "Roles tourist play: An Australian perspective", *Annals of Tourism Research*, 31(2): 408-427.

Gibson, H. and Yiannakis, A. (2002). "Tourist roles—needs and the lifecourse", *Annals of Tourism Research*, 29(2): 358-383.

Gyamtsho, P. (1996). "Assessment of the condition and potential for improvement of high altitude rangelands of Bhutan", In: *PhD Dissertation in Natural Science*, ETHZ, Switzerland.

Kothari, A. (2006). "Community conserved areas. Protected areas programme", *Parks Magazine*, 16(1) Cambridge, IUCN.

Murphy, P. (1985). *Tourism: A Community Approach*. Publisher Methuen.

Nadkarni, S. (2008). "Knowledge creation, retention, exchange, devolution, interpretation and treatment (K-CREDIT) as an economic growth driver in pro-poor tourism", *Current Issues in Tourism*, 11(5): 456-472.

North Eastern Development and Financial Institution (2000). Annual Report 1999-2000. NEDFI, Guwahati, India.

Porter, M. (1985). *Value chain analysis, Competitive Advantage*.

Raufflet, E. and Berranger, A. (2008). *Innovation in business-community partnerships: Evaluating the impact of local enterprise and global investment models on poverty, bio-diversity and development Corporate Governance*, Emerald Group Publishing Limited, ISSN: 1472-0701, Vol. 8, No. 4.

Sarma, M.K. (2004). *A Study on the Demand Pattern of Tourism Oriented Cottage Industry Products in North East India*, Tezpur University, India.

Sproule, K.W. (1996). "Community-based ecotourism development: Identifying partners in the process the ecotourism equation: Measuring the impacts, in Bulletin Series", *Yale School of Forestry and Environmental Studies, No. 99,* Yale University.

The Mountain Institute (2000). *Community-Based Tourism for Conservation and Development: What is Community based Tourism?* Available at http://www.cbt-i.org/travel.php (Accessed: 29 September, 2012).

World-wide Fund for Nature (2001). Available at www.zeitzfoundation.org/userfiles/WWFGuidelines For Community Based Ecotourism Development.pdf (Accessed: 12 December, 2009).

12
Growth of Urbanization and Water Supply Problems in Sikkim

Lakpa Doma Sherpa

Introduction

Urbanization is a process that is associated with growth of urban centres in number as well as in the population occupying these centres. The period of rapid urbanization of the Twenty first century is linked with modernization, industrialization, which reflects the economic development and social transformation of any region. The urbanization pattern is not same everywhere because the various socio-economic and political factors that determine the growth of urban centres vary from country to country and region to region. The urbanization phenomenon is everywhere, but looking at the number of urban centres by size, which vary from 50,000 in Japan, 5000 in India, 2500 in United States and 1000 in Canada (Lollen, 2015). It has been found that the concept of urban centre is also not uniform and same everywhere, but is defined and accepted by respective countries. Apart from the growth of urbanization in the country, it has issue on the sustainability on the existing natural resources such as water, land and air quality. Today, urbanization in India is characterized by unplanned and uncontrolled growth (Banerjee, 2009), leading to further implications on the infrastructure for basic public services such as water supply, urban transport, educational, health institutions and improving the quality of life. The pace and pattern of development and their land use planning for housing and industrial areas have a considerable impact on the environment as well as on the livelihood of the people. Environmental degradation has been very rapid and as a results water pollution, water shortage in water scarce regions (*ibid.*, 2009). When the urban centres started increasing in a very fast manner during the industrial revolution period in the developed world, the provision of clean water became increasingly an important issue (Vo, 2008; Biswas, 2006). The death among six children every minute is caused by consumption of unsafe water and inadequate sanitation in developing countries. On an average 250 million cases of gastroenteritis every year worldwide is because of bathing in contaminated water (Sridhar and Reddy, 2010: 1).

According to the Millennium Development Goals (MDGs) report 2015...

> "Globally, 147 countries have met the drinking water target. Over half of the global population is now enjoying the higher level of services. Despite the success to reduce the number of people unable to reach or affordable safe drinking water, water scarcity affects 40 per cent of people in the world and is projected to increase further."

Theoretical Framework

The basic concept of urban theory is related with agglomeration economies (Henderson, 2002). The growth pattern of urbanization in developing countries is mainly attributed with high concentration of urban population (Mitra and Kumar, 2015; Henderson, 2002). The economic activities in urban centre generate economies of scale in production (Mitra and Kumar, 2015; Mohan and Dasgupta, 2005). The growth of centre in urban areas has either the spillover or feedback effect on its periphery. The urban agglomeration is well explained by rural-urban migration on Lewis and Harris-Todaro model of economic growth. Rural-urban migration is a function of income adjusted for the probability of finding a job in urban areas (Tadaro, 1980).

The growth of centre or primate city faces many challenges and issues related with urbanization. One of the key challenges is the sustainability of urban centre. While measuring sustainability[1] (Martinet, 2012) look the issue of sustainability from the conflict between environmental conservation and economic development along with distribution of resources among present and future generation. One of the important key challenges of urban growth is sustainability of urban centres in developing countries. Urban population in developing countries is much higher than that of developed countries (Mohan and Dasgupta, 2005; Henderson, 2002). The path and pattern of urbanization in developing countries started with much lower income level than comparatively high income in developed countries (Mohan and Dasgupta, 2005). The historical patterns of urbanization in developed countries of European and North America in 19th century tend to urbanized very slowly until they attain urbanization level of around 25-30 per cent. Their pace of economic growth and over all development is higher with rapid structural shift from agricultural to industry and services sectors. Therefore, overall urbanization level is manageable (*ibid.*, 2005). But the growth pattern of urbanization in developing countries is emerging from the problem of non-sustainability, as a key challenge to sustainable development (Dongfeng *et al.*, 2013). Scholars, Chen *et al.*, (2014) concluded that accelerated urbanization does not generate economic growth if urbanization policy is basically initiated by the government only.

Dongfeng, *et. al.*, (2013) established the complicated relationship between urbanization and sustainability through an analysis based on urbanization Kuznets-curve. Their study found that urbanization and sustainability can go together if government adopts a flexible urbanization and extensive regional policy which gives more attention to basic public amenities including education, health security and improving the quality of life with a sustainable urban planning system in different regions of the country. Sridhar and Reddy (2010) studied the growth of urbanization and examined urban services such as water supply, sewerage, sanitation, municipal road, solid waste management and street lighting in the four cities of India. They examined the relationship between expenditure and service delivery to follow acceptable standard to match with the manageable urban centre. Kundu and Thakur (2006) in their study found that lack of water availability in urban areas is due to management failure rather than problem of accessibility.

Growth Pattern of Urbanization in East Sikkim

East Sikkim district is one the most urbanized district of Sikkim. Sikkim is the least populated state of the country with population of 6.07 lakh (Census, 2011). East Sikkim is the most populous district of Sikkim. The district-wise population distribution is as follows; 283,583 in East Sikkim district, 146,850 in South district, 136,435 in West district and 43,709 in North district. Of the total population of the State, 25.15 per cent live in the urban areas. The degree of urbanization particularly, in East Sikkim district in terms of percentage of urban population has increased from 18 per cent in 1991to 43 per cent in 2011. The district covers total area 964 sq.km. The major urban centres in the East Sikkim are: the Gangtok (capital city of Sikkim), Singtam and Rangpo. Urbanization defined by the Population Census of India has got two dimensions: (1) all statutory places with a Municipal Corporation, Cantonment Board or notified town area committee etc., (2) a place satisfying the following three criteria:

(a) a minimum population of 5000 people,
(b) at least 75 per cent of male working population engaged in non-agricultural activities, and
(c) density of population of at least 400 persons per sq. km.

Table 12.1: Degree of Urbanization

Year	*1981*	*1991*	*2001*	*2011*
India (%)	23.34	25.72	27.78	31.16
Sikkim (East District %)	31	18	22	43

Source: Registrar General of India, Census of India (1981, 1991, 2001 & 2011).

Table 12.2: Urban population and growth rate (in brackets) towns of East Sikkim (1981-2011)

Year	*Gangtok*	*Singtam*	*Rangpo*
1981	36747 (176.1)	4043 (109.9)	2452 (37.36)
1991	25024 (–31.9)	3868 (–4.32)	2980 (21.53)
2001	29354 (17.3)	5432 (40.43)	3709 (24.46)
2011	100286 (241.6)	5868 (8)	10450 (181.7)

Source: Registrar General of India, Census of India (1981, 1991, 2001 & 2011).

The decadal growth rate of Gangtok urban population has drastically increased from 17.3 per cent in 2001 to 241.6 per cent in 2011 which is much higher than growth of total urban population of Sikkim. The other urban centres of East Sikkim district such as Rangpo also recorded increase in growth rate from 24.46 to 181.7 per cent. But Singtam recorded decline in growth rate in the same periods. Urban East Sikkim district has the highest density of population which is 4866 persons per sq.km as compared to other districts of the state (Census of India, 2011). The study done by Paul *et al.* (2016) on the demographic and land used pattern of Gangtok town over the period of 1971-2011found that dynamic shift of land use and land cover through remote sensing and Geographic Information System (GSI) technique. Since, any changes in land cover reflect the environmental change. Therefore, land changed pattern in Gangtok urban area reached new development in terms of residential, industrial, commercial etc. The speed of urbanization in Gangtok is ultra high and has become core in urban agglomeration.

Economic development activities is mostly focused in urban areas, and the state has been witnessing a very high rate of migration from rural to urban towns in search for better livelihoods and various opportunities. East Sikkim district is heavily agglomerated with population growth and consequently leading to increasing demand for urban infrastructure and amenities. According to census figures from 1981 to 1991 the percentage of urban population in East district declined given in Table 12.1. This decline in urban population during the decade is due to the re-demarcation of some of the revenue blocks surrounding Gangtok as rural areas. In urban areas of East Sikkim, the growth of buildings is expanding with meager attention to building laws and public amenities. There is no proper policy for the acquisition and disposal of plots in urban areas. Therefore, urban development has been largely unplanned. The existing development of infrastructure and amenities is in response to problem rather than as a result of planning and policy (Lahiri *et al.*, 2001).

Research Objectives

The objectives of the study are:

1. To identify the speed of urbanization in East Sikkim district over the period of 1981 to 2015.
2. To examine the state of finance and expenditure incurred on water supply and sanitation infrastructure in order to sustain the growth of urban centre.

Methodology

This study is based on the secondary data analysis, available from the various government sources, namely population Census, Handbook of statistics of state finance, Reserve Bank of India and published annual data from state government of Sikkim. The Population Census data are available in every 10-year intervals. As we required information on population after 2011 till 2015 extrapolation exercises have been done. We have used exponential interpolation using the growth rate to arrive at the figures for five years between the 2011 and 2015. The urbanization level is defined by various studies (Bhagat and Mohanty, 2009; Bairoch and Goertz, 1986) used the percentage of urban population. The speed of urbanization is calculated by using the same formula used by (Chen *et al.*, 2014) in their study of urbanization pattern.

$$U_{urban} = \frac{(UL2015-UL1981)}{N}$$

Where, U_{urban} represents the annual average speed of urbanization, UL_{2015} and UL_{1981} are urbanization level of 2015 and 1981 respectively and N represents the number of years, urbanization level takes place during the period 1981 to 2015. To understand the state finance on urban infrastructures, we required data from state regarding their expenditure on public services such as water supply and sanitation. Along with this, further information on public service delivery is needed. The concept of public service delivery was well defined, in terms of per capita water available for consumption and the hours for which water is supplied per day (Tiwar and Gulati, 2011). But due to unavailable data on the consumption of water supply in litre term in state of Sikkim, we are taking the percentage of households having safe drinking water and tap water supply connection within premises. The service delivery of water supply in Indian cities over the years is continuously inadequate, poor quality of existing water supply. The sector suffers from chronic operational inefficiency in terms of operations and maintenance expenditure. The problem further aggravated due to uneconomic tariff structure, low collection efficiency and high level of leakage of water supply pipe lying on surface of earth (*ibid.*, 2011). From the analysis will be conforming whether expenditure is a possible cause of public services delivery.

Empirical Results

The detailed classification of speed of urbanization is given in Table 12.3, (Chen, *et al.*, 2014) they have used categorical variables for speed of urbanization into ultra-high, high, medium, low and counter urbanization. The percentage of urban population in East Sikkim district has increased from 31.61 in 1981 to 53.99 in 2015. Urbanization in East Sikkim district have found to be at high speed range of 0.65 during the period from 1981 to 2015.

In order to sustain growth of high speed of urbanization in East Sikkim, there is a need for increasing urban infrastructural demand. At the same time, increasing urban infrastructural demand further generate

Table 12.3: Classification of Speed of Urbanization

Classification	*Range (%)*
Ultra-high speed	0.9–1.5
High speed	0.6–0.9
Medium speed	0.3–0.6
Low speed	0–0.3
Counter-urbanization	< = 0

Source: Chen *et al.*, 2014.

the overburden to existing local government to meet the necessary requirements of the general public services (Sridhar and Reddy, 2010). In Sikkim, the provision of water supply distribution and sanitation in urban areas is the sole responsibility of Water Security and Public Health Engineering Department, government of Sikkim. The expenditure on water supply and sanitation are summarized in Table 12.4 from the period of 1981 to 2015. Percentage of expenditure on water supply and sanitation to total expenditure in Sikkim is less than 1 per cent during the period 2004 to 2015 while the state population is increasing every year.

Therefore, the demand for water will increase due to growth of population. But the expenditure made by State Government on water supply and sanitation infrastructure remains below one per cent is highly inadequate. Rural-Urban migration, the development of towns and low investment in water infrastructure has created a series of crisis in the availability of drinking water in towns and cities (Kundu and Thakur, 2006). The revenue collection from water is taps-based on tariff approach in Sikkim. The domestic households are paying minimum rupees 80 and maximum rupees 250 per month for water tariff as compared to commercial water connections who are paying double the amount per month. The revenue receipts from water supply and sanitation is very low which further worsens the water supply and sanitation services. The physical service delivery is determined on the demand for and supply of water and households population covered with a water supply network. The primary sources of water supply for urban areas of Sikkim are taps, spring and bore wells. Table 12.5 represents figures of access of safe drinking water in urban areas of Sikkim. According to the Census data urban Sikkim falls under high coverage of water supply connection within premises during the period of 1991-2011. Merely having high coverage of water supply connection at household levels does not indicate sufficient water supply to the public. There is no volumetric water consumption system in Sikkim till date. The time period the water received at

Table 12.4: Revenue expenditure on water supply and sanitation of Sikkim, 1981-2015

Year	Water supply and sanitation expenditure (in Lakhs)	Total expenditure (in Lakhs)	% Water supply and sanitation expenditure to Total expenditure	Per capita user charge/ Revenue (Rs.)
1981-82	0	3173	0.00	0.00
1982-83	0	3546	0.00	0.00
1983-84	0	4928	0.00	0.00
1984-85	0	5857	0.00	0.00
1985-86	116	7758	1.50	0.00
1986-87	152	8126	1.87	42.39
1987-88	773	9846	7.85	210.23
1988-89	229	11316	2.02	60.74
1989-90	227	11527	1.97	58.72
1990-91	291	12815	2.27	73.41
1991-92	374	15509	2.41	92.01
1992-93	412	17973	2.29	98.51
1993-94	409	18891	2.17	95.04
1994-95	531	52642	1.01	119.91
1995-96	651	88119	0.74	142.87
1996-97	701	111886	0.63	149.51
1997-98	715	125810	0.57	148.20
1998-99	964	149560	0.64	194.19
1999-00	1089	150997	0.72	213.19
2000-01	1020	76331	1.34	194.06
2001-02	1046	166425	0.63	193.40
2002-03	1161	188262	0.62	212.07
2003-04	1288	118093	1.09	232.44
2004-05	1224	172349	0.71	218.23
2005-06	1400	176761	0.79	246.60
2006-07	1498	188756	0.79	260.68
2007-08	1775	234856	0.76	305.16
2008-09 (RE)	2360	238075	0.99	400.84
2009-10 (BE)	2073	256715	0.81	347.85
2010-11 (Accounts)	2484	290753	0.85	411.79
2011-12 (RE)	2219	355904	0.62	363.43
2012-13 (BE)	1651	357002	0.46	267.14
2013-14 (Accounts)	2219	345796	0.64	354.72
2014-15 (Accounts)	2837	373095	0.76	448.04
2015-16 (RE)	4149	431275	0.96	647.35

Source: Planning Commission, Handbook of Statistics of Indian States, Reserve Bank of India and author's computation. RE = Revised Estimate, BE = Budget Estimate.

Table 12.5: Access of Safe Drinking Water in Urban Sikkim, 1981-2011

Year	*Percentage of Households having tap water*	*Percentage of Households having water within Premises*
1981	71.49	39.56
1991	92.90	74.61
2001	96.79	85.49
2011	92.10	79.80

Source: Registrar General of India, Census of India (1981, 1991, 2001 & 2011).

households and pressure of water supply determined sufficient water received by the public. In 2011, the percentage of households having tap water within premises has declined.

This figure clearly gives some information on shortage of water availability prevailing in urban Sikkim and not matching with the growth of urbanization. The expenditure on water supply and sanitation is almost constant over one decade and the water supply volume showed a consistent pattern of under pricing to the public. Inadequate infrastructure further aggravates the public service delivery in urban East Sikkim. Around 52.82 per cent of the urban populations have access to sanitation facilities and some parts of the urban areas are still covered only by the old system of septic tanks, with waste being thrown into streams or rivers (Lahiri *et al.*, 2001). The present figure is 98.9 per cent of urban household areas are covered with septic tank or flush connection (GOI, 2016).

Conclusion

The speed of urbanization in East Sikkim is very high. The comprehensive measures are prerequisite to sustain the urban centre in long run. To manage this level of speed, public investments on infrastructure are essential. But, the public expenditure on water supply and sanitation as percentage of total expenditure has declined over the decades. This is an unhealthy trend and needs to be reversed to ensure sustainability of water supply and sanitation. Rapid urbanization creates water shortage and water related environmental problems in most cities and towns. During 2001 to 2011, the percentage of households having tap water within premises has declined. Therefore, urban growth needs to be regulated and infrastructure has to be created. The urban land needs well management and planning to sustain the growth of urban towns in the state. Sustainable urban development must look into the issues of access to resources and public investment. The rapidly expanding urban centres require more water for human use and have higher per capita water demand as compared to rural areas. With the growth of urbanization, there is a need for economic optimization of water use. Urban water management policies are important sections which can be linked with laws, institutions and policies management by government or private agency, which itself cover water resources management in planning and environmental issues.

Note

1. It refers to the development that meet the needs of present without compromising the need of future generation to meet their own needs (Brundtland, 1987).

References

Banerjee (2009). "Urban challenges in 21st century India urbanization and its impact on environment and infrastructure", In: Simhadri (Ed.) *Urban Environment and Geoinformatics,* Jaipur: Rawat Publications, pp. 1-37.

Brundtland, G.H. (1987). *Our Common future: World Commission on Environment and Development*, Oxford: Oxford University Press.

Bairoach, P. and Goertz, G. (1986). "Factors of urbanization in the nineteenth century developed countries: A descriptive and econometric analysis", *Urban Studies,* 23: 285-305.

Bhagat, R.B. and Mohanty, S. (2009). "Emerging pattern of urbanization and the contribution of migration in urban growth in India", *Asian Population Studies,* 5(1): 5-20.

Biswas, A. (2006). "Water management for major urban centres", *Water Resources Development. Routledge*, 22: 183-197.

Census 2011. *Post enumeration survey,* New Delhi: Registrar General of India.

Chen, M.; Zhang, H., Liu, W., Zhang, W. (2014). "The Global Pattern of Urbanization and Economic Growth: Evidence from the Last Three Decades", *PLoS ONE* 9(8): e103799. doi:10.1371/journal.pone.0103799.

Dongfeng, Y.; Chengzhi, Y. and Ying, L. (2013). "Urbanization and sustainability in China: An analysis based on the urbanization Kuznets-curve", *Planning Theory,* 12(4): 391-405.

GOI (2016). "Hand Book of Urban Statistics", [accessed:1January 2018: http://www.indiaenvironmentportal.org.in]

Henderson, V. (2002). "Urbanization in developing countries". *The World Bank Research Observer,* 17(1): 89-112.

Kundu, A. and Thakur, S. (2006). "Access to Drinking water in Urban India: An analysis of emerging spatial pattern in the context of New system of

Governance", In: Reddy, V.R. and Dev, S.M (Ed.), *Managing Water Resources Policies, Institutions and Technologies.* Oxford University Press.

Lahiri, A.K.; Chattopadhyay, S. and Bhasin, A. (2001). "Sikkim the People's Vision", New Delhi: Indus Publishing Company.

Lollen, T. (2015). "Urbanization in Arunachal Pradesh", In: Mandal R.K (Ed.), *Development of Tribal People of North East India Issues and Challenges*, Concept Publishing Company Pvt. Ltd., 156-167.

Martinet, V. (2012). *Economic Theory and Sustainable Development: What can We Preserve for Future Generation?*, Routledge, Oxon, United-Kingdom.

Mitra, A. and Kumar, R. (2015). "New Patterns in India Urbanization: Emergence of Census Town", *Environment and Urbanization*, 6(1): 18-27.

Mohan, R. and Dasgupta, S. (2005). "The 21st Century: Asia Becomes Urban", *Economic and Political Weekly*, 40(3): 213-223.

Paul, K.; Sharma, D.; Mukherjee, R.; Sengupta, R. and Tamang, K.L. (2016). "Demographic characteristics and changing landuse pattern in Gangtok, Sikkim (1971-2011)", *International Journal of Geomatics and Geoscience,* 6(4).

Sridhar, K.S. and Reddy, A.V. (2010). *State of Urban Services in India's Cities Spending and Financing*, New Delhi: Oxford University Press.

Tiwari, P. and Gulati, M. (2011). "Efficiency of Urban Water Supply Utilities in India", *International Journal of Water Resources Development,* Taylor and Francis, 27: 361-374.

Todaro, M. (1980). "Internal migration in developing countries: A Survey", *National Bureau of Economic Research,* 361-402, [accessed:12 December 2018: http://www.nber.org/chapters/c9668]

Vo, P.L. (2008). "Urbanisation and water management in Ho Chi Minh City, Vietnam-issues, challenges and perspectives," *GeoJournal* 70, Springer, 75-89.

13
Impact of Colonial Rule and World Wars on the Ecology of Darjeeling Hills

Fr. K.J. Joseph

Introduction

Global environmental concerns have of late led some historians to study the environmental aspects of the past human societies. Environmental change is arguably the most pressing and potentially disastrous problem facing the global community. So far a very few efforts have been made to incorporate information either about how human beings have altered the environment or about how environmental change revised human activity. Changes in civilisation and culture through time resulted in both intentional and unintentional modification of the global environment of which biodiversity constitute the most important component. The awareness of human beings dependence upon nature had long ancestry, but the realisation of the significant role of human being as the maker and un-maker of nature has developed only recently.

One region affected most badly by deforestation with far reaching consequences is the Himalayas. Extending all along the Northern border of India, covering five states from west to east, namely Jammu and Kashmir, Himachal Pradesh, Uttrakhand, Sikkim, Arunachal Pradesh and also the Darjeeling district in the northern part of West Bengal, the mighty mountain range constitutes about 12.84 per cent of the total geographical area of the country. It is the storehouse of glaciers, which provide the perennial river systems, not only for their inhabitants but also for millions of people living downstream for settlements, agriculture and industries. The Himalayan forests are the major suppliers of timber, medicinal plants, oils, spices and condiments, firewood, organic manure, fodder and hydropower. Deforestation and forest degradation in the Himalayas is a major concern worldwide. It was during the British period that the forests in both the Himalayan belt as well as in the adjoining plains were disturbed by human intervention. Since the Himalayan range is one of the most unstable and most fragile mountain areas in the world, deforestation tended to accentuated the disastrous consequences.

Darjeeling, situated in the north-eastern part of India, has always been known for her natural resources. The hills and forests, besides enhancing the beauty of the land, contain valuable flora and fauna, some of which are rare in the world. In course of its historical development, Darjeeling became part of the British India Empire as per the provision of the treaty signed by the British and the Raja of Sikkim. Since the passing of Darjeeling into the sphere of British colonial rule, the area like other parts of British India was subjected to fulfilling the imperial interests and need of the British Empire. Since then the symbiotic relation between man and nature that existed in this part of the world was disrupted. The basic aim of their policy in this country was commercialisation of natural resources so as to earn maximum revenue though it meant wanton destruction of environment and serious ecological imbalance.

Geology of Darjeeling

Nature has a way of writing her own history in her rocks. Indeed, the geological history of any region is a record of all the ancient changes or events, geographical, climatic and pertaining to its life that it has undergone or witnessed. Geographically, the Sikkim-Darjeeling Himalayas is wedged between central Nepal Himalayas to the west and the Bhutan Himalayas to the east. Geological investigation of this region began as far back in 1854 where Hooker in his famous *Himalayan Journal* reported regional gneissic domes, the overlying bedded sedimentary rocks and crinodial limestones at the Tso lhamo Lake during his extensive travels in many parts of Sikkim. Also an excellent account of the geology of the Darjeeling district and its foot hills has been made by Mallet (1875). Geologically the Himalayan Mountain has been classed among the younger mountain ranges of the world. The geological formation of Darjeeling Sikkim Himalayas consists of unaltered sedimentary rocks. Morphologically the area is well defined. The sub-Himalayas are made up of Siwalik deposits of the tertiary age. North of the Siwaliks is coal bearing lower Gondwana formation comparable to Damudas of peninsular

India. A visit of the site of the land-slide in the Darjeeling district will reveal that the soil is composed of soft and loose sandy earth mixed with boulders of various sizes and hardness. The boulders are mostly sandstone, mudstone, and metamorphic rock.

Biodiversity

The most remarkable feature of the forests of Darjeeling is the wonderful variety of species that they contain. There are in fact probably few places in the world in which so many different types of forests exist within so small an area[1]. The configuration of the hills and mountains combined with the differences of altitude, temperature, rainfall and soil type in the region greatly determines the nature of different species found in different parts of the district.

Floristically the eastern Himalayas are one of the richest regions in the world and are literally considered a botanists paradise and have thus attracted a large number of plant hunters and Botanists during the last two centuries. Phyto-geographically it forms a meeting ground of the Indo-Chinese and Indo-Malaysian tropical lowland flora, the Sino-Himalayan east Asiatic flora and the Western Himalayan flora comprising about 9000 plant species with a high percentage of endemic plants. Therefore, the Darjeeling-Sikkim Himalaya, an integral part of the eastern Himalayas region, is a storehouse of biodiversity, boasting of a large number of important, rare and endangered species of flora and fauna. The region exhibits a wide range of altitudinal variations that is instrumental in creating climatic variations ranging from tropical humid to the arctic type which consequently lead to vegetation variations. The region, however, shows predominantly temperate vegetation. Its continuity with other Himalayan ranges and with the plains helped it to host an extremely rich flora. However, like all Himalayan regions, this region remains fragile and its vegetation remains under threat from both natural calamities and severe exploitation.

So far as any inventory of tree species is concerned, we are somewhat better off as we are in a position to prepare a list of tree species on the basis of account left by several historical sources. Since Darjeeling does not have a pre-British history worth name, we do not have any inventory of trees before the British period. The Britishers, after establishing their rule in Darjeeling, took interest in managing the forest resources of Darjeeling; and their inquisitives, combined with their subsequent requirement for forest management led to preparation of inventories listing the various tree species found in the forests of Darjeeling.

The floristically rich Darjeeling Himalayas has attracted plant explorers, botanists and researchers since 18th century. The Indian flora was scientifically and systematically explored since the 1840s. The first two attempts were led by Thomas Thomson who explored the North western Himalayas. It was none other than Sir Joseph Dalton Hooker who introduced the beauty and floristic richness of this region to the outside world for the first time. Sir J.D. Hooker in 1848 took up the third botanical expedition to the eastern Himalayas and in doing so, became the first ever botanical explorer of the eastern Himalayas while writing the Flora of British India as a whole, in all the previous works Darjeeling and Sikkim have been considered together as Darjeeling was then a part of Sikkim.

Since then, explorers from different far and wide have explored the region from time to time and a number of floras included their records and findings contributing outstanding works adding to the knowledge of the vegetation and floristic of the region. The major contributions include J.D. Hooker (1849-51, 1854, 1885, 1872 1897, 1907); T. Anderson (1832-1870); C.B. Clarke (1876, 1885); H.J. Elwes (1877); George Watt (1881); R. Pantling with Sir George King. Various works have put forth the classification of the vegetation of this region and it includes works like Gamble (1875), Cown (1929), Champion (1936). These authors have essentially classified the flora and vegetation according to altitudinal ranges, although they differ considerably in details. Apart from these the statistical account of W.W. Hunter and report on inspection made by forest officers like Dietrich Brandis (1879) and B. Ribbentrop (1889) helps us to a great extent in learning about the forest resources of Darjeeling. Gamble for example in his work trees and climbers of Darjeeling mentioned 90 trees and shrubs directly consumed or used by the *Lepchas* an indigenous tribe of Darjeeling.

Fauna of Darjeeling

The reports of early colonial foresters and settlers and surveyors tell us that a hundred and seventy five years ago, the Darjeeling district was infested with wild animals like elephants, tigers, leopards, and spotted deers. Wild boar, bear and wild goats roamed the dense forests of the Terai, the valleys of the Tista, Rangit and Balasan rivers and even frequented the high forests of the Singalila range. It was estimated that there were between 80 and 90 species of mammals in the district.[2] The best represented was the cat family of which there were 13 known species.

The Darjeeling district was also rich in birds' life. It contained nearly a quarter of the species of birds found in India Burma and Ceylon that means about 550 species.[3] Of the approximately 550 species in the district, more than half are passerine group. Of these groups the largest families are the Timalidae with 61 species of birds including laughing thrushes and babblers.

They report that there were about 51 species of snakes in Darjeeling districts. Of the 51 species of snake found in the district, eleven were poisonous; and six were deadly poisonous.[4] A hundred and twenty five species of fish have been counted in the streams and rivers of the Darjeeling district. The insect fauna is vast, as any collector of beetles and butterflies in Darjeeling will know. Butterflies are found in large numbers mainly in the valleys, along the streams and rivers. The most beautiful specimens belong to the swallow-tail family. Among the moths, the Atlas moth, with its colourful marking attains a span of ten inches or more. There are also two species among the actias that are also very beautiful. The fauna of Darjeeling was also drastically affected by the British intervention in the area. The process of their extinction actually began with the clearing of the forests for developmental activities. They enacted the rules for the protection of wild life since 1912. Rules were framed to preserve animals and birds in the reserve and yet at the same time afforded facilities for shooting at reasonable rates.

How and Why of Ecological Degradation

The colonial period of Darjeeling underwent the industrial colonial mode of resource use which remained in force till independence. In the context of human civilization as a whole, this might be calculated to be only a minor fraction of the time that human being has spent husbanding plants and animals. However, it is very difficult to quantify the environmental impact or harm caused by the colonial policies. Obviously tea and cinchona is different from other means of forest regeneration. The green cover of tea and cinchona plantations is very much different from the diverse species rich natural forests. Therefore, these plantations definitely served as a great destroyer to natural forest cover. Many precious floral species became extinct before they were recorded. This was true for the middle-hill region which was highly disturbed due to tea cultivation. Out of 180 species of Liverworts reported from India by the year 1947, about 140 were from Darjeeling district of which 72 per cent were found to be endemic.

During the colonial period British foresters chiefly tried to replace the natural forests of the districts through the plantation of exotic and commercially important species. Monoculture plantations were thus initiated that soon replaced the natural forests throughout the length and breadth of the district that highly affected the flora and fauna of the district. The fauna of Darjeeling was also drastically affected by the British intervention in the area. The process of their extinction actually began with the clearing of the forests for developmental activities. They enacted the rules for the protection of wild life since 1912 Rules were framed to preserve animals and birds in the reserve and yet at the same time afforded facilities for shooting at reasonable rates.

Earthquake-induced landslides were an additional complicating factor when trying to assess land degradation. A number of earthquakes have occurred over the last 114 years, such as the Bengal earthquakes (14 July, 1885), Assam earthquakes (12 June, 1897; 8 July, 1918), North Bihar earthquakes (15 January, 1934). Earthquakes such as these led to severe flooding and landslide damages in Darjeeling. Although landslides prior to 1899 were not recorded in details it is clear from travellers accounts that landslide scars have always been prominent features. Indeed Joseph Hooker mentioned such scars in his memoirs for 1854. All except the landslips associated with the 1934 Bihar earthquake were caused by rainfall of above average intensities. The landslide of 24 and 25 September, 1899 were caused by 60.96 cm of rain. The town of Darjeeling was badly damaged and nearly 219 persons perished under the falling debris or landslip.[5] On the subject of soil erosion the Divisional Forest Officer of Darjeeling made the following observation:

> Apart from supplying local needs for forest produce, the forests in the Darjeeling hills have a very great indirect effect on the people of lower Bengal. No year passes without land slip occurring to a greater or smaller extent in these hills,......... Though the wood-cutter on the hills hardly realises the effect of felling trees and laying bare the hill slopes, the people hundreds of miles below suffer hardship. It is a great pity that the indirect effect of the existence of forests was not appreciated in olden days and instead of creating reserves on the hills tops and laying bare the whole hill down below, a more even distribution of the forest was not aimed at to prevent soil erosion and its deleterious effect on the rivers of Bengal. The real measure of the importance of the hill forests should always be in terms of their effect on

water supply to the springs and on their prevention of soils erosion.[6]

From the above observation of the Divisional Forest Officer it was obvious that the Britsh forest officers were aware of the evil effect of the deforestation of the hill area. Wherever the forest had been cleared away, the protective covering of the deep soil which was the legacy of the primeval forest had now all been washed away. Sheet erosion, gullies and landslide had started across the Darjeeling Himalayas. Thus the wanton destruction of Darjeeling forest in the early years by the tea planters, contractors, and lately by the industrial class posed a great threat to the station of Darjeeling. The question of the denudation of the hills of Darjeeling district attracted the attention of government as early as 1911.[7] This point had been expressed to the Deputy Commissioner of Jalpaiguri by a tea planter with long experience in the district. According to him the flood of Rehti River became worse than what it was 20 years ago, and the bed of the river near the hills had widened considerably. This particular river often changed its course and the change of the course of the river had much more serious consequence than in the past. As a result of the agitation started by the Indian Tea Association in the year 1905 and of the enquiries made by an officer of the Forest Department deputed in the year 1908, a committee was appointed in the year 1910 to investigate into the mischief caused by deforestation in the District of Darjeeling and to suggest remedial measures.[8]

In a letter No. 1281 dated the 19th March, 1912 the Commissioner of Bhagalpur Division was asked to furnish his opinion on the recommendation made by the Darjeeling Safety Committee.[9] The Commissioner of the Bhagalpur Division was requested to consider, when submitting the report of the Committee to the Government, how far the remedies proposed were politically and economically possible and by what means the necessary regulation could be imposed upon the holders of different classes of property in the District of Darjeeling. Inquiries made by various officers showed that there were certain definite evils to be dealt with, and that in particular the rough cultivation of clearing without precaution and deforestation of slopes too steep for any kind of cultivation and their exposure to unrestricted grazing were causing serious landslips likely to be detrimental to the drainage of the district and to its general welfare. There were also evidence that not only were the hill-sides eroded and the river banks destroyed in this manner, but also that violent floods were causing considerable havoc in the plains.[10] The necessity of dealing with the question throroughly and effectvely was, therefore, apparent. The report of the Committee was submitted by the Commissioner in June 1911.[11]

The Committee recommended the following measures:

1. To reafforest and close to grazing those portions of the hill-side which have slipped or are likely to slip.
2. To prohibit rice cultivation on any but the easiest slopes.
3. To prohibit cardomom growing as much as possible practically everywhere.
4. To restrict grazing on steep and unprotected slopes.
5. To reserve a protective belt of land along the banks of all main streams to a width varying with the size of the stream.

The Deputy Commissioner and the Commissioner were of the opinion that the general adoption of the remedial measures 1 to 4 suggested by the Committee would entail ruin on many raiyats and hardship to nearly all. Any practical scheme for applying remedies for deforestation etc. must be necessarily be framed with reference to the conditions and of the ownership and tenure of land prevailing in the area concerned. In this view the Deputy Commissiner classified the area of district into two groups. Group one consisted of land not under the direct management of Government. They constituted about 303 square miles. Group two constituted of land under direct management of Government like reserved forest, Cinchona reserve Bazar and waste land and Khas mahal land. They were about 861 sq miles. The Deputy Commissioner suggested that legislation should be undertaken to take the necessary power. In paragraph 41 of his report the Deputy Commissioner gave the ouline of the proposed legislation. In the order in council, dated 8th August, 1911, it was directed that the outline Bill be circulated for public opinion in Darjeeling District.

Similarly, in a P.W.D. Resolution No. 483J, dated 25th September, 1911, a committee was duly appointed to consider the safety of Darjeeling station and the steps to be taken for the afforestation of the lower slopes and the more efficient control of the drainage from the Municipal area and of the cultivation and quarrying within this area and on the lower slopes.[12] On the recomendations of these committees a Draft Bill was pioleted in the Bengal Legislative Assembly. In accordance with the orders contained in paragraph 3 of governent letter No. 2622 dated 24th August, 1911, a copy of the proposed Act, together with a request for the expression of opinion on its provisions was sent to prominent citizens of Darjeeling.[13]

Ultimately the Darjeeling Hill-Sides and Rivers Conservation Bill got the sanction of the Government of India for its introduction in 1917 to provide for the Conservation and protection of Hill sides and rivers in the District and to that end to provide facilities, where necessary, for the afforestation of land situated within the District of Darjeeling. The Bill had 21 provisions. In spite of this alarming warning the Forest Department continued the previous mode of operations, which intensified during the First World War and the period after.

First World War and Darjeeling Forests

The Forest Department was called upon to take its part in the First World War which began in August 1914.[14] The Indian Forest Department was asked to supply an enormous amount of timber and other forest produce demanded by the military authorities. They were required for the war fronts in Mesopotamia, Egypt, Salonika, Aden, East Africa, Persian Gulf ports etc.[15] The Indian Munition Board (I.M.B.) was formed in May 1917, and Sir George Hart, Inspector-General of Forest, was appointed a member to control the forest work.[16] A Timber Branch of the Munition Board was created for the supply of timber to the war front. In May 1917 the work of supplying timber to the war front was taken over by the I.M.B. and the Forest Research Officer was appointed Deputy Controller of Timber Supplies under the Board.[17] In a little over a year (April 1917 to October 1918) 228,076 tonnes of timber excluding railway sleepers were supplied by the timber branch of the Monition Board, and 50,000 tonnes of fodder grass exported to help military operations in Egypt and Iraq.[18] The whole of timber despatched was supplied on indent received from the Controller of Timber supplies Simla, and all the sleepers were purchased and despatched according to requisitions from the Railway member of the I.M.B.

Large indents were divided up into portions corresponding to the quantities each Divisional Forest Officer could supply and smaller indents were placed in one Division. The exact amount of war supplies from the Darjeeling District Forest Divisions could not be ascertained from the available sources. The Timber and the Fuel wood extracted from the Darjeeling forest during the First World War was an indication to the extent of the contribution of Darjeeling forests to the war front. Table 5.6 illustrates the amount of timber and fuel wood extracted during the First World War period (1914-15 to 1918-19). Inevitably, First World War had its effect on the forests of India in general and Darjeeling Forests in particular in various ways. The shortage of imported materials caused by the German Submarine campaign made it necessary to develop indigenous materials, and towards this end the F.R.I. undertook different tests regarding the suitability of local materials, many of which were recognized later as good substitute for the imported materials.[19] The end of the First World War saw great strides in the reorganisation of forest research for the development of forestry, and the role of the forests in the national economy came to be recognised. The Forest Department realised the need for expansion and enrichment of forest resources to provide incentive to the newly emerging industries. As result, period after First World War marked the beginning of mechanical way of extraction of forest produce and its effective transportation.[20]

Second World War and Darjeeling Forests

The Second World War came physically much nearer to India in general and to Bengal and Darjeeling in particular. The demands made on the forests of Darjeeling were of much greater magnitude than the demands during the First World War.[21] When Britain engaged in War with Hitler's Germany, India was unprepared both materially and emotionally to respond with any weighty contribution. There was little to indicate that India herself would be involved. Egypt and the Middle East, did not immediately, require their garrison to be strengthened, for which troops and supplies were moved from India.[22] Hutting timber, box shooks and package material, bamboos and poles were early in demand. As early as 1940 a Timber directorate was set up at Delhi to channel the bulk supplies of forest products to the armed forces and to coordinate the work of the Forest Department in provinces and native states. This timber Supply organisation rapidly expanded as the war progressed. Mr. Stewart, who was the officiating Utilization Officer at the F.R.I., was transferred in September 1939 to Delhi in the post of joint Timber Adviser to the Railway and Defence Departments. Soon an immediate demand arose for suitable India woods for such article as shuttles and bobbins for textile mills, packing cases, plywood etc. as well as for electric transmission poles. India was recognised as the chief source of supply to the Middle East Theatre of War (*see* Table 13.1).

World Wars intervened and spurts of forest activity were noticed mainly in the overcutting of forests in the name of war supply. Inevitably, First World War (1914-18) had its effect on the forests of Darjeeling. The shortage of imported materials caused by German Submarine

Table 13.1: The Amount of Timber and Fuel Wood Extracted from Darjeeling District Forests During the First World War (1914-1919)

Division	*Year*	*Timber in C.ft*	*Fire wood in C.ft*	*T&F Wood in C.ft*	*Per cent Annual timber*	*Per cent Annual Fuel*	*Per cent of total production*
Darjeeling	1914-15	269812	1106006	1375818	19.61	80.39	6.96
	1915-16	353764	716707	1070471	33.05	66.95	5.42
	1916-17	231725	1038070	1269795	18.25	81.75	6.43
	1917-18	181000	980000	1161000	15.59	84.41	5.88
	1918-19	171369	959392	1130761	15.16	84.84	5.72
Total	**1914-19**	**1207670**	**4800175**	**6007845**	**20.10**	**79.90**	**30.41**
Teesta	1914-15	349599	1416190	1765789	19.80	80.20	8.94
	1915-16	286167	910464	1196631	23.91	76.09	6.06
	1916-17	362050	1485865	1847915	19.59	80.41	9.35
	1917-18	312385	1202089	1514474	20.63	79.37	7.67
	1918-19	463852	1045464	1509316	30.73	69.27	7.64
Total	**1914-19**	**1774053**	**6060072**	**7834125**	**22.65**	**77.35**	**39.66**
Kurseong	1914-15	191784	952273	1144057	16.76	83.24	**5.79**
	1915-16	202892	1041119	1244011	16.31	83.69	6.30
	1916-17	233306	884382	1117688	20.87	79.13	5.66
	1917-18	275386	1040950	1316336	20.92	79.08	6.77
	1918-19	178075	912490	1090565	16.33	83.67	5.52
Total	**1914-19**	**1081443**	**4831214**	**5912657**	**18.29**	**81.71**	**29.93**
G.T.		**4063166**	**15691461**	**19754627**			

Source: Annual Administrative Reports of the Respective Years.

Table 13.2: Timber and Fire Wood Extracted from Darjeeling, Teesta and Kurseong Forests Divisions during the Second World War (1940-1945)

Division	*Year*	*Timber In C.Ft*	*Fire Wood In C.Ft*	*T&F.Wood In C.Ft*	*Per cent Annual Timber*	*Per cent Annual Fuel*	*Per cent of Total Production*
	1940-41	166000	1369000	1535000	10.81	89.19	5.87
	1941-42	159000	1414000	1573000	10.11	89.89	6.01
	1942-43	189334	1551889	1741223	10.87	89.13	6.66
	1943-44	243000	1872667	2115667	11.49	88.51	8.09
	1944-45	287000	2868000	3155000	9.10	90.90	12.06
Tota	Five Years	**1044334**	**9055576**	**10119890**	**10.32**	**89.48**	**38.68**
Teesta	1940-41	233000	1013000	1246000	18.70	81.30	4.76
	1941-42	265000	1057000	1322000	20.05	79.95	5.05
	1942-43	300334	1344800	1645134	18.26	81.74	6.29
	1943-44	403000	2230000	2633000	15.31	84.39	10.06
	1944-45	270000	1370000	1640000	16.46	83.54	6.27
Tota	Five Years	**1471334**	**7014800**	**8486134**	**17.34**	**82.66**	**32.44**
Kur	1940-41	403000	725000	1128000	35.73	64.27	4.31
	1941-42	457000	789000	1246000	36.68	63.32	4.76
	1942-43	518600	923000	1441600	35.97	64.03	5.51
	1943-44	589000	1360000	1949000	30.22	69.78	7.45
	1944-45	737000	1054000	1791000	41.15	58.85	6.85
Tota	Five Years	**2704600**	**4851000**	**7555600**	**35.80**	**64.20**	**28.88**
G.T.				**26161624**			

Source: Annual Progress Reports of the Forest of West Bengal.

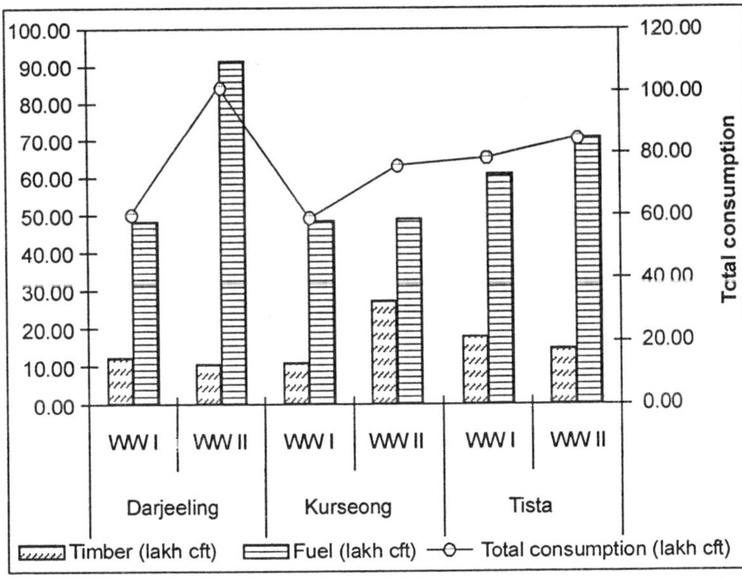

Fig. 13.1: Comparative Account of Consumption of Timber and Fuelwood Per Lakhs cft. During World War I & II

Source: Based on data shown in Tables 1:a and 1:b.

Campaign made it necessary to develop indigenous materials, and towards this end the Forest Research Institute undertook different tests regarding the suitability of local materials. Many of which were recognised later as good substitute of the imported materials. The impact of the Second World War was more severely felt on the forests of Darjeeling. India was the sole supplier of timber to the Middle East theatre, and later to the Allied forces in Iraq and the Persian Gulf. To meet the exigencies of war, fellings and sawing were pushed to remotest corners of the forest divisions of the Darjeeling district. The Forest Department's instructions were to produce the maximum outturn possible. Not surprisingly, working-plan prescriptions in the reserved forests were considered upset during the wars. Tables 13.1 and 13.2 gives some indication of the First and Second World War demand of the Darjeeling forests and efforts to meet it. The felling recorded show an increase, over pre-War outturn. However, it was admitted that due to the varying circumstances in which felling took place, an accurate estimate of the damage done to forest capital was not possible. For the reserved forests, these excess felling were estimated to be on an average as much as six annual yields. During First World War maximum extraction was done from Teesta Division. Similar trend could be seen in Darjeeling and Kurseong Divisions also. Maximum timber extraction was experienced by Teesta Division during the World War period till 1919. This was followed by Kurseong Division. This may be attributed to easy accessibility and valuable timber species like Sal and Teak in the Division.

During the Second World War, Darjeeling Division saw a huge tree felling continuously from 1940-1945. Fuel wood requirement was the major factor for felling. Teesta and Kurseong Division also suffered the onslaught of World War but to lesser degree compared to Darjeeling. Analysis of timber extraction during the Second World War showed that the Kurseong Division suffered the most due to its good connectivity and high timber value tree species. Analysis of the data for timber and fuel wood extraction during the two World Wars revealed maximum felling occurred in the Darjeeling Division followed by Teesta Division. The data also reveals that maximum fellings were done for fuelwood requirement. This requirement was more in Darjeeling Division. For timber, British heavily relied on Kurseong and Teesta Divisions.

After a careful study of the deforestatrion during the World Wars in Darjeeling, the researcher had observed that the unresticted deforestation of the forest areas in Darjeeling District must have led to significant change in the soil composition of the district. The denudation and weathering of exposed soil was a well known fact. At the same time, landslides in the hills and floods in the plains, which was a common phenomenon in Darjeeling Disrict might have led to more transportation and disposition of soil. Environmental degradation and associated phenomena were the most pervasive of natural problems that undermined the economic and cultural development of the Darjeeling District of Sub-Himalayan West Bengal. Deforestation along with high intensity rainstorm induced accelerated soil erosion, mass movement in the upper catchment and massive flood in the lower parts of the catchment area.[23] For example, in 1918, the Rakti and Chel rivers broke out a new channel into Ghish and caused immence damage to the cultivation in the plains. Much valuable land was silted over by the rivers Chel and Ghish combined and the Bengal duars railway embarkment swept away close to Udlabari station.[24] Implementation of various development schemes, construction of human settlement and roads to cater the smooth movement of forest produce to the supply line, boosting of tea plantation, quarrying, on the Himalayan immature geology triggered the disaster, huge and complex, never encountered before the advent of the British. The situation was different before the advent of the British. The hills were densely covered by natural vegetation with very thin population and the harmonious relation between the upper and lower catchment was well preserved. Darjeeling District Revenue maximisation being the prime concern of the Forest Department, ecological concern failed to get the necessary attention.

The Himalayas compose one of the lofty mountain chains of the world. Darjeeling is a part of the eastern Himalayas. Ecologically, these constitute a fragile and unique terrestrial system. The Darjeeling Himalayas is different from the rest of the Himalayas with regard to its ecological set up. Erosion of soils and sinking of landmass are the two basic causes of landslip in Darjeeling District.[25] The Mountains of Darjeeling consist of rocks of different stages. Of these the Damuda Stage of lower Gondwana, Nahan Stage of Siwalik system, Daling series and Darjeeling Gneisses are important. Major rock types are quartzites, slates, phyllite, foliated rocks composed of flaky minerals and partly sedimentary and partly igneous banded metamorphic rocks. These gneissic and schistose rocks mainly are subjected to severe weathering and erosion Mica-schist are easily carried out by flowing water. Naturally, they help vigorous erosion and slip of lands. Soil erosion in Darjeeling Himalayas is unfortunately a man-made problem being aggravated by natural erosion.

Natural erosion is mainly pronounced in areas where the land is steep giving run-off a good momentum. High rainfall and steep slopes created favourable conditions for the initiating of run-off. Soils originating from schistose and gneissic rocks do not contain any cementing material to hold them firmly enough. As a result, immediately after rain, wherever the top soil bare enough, it is washed away by rain water. The steepness of the terrain, the tectonic instability of the area, as well as the relatively young age of the mountains all contribute to the erodability of the slopes. Besides, seepage of water within the soil layers makes the schistose parent rock slippery enough and help landslides in all small catchment areas.[26] This is equally true in case of big rivers—the Teesta catchment, the Balasan catchment, the Rangit catchment, the Lish catchment etc.

Conclusion

Whenever human agency interfered with the system of equilibrium in nature, disasters happened. The colonial intervention and the developmental activities that followed were primarily responsible for this ecological degredation of the Darjeeling Himalayas. Of all factors, deforestation was primarily responsible for rapid erosion of soil. Mass felling of trees as has already been dealt with, has had left the land bare, and prey to run-off along the steep slopes. It was said that deforestation in Darjeeling mountain was always followed by afforestation. But, it was not true in all cases. In some places Forest department had planted trees like Dhupi (*Cryptomeria japonica*). But, these gathered sufficient strength to hold the soil not before fifteen years after the plantation. Within the span of these fifteen years the soil layers were partly on totally carried away. The clear felling of trees and taungya cultivation kept the mountain bare for a substantial period there by accelarating soil erosion.

The people of Darjeeling usually got their supply of water from mountain springs and othe water channels. Even before independence they had to fetch water from a greater distance than before. Many springs had dried up and many channels had retreated. Deforestation had a direct bearing on this development. Deforestation fostered runoff as well as restricted infiltration of water into soil layer.

Hence, it can be concluded that the colonial intervention and world Wars marked an ecological watershed in the history of Darjeeling. They led to the loss of forests and consequent ecological catastrophe, the impact of which are still felt in the region. Despite several odd attempts at regeneration of forests and ecological conservation since the British days, the negative impacts produced in Darjeeling by the colonial intervention and deforestation especially during the World Wars has always remained producing frequent environmental hazards even today.

Notes

1. O. Malley, L.S.S. (1907). *Bengal gazetteers*, Darjeeling, Alipore: Government printing Press, p. 87.
2. Dash, A.J. (1947). *Bengal District gazetteers*, Darjeeling, Calcutta: Bengal Government Press, p. 28.
3. Ray, B. (1961). *District Handbook*, Darjeeling. Deputy Superintendent of Census Operation, West Bengal, Calcutta: Mudrani Press, pp. 17-18
4. *Ibid.*, p. 19.
5. E.C. Dozey, (1922). *A Concise History of the Darjeeling District Since 1835*, Varanasi: Deepak Press, p. 140.
6. Dash, Arthur Jules, *Op. cit.*, p. 136.
7. A letter from D.H. Lees Esq; Deputy Commissioner of Jalpaiguri to the Commissioner of the Rajashahi Division, No. 1232 G; dated Jalpaiguri the 1st August, 1911, File 4-W/1-No. 1-2.
8. The Proceeding (A) of the Hon'ble L.t. Governor of Bengal Revenue Department, Forest Branch on the Darjeeling Hill Side and River Conservation Bill, 1917, Proceeding Volume of July 1917, No. 1-8.

9. A Letter from R.N. Reid Esq, Under Secretary to the Government of Bengal, Revenue Department to the Commissioner of Bhagalpur Division, No. 1281, dated Calcutta, the 19th March, 1912, File 10R/1-2 of 1912.
10. The Proceeding (A) of the Hon'ble L.t. Governor of Bengal Revenue Department, Forest Branch on the Darjeeling Hill Side and River Conservation Bill 1917, Proceeding Volume of July 1917, No. 1-8.
11. Proceeding (A) of the Hon'ble Lt. Governor of Bengal Revenue Department Forest Branch, On deforestation in the district of Darjeeling, dated 30th March, 1912 from the Commissioner of Bhagalpur Division to the Secretary to the Government of Benga, File 10R/1-8.
12. Memo by B.K. Finnimore Esq., Secretary to the Government of Bengal, Public Work Department, No. 250 M.P.I., dated Calcatta the 19th February, 1912.
13. Proceeding (A) of the Hon'ble Lt. Governor of Bengal, Revenue Department Forest Branch, dated 30th March, 1912 from E.H.C. Walsh Esq., Commissioner of Bhgalpur Division to the Secretary to the Government of Bengal, Revenue Department, File 10R/1-No. 3-4.
14. Stebbing, E.P. (1926). *The Forests of India*, Vol. III, New Delhi (A.J. Rpt. 1982), p. 531.
15. *Ibid.*, p. 533.
16. *Ibid.*
17. *Ibid.*, p. 536.
18. *Ibid.*
19. Government of India. *Hundred Years of Indian Forestry, 1861-1961*. Vol. I, *op. cit.*, p. 79.
20. Stebbing, E.P., *op. cit.*, p. 561.
21. Government of India. *Hundred Years of Indian Forestry, 1861-1961*. Vol. I, *op. cit.* p. 81.
22. Stebbing, E.P., *op. cit.*, p. 147.
23. A letter from D.H. Lees Esq., Deputy Commissioner of Jalpaiguri to the Commissioner of the Rajashahi Division, No. 1232 G; dated Jalpaiguri the 1st August, 1911, File 4-W/1-No. 1-2.
24. Farrigton, H.A. *Annual Progress Report of Forest Administration in Bengal for the year, 1918-19*. Conservator of Forests in Bengal, Calcutta: Bengal Secretariate Press, 1919, p. 6.
25. Gerrard, J. (1990). *Mountain Environment*, Cambridge, MA: The MIT Press, p. 257.
26. *Ibid.*, p. 62.

14
Political Changes and Economic Development in Sikkim

Dhanraj Rai and *Surendra Rai*

Introduction

The state of Sikkim is second smallest state of India. With a total area of 7,096 sq. km, it constitutes 0.22 per cent of the total geographical area of the country. The state is bounded by vast stretches of Tibetan Plateau in the North, the Chumbi Valley of Tibet and Bhutan in the East, Nepal in the West and Darjeeling District of West Bengal in the South. It stretches over 112 kms. from North to South and 64 kms from East to West. It lies between 27° 00′46″ to 28° 07′48″ North Latitude and 88° 00′58″ to 88° 55′25″ East Longitude. Sikkim was ruled by the Chogyal since 1642 till its merger with India in 1975. After the treaty of 1950 Sikkim became the protectorate state of India which meant that Sikkim was a sovereign state retaining control over its internal affairs while India was responsible for its defence and territorial integrity. On 26 April, 1975 Sikkim was merged with the Indian Union, thus becoming the 22nd state of the Indian Union. The merger with India ushered in not only political changes in terms of monarchy being replaced by parliamentary representative democracy, but it also lead to demographic and socio-economic changes.

This chapter attempts to accommodate the basic problems of development on political superstructure and economic base. Political economy refers to research which attempts to answer two questions— How do institutions evolve in response to the individual incentives, strategies and choices? and How do institutions affect the political and economic system? (James E. Alt and Alberto Alesina, 1996, 1998)[1]. It comprehends the relationship between political institution of local governance and economic base and financial system of the institution, political economic planning, and political economy of institutions, approaches and theories, legislature of political economy, political economy of the formation of government, bureaucratic political economy, public policy and political economy of budgeting. Political economy constitutes the collaborative function of politics and economy.

After 1975 different political parties emerged having democratic ideologies and principles. Since 1990s the state instigated the negation within the democratic pattern of governance from representative into neo-liberal economy wherein power project introduced, state opened the door to pharmaceutical industries to establish their companies. The introduction of liberal economic development in the state of Sikkim has many flaws which only benefited the companies and industrialists rather than local proletariat. Establishment of Hydro power companies has many environmental threats etc. and they have been resisted by the people. This chapter tries to study the causal relation between politics and economy of the state and causation of development policies and welfare of the indigenous people and also focused how changes in economic policies changed the economic development in the state. This chapter is based on primary sources of data and also used secondary data as well.

Objectives

The objectives of the study are:

1. To define the theoretical concept of the diversities of political economic development proposing different theories of development accommodating liberal theory of development.
2. To study the causal relationship between development and welfare of the people.
3. To find out the different development programmes and policies in the state.
4. To find out the major challenges of development initiatives in the state of Sikkim.

Methodology

The study has been conducted in the state of Sikkim which is located in North Eastern parts of India. Sikkim is divided into four districts, viz. East, West, North and South respectively. It is exploratory and descriptive study. It is exploratory study because it tries to diagnose the problems in development of politics and economic policies and find out the major challenges. It is descriptive study because it tries to describe the existing phenomena on development and its impact on welfare of the people. The study employed the combination of both qualitative and quantitative methodology. Secondary data has been collected from books, journals, articles, governmental and institutional data etc.

Political History of Sikkim

In the year 1642 Phuntso Namgyal, by proclaiming himself as king of Sikkim, started the dynastic rule that was to last for nearly 330 years. Sikkim was ruled by Chogyals (kings) since 1642-1975. Chogyals were the monarchs of the former kingdoms of Sikkim which were ruled by separate branches of the Namgyal family. The Chogyal or divine ruler was the absolute potentate of Sikkim from 1642 to 1975, when monarchy was abrogated and its people voted in a referendum to make Sikkim India's 22nd State. However, Chogyal meaning "Dharma Raja" or "Religious King" is a title which was also conferred upon a special class of temporal and spiritual rulers. From 1642 to 1975, Sikkim was ruled by the Namgyal Monarchy (also called the Chogyal Monarchy or Dharma Raja), founded by the fifth-generation descendants of Guru Tashi, a prince of the Minyak House who came to Sikkim from the Kham district of Tibet. Chogyal means "righteous ruler", and was the title conferred upon Sikkim's Buddhist king during the reign of the Namgyal Monarchy.

The reign of the Chogyal was foretold by the patron saint of Sikkim, Guru Rinpoche. The 8th century saint had predicted the rule of the king when he arrived in the State. In 1642, Chogyal Phuntsog Namgyal was crowned as Sikkim's first ruler in Yuksom, West Sikkim. The crowning of the king was a great event and he was crowned by three revered lamas who arrived there from three different directions, namely the north, west and south.

Emergence of Democracy in Sikkim

The political upheavals of 1940s precipitated into protest movement of 1973 that finally led to the merger of Sikkim into Indian Union in 1975 and led to establishment of representative democracy. As the political era from 1919 up to 1947 is referred as Gandhian era in the Modern Indian History, the period of 30 years, i.e. from 1945 up to 1975 can be regarded as Kazian era in the Democratic History of Sikkim. It is because from 1945, late L.D. Kazi single handedly guided the democratic movement of Sikkim till its merger. Though monarchy exist under Namgyal Rule in Sikkim till 1975 but the amalgamation of the three petty political organizations of Sikkim Rajya Praja Mandal, Rajya Praja Sammelan and Praja Sudhar Samaj in 7th December, 1947 already gave birth of protest movement against feudal monarchy. On the very date, that is on 7th December, 1947 they held a joint meeting at today's Palzor Stadium (then Polo Ground) and decided to form a compact body to combat lawless feudalism. The huge gathering of 7 December, 1947 led to the birth of first ever political Party of Sikkim known as Sikkim State Congress. Tashi Tshering also popularly known as Tashi Babu of Gangtok was the elected President of Sikkim State Congress.

In 1953, Kazi Lhendup Dorjee Khangsarpa (people of his native place fondly called him Kancha Kazi) became the President of Sikkim State Congress and held that post till 1958. During his President ship he led a delegation to Delhi in 1954 to call on the Prime Minister of India, Pandit Jawaharlal Nehru. The Sikkimese had been fighting for political and economic reforms and these were discussed by the delegation with Pandit Nehru, who was deeply impressed by the sincerity of Kazi Lhendup Dorjee. The Indian Prime Minister promised to give assistance for the progress and economic welfare of the Sikkimese populace and assured Government of India's support towards political reform in Sikkim. Above protest movement against Namgyal Dynasty led to the merger of Sikkim with India in 1975.

Post-Merger Political Scenario: A Paradigm Shift

Sikkim Janata Parishad was formed in 1977 by the Nar Bahadur Bhandari which won the state assembly election held in 1979 and he became the Chief Minister on 18 October, 1979. In 1984, he also served briefly as Member of Parliament from Sikkim constituency in the 8th Lok Sabha as an independent candidate. In 1984, Bhandari dissolved the Sikkim Janata Parishad and formed a new party called Sikkim Sangram Parishad (SSP). The Sikkim Sangram Parishad is a political party emerged in Sikkim after the merger of Sikkim with India in 1975. Nar Bahadur Bhandari is a former Chief Minister and great leader of the party SSP in the state of Sikkim who was in power since 1979 to 1994. He was the founder leader of Sikkim Sangram Parishad party. His wife Dil Kumari Bhandari is a former Member of Parliament (Lok Sabha) from Sikkim.

She is the current president of Bharatiya Gorkha Parisangh, an organisation of the Indian Gorkhas.

In 1994, Bhandari's party Sikkim Sangram Parishad lost the assembly elections to Pawan Kumar Chamling led Sikkim Democratic Front (SDF). Sikkim Sangram Parishad also lost the 1999 assembly election. In the 2004 state assembly elections, Bhandari contested under the Congress party but the party lost the election, winning only one seat. Again in the 2009 assembly elections the Congress party under Bhandari failed to win any seat in the state assembly. But, there are cases pending in the Court of Law regarding the conduct of elections. There are charges of elections being rigged.

1. Media was totally banned.
2. Existence of Single powerful party which lead absolute government.
3. Freedom of speech and express was restricted under this party.
4. Choice of the people's representative was limited which made party one man rule within the democracy.

In 1994, Sikkim Democratic Front (SDF) formed the government under Pawan Kumar Chamling as Chief Minister. The party was formed in 1993. Main Ideology of the party is **Democracy, Secularism, Socialism, Welfarism, Rule of Law etc. and Liberalisation in Democracy.** The Policies are democratic-oriented for the welfare of the people from grass-roots level. The Party, the Sikkim Democratic Front, firmly upholds the cause of Sikkimese people in their struggle for Democracy and Rule of Law. This party truly stands Democratic Principles, which always strive to protect and preserve the democratic rights and privileges of the people; it has ruled the state since 1994 with Pawan Kumar Chamling as the Chief Minister. The party consolidated its position sweeping the 1999 and 2004 state elections. It won 31 out of the 32 assembly seats in the 2004 election. In the 2009 assembly election, the party made a clean sweep, winning all 32 seats. It also retained the lone Lok Sabha seat.

Political and Economic Relation in Sikkim Since 1990

The politics in the state of Sikkim is moving towards liberal democracy since 1990 with the emergence of Sikkim Democratic Front (SDF). Sikkim, a tiny Himalayan state of India which is located in North Eastern parts of the country after merger with Indian Union in 1975 has shown tremendous changes in different aspects, whether it could be of development of economy or political changes after 1990s wherein various Power Projects, Pharmaceutical companies and other industries and educational institutions was setup, the major factors led to liberalised democracy are: Opening up the gateway of Establishment of Different Hydro-Power Projects, Promotion of Establishment of Private Pharmaceuticals Companies and Opening up of International Border Trade between India and China (Nathula pass in 1996). Despite of open economic policies in the state

Impact of Hydro Power Projects in Sikkim

The developmental projects drastically redefine the land use pattern like hydro power projects that not only induced displacement of people from their ancestral habitats and caused large-scale loss of traditional culture and occupations but also bring about socio-economic and demographic changes which are not easily acceptable to the local population resulting to turmoil and conflicts in a relatively peaceful area. Despite the opposition of the Lepcha community (an indigenous tribe) residing in the Dzongu region of Sikkim against the construction of Teesta power projects is an example of how developmental projects in order to enhance better *socio-economic opportunities is alienating the local population from their land and culture and bringing about changes* which are not easily acceptable to the local population leading to ripples of protests which at present is more Gandhian but may soon turn violent and disturb the peace in a relatively peaceful state of the North East India (which is usually in a turmoil having insurgency problems).

Hydro Power Potential in Sikkim

India's hydropower potential is about 148,700 MW and currently only 21 per cent (32,442 MW) is under operation. The state of Sikkim has a potential of about 8000 MW peak with a firm base of 3000 MW. The Teesta and Rangit are the two main rivers of Sikkim where considerable hydro potential is available. In 1974, a committee was constituted to study the hydropower potential in Sikkim. According to the preliminary reconnaissance survey, the river Teesta could be harnessed under a cascade development for hydropower generation in six stages, i.e. Teesta Stage-I to Stage-VI. Besides river Teesta other tributaries of the river such as Rangit, Rangpo, Lachen etc. have high potentiality for the hydro power development. National Hydroelectric Power Corporation Limited (NHPC) and other private developers are entering in hydropower sector in Sikkim as the state government encourages hydropower development which is being considered as one of the main sources for enhancing socio-economic development of the state. It is envisaged that hydropower development will eventually lead to the overall infrastructural development of the state as hydropower generation involves construction of dams, tunnel, power station etc. which involves developing transport linkages, opens up employment opportunities and generates income.

At present about 600 MW (7.5%) of hydropower potential has been developed in the state by constructing mini and micro Hydel projects. More than 5000 MW hydro power potential is under development in different stages. Out of 3315 MW in its power system 17.19 per cent (570 MW) has already been commissioned. The Sikkim Power Development Corporation Limited has granted permission for more than 24 different hydropower projects, which will generate at least 5494 MW. The list of upcoming hydropower projects are shown in Table 14.1. The total estimated cost of these projects is about Rs. 25,000 crore (US $ 62 billion).

Pharmaceutical Companies in Sikkim

Today, Sikkim is home to as many as major pharma companies, which have significant investments in the state. It took very little effort and time for investor in pharma industries sector in the state to decide on its manufacturing hub. The tax incentives which thishilly state offered on the table were quite attractive and easily comparable to the so-called pharma-hub. The major pharmaceutical companies includes CIPLA, INDICHEMIE and ALKEM is located Kumrek, near Rangpo, east Sikkim, ZYDUS CADILLA, INTAS PHARMA and UNICHEM is located at BagheyKhola. SUN PHARMA is at Ranipool, 12 km distance from capital of Sikkim; Gangtok. TORRENT PHARMA is at 32 mile, NH31A to Gangtok. GOLDEN CROSS is located at Rorathang, 12 km from Rangpo. STP PHARMACEUTICAL is planted at Sangkhola, near Singtam, East Sikkim. Sikkim which is the least populous state in the country and the second-smallest after Goa has already attracted pharma investment upwards of Rs. 2,500 crore. After Gujarat, Goa and Baddi, Sikkim is now attracting the most attention in this regards. This could have big implications, considering the fact that the country is the world's fourth largest producer of pharmaceuticals by volume.

Table 14.1: Total Power Projects in Sikkim

Upcoming and completed Hydropower Projects in Sikkim					
Sl. No	*Project Name*	*Capacity (MW)*	*Developer*	*Probable date of commissioning*	*Present status*
1.	Teesta Stage-I	280	Himalayan Green Energy (P) Ltd.	2012-13	Under investigation
2.	Teesta Stage-II	330	Him Urja Infra (P) Ltd.	2011-12	Under investigation
3.	Teesta Stage-III	1200	Teesta Urja Ltd.	2011-12	DPR Ready
4.	Teesta Stage-IV	495	NHPC	2011-12	Under investigation
5.	Teesta Stage-V	510	NHPC	2008-09	Commissioned
6.	Teesta Stage-VI	500	Lanco Energy (P) Ltd.	2011-12	Under investigation
7.	Lachen	210	NHPC		Under investigation
8.	Panan	280	Himgiri Hydro Energy (P) Ltd.	2011-12	DPR Ready
9.	Rangyong	Approx 300	—	2011-12	Stopped
10.	Rukel			2005	Stopped
11.	Ringpi			2005	Stopped
12.	Lingzya			2005	Stopped
13.	Rongnichu	96	Madhya Bharati Power Co.	2011-12	Under investigation
14.	Chuzachen	71	Gati Infrastructure Ltd.	2011-12	Under Construction
15.	Teesta Stage-I	280	Himalayan Green Energy (P) Ltd.	2012-13	Under investigation
16.	Teesta Stage-II	330	Him Urja Infra (P) Ltd.	2011-12	Under investigation
17.	Teesta Stage-III	1200	Teesta Urja Ltd.	2011-12	DPR Ready
18.	Teesta Stage-IV	495	NHPC	2011-12	Under investigation
19.	Teesta Stage-V	510	NHPC	2008-09	Commissioned
20.	TeestaStage-VI	500	Lanco Energy (P) Ltd.	2011-12	Under investigation
21.	Lachen	210	NHPC		Under investigation
22.	Panan	280	Himgiri Hydro Energy (P) Ltd.	2011-12	DPR Ready
23.	Rangyong	Approx 300	—	2011-12	Stopped
24.	Rukel			2005	Stopped
25.	Ringpi			2005	Stopped
26.	Lingzya			2005	Stopped
27.	Rongnichu	96	Madhya Bharati Power Co.	2011-12	Under investigation
28.	Chuzachen	71	Gat Infrastructure Ltd.	2011-12	Under Construction

Major factors contributing Sikkim as pharmaceutical hubs in the recent past are: it is a peaceful state and has huge potential for the manufacturing sector, minimal interference by the state government. It is true the state took some time to develop and attract the pharma companies. But now it is surely at a tipping point. The company is also finding labour, power and overall cost of manufacturing to be lower in Sikkim as compared to states like Gujarat and Maharashtra. Sikkim's attractiveness lies in the multitude of tax benefits it has on offer. As part of this, all new units as well as existing units which go in for substantial expansion in Sikkim will be eligible for incentives for a period of ten years from the date of commencement of commercial production. Some of the incentives include 100 per cent excise duty exemption on finished products manufactured there, 100 per cent exemption on income tax, capital investment subsidy of 30 per cent on the investment in plant and machinery, interest subsidy at 3 per cent on working capital loan and even reimbursement of 100 per cent insurance premium. On the top of it all, Sikkim also offers attractive freight subsidy. The benefits which the companies are accommodating in Sikkim are truly attractive and in some cases even better than any part of the nation. However, the freight benefit may not have a huge impact on the pharma industry as freight cost in the domestic market accounts for just 1-2 per cent. Even if excise benefits at Sikkim as such benefits are now also available in several states, the biggest draw for the state is its ten-year income tax holiday.

However, a section of the industry feels the state needs to work on certain grey areas to emerge as a major pharma cluster. Infrastructure is still the biggest concern in Sikkim. The State is also addressing the power situation. The recent announcement of constructing the rail link in Sikkim will provide a further fillip. Certain vital factors are still missing in Sikkim. The state government needs to come up with a dedicated policy to support the pharma industry. Plus, there are issues with availability of skilled workers which again the state government can address by setting up training institutes. The state has another latent edge the Silk Route of India or the Nathu La Pass. The industry believes this could act as a shortcut for the Indian industry to tap the highly potential Chinese and CIS countries. If Sikkim can effectively market itself and the benefits it offers, there can be no reason why it cannot emerge as the next generation pharma hub of the nation.

India-China Trade at Nathu La Region: Economic and Political Impact

Nathu La is located on the 563 km Old Silk Route, an offshoot of the historic Silk Road. The Old Silk Route connects Lhasa in Tibet to the plains of Bengal to the south. In 1815, the trade volumes increased after the British annexed territories belonging to the Sikkimese, Nepalese, and Bhutanese. The potential of Nathu La was released in 1873, after the Darjeeling Deputy Commissioner published a report on the strategic importance of mountain passes between Sikkim and Tibet. In December 1893, the Sikkimese Monarchy and Tibetan rulers signed an agreement to increase trade between the two Nations. The agreement culminated in 1894 when the trade pass was opened. Nathu La is a mountain pass in the Himalayas. It connects the Indian state of Sikkim with China's Tibet Autonomous Region. The pass at 4310 m (14,140 ft.) above mean sea level forms a part of an offshoot of the ancient Silk Road. Nathu means "listening ears" and La means "pass" in Tibetan. On the Indian side, the pass is 54 km 34 (miles) east of Gangtok, the capital of Indian state of Sikkim on J.N. Marg and only citizens of India can visits the pass, that too after obtaining a permit in Gangtok.

Nathu La is one of the three open trading border posts between China and India; the other two are Shipkila in Himalchal Pradesh and Lipulakh (or Lipulech) in Uttarakhand. Sealed by India after the 1962 Sino-India war, Nathu La was re-opened in 2006 following numerous bilateral trade agreements. The opening of the pass was expected to bolster the economy of the region and play a key role in the growing Sino-Indian trade but that has not happened. Currently, agreements between the two nations limit trade across the pass to 29 types of goods from India and 15 from the Chinese side. The opening also shortens the travel distance to important Hindu and Buddhist pilgrimage site in the region.

Until the year 1962, before the pass was sealed, goods such as pens, watches, cereals, cotton cloth, edible oils, soaps, building materials, and dismantled scooters and four-wheelers were exported to Tibet through the pass on mule-back. Two hundred mules, each carrying about 80 kg of load were used to ferry goods from Gangtok to Lhasa, which used to take 20-25 days. Upon return, silk, raw wool, musk pods, medicinal plants, country liquor, precious stones, gold and silver ware were imported into India. Most of the trade in those days was carried out by the Marwari community, which owned 95 per cent of the 200 authorised firms.

Since July 2006, trading is open Mondays through Thursdays. Exports from India exempted from duty include agricultural implements, blankets, copper products, clothes, cycles, coffee, tea, barley, rice, wheat, flour, dry fruits, vegetables, vegetable oil, tobacco, snuff, spices, shoes, kerosene oil, stationery, utensils, milk processed products, canned food, dyes, and local herbs. Chinese exports to India exempted from duty include goat skin, sheep skin, wool, raw silk, yak tail, yak hair, china clay, borax, butter, common salt, horses, goats, and sheep. Restrictions are placed on traders, with permits only given to those who were Sikkimese citizens before the kingdom merged with India in 1975.

There were fears among some traders in India that Indian goods would find a limited outlet in Tibet, while China would have access to a ready market in Sikkim and West Bengal. The reopening of the pass was expected to stimulate the economy of the region and bolster Indo-Chinese trade but this has not happened. Figures released by the Tibet Autonomous Regional Bureau of Commerce show that in the 51 days of trading in 2006, only US$186,250 worth of trade passed through Nathu La. Nathu La as far as India's National Security as well as National Development is concerned is a strategic place. It is strategic place because out here India shares its border with China which means it is strategic and as we can say it is war prone zone. At the same time it is the trade centre between two super powers India and China which determines the economic goals.

After the People's Republic of China took control of Tibet in 1950 and suppressed a Tibetan uprising in 1959, the passes into Sikkim became a conduit for refugees from Tibet. During the 1962 Sino-Indian War, Nathu La witnessed skirmishes between soldiers of the two countries. Shortly thereafter, the passage was sealed and remained closed for more than four decades. Between 7 and 13 September 1967, China's People's Liberation Army and the Indian Army had six-day "border skirmishes" including the exchange of heavy artillery fire. In 1975, Sikkim acceded to India and Nathu La became part of Indian Territory. China, however, refused to acknowledge the accession at that time.

Doklam Standoff

The standoff between Indian and Chinese armies in the Doklam area on 2017 adversely affected the international trade through Nathu La pass which is located in East Sikkim and lying on the Old Silk Route. Unless the continuing border tension is defused, it is likely to adversely affect the progress of trade made over the last decade. Economic development is the key to peace and security. Therefore, both countries should liberalise border trade, increasing trading opportunities. The trade includes Chinese imports like wool, goat skins, sheep skins, yak tails, goats, sheep, yak hair, horses, salt, borax, silk, readymade garments, shoes, quilt/blankets, carpets, local herbal medicine and export of locally produced commodities like vegetable oil, textiles, copper items, blankets, carpets, tea, and coffee. The export of iron ore and livestock products from India and wool, herbs and electric appliances from China is convenient to transport through this land pass.

The Nathu La Trade Study Group Report of 2005 estimated significant bilateral trade flow of Rs. 2266 crore (US$ 580 million) between 2010 and Rs. 12203 crore (US$ 2 billion) 2015. In 2010, the export from India crossed Rs. 4.02 crore while the import from China was zero. The border trade statistics till 2012 show that there has been a significant increase in the export of good to China. The overall border trade in 2012 constituted approximately US$ 200,000 and total exports of US$ 1.125 million. The highest export record to China, ever since the border trade resumed, was in the year 2016 with exported goods worth Rs. 63.38 crore and imported goods worth Rs. 19.30 crore. Moreover, it has also helped promote a friendlier relationship.

There are, however, a few hurdles, which hinder the smooth flow of trade. The items allowed for trade are limited and trading communities on both sides have been pressing their respective governments to expand the list of the number of tradable items. The items traded in the 1950s and early 1960s are the same as the goods traded today. Thus, many of the permitted tradable items are unnecessary in today's market. Moreover, the present list is insufficient due to its low commercial value. At present, India allows the export of 29 items and the import of 15 items from China. There is a need to expand the trade in goods to increase the volume of two-way trade through this land route. Being one of the leading organic farming States in India, Sikkim can contribute immensely to trade in items like flowers, herbs and crops.

There are major transportation problems during the monsoon season between May and September. The roads are frequently in disrepair and landslides block the roads, thereby, making it difficult to commute and transport goods. The collaboration of State Public Works Department (SPWD) and Border Roads Organisation-General Reserve Engineer Force (BRO-GREF) to maintain roads for efficient transportation is restricted due to the overlap between the trade and the tourist seasons. The lack of proper accommodation facilities also becomes a problem for traders who travel from China to Sikkim. Despite the infrastructural limitations, the Nathu La pass remains an important trading route for India with China.

Conclusion

The above discussion shows that Sikkim has been a dynamic State in terms of its formulation of policies, ideologies, forms of governance etc. Since 1994 Sikkim witnessed the emergence of liberalisation and followed the path of it for the overall development of the State. The State legitimately sanctioned liberalisation wherein various Power Projects, Pharmaceutical companies and other industries and educational institutions were set up. The major factors which led to liberalised democracy are: opening up the gateway for establishment of different Hydropower Projects, Promotion of establishment of Private Pharmaceuticals Companies and opening up of International Border Trade between India and China (Nathula pass in 2006). With exploratory and descriptive methods, the study made an attempt to diagnose the problems in development of politics and economic policies and find out the major challenges in the procedural development. It also studied three dimension of development, viz. causation of hydro project in the people's welfare in the State, political significance of international trade between India and China at Nathula Region of Sikkim and economic impact of pharmaceuticals companies in the State.

Note

1. Part VIII, Chapter 28-31 of A New Handbook of Political Science, Oxford University Press, 1996, 1998 included the new chapter titled "Political Economy" contributed by various authors.

References

Arora, V. (2006). "Roots and Route of Secularism in Sikkim", *Economic and Political Weekly*, 41.

Arora, V. (2007). "Assertative identities, indegenity and politics of recognizing as a tribe: The Bhutias, the Lepchas and the Limbus of Sikkim", *Indian Sociological Society* (Sociological Bulletin), 56(02): 195-220.

Arora, V. (2008). "Gandhigiri in Sikkim", *Economic and Political Weekly, 43*(38): 27-28.

Arora, V. (2009). "They are all set to dam (n) our future: Contested hydel power in democratic Sikkim", *Indian Sociological Society, 58* (01): 94-114.

Bora, B. (2004). "Pro-Incumbency Factor", *Economic and Political Weekly, 39*, pp. 5536-5544.

Brass, P.R. (2010). *Routlegde Handbook of South Asian Politics.* London and New York: Routledge Taylor and Francis Group.

Lama, M.P. (2001). *Sikkim Human Development Report.* Human Resource Development Department, Delhi: Government of Sikkim.

Sinha, A.C. (1973). "The feudal polity and political development in Sikkim", *Indian Anthropological Association, 3*(2): 71-87.

Sinha, A.C. (1975). "The Kazi Patrician in the Sikkemese Polity", *Indian Anthropoligical Association, 5*(2): 7-11.

Sinha, A.C. (2008). *Sikkim: Feudal and Democratic* (1st edn.). New Delhi (India): Indus Publishing House.

15
Migration and Sustainability in Uttarakhand
Issues and Challenges

Manoj Shukla

Introduction

Myriad research work has gone into the human urge of leaving the place of origin for settlement in far of places. Economic History abounds with the tales of migrants who have earned fortune and fame after migration and the remittances have brought prosperity to the state of origin. At different places, in different times, there have been pull and push factors at work for migration, which may be categorised into economic social and political. People migrate either to leverage their skills for quality livelihoods or to fill the void of non-availability of manual labour which has zero opportunity cost in their place of origin. Inter-state migration in India has become a crucial phenomena which is a by-product of uneven development due to neglect of certain regions as such regions have least heft in political arena. Hill states in India comes under this category. The present study covers the state of Uttarakhand to highlight the ill effects of migration on the state of origin of the migrants. There are instances in India when the inter-state migration has culminated in to higher productivity, prosperity and empowerment in the state of origin. Uttar Pradesh and Bihar are the two states where migrants remittances helped in asset formation and increase in per capita income in both these states. Not only that the migrants from these two have been able to create pressure groups in the state of settlement and carries political heft and hence derive dividends. Migration from hill state of Uttarakhand showcases a complete different scenario where migration has not only been counter-productive but has challenged the sustainability of the state itself. The mass exodus of the people particularly to the National Capital Region-Delhi (Henceforth NCR-Delhi) has deprived the state of its skilled and value oriented human resource and jeopardised the sustainable livelihoods. According to the 2011 Census there are 1053 uninhabited villages in Uttarakhand and a total of 3.36 lakh houses are located in villages of the 13 districts of Uttarakhand. It is strange paradox that the successive governments in Uttarakhand have to start a special campaign to curb it. There is a common belief in Uttarakhand that quality of life can be improved only if we get employment in the plain areas particularly in the NCR-Delhi. The migration of productive manpower comes at a huge economic cost as low demand discourages investment and hence low capital formation further depleting the sustainability of livelihoods in the state Land which is considered the most durable prized asset suffering drastic fall in its value except in the tourist centric urban areas. Tourism being the only sustainable source of income has never been benefiting the locals as most of the properties are owned by the people from Delhi and Punjab and the local people get menial jobs which are underpaid and seasonal. Tourism industry is found to be making huge profits without involving local people, depleting the resources ignoring sustainability. A seasonal occupation like tourism has to be complemented with agro food sector for creating sustainable livelihoods. We have to rethink and reimaging that how sustainability is restored and leveraged for improving the quality of life in this hill state through promoting sustainable livelihoods. Creating and sustaining opportunities of quality livelihoods in natural resource rich state can be a major driver for retaining and utilizing human resource of the state for achieving higher productivity and shared prosperity. Agro food sector is one of such sectors which has the potential to create entrepreneurship at the bottom of pyramid and can be source of sustainable livelihoods for people having different skills. Local latent resources can be leveraged through this sector.

Literature Review

Inter-state and inter-regional migration has been on the rise as it provides opportunities for improving quality of life for masses. The inter-state migration of workers in India has increased substantially to 90 lakh annually between 2011-2016 compared to previous years. The largest recipient of migrant workers was the NCR-Delhi region, which accounted for more than half of migration in 2015-16. Uttar Pradesh and Bihar together accounted for half of total outmigration in 2015-16 (The Economic Survey, 2016). Infrastructures development projects that directly induce population displacement and resettlement for those who migrate become permanent residents (McDowell, 1996). Ravenstein (1885) while explaining the five stages of migration explains that migration accelerates with growth in mean of transport and communication and expansion of trade and commerce. Poros (1995) argues that migrant networks are sets of interpersonal ties that connect migrants, former migrants and non-migrants in origin and destination areas through ties of kinship, friendship, and share communities origin. The state of Uttarakhand carved out in 2000 has 9 hill districts out of thirteen and suffering from ill effects of migration. Uttarakhand which shares 350 km long border with China has been facing problem of people migrating from villages, Mr. Rajnath Singh, Home Minister commented that people are strategic asset and so migration need to be curbed (Times of India; October 1, 2017). An article in on line journal *Down to Earth* shows that 3500 villages in Uttarakhand have no population. A distinguish feature of out-migration in Uttarakhand is its being predominantly longer duration and largely to big cities and towns within as well as outside the State (Mamgain & Reddy, NIRDP, Hyderabad, 2015). This is in contracts to the pattern observed in other parts of country which report the preponderance of short duration migration (Srivastava, 2011; Unesco, 2013). Development pattern influence national and worldview the kind of government elected the way natural and financial resources are used and the development of transportation system (Herbers, 1986). These forces can be classified as either 'Push' or 'Pull'. The push factors are those life situations that give one reason to be dissatisfied with one's present locale; while the pull factors are those attributes of distant places that make them appear appealing (Dorigo and Tobler, 1983). In case of Uttarakhand there is dire need to adopt development strategies to counter-migration—an example would be so called *stay-at-home* development strategies which are designed to promote development and at the same time reduce emigration strategy (Ghosh, 1992). It is always presumed that the contribution of remittances in GDP is significant. Due to paucity of authentic data regarding national remittances the actual impact in indiscernible. However, a study by Stark, O., 1991 and Adams, R.H., 1991 established that international remittances increase inequality but national remittances reduces inequality. There is, therefore, the need to look into the contribution of remittance in SGDP of Uttarakhand. The contribution, migration and remittances can make to social development depends on policies for people's welfare, creating infrastructure market (Hein de Haas, 2007). The out-migration has become so critical that

Uttarakhand is the only state which is running a special drive to curb migration. In this context Uttarakhand C.M. Trivender Singh Rawat said "Migration should be by choice, not by compulsion". Agro-food sector holds the key for sustainable livelihoods in the hilly regions. Food processing sector not only leads to income generation but also helps in reduction of wastage, value addition and enhance manufacturing competitiveness (Rais, Acharya & Sharma, 2013).

Objectives of the Study

1. To know and verify the motives for outmigration and its impact on hill economy.
2. To study socio-economic behaviour of hill people *vis-à-vis* migrants from other states.
3. To present a conceptual framework of agro-food sector in Uttarakhand.
4. To apply this framework for promoting and creating sustainable livelihoods.

Research Methodology

The study seeks to identify and verify the motives of migration and the socio-economic behaviour of emigrants. An ethnographic survey was conducted in NCR-Delhi where migrants from Uttarakhand are settled. A sample size of eighty people (twenty from each District) settled in NCR-Delhi has been taken. The respondents' views were taken through a combination of qualitative research methods—interview and discussions. The household were randomly selected so as to be able to draw some comparative insight. The study has taken secondary data from the web site of Government of Uttarakhand and various publications in journal and research articles.

Outmigration: Trends and Factors

In the state of Uttarkhand there is a common phrase that get skilled or acquire academic excellence and migrate to the NCR-Delhi. National capital region of Delhi which is one of the world largest agglomeration with the population of 47000000 (Census 2011) comprising Delhi as well as area of twenty two districts surrounding it on states of Haryana, Uttar Pradesh and Rajasthan witnessing a phenomenon where rural urban connectivity is a major factor influencing the economic development and shared amenities and prosperity. So proudly the parents of migrants claim that our wards have at last settled in Delhi and NOIDA and we are shifting our base enticing others to imbibe. Nine out of Thirteen districts in Uttarakhand are in hills. Tourism, a major source of informal employment for people and source of revenue for the government, have never been developed in structured manner and its potential remained untapped. Moreover the employment and income derived is seasonal and highly uncertain. Besides the major dividends from tourism has been taken away by developers and promoters from neighbouring rich states. The migrants from Nepal takes most of the jobs at low wage rates. The hotel developers and promoters prefers to higher labour from outside rather than locals and scope of employment of local hill people diminishes. During the last decade the state of Uttarakhand has sown a phenomenal progress in creating infrastructure for education and both the government and private sector have contributed significantly. This has provided ample opportunities to the people to acquire skills as per their aptitude and resource available Uttarakhand's literacy rate (http://des.uk.gov,in/files/statistical-Diary-2014-2015.pdf) at 78 per cent is higher than the national average of 73 per cent. The teacher to student ratio in primary section is 1:23 compared to the national figure of 1:41. Jobs availability could not match the supply of job seekers. In such a scenario the only escape is seeking white collar jobs in the NCR-Delhi where is there no dearth of such opportunities In 2015, the National Institute for Rural Development and Panchayat Raj (Hyderabad) conducted a survey and found that the top reason for migration was employment—47 per cent of migrants cited the lack of job opportunities in their home districts. Another 18 per cent have migrated anticipating better jobs in cities. This study further commented "The attraction to cities arising due to hardships of village life in hills such as poor transport connectivity, lack of water, inadequate medical facilities, poor facilities for higher education in some area and inaccessibility have further accelerated the process of migration of youth". Table 15.1 shows the number of migrants from the covered districts.

The severity of the situation can be gauged from the fact that 9 per cent of the villages of the state are virtually uninhabited. As per Census 2011, of Uttarakhand's 16,793 villages, 1,053 have no inhabitants and another 405 have a population of less than 10. The people moves in the hope of sustainable livelihood in the NCR-Delhi at the cost of comprising sustainably in the hilly regions. There are research findings establishing that the emigrants has brought prosperity to the state of origin. Internal

Table 15.1: Number of Families Migrated

District	*Number of Families*
Nanital	15075
Pithoragarh	22936
Tehri Garwal	33689
Chamoli	18536

Source: Census 2011.

migration has the potential for improving quality of life and reducing inequality in the state of origin. Bihar and Uttar Pradesh are the two states which have gained maximum dividends from migration. The emigrants from these two states have not only earned economic empowerment but have also created a pressure group. A unique feature of theses emigrants from these two states is that they continue to maintain a proper linkage with their respective states. The remittance from these people has influenced the state gross domestic capital formation. Inequality in land distribution in both these states have vastly diminished as the remittances are used to buy small landholdings in towns and semi-urban areas. This has influenced the pace of urbanisation in these two states as people move from rural areas to towns after acquiring land this establishes the fact migration has been able to promote sustainable livelihoods in the state of origin.

Paradox of Outmigration

The state of Uttarakhand presents a study in contrast on two counts. First, it is assumed that poverty and inequality entice people to other states where here are sustainable livelihoods. Secondly, the remittances have improved private asset ownership and hence state gross capital formation in the state of origin. Both Bihar and Uttar Pradesh are quintessential for this. On both these counts Uttarakhand shows dismal picture. The Uttarakhand state is second fastest growing in India. The real GDP grew at 13.7 per cent (CAGR) during the FY 2006-FY 2012. Its state gross state domestic product (GSDP) stood at 8.7 per cent in FY-16 higher than the all India GDP growth of 7.56 per cent. The state outlay for development in period between 2013-14 and 2015-16 is 50 per cent where for other states it is 49.4 per cent (*Indian Express*, March 13, 2017) The state has improved its rank and stands at 9 in ease of doing business. Secondly, those who migrate from states no longer maintain any linkage with the state and hence remittances are insignificant. During the visits to these households settled in NCR-Delhi a number of reasons were found for outmigration Table 15.2 shows the economic profile of emigrants from Uttarakhand.

Table 15.2: Education Profile of the Emigrants

Educational Qualification	*% of respondents*
Matriculate	10
Graduate	12
Technical Graduate	22
Vocational (Tourism and Pharmaceutical)	43
Post Graduate	13

Source: Field Survey.

Table 15.2 clearly reflects that skilled manpower comprises the bulk of out-migrants. These people have been benefited by state education infrastructure and then out-migrated. Table 15.3 shows the reasons for out-migration.

Table 15.3: Reasons for Outmigration

Reasons	*% of respondents*
Number employment opportunities	12
Underemployment	20
Higher salaries	22
Scope for advance learning and earning	24
Sibling have settled	15
Comfort and convenience	7

Source: Field Survey.

Table 15.3 shows that 24 per cent of respondents have out-migrated in the hope of earning high and at the same time for continuous learning as there is not much scope for advance learning and earning more and this is more apt in computer software and hardware. 22 per cent of respondents opined that within the same occupation if they move to the NCR-Delhi they will get higher salaries. This is found in school teachings where majority of migrants are employed. The figure of 12 per cent and 20 per cent for unemployment and underemployment shows that there is no dearth of employment opportunities in Uttarakhand. Most of the emigrants no longer maintain any contact with the state as they have permanently settled in the NCR-Delhi region. Table 15.4 shows the asset profile after out-migration.

Table 15.4: Asset Profile of Emigrants

Land and House ownership	*% of respondents*
Still owning agriculture land	23
Still owning house in state	13
Sold house in the state	12
Owning house and land in NCR-Delhi	42
Owning 2 to 3 houses in NCR-Delhi	10

Source: Field Survey.

Table 15.3 reflects that 42 per cent of respondents have been able to own their own house after migration. This they could do because of higher earnings and they feel safe and secure. Only 23 per cent own agriculture land. This also shows the land is non cultivable due to geographical terrain. 12 per cent of respondents disclosed that they could acquire land after disposing of their house in the state or they have sold out because no family member lives there.

Impact of Out-migration

In most of the State out-migration has given lots of dividends and which have been leveraged for creating sustainable livelihoods in the state of origin. In case of Uttarakhand out-migration has been counter-productive. Bihar and Uttar Pradesh are two states where internal remittances have been the major driver of growth in the state, the remittances in these two states have been fuelling demand and hence incentives to invest which has a multiplier effect on demand and opportunities for employments are created. The emigrants from Uttarakhand are no longer sending remittances. They do not maintain bank accounts in the state. This deprives the state from potential savings which could have channelized in investment. Out-migration has also made its impact on demand for goods and services in the hilly regions. Informal sector which is a major source of employment for rural people and semi skilled people no longer spreads or due to large supply of labour wages come down further reducing demand for goods and services. The other phenomenon which is by product of outmigration is that people from Nepal and Tibet have started settling in Uttarakhand. The State has achieved 97 per cent electrification of villages and 725 of villages are connected by *pucca* roads. The health and educational facilities are made available effectively even in the remotest corner of the state remotes. There is hardly any district in Uttarakhand which do not have separate settlement for these people. These migrants provide cheap labour in the informal sector further aggravating the declining wages situation. As most of these migrants have no scope of permanent settlement in Uttarakhand, they send remittances to their home state. Even strategically the out-migration compromises the security of the nation. After taking oath Uttarakhand CM T. S. Rawat commented: "Stopping migration is also necessary for our state given our geographical location as a border state. We need civilian population in border villages to ensure there is no Kargil-type situation." Besides once the state is infested with migrants who have long term affiliation with the state sustainability is compromised. Tourism and religion, the sources of employment and revenue have also suffered in the absence of local populace not involved or are indifferent. That is the reason that vast hidden potential in spiritual and leisure tourism has remained untapped till today. In the absence of gainful employment in informal sector the local who are unskilled and semi-skilled have to opt trading for survival. The towns and shops in Uttarakhand are full of shops selling daily need items. There are villages on the state highways where there are less than fifty households and every house on the main road have opened a shop selling daily needs items and eatables. They are disguised shopkeeper as rate of return is very low for the whole family.

Promoting Sustainable Livelihood through Agro-food Industry

Agro-Food sector is vital for food security, reducing inequality and enhancing sustainable livelihoods and hence a key to inclusive growth. Sustainable agro food sector in South Asia is important not only for the security of the livelihood of the people living in the region and downstream, but also for the sustainability of the mountain ecosystem (Upadhyay, 2008). Agro-Food sector being a value addition sector holds a lot of potential for promoting entrepreneurship at each stage of processing and for every class ranging from unskilled to semi-skilled and highly skilled technical manpower. The cumulative effects of employment at one stage will create opportunities in related field at other stages by many times. This industry will catalyze supplementary and complimentary tiny industry. Development of agro-food industry will leverage the resources available in forest, pastures, crops, horticulture and livestock. Promoting agro-food sector serves dual benefits—assured fair price and demand to cultivators and assured supply of hygienic food to the consumers.

Agro-Food Processing Sector: A Value Addition Venture

Adding value to any product creates both utility and employment. Food processing sectors has the potential to add value to intermediate goods at various stages before it reaches to final consumers. From sapling stage to harvesting, processing, packaging and delivery, there is value addition and employment generation for persons of varied skills. The income generated through value addition gets evenly distributed among persons involved at each stage and share depends upon skill required to do that job and availability of persons having that skill. The three stages of food processing, viz. primary, secondary and tertiary have enormous job potential and scale and magnitude in one stage has a multiplier effect on successive stages. The mechanism in three stages is a brilliant example of agriculture-industry interrelationship and interdependency. Food processing industry is a classic case, where the output of one sector becomes input for other and during this process basic employment (B) generation leads to non-basic employment (NB) generation in other related sectors [Total Employment (T) = B+NB]. According to MOFPI commissioned vision document for the industry—"The triple of size of industry is estimated to generate a direct employment of 0.28 crore and indirect employment of 0.74 crore persons.

Total Linkage Maximum

Prof. Hirschman in the theory of "Unbalanced Growth" recognised the inter-relation of different economic activities and suggests that such Industries should be taken up whose total linkage (combined effect of forward and backward linkage) is maximum. The forward and backward linkage effect is relatively high for food processing industry as compared to the other industry. The setting up of food processing units develops a source of raw material from farmhouses and farmers are assured of demand for their products and they will produce more quality food. There exists a vast potential to improve productivity in fruits as it is very low compare to other fruits producing states Uttarakhand has absolute advantage because of favourable climatic condition and fertile soil.

Scope and Challenges in Agro-food Industry

The vast natural resources and favourable agro climatic condition are very conducive for nurturing and promoting entrepreneurship in agro-food industry Table 15.5 shows Uttarakhand relative ranking in fruit production in India.

Table 15.5: Uttarakhand Ranking in India in Fruits Production

Rank	*Fruits*
1st	Pears, Peach, and Plum
2nd	Walnuts
3rd	Apple
10th	Cut Flower Cultivation

Source: Investor Portal, Government of Uttarakhand.

Besides, the state has highest production of spice at (7.2MT/ha) as against 1.80MT/ha of national average of. Livestock, Dairying, Poultry and Fisheries are the primary activities which have a tremendous potential in generating livelihoods at secondary and tertiary level. In all these sectors jobs can be created from different stages sapling, sowing, harvesting, transporting, storing, processing and packaging and above all marketing. Once the farmers are assured of demand around the year they will not hesitate to produce more. There is a vast scope of innovation at each stage for creating values. The state can be the source of supply of packaged food to the neighbouring state and even for export.

Conclusion

In a democratic country like India no legislation can proscribe the movement of people for quality livelihood. This is more apt when skilled people want to move to other areas to enhance their future prospects. Still the State can play an important role in nudging people to stay through development strategies or calling back people with experienced and resources to be used in the development of the state. It is a known fact that human resource is both a source of demand and capital formation. Government needs to make strenuous efforts to involve skilled manpower in the development process. Here in lies the need for incubating, nurturing and promoting entrepreneurship in the agro-food sector.

References

Adams, R.H. (1996). "The economic uses and impact of international remittances in rural Egypt", *Economic Development and Culture Change*, Vol. 39, November, 695-722.

Ghosh, B. (1992). "Migration-Development linkage: Some specific issues and practical policy measures", *International Migration*, Vol. xxx no. 3/4.

Mangain and Reddy (2015). *Outmigration from Hill Region of Uttarakhand: Magnitude, Challenges and Policy Options.*

Poros, Maritsa V. (1995). *Modern Migrations: Guajarati Indian Networks in New York & London.*

Raism, Acharya S. and Sharma, N. (2013). "Food Processing Industry in India S and T Capabilities, Skills and Employment Opportunities." *J Food Technology.*

Srivastava, Ravi (2011). *Internal Migration in India: An Overview of its Features, Trends and Policy Challenges*, Paper presented at UNESCO-UNICEF National workshop on Internal Migration and Human Development in India 6-7 December, 2011 Niscel.

Hein de Haas (2007). *Remittances, Migration and Social Development: A Conceptual Review of Literature.*

Stark, O. (1991). *The Migration of Labour*, Cambridge Mass, Harvard University Review.

Upadhya, H.K. (2008). *Economic Policies for Sustainable Land Use in HKH Region in securing Sustainable Livelihood in the Hindu-Kush-Himalaya, Direction for Future Research: Development and Cooperation* (ed.) Gyanmatish ICIMOD.

16
Fiscal Governance and Resources for Development in the Hilly States of India

Subrata Dutta

Introduction

Developing countries often face resource constraint and foreign exchange constraint to sustain growth. These constraints can limit investments (Stiglitz *et al.*, 2006: 54-55).[1] During the last two decades India has been able to accumulate substantial amount of foreign exchange reserves by liberalising its economy. But, scholar like Patnaik (2004: 5565) cautions, reminding us about what happened in East and South-East Asian countries, that most of it is short-term speculative capital inflow which should not be used for long-term investment, e.g. in infrastructure, since sudden outflow of such capital caused by some real reason or speculation, can create "a massive liquidity crisis". In this context, Chandrasekhar (2008) notes that "unlike China which earns a significant share of its reserves by exporting more than it imports, India either borrows or depends on foreign portfolio and direct investors to accumulate reserves. Its surplus foreign exchange is not earned, but reflects a liability."[2] But, what happens when India really runs current account surplus? As *EPW* editorial (2005) has noted, in the first half of the last decade (2001-02 to 2003-04) India had had a current account surplus on its balance of payments (implying exports greater than imports) whereas it has simultaneously experienced capital exports (implying an investment of part of its reserves in foreign countries). This indicates unreliability of such surplus in open economy as far as domestic asset/infrastructure creation or domestic capital formation is concerned. Thus, domestic saving assumes enormous significance as far as further investment in infrastructure is concerned. Especially, investment in rural infrastructure is the need of the hour in order to alter income distribution patterns. Public investment could channelize investible resources to sectors short of capital (such as agriculture/irrigation and other rural infrastructure), thereby creating an atmosphere conducive to inducement of private investment in agriculture and industry in rural districts (Mazumdar, 2008). Mazumdar found that while the organised manufacturing sector has experienced an enhanced capital formation process (greater investment) during the liberalised era, "the output structure has increasingly moved in favour of services in response to the demand expansion pattern" (p. 75). Thus, he suggests that investment in agriculture and (rural) infrastructure could both absorb capital and expand the market for manufactured products. The fallacy that manifests in this proposition is that the author has himself found an investment bias of the private capital towards the organised, corporate manufacturing sector. Diversion of this investment towards irrigation or other rural infrastructure is thought to be an extremely difficult task. Government savings may be considered to be the suitable alternative to fill up the void in rural infrastructure investment. But, India's public savings, as Shome (2006) argued, did not perform well while private savings—in particular household savings—experienced phenomenal growth. Total gross domestic savings as percentage of GDP rose continuously from about 10 per cent in 1950-55 to around 30 per cent in the last decade. This rise in private savings did not reflect upon rural investment as it has also been indicated in Mazumdar's (2008) study. Further risk in this regard draws attention of many scholars when private savings rate tends to fall, as it happened in the year 2008-09 (Government of India, 2011).[3] Rangarajan and Srivastava (2005) raise concern over the issue, arguing that if the reduction in government saving is not fully offset by a rise in private saving then the ultimate effect is the fall in overall saving rate, which will have detrimental effect on growth. However, at this point of debate, scholars of different views (e.g. Patnaik, 2004) favoured public investment in rural infrastructure through borrowing, not by generating savings, as saving in revenue account is often expected to cause shrinkage in social sector spending or development expenditure (*see* also Amiya K. Bagchi, 2004). Amaresh Bagchi (2006), however, argues that a level of fiscal responsibility or discipline should be maintained by the governments—not through the means of expenditure cut in the development sector, but through raising additional revenues from various untapped sources (e.g. agricultural income, purely cotton-based textiles etc.) and by empowering local bodies to generate own revenues.[4] Let us now extend the discussion in the light of the debate concerning government saving *versus* government borrowing.

Government Saving *Versus* Government Dissaving: The Debate

Economists generally do not disagree with the view that government should afford deficits and thus stimulate demand through greater expenditure (to compensate the shortfall in aggregate demand) while in slump, but should run surpluses to check inflation caused by excess demand while in boom (when output demanded is greater than its full employment level). In demand deficient economies, as Rakshit (2005: 3444) asserts, it is higher expenditure (even at the risk of higher borrowing) "which drives saving and growth, not the other way round." On the other hand, Rakshit (2006) also points out the supply-side shocks such as variations in monsoon or oil prices that are often important determinants of economic cycles. The cyclical components would involve variations in public investments *via* decisions on borrowing. However, Govinda Rao (2009) argues that when there are long-term deficit trends, the problem manifests as structural rather than cyclical. Let us give an example. Rajasthan went through revenue deficits continuously for about one-and-a-half decades, starting from 1992-93 to 2005-06. This cannot be characterised as cyclical feature; rather it reflects a robust structural feature of revenue deficit. Adopting a strategy of maintaining revenue deficit for long-term—irrespective of business cycle—to make the economy demand-driven may not always be straightway correct. If greater problems arise from the supply side rather than the demand side, then higher public spending through revenue account (often creating higher revenue deficit) might be counter-productive as this would result in higher inflation by stimulating demand. Supply-side problems cannot be addressed by demand-side remedies. The former entails higher level of public investment, especially in those areas (e.g. backward rural areas) which have drawn less attention of private investment and have been trapped in supply-side bottlenecks. Hence, surplus in revenue account may result in creation of greater or improved infrastructure induced by higher public investment through capital outlay. Furthermore, this may help in keeping a check on the fiscal deficit as well.

There has been long-standing debate concerning propositions of savings-driven growth and deficit-financing-driven growth. As far as the fiscal measures with a view to achieving higher growth are concerned, the former seeks to address the supply side bottlenecks (for example, power cuts, lack of good roads, inadequate transport systems, shortage of specific inputs etc.) whereas the latter emphasizes the demand stimulants in a demand deficient (i.e. low purchasing power) economy. In this connection, the neo-classical approach, as sternly reflected through the reports of the Twelfth Finance Commission (TFC), is said to have a primary focus on the reduction of unsustainable debt by the means of reducing fiscal deficit (thus, leading to less borrowing) that would further help in eliminating revenue deficit (through reduction in interest payments) or even in generating revenue surplus (thus, producing 'savings') that would finally be 'invested' (through capital outlay, the falling rate of which had worried many scholars) in tangible asset creation (Government of India, 2004). Thus, (public) saving turns into investment and provides, at least partially (since private investment contributes the rest), the impetus to growth, without allowing uncontrollable rise in public debt and consequent servicing costs (Srivastava, 2006). A brief schematic presentation is given in Chart 16.1 on expected negative as well as positive impacts of fiscal deficit.

The perpetrators of the Eleventh Five-Year Plan found it problematic to deal with government savings (i.e. removal of revenue deficit) since, as they explained, "the grant component of transfers from the Centre to the States is revenue expenditure" (Government of India, 2008: 50). Similarly, it is the same for the transfers from the states to the local bodies. Thus, the Eleventh Five-Year Plan Approach Paper cautioned that elimination of revenue deficit "will limit the extent and pace of devolution" to the rural and urban local bodies (Government of India, 2006: 69). However, at this point of debate, Rakshit (2005: 3443) argues that while both supply constraints and demand deficiency do coexist in low income regions, there is a need to adopt an "intertwining" approach. Rakshit (2006: 4551) shows the way, saying that although "there is not much scope of reducing public consumption expenditure" (i.e. revenue expenditure), cutbacks in various forms of subsidies, in his opinion, may be allowed since much of them are enjoyed by the rich. However, he emphatically cautioned us about the negative welfare implications of eliminating revenue deficit and reducing fiscal deficit in the public budget, since such measures are supposed to scale down overall welfare through reducing economy's consumption, saving, investment and the subsequent growth effects. During recession, governments (Centre and States) had to increase their overall expenditures to add on to aggregate demand and

Expected positive impact of high fiscal deficit	***Expected negative impact of high fiscal deficit***
High fiscal deficit ⇩ Higher public expenditure ⇩ Higher private demand ⇩ Higher GDP ⇩ Higher revenue receipt ⇩ Higher public expenditure again	High fiscal deficit ⇩ Greater borrowing ⇩ Greater interest payment ⇩ Higher revenue expenditure ⇩ Shrinkage in capital outlay ⇩ Development of physical infrastructure is compromised (underdeveloped regions get adversely affected) ⇩ Low level of economic activity, especially in the backward region ⇩ Low revenue in public exchequer ⇩ Higher deficit again ⇩ Higher borrowing again ⇩ Unsustainable debt accumulation/Debt trap

Chart 16.1: Expected Positive and Negative Impacts of High Fiscal Deficit

also to boost private demand (Table 16.1 briefly presents fiscal situations/ strategies—before, during and after the recession). However, there is a need to take a stock of the fiscal trends of the States with respect to fiscal deficit, capital outlay, outstanding liabilities, interest payment, non-development revenue expenditure, and development revenue expenditure, as it is often argued that there are serial links between them (Rangarajan and Srivastava, 2005).

Table 16.1: Fiscal Situations/Strategies—Before, During and After the Recession

Before 2005-06	*In and around 2005-06 (adoption of fiscal consolidation)*	*From 2005-06 till economic slowdown*	*2008*	*Post 2008-09*
High revenue as well as fiscal deficits; unsustainable debt	Fiscal Responsibility and Budget Management (FRBM) enactment*	Deficit reduction exercises undertaken and maintainned	Beginning of world-wide recession; FRBM amended (i.e. time-frames revised)#	Reinstatement of fiscal reforms within the revised time frames

Notes: * This enactment entailed the governments to meet the deficit reduction targets (revenue deficit to be zero by 2008-09 and fiscal deficit to gradually come down to 3 per cent of GSDP), among others, as specified by the TFC.

For some well-performing states, time for both the deficits has been extended till 2011-12; and for others the time limits are 2013-14 and 2014-15 for fiscal deficit and revenue deficit, respectively. For further details, see RBI (2011: 36).

Surplus Revenue, Fiscal Deficit and Capital Outlay

As shown by Govinda Rao (2009) and Chakraborty (2009), aggregate revenue deficit of all states as percentage of their aggregate GSDP (gross 'state' domestic product) started consistently declining from 2002-03, and surplus in revenue account started getting generated since 2006-07. This has resulted in the decline in the ratio of gross fiscal deficit (GFD)-to-GSDP on the one hand and raised the ratio of capital outlay-to-GSDP on the other. More importantly, in the case of the non-special category states, the average GFD/GSDP ratio is observed to remain lower than the average capital outlay-to-GSDP ratio for the consecutive three years (from 2006-07 to 2008-09) (see Fig. 16.1). Especially, remarkable improvements are seen in the two consecutive years, i.e. 2006-07 and 2007-08, after which the average ratio of GFD-to-GSDP started rising again as a response to the global economic downturn. And, interestingly, average ratio of capital outlay-to-GSDP started falling simultaneously. Such inverse relationship between these two ratios is again evident in 2010-11 (BE) as against the previous year. It is worth mentioning here that the average GFD/GSDP ratio for the non-special category states has experienced continuous downward trends from 5.31 per cent in 2003-04 to 2.30 per

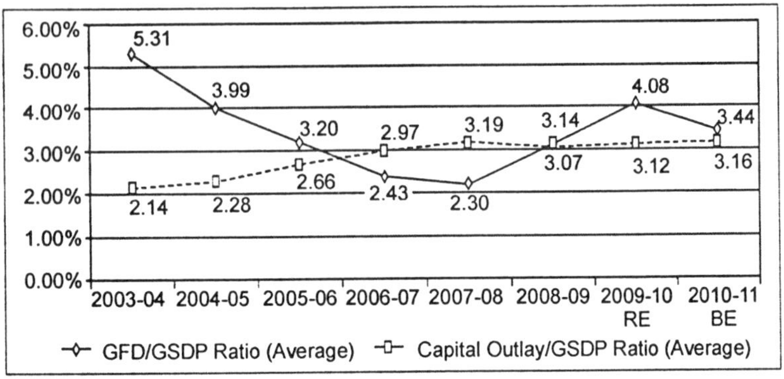

Fig. 16.1: Average GFD/GSDP Ratio and Average Capital Outlay/GSDP Ratio (Non-special Category States)

Notes: RE = revised estimate; BE = budget estimate

Source: Estimated from the Reserve Bank of India (RBI) budget data and the Central Statistical Organisation (CSO) GSDP data.

cent in 2007-08, showcasing a reduction by 3 percentage points. This observation receives support from that of Govinda Rao (2009: 81) as well. Moreover, for the two consecutive fiscal years—i.e. 2006-07 and 2007-08—the ratio remained below the 3 per cent level (according to the TFC as well as the FRBM rule, the GFD/GSDP ratio should not rise beyond the 3 per cent level). The ratio of capital outlay-to-GSDP went up by 1.05 percentage points during 2003-04 to 2007-08. However, more importantly, capital outlay/GSDP ratio (non-special category average) is found to be much higher than the GFD/GSDP ratio (non-special category average) for the two consecutive years, i.e. for 2006-07 and 2007-08 (and marginally higher in 2008-09). Thus, the positive impact of generating surplus fund in revenue account is clearly evident. This finding receives further empirical support when we look at Table 16.2.

In Table 16.2, a comparison has been drawn of the proportional shares of different components of GFD between 2003-04 and 2007-08. The rationale for selecting these two fiscal years is that the former precedes the enactment of the FRBM while the latter is expected to manifest as the latest outcome of the fiscal consolidation policies just prior to (or just at the beginning of) the recession. Additionally, we have presented the absolute values of the GFD components in parentheses as well. The 2007-08 figures as compared to that of 2003-04 would help us understand better the contribution of the surplus revenue in capital outlay. As regards special category states, seven out of eleven states were found to be revenue

Table 16.2: Revenue Deficit, Capital Outlay, Net Lending and Non-debt Capital Receipt as Percentage of GFD, 2003-04 and 2007-08

	2003-04				*2007-08*				
	Revenue Deficit	*Capital Outlay*	*Net Lending*	*Gross Fiscal Deficit*	*Revenue Deficit*	*Capital Outlay*	*Net Lending*	*Non-debt Capital Receipt*	*Gross Fiscal Deficit*
1	2	3	4	5 = [2+3+4]	6	7	8	9	10 = [6+7+8-9]
Arunachal Pradesh	-73.60	173.20	0.40	100	-4,953.33	4,846.67	6.67	0	(-)100
	(-184)	(433)	1)	(250)	(-743)	(727)	(1)		(-15)
Assam	49.14	44.62	6.24	100	-326.71	213.67	13.04	0	(-)100
	(685)	(622)	(87)	(1394)	(-2,581)	(1,688)	(103)		(-790)
Himachal Pradesh	67.41	32.93	-0.34	100	-153.99	255.98	-2.17	0	100
	(1,607)	(785)	(-8)	(2,384)	(-850)	(1,413)	(-12)		(552)
Jammu and Kashmir	-11,235.29	10,817.65	317.65	(-)100	-84.94	183.40	1.49	0	100
	(-1,910)	(1,839)	(54)	(-17)	(-2,216)	(4,785)	(39)		(2,609)
Manipur	15.44	84.21	0.35	100	-1,192.16	1,086.27	5.88	0	(-)100
	(44)	(240)	(1)	(286)	(-1,216)	(1,108)	(6)		(-102)
Meghalaya	-42.08	116.34	25.74	100	-87.85	183.18	4.67	0	100
	(-85)	(235)	(52)	(202)	(-188)	(392)	(10)		(214)
Mizoram	-27.12	121.57	5.56	100	-33.42	138.78	-5.36	0	100
	(-83)	(372)	(17)	(306)	(-131)	(544)	(-21)		(392)
Nagaland	-346.20	247.47	-1.27	(-)100	-106.80	206.80	0	0	100
	(-547)	(391)	(-2)	(-157)	(-424)	(821)			(397)
Sikkim	-320.00	422.00	-2.00	100	-548.44	648.44	0	0	100
	(-160)	(211)	(-1)	(50)	(-351)	(415)			(64)

(Contd.)

Table 16.2: *(Contd.)*

1	2	3	4	5 = [2+3+4]	6	7	8	9	10 = [6+7+8-9]
Tripura	-31.09	130.50	0.59	100	-5,317.65	5,435.29	-17.65	0	100
	(-106)	(445)	(2)	(341)	(-904)	(924)	(-3)		(17)
Uttarakhand	54.09	37.88	8.03	100	-36.57	128.30	8.27	0	100
	(761)	(533)	(113)	(1,407)	(-637)	(2,235)	(144)		(1,742)

Notes: (1) Figures in parentheses are expressed as Rupees in crore at current price; (2) Figures with negative sign (-) indicate surplus/saving. Note that there are several 100s with negative sign in columns 5 and 10. For simple arithmetic reason, this sign has been attached to them, meaning only 'gross fiscal surplus' (rather than deficit) and nothing else; (3) Figures for Jammu and Kashmir and Jharkhand for the years 2003-04 and 2007-08 relate to revised estimates (RE). Figures for Bihar in 2003-04 relate to RE.

Source: RBI Publication entitled *State Finances: A Study of Budgets (2005-06 and 2009-10).*

surplus states in 2003-04 (the seven states include Arunachal Pradesh, Jammu and Kashmir, Meghalaya, Mizoram, Nagaland, Sikkim and Tripura) whereas in 2007-08 all states have been found to be in surplus group.[5] Especially, Tripura, Arunachal Pradesh and Manipur have made extraordinary performance in terms of generating revenue surplus.

Let us now look back at Figure 16.1 where we presented average GFD/GSDP ratio and average capital outlay/GSDP ratio (both the ratios for the non-special category states), and conclude our earlier discussion. If we look at the two fiscal years, i.e. 2008-09 and 2009-10 (RE), the effects of economic slump become evident. Both the ratios have been adversely affected during the economic slowdown. The GFD/GSDP ratio surpassed the 3 per cent level—i.e. its upper limit—in 2008-09 and further shot up to 4.08 per cent in 2009-10 (RE). The capital outlay/GSDP ratio has also been adversely affected in 2008-09. However, both the ratios show improvements in 2010-11 (BE), implicating recovery from economic downturn.

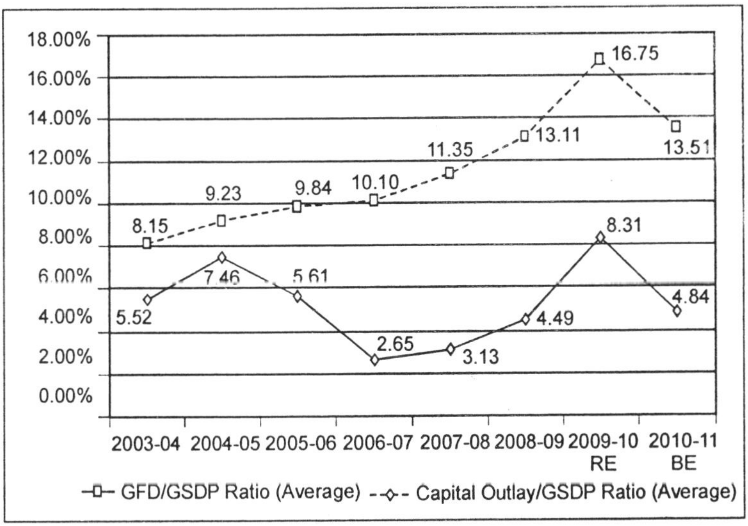

Fig. 16.2: Average GFD/GSDP ratio and average capital outlay/GSDP ratio (special category states)

Note: RE = revised estimate; BE = budget estimate

Source: Estimated from the RBI budget data and the CSO GSDP data.

Let us now take a look at the special category states (*see* Fig. 16.2). Prior to 2005-06, high average GFD/GSDP ratio had been a concern of worry (e.g. 7.46 per cent in 2004-05). Fiscal consolidation strategies resulted in remarkable improvement by bringing the average GFD/GSDP ratio down to 2.65 per cent in 2006-07. But, just in the immediate following year it again rose above the 3 per cent level (the upper limit as set by the TFC), and by 2009-10 (RE) it shot up to 8.31 per cent, which is an alarmingly high level. During the economic slowdown several governments found it difficult to afford savings and therefore, some state governments had to revert back to dissaving to sustain their consumption expenditure with a view to making an effort to stimulate individual demand during the slump. However, further improvement of the fiscal situation is called for. The average GFD/GSDP ratio in 2010-11 (BE) shows significant improvement, but mainly at the cost of the average ratio of capital outlay-to-GSDP. In addition to all this, one finding deserves due attention as far as the special category states are concerned. The average GFD/GSDP ratio is not seen to be higher than the average ratio of capital outlay-to-GSDP even for a single year in the study period, implying the fact that surplus revenue of the special category states have been consistently contributing to their capital outlay, and this becomes evident when we look at Table 16.5 and see the difference between the average ratio of capital outlay-to-GSDP for all the special category states and that for all the non-special category states in each year. But, are we drawing a perfect conclusion about the special category states? See the "End Note 5" of this article, which explains that higher devolution and transfers from the Central Government have largely contributed to the fiscal corrections for the special category states. This is the reason why special category states are separately considered when some analysis on such topics is undertaken.

However, in this connection, there is a need to examine the trends of individual states that belong to both the non-special and special categories. Before doing so, for a brief appraisal of the states in terms of the saving/dissaving status (revenue account) during the post-recession period, let us take a look at Table 16.3. In terms of the two years' status (i.e. after the recession hit the economy in 2008), Type D states are seen to be facing challenges in generating surplus in their revenue account.

Analysis of Trends of GFD/GSDP Ratio of Individual States

Table 16.4 gives us an estimate of the GFD/GSDP ratio for the individual states in the hilly region. The states which were in bad shape in 2003-04 include Arunachal Pradesh, Himachal Pradesh, Manipur, Mizoram, and Uttarakhand. Only in the case of Mizoram, the trends from 2003-04 to

Table 16.3: Saving/Dissaving Status of the States During the Post-recession Period

Type A Saving in both 2009-10 (RE) and 2010-11 (BE)	*Type B* Saving in 2009-10 (RE), but dissaving in 2010-11 (BE)	*Type C* Dissaving in 2009-10 (RE), but saving in 2010-11 (BE)	*Type D* Dissaving in both 2009-10 (RE) and 2010-11 (BE)
Jammu & Kashmir, Manipur, Arunachal Pradesh, Meghalaya, Mizoram, Nagaland, Sikkim, and Tripura	None	Uttarakhand	Assam and Himachal Pradesh

Note: West Bengal and Sikkim have enacted the FRBM legislation just recently, i.e. in the Fiscal Year of 2010-11.

2010-11 (BE) do not suggest us to make any conclusive remarks (due to its highly volatile trends), but the other four states are seen to have affirmatively responded to the fiscal restructuring efforts. Tripura's trends look similar to that of these four states. However, the effects of economic downturn are also evident from the trends. Also, by and large, similar trends are seen in the cases of Assam, Meghalaya, and Sikkim. Nagaland was in surplus position in 2003-04, but could not reach a similar position once again later on (in 2006-07 its position was reasonably good though). Jammu and Kashmir does not seem to be responsive either to the fiscal correction measures or to the economic downturn.

Table 16.4: GFD/GSDP Ratio—Performance of Individual States

	2003-04	*2004-05*	*2005-06*	*2006-07*	*2007-08*	*2008-09*	*2009-10 (RE)*	*2010-11 (BE)*
Arunachal Pradesh	10.56	13.53	8.77	-3.11	-0.41	7.27	3.79	1.86
Assam	2.95	3.92	-0.62	-1.10	-1.10	-1.78	11.45	9.46
Himachal Pradesh	11.51	7.85	2.80	3.22	1.71	6.17	5.42	5.08
Jammu & Kashmir	-0.08	4.15	5.98	5.03	8.21	6.68	5.81	4.63
Manipur	7.19	9.83	5.35	8.79	-1.74	3.42	4.76	3.48
Meghalaya	3.83	5.39	2.78	1.02	2.53	4.53	5.60	2.99
Mizoram	13.16	9.53	14.59	6.38	11.86	2.47	9.05	0.88
Nagaland	-3.26	4.24	5.57	2.61	5.52	4.83	12.12	3.54
Sikkim	3.50	11.61	8.14	4.76	2.79	8.96	11.97	10.87
Tripura	4.52	2.89	1.17	-1.27	0.16	2.28	13.21	7.18
Uttarakhand	6.88	9.15	7.17	2.82	4.89	4.58	8.28	3.26
Special category average	**5.52**	**7.46**	**5.61**	**2.65**	**3.13**	**4.49**	**8.31**	**4.84**
All states average	**5.39**	**5.35**	**4.15**	**2.51**	**2.63**	**3.63**	**5.74**	**3.99**

Note: RE = revised estimate; BE = budget estimate

Source: Estimated from the RBI budget data and the CSO GSDP data.

Trends of Capital Outlay/GSDP Ratio of Individual States

Let us take a look at the trends of ratio of capital outlay-to-GSDP for each state as illustrated in Table 16.5. The states that have shown consistency in remaining above the average of the hilly states are Arunachal Pradesh, Sikkim, Jammu & Kashmir, Manipur (except for 2003-04), and Mizoram (until 2007-08). The states which need considerable improvements when compared to the hilly states average in each year are Assam, Himachal Pradesh, Meghalaya, and Uttarakhand. By and large, Tripura has shown gradual improvements, but, however, it has not been successful in lifting its position above the average during the study period. As a whole, Nagaland does not display a poor situation; especially after 2005-06 it has been able to maintain above average position (except for 2008-09).

Table 16.5: Capital Outlay/GSDP Ratio—Performance of Individual States

	2003-04	*2004-05*	*2005-06*	*2006-07*	*2007-08*	*2008-09*	*2009-10 (RE)*	*2010-11 (BE)*
Arunachal Pradesh	18.30	13.14	15.00	17.16	18.70	28.43	35.96	30.81
Assam	1.31	4.15	1.88	2.26	2.36	3.00	5.35	3.36
Himachal Pradesh	3.79	2.84	3.20	3.88	4.39	5.63	4.99	3.67
Jammu and Kashmir	8.29	10.45	12.67	11.47	15.05	16.23	17.27	16.70
Manipur	6.04	11.41	12.16	16.05	18.95	23.13	27.37	21.75
Meghalaya	4.46	4.23	4.02	4.37	4.62	5.53	7.40	5.52
Mizoram	15.99	13.42	16.59	15.57	16.47	11.58	15.19	8.12
Nagaland	8.13	7.38	9.43	11.88	11.41	12.09	17.32	15.37
Sikkim	14.79	22.07	18.89	16.01	18.08	23.44	32.67	26.76
Tripura	5.89	7.67	7.93	7.00	8.54	10.16	14.63	12.78
Uttarakhand	2.61	4.75	6.51	5.42	6.28	5.01	6.11	3.74
Special Category Average	**8.15**	**9.23**	**9.84**	**10.10**	**11.35**	**13.11**	**16.75**	**13.51**
All states average	**4.50**	**5.01**	**5.48**	**5.77**	**6.39**	**7.06**	**8.47**	**7.22**

Note: RE = revised estimate; BE = budget estimate.
Source: Estimated from the RBI budget data and the CSO GSDP data.

Outstanding Liabilities of States

The question as to whether the FRBM measures have had any favourable impact on the debt burden of the states can be examined from the trends presented in Figure 16.2. It is crystal clear that all the three curves—i.e. average debt/GSDP ratio of the non-special category states, average debt/GSDP ratio of the special category states, and average debt/GSDP ratio of all states—fell sharply in 2006-07 as against 2005-06. Taking the two point-of-time figures between 2005-06 and 2010-11 (BE), we observe that the average debt/GSDP ratios for the non-special category states and special category states have fallen by 7.7 percentage points and 6.1 percentage points, respectively. However, after 2005-06, the performance of the general category states has remained more consistent than that of the special category states (*see* Figure 16.3). This is because the latter experienced higher trends during 2007-08 to 2009-10 (RE) as against the 2006-07 level, which is not the case for the non-special category states. In general, as we observe, the average debt/GSDP ratio for the special category states in each year is very high as compared to that of the non-special category states. This is a phenomenon which is worrisome for the special category states. For example, in 2010-11 (BE) the average debt/GSDP ratio for the special category states is higher than that of the non-special category states by 27 percentage points.

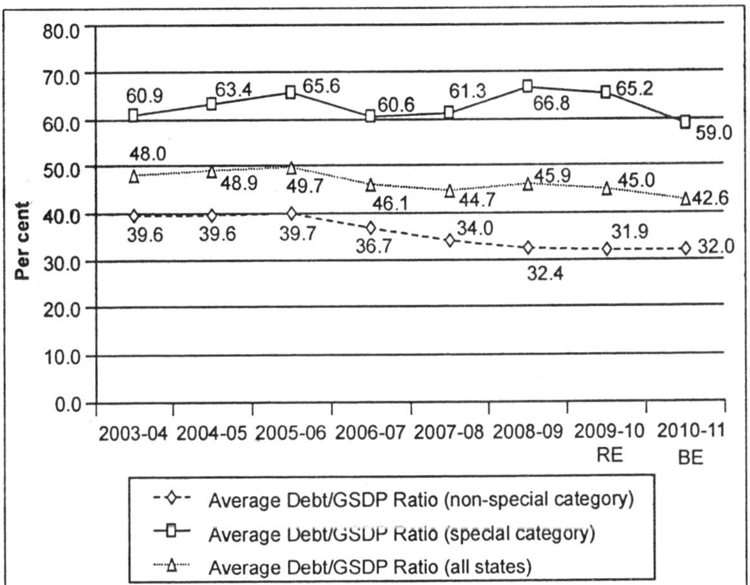

Fig. 16.3: Trends of Average Debt/GSDP Ratio

Note: RE = revised estimate; BE – budget estimate
Source: RBI (2011), p. 153.

Now, we will take a look at the individual mountain states (Table 16.6). A number of hilly states are in very poor condition in terms of debt/GSDP ratio (Table 16.6). Mizoram's total liability has been even found to be more than its GSDP for consecutive seven years in the last one decade. Arunachal Pradesh's situation has worsened rapidly and it has recorded its debt/GSDP ratio to be more than 100 per cent for two years—2008-09 and 2009-10 (RE). Only Assam has been consistently improving its position after 2003-04. However, by and large, some favourable impacts of fiscal consolidation are seen in the cases of Himachal Pradesh, Manipur, Tripura, and Uttarakhand.

In this regard, we should keep in mind that, according to the TFC, the long-term goal for the states (and for the Centre as well) for the debt/GSDP ratio should be 28 per cent. On this note, except Assam, all other states are found to be in uncomfortable situation.

Table 16.6: Trends of Debt/GSDP Ratio—Performance of Individual States

State	*2001-02*	*2002-03*	*2003-04*	*2004-05*	*2005-06*	*2006-07*	*2007-08*	*2008-09*	*2009-10 (RE)*	*2010-11 (BE)*
Arunachal Pradesh	37.5	46.6	73.3	72.5	82.7	69.7	77.0	130.6	115.9	77.8
Assam	31.3	30.2	33.2	32.4	31.8	30.6	28.7	28.8	28.0	27.8
Himachal Pradesh	58.6	64.7	69.4	71.5	67.7	63.4	60.5	59.3	55.7	53.2
Jammu & Kashmir	53.4	51.8	66.4	65.4	69.4	67.8	69.5	72.0	70.1	67.1
Manipur	55.5	53.9	61.4	70.9	80.2	78.3	79.4	77.0	77.4	66.3
Meghalaya	34.1	38.2	40.2	41.5	41.3	40.5	42.3	38.5	37.3	36.2
Mizoram	88.0	90.8	112.1	119.0	115.9	111.9	119.5	108.9	109.1	98.1
Nagaland	45.2	50.9	47.4	49.3	53.0	50.5	49.7	59.3	59.4	58.0
Sikkim	81.8	77.5	70.6	71.8	70.5	68.1	72.5	77.3	80.6	82.2
Tripura	44.2	48.7	53.7	58.5	57.1	45.0	40.4	39.8	42.2	43.2
Uttarakhand	31.7	34.0	40.5	42.7	45.9	44.8	41.2	42.8	41.1	39.5

Note: RE = revised estimate; BE = budget estimate
Source: RBI (2011), p. 153.

Interest Payment *vis-à-vis* Non-development as well as Development Revenue Expenditures

A decrease in interest payment (IP) will result in a decrease in non-development revenue expenditure (NDRE) (since the former is a part of the latter)[6] if the sizes of other outlets within NDRE remain unchanged. This will leave a scope for greater contribution to development revenue expenditure (DRE) if the size of available funds for total revenue expenditure does not reduce. As regards the non-special category states, the trends of average NDRE/GSDP ratio, the trends of average DRE/GSDP ratio, and the trends of average IP/GSDP ratio are presented in Figure

16.4. The average IP/GSDP ratio has not experienced a rise even for a single year from 2003-04 till 2010-11 (BE). This has had a favourable impact on NDRE/GSDP ratio, which has shown decreasing trends till 2008-09. For the latest two years, it has been on the rise again, indicating the increase of other components of NDRE. However, the downward trend in NDRE/GSDP ratio, as stated above, has left some scope for the DRE/GSDP ratio to rise. In this connection, we observe an inverse linkage between the average NDRE/GSDP ratio and the average DRE/GSDP ratio in Figure 16.4, except for the year 2009-10 (RE). The most favourable situation occurred during 2005-06 to 2008-09 when the former uninterruptedly went down and, in response, the latter went up. But, the exception of 2009-10 shows that such (an inverse) relationship may not always take place due to certain reasons and this needs further elaboration. As observed by some researchers (e.g. Chakraborty and Bhadra, 2010), the sudden spurt in overall revenue expenditure in and after 2008-09 was due to the hike in salary based on the recommendation of the Sixth Pay Commission. Moreover, many States announced stimulus packages to counter recessionary effects, though the quantum of packages remained unspecified except for a few states such as Kerala, Haryana, and West Bengal (Chakraborty and Bhadra, 2010). However, for the special category states too, similar explanations (i.e. combined effects of Pay Commission and stimulus package) are applicable for the sudden steep rise in NDRE/GSDP ratio as well as DRE/GSDP ratio in 2009-10 (RE) (see Figure 16.5).

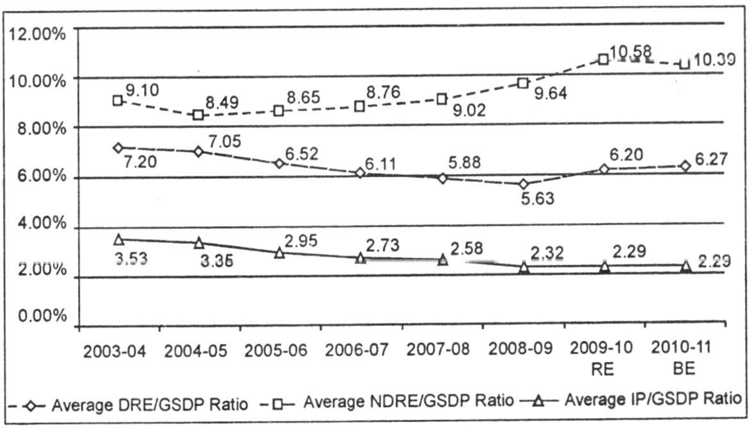

Fig. 16.4: Average IP/GSDP Ratio, Average NDRE/GSDP Ratio and Average DRE/GSDP Ratio (Non-special Category States)

Note: RE = revised estimate; BE = budget estimate

Source: Estimated from the RBI budget data and the CSO GSDP data.

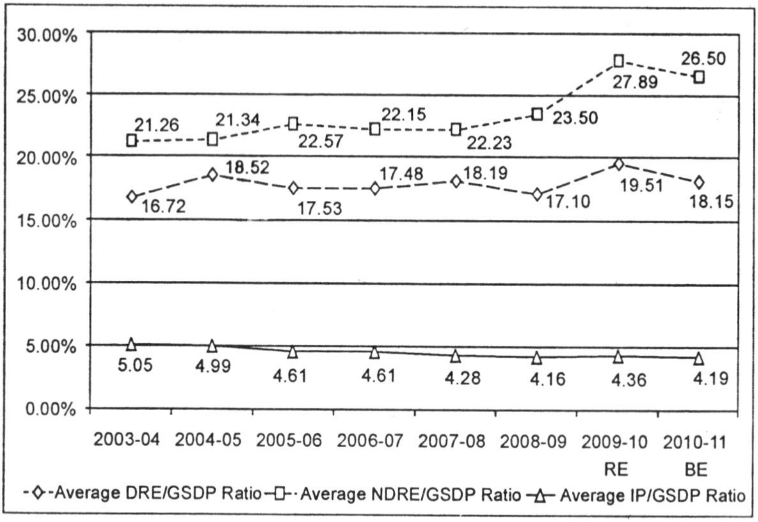

Fig. 16.5: Average IP/GSDP Ratio, Average NDRE/GSDP Ratio and Average DRE/GSDP Ratio (Special Category States)

Note: RE = revised estimate; BE = budget estimate.

Source: Estimated from the RBI budget data and the CSO GSDP data.

As far as the special category states are concerned, the average IP/GSDP ratio (the curve at the bottom in Figure 16.5) shows overall downward trends till 2008-09. This might have helped the average NDRE/GSDP ratio to remain below its 2004-05 level for the succeeding four years (i.e. from 2005-06 to 2008-09).[7] The average DRE/GSDP ratio (the curve at the top) displays by and large upward trends (though the levels in 2006-07 and 2007-08 are lower than that of 2005-06 and then the ratio fell again in 2010-11 BE against its 2009-10 RE level). During the span of 2004-05 to 2008-09, the inverse relationship between non-development and development expenditures are *only* observed at two points in time—i.e. in 2005-06 and 2008-09. Note that the relationships between the three ratios are not as consistent as found in general category states. The inconsistency first started with the fact that the NDRE/GSDP ratio did not respond favourably to the declining trends in IP/GSDP ratio. In this respect, let us keep in mind that the special category states are "special" from various perspectives and thus are very different from the general category states (see the end note 5 again). As we have already seen in the "End Note 5" of this article that on revenue side they receive high amount of devolution and transfers from the central government as compared to the general category states. Similarly, on expenditure side, they perhaps often found it hard to compress their NDRE, even when they were not in uncomfortable position in terms of their IP/GSDP ratio. Apart from interest payments, there remained some other elements in the basket of non-development revenue budget (under the broad classification of 'general services'), which did also have *strong* influence on the trends of the NDRE/GSDP ratio for the special category states. Especially, as often argued, increasing security-related expenditure has crucially constricted available levels of development finance with the various state governments of the North-Eastern region.

Trends of IP/GSDP Ratio of Individual States

If we look at the IP/GSDP ratio for the individual states (Table 16.7), Sikkim displays the poorest position (i.e. highest percentage), among all, followed by Jammu & Kashmir and Mizoram, respectively, in 2010-11 (BE). Except for 2007-08 and 2010-11 (BE), Mizoram has retained the poorest position all through the study period, whereas Assam, Meghalaya, and Uttarakhand demonstrated extraordinary performance by keeping their IP/GSDP ratio lower than the *all states average* (which is further a bit lower than the special category average) in each year during 2003-04

Table 16.8: Interest Payment as Percentage of GSDP—Performance of Individual States

	2003-04	*2004-05*	*2005-06*	*2006-07*	*2007-08*	*2008-09*	*2009-10 (RE)*	*2010-11 (BE)*
Arunachal Pradesh	6.00	5.15	5.35	5.51	3.99	4.76	4.78	4.51
Assam	3.06	2.67	2.61	2.35	2.11	2.01	2.42	2.44
Himachal Pradesh	7.11	7.11	6.09	5.84	5.29	5.13	4.69	4.65
Jammu and Kashmir	4.96	4.84	4.90	4.14	6.39	4.59	5.28	5.30
Manipur	5.40	5.82	4.70	5.35	5.11	4.95	4.94	4.45
Meghalaya	3.22	3.05	2.96	2.77	2.23	2.21	2.24	2.12
Mizoram	7.18	7.41	6.80	7.64	6.29	5.93	6.07	5.15
Nagaland	4.88	4.86	4.63	4.68	3.75	4.45	4.84	4.93
Sikkim	6.50	6.18	5.63	5.64	5.14	5.48	5.78	5.87
Tripura	4.41	4.29	3.95	3.76	3.66	3.33	3.64	3.73
Uttarakhand	2.92	3.44	3.09	3.07	3.08	2.95	3.22	2.95
Special category average	**5.06**	**4.99**	**4.61**	**4.61**	**4.28**	**4.16**	**4.36**	**4.19**
All states average	**4.13**	**3.99**	**3.60**	**3.47**	**3.25**	**3.04**	**3.10**	**3.03**

Note: RE = revised estimate; BE = budget estimate
Source: Estimated from the RBI budget data and the CSO GSDP data.

to 2010-11 (BE). Although Himachal Pradesh has been improving over time, it has not been able to do so against the special category states average. Tripura has consistently improved till 2008-09. As compared to the special category states average, Arunachal Pradesh and Manipur need improvement, whereas Nagaland's position was not found much poor before 2008-09.

Development Revenue Expenditures and Non-development Revenue Expenditures (Individual States)

Among the special category states, Sikkim portrays poor illustration, registering its NDRE/GSDP ratio to be extremely high throughout the study period (Table 16.8)—even more than 70 per cent in 2004-05. In spite of maintaining high NDRE/GSDP ratio, it went on affording relatively high DRE/GSDP ratio (Table 16.9). As regards the latter ratio, among the special category states, Arunachal Pradesh and Mizoram are seen to be in impressive position as compared to the special category averages over the years. For these phenomena, "End Note 5" is again referred to.

Table 16.8: Non-Development Revenue Expenditure (NDRE) as Percentage of GSDP—Performance of Individual States

	2003-04	*2004-05*	*2005-06*	*2006-07*	*2007-08*	*2008-09*	*2009-10 (RE)*	*2010-11 (BE)*
Arunachal Pradesh	18.51	17.14	16.75	16.40	15.95	17.06	23.11	15.64
Assam	7.46	7.02	7.27	6.68	6.88	6.77	14.22	10.12
Himachal Pradesh	11.98	11.80	10.97	11.54	10.64	10.61	10.28	10.79
Jammu and Kashmir	15.27	14.28	14.14	14.24	16.58	15.35	17.07	18.71
Manipur	15.74	15.35	14.20	16.16	15.94	17.26	17.89	18.73
Meghalaya	9.96	10.11	9.70	9.59	9.19	9.76	9.64	9.22
Mizoram	19.89	20.97	19.91	20.59	19.54	21.11	23.71	22.25
Nagaland	18.18	16.70	17.12	17.07	16.58	19.11	20.72	22.76
Sikkim	48.20	71.19	63.57	61.23	69.18	52.06	54.12	48.01
Tripura	11.60	11.18	11.45	11.19	12.13	11.30	14.73	15.78
Uttarakhand	7.14	8.01	7.74	7.58	7.46	7.71	9.15	7.67
Special Category Average	**16.72**	**18.52**	**17.53**	**17.48**	**18.19**	**17.10**	**19.51**	**18.15**
All states average	**10.94**	**11.56**	**10.85**	**10.57**	**10.72**	**10.14**	**11.43**	**10.94**

Note: RE = revised estimate; BE = budget estimate

Source: Estimated from the RBI budget data and the CSO GSDP data.

Table 16.9: Development Revenue Expenditure (DRE) as Percentage of GSDP—Performance of Individual states

	2003-04	2004-05	2005-06	2006-07	2007-08	2008-09	2009-10 (RE)	2010-11 (BE)
Arunachal Pradesh	40.28	35.77	40.40	39.19	42.16	46.22	53.11	39.39
Assam	10.38	12.42	10.94	11.09	10.91	10.45	16.56	19.25
Himachal Pradesh	14.97	13.30	14.18	15.18	15.08	14.94	15.01	14.40
Jammu & Kashmir	14.44	19.47	22.51	20.43	20.17	20.39	22.36	22.39
Manipur	21.04	20.80	25.37	28.53	23.27	24.09	27.69	30.10
Meghalaya	14.92	17.39	16.28	16.43	17.42	18.16	23.07	23.09
Mizoram	35.49	35.84	38.46	36.73	38.21	39.65	45.60	38.69
Nagaland	19.49	16.09	20.41	20.10	19.16	21.83	25.31	29.52
Sikkim	34.40	36.38	33.02	31.37	33.02	35.79	42.79	43.23
Tripura	15.20	14.69	13.45	12.38	13.11	14.48	19.59	17.77
Uttarakhand	13.21	12.62	13.24	12.20	12.05	12.47	15.74	13.69
Special Category Average	**21.26**	**21.34**	**22.57**	**22.15**	**22.23**	**23.50**	**27.89**	**26.50**
All states average	**13.88**	**13.54**	**14.12**	**14.02**	**14.21**	**15.08**	**17.38**	**16.72**

Note: RE = revised estimate; BE = budget estimate
Source: Estimated from the RBI budget data and the CSO GSDP data.

Conclusion

This study, at the first place, has investigated the policy of government saving in revenue account and checked the impact of this on the capital outlay which is required for the improvement of the infrastructure. Infrastructure is urgently needed to address the supply-side constraints which the economy has been severely suffering from. Taking two points-in-time figures (i.e. 2003-04 and 2007-08) of GFD components for each state, the study shows that fiscal consolidation has improved both revenue balance-sheet and capital budget of many states. Second, the study has made an attempt to examine as to whether fiscal consolidation has had any favourable impacts on states' outstanding liabilities, debt service, and revenue expenditures (both non-development and development). It was found that fiscal consolidation has helped to reduce outstanding liabilities, interest payments, reduce revenue expenditure and promote developmental expenditures.

Notes

1. Stiglitz *et al.* (2006) argue that none of these two constraints is important for

developed countries. If they opt for greater investments, they can borrow on international markets, with flexible exchange rates and open capital markets.

2. Typically, a country with a current account deficit will have a capital account surplus, because the deficit has to be financed with capital imports (Chandrasekhar, 2008).
3. According to *Economic Survey 2009-10*, India's savings rate (as per cent of GDP) registers the following growth trends in recent times: 32.2 per cent in 2004-05; 33.1 per cent in 2005-06; 34.4 per cent in 2006-07; 36.4 per cent in 2007-08; and 32.5 per cent in 2008-09.
4. In another context, Dasgupta (1993) argues that, for very poor regions, infrastructure has to be supplied by the government, the expenditure being financed by general taxation.
5. "Special category States account for nearly one-tenth of the total size, measured in terms of aggregate expenditure, of all State governments. The typical features of a special category State, i.e. hilly terrain, sparsely populated habitation and high transport costs etc. lead to high cost of delivering public services. With the relatively lower level of economic activity in most special category States, their tax base is limited *vis-à-vis* non-special category States. These States, to a large extent, depend on transfers from the Centre (comprising grants and tax devolutions) for their resource needs. The fiscal correction observed in special category States during 2004-05 to 2007-08 was largely on account of higher devolution and transfers from the Centre, while there was some improvement in own revenue receipts as well" (RBI, 2011: 36-7).
6. Debt service accounts for a major share of recurrent spending (World Bank, 2005).
7. Although—while further observed—this ratio is seen to be passing through fluctuating trends in those four years.

References

Bagchi, Amaresh (2006). "India's fiscal management post-liberalisation: Impact on the social sector and federal fiscal relations", *Economic and Political Weekly*, 30 September, pp. 4117-21.

Bagchi, Amiya K. (2004). "Neo-Liberal Reforms with Cosmetic Changes?", *Economic and Political Weekly*, 7 August, pp. 3572-4.

Chakraborty, L. and K. Bhadra (2010). "Subnational Public Finance in Times of Recession", *Economic and Political Weekly*, Vol. XLV, No. 35, 28 August, pp. 15-9.

Chakraborty, P. (2009). "Intra-regional Inequality and the Role of Public Policy: Lessons Learnt from Kerala", *Economic and Political Weekly*, Vol. XLIV, Nos. 26 and 27, 27 June, pp. 274-81.

Chandrasekhar, C.P. (2008). "India and the world economy," *Macroscan*, 12 January. Available at: www.macroscan.org

Dasgupta, P. (1993). *An Inquiry into Well-Being and Destitution*; New York: Oxford University Press Inc.

Dutta, S. (2012). *The Economics of Government Savings: A Note on Indian State-level Fiscal Restructuring*, SPIESR Working Paper Series No. 10; Ahmedabad: Sardar Patel Institute of Economic and Social Research (SPIESR).

EPW editorial (2005). "Saving and investment: How buoyant?" *Economic and Political Weekly*, 12 February, pp. 587-8.

Government of India (2004). *Report of the Twelfth Finance Commission (2005-10)*, New Delhi: Government of India.

Government of India (2006). *Towards Faster and More Inclusive Growth: An Approach to the 11th Five-Year Plan*; New Delhi: Planning Commission.

Government of India (2008). *Eleventh Five Year Plan (2007-2012)*; New Delhi: Planning Commission and Oxford University Press.

Government of India (2011). *Economic Survey 2009-10*; New Delhi: Government of India.

Govinda Rao, M. (2009). "The Fiscal Situation and a Reform Agenda for the New Government", *Economic and Political Weekly*, Vol. XLIV, No. 25, 20 June, pp. 77-85.

Mazumdar, S. (2008). "Investment and growth in India under liberalisation: Asymmetries and instabilities", *Economic and Political Weekly*, 6 December, pp. 68-77.

Patnaik, P. (2004). "On financing infrastructure on the strength of reserves", *Economic and Political Weekly*, 25 December, pp. 5565-7.

Rakshit, M. (2005). "Some analytics and empirics of fiscal restructuring in India", *Economic and Political Weekly*, Vol. 40, No. 31, 30 July, pp. 3440-9.

Rakshit, M. (2006). "Budgetary rules and plan financing", *Economic and Political Weekly*, Vol. 41, No. 43, 4 November, pp. 4547-53.

Rangarajan, C. and D.K. Srivastava (2005). "Fiscal Deficits and Government Debt in India: Implications for Growth and Stabilisation"; *NIPFP Working Paper No. 35*; New Delhi: National Institute of Public Finance and Policy (NIPFP).

Reserve Bank of India (various years). *State Finances: A Study of Budgets*; Mumbai: Reserve Bank of India (RBI).

RBI (2011). *State Finances: A Study of Budgets of 2010-11*; Mumbai: Reserve Bank of India (RBI).

Shome, P. (2006). "At the threshold of 10 per cent economic growth?" *Economic and Political Weekly*, 18 March, pp. 913-7.

Srivastava, D.K. (2006). "FRBM Act and Eleventh Plan Approach Paper", *Economic and Political Weekly*, 4 November, pp. 4553-9.

Stiglitz, J., J.A. Ocampo, S. Spiegel, R. Ffrench-Davis, D. Nayyar (2006). *Stability with Growth: Macroeconomics, Liberalisation and Development*; New Delhi: Oxford University Press.

World Bank (2005). *State Fiscal Reforms in India: Progress and Prospects (A World Bank Report)*; New Delhi: Macmillan India Ltd.

17
State Finances of Arunachal Pradesh in the Post Reform Period

Anup Kumar Das and *Bhabesh Hazarika*

Introduction

The resource poor State of Arunachal Pradesh is highly dependent on central transfer of fund. It is having difficult hilly terrain and remoteness in the location. The State is backward in physical and social infrastructure due to high cost of production and resource constraints. Transportation is other major inherent challenge which has handicapped the state in a variety of ways. In this state, while the lack of own resources creates a budgetary hardship, the provisioning of public goods is very costly. For instance, Sarma *et al.* (2006) found that the per unit cost of provisioning merit goods like education and health in Arunachal Pradesh is two and half times more as compared to the plain areas (Nayak *et al.*, 2013). Considering the problems mentioned above, Arunachal Pradesh was accorded the 'Special Category' status along with other ten States by the National Development Council (NDC) as per there commendation of the Planning Commission. However, the State has not made any remarkable progress in its development by utilising the advantages of special category status. Recently, the transfer of fund under special category status has been stopped by the Union Government after coming to power in May 2014.

The economic reforms initiated in 1991could hardly make any contribution to Arunachal Pradesh and other special category States (Bhattacharjee, 2014). In fact, it constrained the States regarding access to soft central resources (Nayak *et al.*, 2013). The reform enhanced the growth of the country as a whole in general and the already developed

States in particular only. Thus, the reforms have increased the inter-state disparities in growth as mentioned by Ahluwalia (2000). Such disparity increased even more between developed and poor States (Kurian, 2000). Moreover, the implementation of 6th Pay Commission again deteriorated the fiscal health of Arunachal Pradesh by enhancing outstanding liability by a big margin. Hence, considering these inherent problems and challenges posed by policies of the Union Government, an attempt has been made to give an overview of the state finances in Arunachal Pradesh. Given the greater scope for the state level activities due to reduced degree of control by the Central Government as induced by the fiscal liberalisation, it is also important to address some of the expenditure priority of the State especially in the social sector areas.

Fiscal Situation in the State

The State of Arunachal Pradesh has been maintaining a surplus in revenue account from 2005-06, i.e. from the pre FRBM Act[1] period and it is continuing. However, as a percentage of the GSDP surplus in revenue account has been fluctuating, and it ranges from -4.8 per cent to -18.6 per cent during 2005-06 to 2014-15 (Table 17.1). The surplus in the revenue account of the state is because of large scale central transfers in the form of grant. Because of special category status, the state receives 90 per cent of Plan assistant as grant. During the reference period in most of the years, there was a gross fiscal deficit. The state also experienced primary deficit number of times during the period 2004-05 to 2014-15. As a percentage of GSDP, gross fiscal deficit and primary deficit were -3.3 per cent and -5.6 per cent respectively by the end of the study period.

The outstanding debt has increased from INR 2070 crore in 2004-05 to INR 5761 crore in 2014-15, but it has declined as a percentage of GSDP. The outstanding debt as a percentage of GSDP was 59.4 per cent in 2004-05 which has declined to 37.0 per cent in 2014-15 which is a good sign for the state economy. The outstanding debt as a percentage of GSDP was highest in 2005-06 and thereafter declining continuously till 2013-14 and in next year it increased slightly. The interest payment has increased from INR147 crore in 2004-05 to INR 351crore in 2014-15 with some fluctuations. However, as a percentage of GSDP, it has decreased from 4.2 per cent at the beginning of the study period to 2.3 per cent at the end of the study period (Table 17.1). As a whole, the state has made some improvement in the fiscal situation in last few years.

With the increase of per capita NSDP over the period, the gross fiscal deficit in Arunachal Pradesh has been improving. Fig. 17.1 depicts

Table 17.1: Financial State of Arunachal Pradesh in Last Few Years (*in INR Crore*)

Year	*2004-05*	*2005-06*	*2006-07*	*2007-08*	*2008-09*	*2009-10*	*2010-11*	*2011-12*	*2012-13*	*2013-14*	*2014-15*
Revenue Deficit	8	–182	–695	–743	–961	–599	–1678	–1081	–975	–89	–1979
Gross Fiscal Deficit	386	257	–112	10	354	434	–25	991	232	1606	–519
Primary Deficit	239	100	–300	–145	139	207	–425	710	–40	1293	–870
Outstanding Debt	2070	2410	2371	2639	2955	3119	3547	3873	4179	4531	5761
Interest Payment	147	156	188	155	216	227	400	282	272	313	351
As a percentage of GSDP at current prices											
Revenue Deficit	0.2	–4.8	–16.9	–15.5	–16.9	–8.0	–18.6	–10.0	–8.2	–0.7	–12.7
Gross Fiscal Deficit	11.1	6.8	–2.7	0.2	6.2	5.8	–0.3	9.2	2.0	11.9	–3.3
Primary Deficit	6.9	2.7	–7.3	–3.0	2.4	2.8	–4.7	6.6	–0.3	9.6	–5.6
Outstanding Debt	59.4	64.2	57.7	54.9	52.0	41.7	39.3	36.0	35.3	33.5	37.0
Interest Payment	4.2	4.2	4.6	3.2	3.8	3.0	4.4	2.6	2.3	2.3	2.3

Note: '+' indicates deficit and '–' indicates surplus.
Source: Finance Accounts, CAG, GOI.

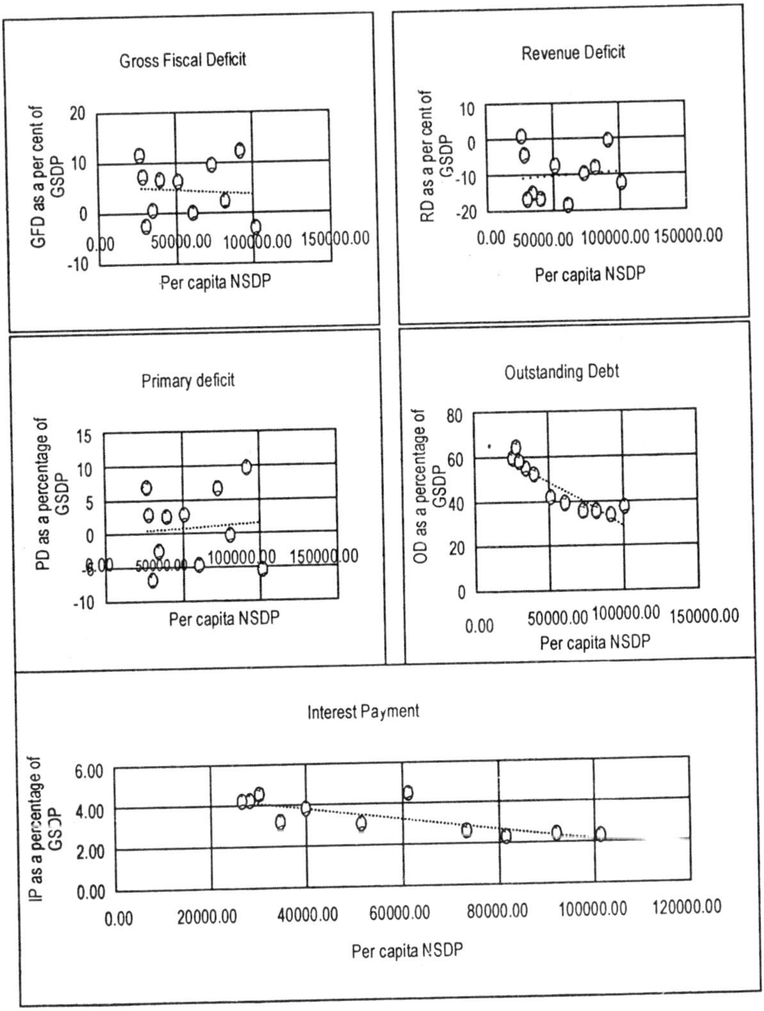

Fig. 17.1: Economic Growth and Fiscal Situation in Arunachal Pradesh (in INR Crore)

Note: Up to 2010-11, base year is 2004-05 prices and from 2011-12, base year is 2011-12

Source: Finance Accounts, CAG & Study of State Budgets, RBI.

that the there is a declining trend of gross fiscal deficit as a percentage of GSDP with the increase of per capita NSDP. In contrast, there has been deterioration in case of revenue account and primary account. As a percentage of GSDP, with the increased per capita NSDP, revenue surplus has been decreasing while primary deficit has been increasing. The outstanding debt and so the interest payment as a percentage of GSDP have shown a downward trend in the higher economic growth. It indicates the improvement of state debt situation in the state.

Trend and Pattern of Receipts and Expenditure

Revenue Receipts and Its Composition

While revenue receipts of the government of Arunachal Pradesh have been increasing continuously during the period 2004-05 to 2014-15, its share in the GSDP has been fluctuatingin the period (Table 17.2). As a percentage of the GSDP, revenue receipts increased from 43.1 per cent in 2004-05 to 58.6 per cent in 2014-15. The share of revenue receipts to the GSDP was highest in 2008-09 and lowest in 2013-14 but sharply increased it in the next year. The annual growth rate of revenue receipts increased to 57.0 per cent in 2014-15 which was 43.1 per cent at the beginning of the reference period. However, the growth of revenue receipts was quite low during 2011-12 to 2013-14. The decreased interest receipts and revenue from power sector brought down the growth of revenue receipts in 2011-12 to 2012-13. The reduction of grant from the centre led to the growth of revenue receipts to be almost stagnant in the successive years. Moreover, reduction of revenue receipts under VAT also contributed to the lower growth of revenue receipts in 2012-13.

Looking into the components of revenue receipts, all have increased by the end of the period compared to the initials fiscal years. However, as a percentage to the GSDP, central transfers have increased sharply while the other component, i.e. own revenue (tax) has declined. It shows the inability of the state to move forward to become self-sufficient. All the components of revenue receipts have also experienced a negative growth rate in some times in the study period. More importantly, the growth rate of central transfers has increased in 2014-15 compared to that in 2005-06 while the growth of own revenue decreased at the end of the period compared to the beginning of the period.

Regarding the composition of revenue receipts in the state, the bulk of it is coming from the central transfer. Throughout the study period, the central transfers contributed more than three-fourth of the revenue receipts of the state while own revenue contributed less than one-fourth of it. Moreover, the share of central transfers in revenue receipts has

Table 17.2: Trend of Revenue Receipts

(in INR Crore)

Heads	*2004-05*	*2005-06*	*2006-07*	*2007-08*	*2008-09*	*2009-10*	*2010-11*	*2011-12*	*2012-13*	*2013-14*	*2014-15*
Amount in crore											
Revenue Receipts	**1502**	**1849**	**2592**	**3003**	3856	**4295**	**5422**	**5499**	**5762**	**5820**	**9136**
Own Revenue	**219**	**264**	**376**	**755**	**908**	**685**	**745**	**678**	**601**	**840**	920
Own Tax Revenue	49	61	78	98	136	173	215	318	317	435	462
Own Non-Tax Revenue	170	202	297	657	772	511	530	361	284	405	458
Central Transfers	**1283**	**1586**	**2217**	**2248**	**2948**	**3610**	**4677**	**4821**	**5161**	**4981**	**8216**
Tax Devolution	193	273	347	438	462	475	720	839	958	1046	1110
Grants	1090	1313	1870	1810	2486	3135	3957	3982	4203	3935	7106
As a percentage of GSDP at current prices											
Revenue Receipts	**43.1**	49.3	63.1	62.4	67.8	57.5	**60.1**	**51.0**	48.7	**43.0**	**58.6**
Own Revenue	**6.3**	**7.0**	**9.1**	**15.7**	**16.0**	**9.2**	**8.3**	6.3	5.1	**6.2**	**5.9**
Own Tax Revenue	1.4	1.6	1.9	2.0	2.4	2.3	2.4	3.0	2.7	3.2	3.0
Own Non-Tax Revenue	4.9	5.4	7.2	13.7	13.6	6.8	5.9	3.4	2.4	3.0	2.9
Central Transfers	**36.8**	**42.2**	**54.0**	**46.7**	**51.8**	**48.3**	**51.8**	**44.7**	**43.6**	**36.8**	**52.7**
Tax Devolution	5.5	7.3	8.5	9.1	8.1	6.4	8.0	7.8	8.1	7.7	7.1
Grants	31.2	35.0	45.5	37.6	43.7	41.9	43.9	37.0	35.5	29.1	45.6
Annual growth rate											
Revenue Receipts		**23.1**	**40.2**	**15.9**	**28.4**	**11.4**	**26.3**	**1.4**	**4.8**	**1.0**	**57.0**
Own Revenue		**20.2**	**42.5**	**101.0**	**20.3**	**–24.6**	**8.8**	**–9.0**	**–11.5**	**39.8**	**9.6**
Own Tax Revenue		24.8	28.0	25.0	39.2	27.2	24.0	47.8	–0.4	37.3	6.4
Own Non-Tax Revenue		18.9	46.9	121.1	17.5	–33.8	3.7	–32.0	–21.2	42.5	13.0
Central Transfers		**23.6**	**39.8**	**1.4**	**31.1**	**22.5**	**29.6**	**3.1**	**7.1**	**–3.5**	**65.0**
Tax Devolution		41.5	27.1	26.2	5.5	2.9	51.5	16.5	14.2	9.2	6.1
Grants		20.5	42.4	–3.2	37.3	26.1	26.2	0.6	5.6	–6.4	80.6

Source: Compiled and calculated from Finance Account, CAG.

increased from 85 per cent in 2004-05 to 90 per cent in 2014-15. In 2007-08, there was a decrease of share of central transfers in total revenue receipts which again increased from the next year and continued till 2012-13. The reduction in the contribution of central transfers in 2007-08 was due to marginal increase in central transfer as well as due to increase own revenue generation primarily from the power sector. However, fall of revenue collection from the power sector in successive years again enhanced the dependency of the State on Centre. The reduction of the share of Central transfers again in 2013-14 was brought both by a decrease of grant from the centre and increased contribution from the power sector. Thus, it has been found that power sector is a significant contributor to the revenue generation of Arunachal Pradesh. Regarding the shares of own tax revenue and own non-tax revenue, some changes have been noticed. It has been found that before 2011-12 own non-tax revenue contributed more than that of own tax revenue but thereafter the contribution from own tax revenue surpassed the contribution from own non-tax revenue. Thus, some changes in the composition of revenue receipts (own) have taken place because of increase in revenue collection through VAT.

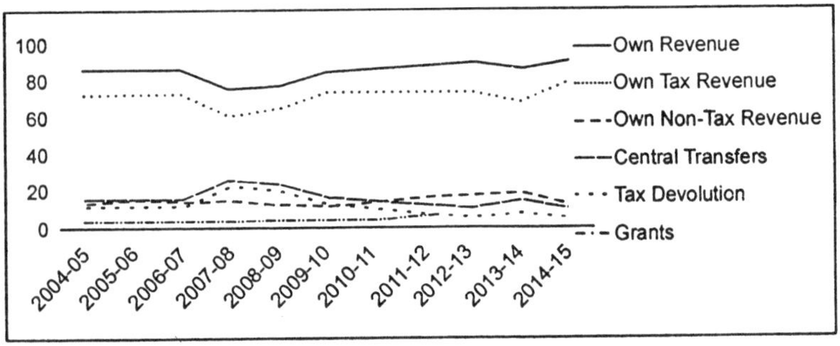

Fig. 17.2: Composition of Revenue Receipts (in INR Crore)

Source: Compiled and calculated from Finance Accounts, CAG.

Expenditure and Its Composition

The total expenditure of the government of Arunachal Pradesh has increased from INR1891 crore in 2004-05 to INR 8645 crore in 2014-15. This increase in government expenditure has been accompanied mainly by continuously increasing revenue expenditure. However, in 2012-13 there was a reduction of the total expenditure because of reduction of developmental capital expenditure (both social and economic). As a percentage of GSDP, the total expenditure of the state has remained same at the end of the reference period as compared to the beginning of the period but fluctuated significantly in between. The total expenditure as a per cent of GSDP reached 74.1 per cent in 2008-09 and in that year growth rate of it was also highest. It was because of substantially increased developmental expenditure on energy, roads and bridges. While both revenue expenditure and capital expenditure have increased in an absolute sense at the end of the study period compared to the initial period, as a percentage of GSDP only former has been increased. In fact, while there was always positive growth of revenue expenditure which also increased from 10.5 per cent in 2004-05 to 24.9 per cent in 2014-15, a number of times, capital expenditure experienced negative growth rate and at the end of the period too it was negative. Thus, the negative growth of capital expenditure indicates declining of government's interest and/or effort for further asset creation in the state whereas inadequate infrastructure facilities are still one of the major causes of lower development of the state (*see* Table 17.3).

The revenue expenditure has been dominating the total expenditure of the state Arunachal Pradesh. The share of revenue expenditure in the total expenditure ranges from 68.04 per cent to 82.79 per cent. There was a declining trend of the share of revenue expenditure from 2005-06 to 2011-12 because of relatively more increased of capital expenditure. In the successive years, again the share of revenue expenditure in the total expenditure increased because of absolute increased of revenue expenditure and decreased of capital expenditure. Across components of revenue expenditure, it has been foundeconomic continued to account for the largest share followed by social services. The shares of different components in the total expenditure have beenmore or less the same throughout the study period. A positive sign for the economy of the state noticed is that the interest payment as a percentage of total expenditure has been going down (*see* Fig. 17.3).

Tax Buoyancy

Table 17.4 depicts that tax buoyancy in Arunachal Pradesh is very low during the reviewed period. It indicates the inefficient tax revenue mobilisation in the state. Thus, while tax is the sustainable source of government revenue, Arunachal Pradesh has been suffering from two serious challenges with regard to tax revenue. On the one hand, the share

Table 17.3: Trend of Expenditure

(in INR Crore)

Year	*2004-05*	*2005-06*	*2006-07*	*2007-08*	*2008-09*	*2009-10*	*2010-11*	*2011-12*	*2012-13*	*2013-14*	*2014-15*
Total Expenditure	**1891**	**2110**	**2485**	**3016**	**4213**	**4931**	**5400**	**6493**	**5997**	**7430**	**8645**
Revenue Expenditure	**1510**	**1668**	**1897**	**2260**	**2896**	**3696**	**3744**	**4418**	**4786**	**5731**	**7157**
General Services	489	489	560	620	774	1161	1265	1285	1424	1780	2063
Interest Payment	*147*	*157*	*188*	*155*	*216*	*227*	*400*	*282*	*272*	*313*	*351*
Social Services	473	571	634	707	981	1197	994	1385	1506	1770	2358
Economic Services	548	608	704	933	1141	1338	1485	1748	1857	2181	2736
Capital Expenditure	**381**	**442**	**588**	**756**	**1318**	**1236**	**1656**	**2076**	**1210**	**1698**	**1488**
Capital Outlay	375	438	586	753	1290	1030	1649	2066	1206	1680	1483
As a percentage of GSDP at current prices											
Total Expenditure	**54.2**	**56.2**	**60.5**	**62.7**	**74.1**	**66.0**	**59.9**	**60.3**	**50.7**	**54.8**	**55.5**
Revenue Expenditure	**43.3**	**44.4**	**46.2**	**47.0**	**50.9**	**49.4**	**41.5**	**41.0**	**40.4**	**42.3**	**45.9**
General Services	14.0	13.0	13.6	12.9	13.6	15.5	14.0	11.9	12.0	13.1	13.2
Interest Payment	*4.2*	*4.2*	*4.6*	*3.2*	*3.8*	*3.0*	*4.4*	*2.6*	*2.3*	*2.3*	*2.3*
Social Services	13.6	15.2	15.4	14.7	17.2	16.0	11.0	12.9	12.7	13.1	15.1
Economic Services	15.7	16.2	17.1	19.4	20.1	17.9	16.5	16.2	15.7	16.1	17.5
Capital Expenditure	**10.9**	**11.8**	**14.3**	**15.7**	**23.2**	**16.5**	**18.4**	**19.3**	**10.2**	**12.5**	**9.5**
Capital Outlay	10.8	11.7	14.3	15.7	22.7	13.8	18.3	19.2	10.2	12.4	9.5
Annual growth rate											
Total Expenditure		**11.6**	**17.8**	**21.3**	**39.7**	**17.1**	**9.5**	**20.3**	**–7.7**	**23.9**	**16.4**
Revenue Expenditure		**10.5**	**13.8**	**19.1**	**28.1**	**27.6**	**1.3**	**18**	**8.3**	**19.7**	**24.9**
General Services		–0.1	14.5	10.8	24.9	50	9	1.5	10.8	25.1	15.9
Interest Payment		*6.5*	*20*	*–17.5*	*39.1*	*5.3*	*76.2*	*–29.5*	*–3.5*	*15*	*12.3*
Social Services		20.8	11	11.5	38.8	22	–16.9	39.3	8.7	17.5	33.2
Economic Services		10.9	15.8	32.5	22.3	17.3	11	17.7	6.2	17.5	25.4
Capital Expenditure		**16**	**33**	**28.6**	**74.2**	**–6.2**	**34**	**25.4**	**–41.7**	**40.3**	**–12.4**
Capital Outlay		16.7	33.8	28.6	71.3	–20.1	60.1	25.3	–41.6	39.2	–11.7

Source: Compiled and calculated from Finance Accounts, CAG.

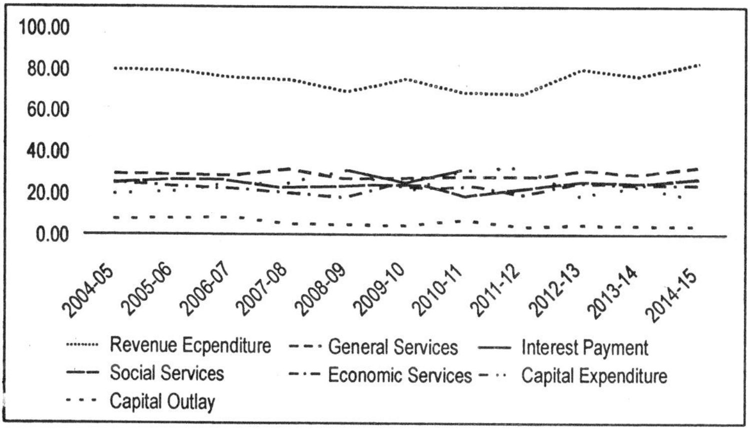

Fig. 17.3: Composition of Expenditure

Source: Compiled and calculated from Finance Accounts, CAG.

of own tax in the total revenue receipts is very low and at the same time there is also inefficiency in mobilisation of own tax revenue and its major components.

Table 17.4: Tax Buoyancy during 2004-05 to 2014-15

Own Tax Revenue	0.0002
Sales Tax	0.0001
State Excise Duties	0.0002
Motor Vehicle Tax	0.0002
Taxes on Goods and Passengers	0.0013
Stamp Duty and Registration Fees	0.0002
Other Taxes	0.0002

Source: Calculated using CAG and RBI data.

The FRBM Act in Arunachal Pradesh

With regard to achievement of the APFRBM Act, it has been found that all the targets set under this Act have not been achieved fully by the state. The target of maintenance of surplus in the revenue account at least at the level of an average of base years[2] as per APFRBM Act, 2006 has been achieved right from the beginning of the effective year. The APFRBM Act after amendment inDecember 2011 has also set the target of maintenance of revenue surplus from the financial year beginning on the 1st day of April 2010 and ending on 31st March 2015 which has been achieved throughout the period. The targets of keeping the fiscal deficit below 3 per cent of GSDP from 2008-09 of both APFRBM Act, 2006 and APFRBM Act, 2011 were not satisfied in most of the years. Further the target of reduction of the fiscal deficit by a minimum of 0.3 per cent of GSDP by the end of each financial year as per APFRBM Act, 2006 has been achieved in three years out of the five effective years. As per outstanding debt is concerned, the limit set under the APFRBM Act, 2011 has not been crossed in any year (see Table 17.4).

Public Expenditure on Social Sector: 2004-05 to 2016-17 (BE)

This section focused on the social sector expenditure for the last 10 years in the state. Social sector expenditure is considered in the present study as the total expenditure on social services that includes education, sports and youth welfare, arts and culture, health and family welfare, water supply and sanitation, housing, information broadcasting, and few other aspects as given in the state finance accounts and budget documents. The present analysis considers the aggregate expenditure (revenue expenditure plus capital expenditure) and also refers both the plan and non-plan expenditure instead of considering only revenue account as done by some earlier studies (Prabhu, 2001, 2005). Such definition is also used by some other studies such as Dev and Mooij (2002), Mooij and Dev (2004), and Goswami and Bezbaruah (2011).

Table 17.5 reflects the commitment of the government of Arunachal Pradesh towards the development of the social sector in the state. It presents an overview of the social sector expenditure in the state as a percentage of GSDP, as a percentage of aggregate expenditure, and per capita expenditure for the period of 2004-05 to 2016-17 (BE). It can be seen from the table that there has been a fluctuation in the social sector spending over the last few years and the state spends about 15-18 per cent of GSDP annually. It was 15.61 per cent in 2004-05 which reached a peak of 20.09 per cent in 2008-09 and then came down to 17.97 per cent 2014-15. The rise in expenditure in 2008-09 was mainly due to the implementation of 6th State Pay Commission award which almost doubled the pay level of the government employees. The rise in the expenditure was also given a push by of the additional (temporary) fiscal stimulus to keep the unaffected from the global financial crisis. However, the expenditure experienced a sharp decline in 2010-11 as a result of the amendment of state FRBM Act. In order to achieve the new FRBM targets, the state had cushioned the various expenditures including the social sector

Table 17.4: Targets and Achievements under APFRBM Act

		2005-06	2006-07	2007-08	2008-09	2009-10	2010-11	2011-12	2012-13	2013-14	2014-15
Revenue deficit (in INR Crore)	Actual	-182	-695	-743	-961	-599	-1678	-1081	-975	-89	-1979
	Target	Surplus	Surplus	Surplus	Surplus	Surplus	Surplus	Surplus	Surplus	Surplus	Surplus
Fiscal deficit as a % of GSDP	Actual	6.8	–2.7	0.2	6.2	5.8	–0.3	9.2	2.0	11.9	–3.3
	Target				3	3	3	3	3	3	3
Δ of Fiscal deficit as a % of GSDP	Actual[1]	4.2	9.6	–2.9	–6.0	0.4					
	Target	0.3	0.3	0.3	0.3	0.3					
Outstanding debt as a % of GSDP	Actual	64.2	57.7	54.9	52.0	41.7	39.3	36.0	35.3	33.5	37.0
	Target						63.1	58.2	55.2	52.5	50.1

Note: '+' indicates deficit and '-' indicates surplus.
Source: Finance Account, CAG, GOI.

Table 17.5: Social Sector Expenditure by Government of Arunachal Pradesh

Year	*Social Sector Expenditure (Revenue Account + Capital Account)*			*Social Sector Expenditure (Revenue Account)*		
	Percentage of GSDP	*Percentage of Public Expenditure*	*Per Capita Expenditure (in INR)**	*Percentage of GSDP*	*Percentage Total Revenue expenditure*	*Per Capita Expenditure (INR)*
2004-05	15.61	28.89	4714.85	13.55	25.08	4092.38
2005-06	17.61	30.88	5656.64	15.21	26.67	4884.93
2006-07	18.83	31.15	6532.47	15.42	25.52	5351.28
2007-08	17.77	28.38	7135.82	14.69	23.45	5897.97
2008-09	20.09	27.29	9425.92	17.24	23.43	8091.88
2009-10	18.07	28.57	11,004.60	16.01	25.32	9752.74
2010-11	15.56	26.03	11,313.07	11.02	18.43	8011.89
2011-12	17.92	29.78	15,386.53	12.86	21.37	11039.18
2012-13	15.09	29.80	14,063.36	12.73	25.14	11860.50
2013-14	16.79	30.68	17,709.96	13.07	23.89	13786.27
2014-15	17.97	32.42	12,737.18	15.13	27.30	10724.85
2015-16 (RE)	20.40	30.02	26,809.61	16.74	24.63	21997.01
2016-17 (BE)	23.80		34,241.74	20.60	29.88	29631.54

Note: *Per capita expenditures are at current prices
Source: Compiled and calculated from Finance Account, CAG.

heads such as *elementary education, art* and *culture*, and *water supply and sanitation*. By the end of the fiscal year 2009-10, the state not only had a huge revenue surplus (-18.6%) but also became fiscal surplus (-0.3%). The fiscal year 2011-12 onwards, there is a gradual increase in the social sector expenditure. Overall, the average social sector expenditure during 2009-10 to 2013-14 had been lower as compared to the period 2004-05 to 2009-10. This deviation is explained by the deviation in the GSDP growth rate. The state was growing faster during the period 2004-05 to 2008-09 as compared to the period 2009-10 to 2014-15. Considering the initial years of 14th Finance Commission, the figures are quite impressive and reflects that the state is putting money into the sector being one of largest beneficiaries of the tax devolution.

As a percentage of the total public expenditure, the state spends about 28-30 per cent on the sector (Table 17.5). There had been a fluctuation too in the expenditure level during 2004-05 to 2009-10 but 2010-11 onwards it has shown an increasing trend in the allocation to the social sector implying that a higher percentage of total public expenditure has been devolved in to the sector. Similarly, in terms of per capita expenditure (in current prices), there has been a continuous rise in the sector. It has increased from INR 4714.85 in 2004-05 to INR 17,709 in 2013-14 with a slight dip in 2014-15 where it stood at INR 12737.18. However, the 2015-16 (RE) and 2016-17 (BE) figures show a considerable level of per capita expenditure in the state. Considering the public expenditure in the revenue account as a percentage of GSDP and total public expenditure, the trend appears similar to that of the aggregate social sector expenditure.

Figure 17.4 depicts that the revenue expenditure component has an overwhelming share in the total expenditure. The revenue expenditure reached a peak in 2008-09 as a result of the 6th State Pay Commission and then affected by the FRBM target in 2010-11. There has been an effort to spend more on capital heads in 2010-11 as well as 2011-12 under different heads as compared to the previous few years. After that, there has been a considerable improvement in the revenue expenditure in the recent years whereas the capital expenditure has not been matched the growth of the expenditure in revenue account. Even after the award of the FFC, the figures clearly indicate that the expenditure in the sector has been mostly meant for the revenue account.

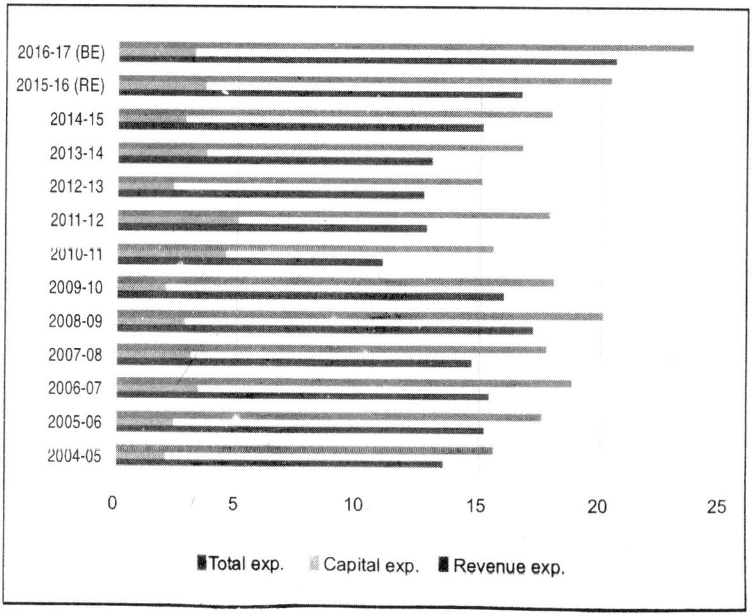

Fig. 17.4: Revenue and Capital Expenditure in Social Sector as a Percentage of GSDP

Expenditure on Major Heads

Public expenditures as a percentage of GSDP for the major heads are presented in Table 17.6. Education continues to be the important major head in the social sector in the state. About INR 212.42 crore was allocated for education in 2004-05 which had gone up to INR 564.17 in 2009-10 and further increased to INR 1015.76 in 2014-15. It can be seen from Table 17.2 that the public expenditure on *education* (inducing *sports* and *culture*) was around 6.42 per cent of GSDP in 2004-05 which has increased to 7.46 per cent in 2014-15 showing a gradual increase over the last decade. The allocation for the education has been shown a much higher percentage in the 2015-16 (RE) and 2016-17 (BE). However, in terms of the percentage of aggregate expenditure, the state's spending on education is one of lowest for the last couple of years. In 2013-14, the state spent 11.5 per cent against the national level of 16.5 per cent (RBI, 2016).

Concentrating on health expenditure, it was around 2.58 per cent of the GSDP of the state which has increased to 3.47 in 2014-15. The state budget estimated an expenditure of 4.67 per cent of GSDP for the fiscal year 2016-17 which a considerable figure as compared to many states of India. Looking at the 2015-16 (RE) and 2016-17 (BE) estimates, there is a significant increase in the allocation in education as compared to health and rural development. However, the increased allocation is mostly in the form of non-plan expenditure under revenue account which is meant for creation of new posts and provision of state scholarships.

The expenditure on rural development as a percentage of GSDP has not changed much over the years and kept around 6-7 per cent for the last couple of years. Among the different major heads under rural development, the expenditure on water and sanitation has come down from 3.74 per cent of GSDP in 2004-05 to 3.18 per cent in 2014-15. Against that, the allocations in housing and urban development have gone up from .067 per cent of GSDP to 1.53 per cent in 2014-15. Similarly, the social security and welfare programmes have also been focused in the recent five years through various CSS and state plans for the people of the state.

Table 17.7 provides the changes in the compositions of social sector expenditure. Education appears as the major head where consistently more than 40 per cent of the total social sector expenditure has been spent in most of the years of the last decade. The 2015-16 (RE) and 2016-17 (BE) shares also suggest the priority of the state government towards universalisation of education especially through the promotion of

Table 17.6: Expenditure on Social Sector as Percentage of GSDP at Current Prices: Major Heads from 2004-05 to 2016-17

	2016-17 (BE)	*2015-16 (RE)*	*2014-15*	*2013-14*	*2012-13*	*2011-12*	*2010-11*	*2009-10*	*2008-09*	*2007-08*	*2006-07*	*2005-06*	*2004-05*
Education, Sports, Culture, and Youth Welfare	11.15	9.03	7.46	6.59	6.53	7.08	6.68	8.53	8.54	6.91	7.22	6.40	6.42
General Education	10.37	8.57	6.42	5.65	5.88	5.90	5.60	7.51	7.32	6.09	6.53	5.55	6.09
Technical Education	0.08	0.08	0.09	0.15	0.06	0.39	0.22	0.04	0.05	0.04	0.04	0.36	0.00
Sports and Youth Services	0.46	0.20	0.48	0.32	0.32	0.35	0.45	0.24	0.96	0.49	0.40	0.16	0.14
Art and Culture	0.24	0.18	0.46	0.47	0.28	0.44	0.42	0.74	0.20	0.28	0.25	0.33	0.19
Public Health and family welfare	4.67	3.72	3.72	2.51	2.30	2.71	2.66	2.91	3.22	2.43	2.99	2.02	2.70
Medical and Public Health	4.67	3.56	3.47	2.41	2.19	2.60	2.57	2.75	3.11	2.29	2.86	1.92	2.58
Family Welfare	—	0.15	0.25	0.10	0.11	0.10	0.09	0.17	0.12	0.14	0.13	0.11	0.12
Rural Development	7.90	7.58	6.70	7.61	6.17	8.05	6.13	6.51	8.22	8.34	8.53	9.07	6.38
Water Supply and Sanitation	2.21	3.04	2.18	2.19	1.97	2.14	2.24	2.96	4.50	4.47	4.11	4.26	3.74
Housing and Urban Development	2.87	1.95	1.53	2.36	1.20	2.17	1.89	1.38	1.37	1.72	1.28	1.01	0.67
Broadcasting	0.13	0.16	0.10	0.12	0.11	0.14	0.14	0.14	0.11	0.11	0.11	0.11	0.10
Labour and Employment	0.20	0.18	0.12	0.11	0.10	0.08	0.08	0.10	0.10	0.11	0.07	0.07	0.07
Social Security and Welfare	1.91	1.19	1.21	1.43	1.28	1.74	1.18	0.98	1.03	1.03	1.02	1.02	0.76
Nutrition and Relief on Account of Natural Calamities	0.57	0.71	1.55	1.40	1.50	1.76	0.59	0.95	1.13	0.89	1.94	2.61	1.03
Others	0.08	0.09	0.08	0.09	0.08	0.09	0.09	0.11	0.10	0.09	0.09	0.11	0.12
Total	23.80	20.40	17.97	16.79	15.09	17.92	15.56	18.07	20.09	17.77	18.83	17.61	15.61

Source: Compiled and Calculated from Finance Accounts, CAG.

Table 17.7: Changes in the Composition of the Social Sector Expenditure from 2004-05 to 2016-17 (BE)

	2016-17 (BE)	*2015-16 RE)*	*2014-15*	*2013-14*	*2012-13*	*2011-12*	*2010-11*	*2009-10*	*2008-09*	*2007-08*	*2006-07*	*2005-06*	*2004-05*
Education, Sports, Culture, and Youth Welfare	46.85	44.23	41.53	39.23	43.30	39.51	42.92	47.20	42.51	38.89	38.37	36.36	41.12
General Education	43.58	41.99	35.74	33.65	38.98	32.92	35.96	41.55	36.46	34.28	34.71	31.54	39.01
Technical Education	0.34	0.38	0.53	0.88	0.41	2.17	1.42	0.23	0.24	0.25	0.22	2.04	0.00
Sports and Youth Services	1.92	0.97	2.70	1.89	2.09	1.96	2.88	1.34	4.80	2.78	2.13	0.88	0.90
Art and Culture	1.01	0.90	2.56	2.80	1.83	2.46	2.67	4.08	1.02	1.57	1.32	1.90	1.21
Public Health and Family Welfare	19.63	18.22	20.72	14.96	16.10	15.10	17.08	16.12	16.05	13.70	15.89	11.48	17.26
Medical and Public Health	19.63	17.47	19.33	14.38	15.35	14.53	16.50	15.20	15.46	12.91	15.22	10.88	16.50
Family Welfare	—	0.75	1.38	0.58	0.75	0.58	0.58	0.92	0.59	0.79	0.67	0.60	0.76
Rural Development	33.18	37.13	37.29	45.30	40.89	44.90	39.40	36.06	40.94	46.91	45.29	51.52	40.86
Water Supply and Sanitation	9.30	14.92	12.13	13.03	13.05	11.96	14.40	16.38	22.39	25.16	21.81	24.19	23.95
Housing and Urban Development	12.06	9.54	8.53	14.06	7.98	12.14	12.14	7.64	6.81	9.70	6.78	5.76	4.28
Broadcasting	0.56	0.76	0.55	0.70	0.74	0.80	0.92	0.80	0.54	0.63	0.57	0.60	0.67
Labour and Employment	0.84	0.89	0.69	0.65	0.69	0.44	0.54	0.55	0.48	0.61	0.39	0.38	0.46
Social Security and Welfare	8.03	5.85	6.74	8.49	8.49	9.72	7.59	5.41	5.12	5.82	5.43	5.78	4.88
Nutrition and Relief on Account of Natural Calamities	2.40	3.50	8.64	8.36	9.95	9.84	3.80	5.28	5.61	5.00	10.31	14.82	6.62
Others	0.34	0.42	0.47	0.51	0.56	0.49	0.59	0.63	0.49	0.50	0.45	0.64	0.76
Total	100.00	100.00	100.00	100.00	100.00	100.00	100.00	100.00	100.00	100.00	100.00	100.00	100.00

Source: Compiled and calculated from Finance Account, CAG.

elementary education. Public provision for health in the state is financed at around 15 per cent over the last 10 years with a maximum of 17.08 per cent in 2010-11 and a minimum of 11.48 per cent in 2005-06. The share of health in total social sector expenditure has not improved much despite a higher devolution in the union taxes during the initial years of FFC (Table 17.8). The expenditure on the rural development heads is mainly driven by the water supply and sanitation as well as the housing and urban development. Although there are declining share of water and sanitation over the years, it appears top in the priority list of the state government among different rural development programmes. Looking at the share of rural development, it can be seen that the public expenditure on the rural development programmes had been dominated in the initial few years up to 2007-08. After that, the expenditure on education started to take over the bulk of the social sector expenditure. In the first year of FFC (2014-15), the share of education in the total social sector expenditure was 41.53 per cent as compared to 37.29 per cent for rural development. The 2015-16 (RE) and 2016-17 (BE) figures also reveal priority of the government towards education, especially in elementary and secondary education.

Inter-sectoral Composition

From the inter-sectoral composition, it can be seen from Table 17.8 that the share of elementary education has been kept consistently over 60 per cent of the total expenditure on education which slightly dipped during 2010-11 and 2011-12. Such decline in the elementary education due to cuts under the heads of Teacher Training and Text Books as well as a substantial increase in the technical education and expenditure related to other heads including physical education during the fiscal years 2010-11 and 2011-12. On the other hand, the consistent higher share of the elementary education is partly explained by the SSA towards universalization of education and improving the nutritional level of the students in the elementary level.

Secondary education in the state has gained importance after the implementation of RMSA in 2009-10 (INR 393.35 crore has been allocated as compared to INR 129.54 crore in 2004-05) (Table 17.8). The fiscal year 2009-10 onwards, there has been a significant allocation in the secondary education though there have not many changes in terms of inter-sectoral share as well as the percentage of GSDP. The emphasis in elementary and secondary education led to a decline in the shares of

Table 17.8: Intra-Sectoral Allocation (in percentage) in Education, Health, and Rural Development

	2016-17 (BE)	*2015-16 (RE)*	*2014-15*	*2013-14*	*2012-13*	*2011-12*	*2010-11*	*2009-10*	*2008-09*	*2007-08*	*2006-07*	*2005-06*	*2004-05*
Education	100	100	100	100	100	100	100	100	100	100	100	100	100
Elementary Education	0.00	0.00	68.87	59.23	63.73	52.26	52.80	69.72	57.18	65.40	59.81	61.95	60.98
Secondary Education	0.00	0.00	17.18	22.65	21.01	19.94	20.25	20.86	25.00	23.41	27.12	20.10	16.23
Higher Education	0.00	0.00	7.41	7.35	6.67	6.06	6.45	5.84	6.60	6.18	9.12	9.32	14.42
Adult Education	0.00	0.00	0.89	1.57	0.77	0.80	1.02	0.68	0.73	0.79	0.86	0.95	0.90
Others General	94.57	83.75	4.20	6.64	6.77	14.77	15.70	2.33	9.84	3.49	2.45	1.60	7.46
Technical Education	0.78	0.89	1.45	2.56	1.04	6.18	3.79	0.56	0.65	0.73	0.64	6.07	0.00
Public Health and Family Welfare	100.00	100.00	100.00	100.00	100.00	100.00	100.00	100.00	100.00	100.00	100.00	100.00	100.00
Public Health	0.00	0.00	36.68	96.15	15.89	14.87	16.49	19.81	0.71	16.37	13.20	18.14	14.90
Medical Education	0.00	0.00	2.80	0.64	0.77	0.62	0.83	0.90	12.36	1.05	0.96	0.91	1.05
Others	100.00	95.88	53.84	70.64	68.84	80.69	79.28	73.60	83.28	76.79	81.61	75.74	79.65
Family Welfare	0.00	4.12	6.68	3.85	4.67	3.82	3.40	5.70	3.65	5.78	4.23	5.21	4.40
Rural Development	100.00	100.00	100.00	100.00	100.00	100.00	100.00	100.00	100.00	100.00	100.00	100.00	100.00
Water Supply and Sanitation	28.02	40.17	32.52	28.77	31.92	26.64	36.53	45.43	54.67	53.63	48.16	46.95	58.61
Housing and Urban Development	36.36	25.70	22.88	31.04	19.52	27.03	30.82	21.20	16.63	20.68	14.97	11.18	10.48
Broadcasting	1.69	2.05	1.48	1.55	1.81	1.79	2.34	2.21	1.33	1.34	1.27	1.17	1.64
Labour and Employment	2.52	2.41	1.86	1.44	1.68	0.97	1.38	1.52	1.16	1.29	0.87	0.73	1.12
Social Security and Welfare	24.20	15.75	18.09	18.74	20.75	21.65	19.27	15.01	12.50	12.40	11.98	11.21	11.95
Nutrition and Relief on Account of Natural Calamities	7.22	9.43	23.18	18.46	24.32	21.92	9.66	14.63	13.71	10.66	22.76	28.76	16.20

Source: Compiled and calculated from Finance Accounts, CAG.

higher education, adult education, and other expenditure. The share of higher education has declined from 14.42 per cent in 2004-05 to 7.41 per cent in 2014-15 (Table 17.8). In the current environment which is driven by information technology, it is important to go beyond the primary and secondary education and give some priority to build institutions for higher and technical education towards the creation of knowledge-based economy (IGIDR, 1999).

The intra-allocation for the health and family welfare reveals that the share of public health was around 16-17 per cent from 2004-05 to 2013-14. In 2014-15, there had been a significant increase in the intra-allocation for public health to a whopping 36.68 per cent as compared to 16.57 per cent 2013-14. The share of "others" that comprises Rural and Urban Health Services, System of Medicines, Hospital and Dispensaries and others consistently dominated over there years until 2014-15. In the case of family welfare, its intra-allocation share was increased from 4.40 per cent in 2004-05 to 5.70 per cent in 2009-10, and thereafter it showed a declining trend to be 3.85 per cent in 2013-14. However, the fiscal year 2014-15 had seen a better intra-allocation of 6.68 per cent as compared to the previous few years.

Comparing the share of the rural development, it can be seen that the priority of the state government has slightly shifted from water supply and sanitation to housing and urban development. The government used to spend about 50 per cent of the total expenditure devoted to rural development for water supply and sanitation up to 2008-09 and thereafter it experienced a gradual decline to 32.52 per cent in 2014-15. On the other hand, there has been an increase in the intra-allocation under the head of housing and urban development 2009-10 onwards, and it was 22.88 per cent in 2014-15 as compared to 10.48 per cent in 2004-05. However, much of the expenditure has been made at the expense of water supply and sanitation programmes. Focus has also been given in the areas of social security and welfare measure in the last couple of years. The intra-allocation in social security and welfare had gone up from 11.95 per cent in 2004-05 to 21.65 per cent in 2011-12 and then experienced a decline to 18.09 per cent 2014-15. The priority of the aspect is again restored, and the 2016-17 (BE) allocates 24.20 per cent of the aggregate expenditure under rural development heads (Table 17.9).

Conclusion

The above discussion and findings show that the fiscal health of the state has been improving in the last decade. The improvement of fiscal health of Arunachal Pradesh is to a great extent due to the implementation of FRBM Act. However, the contribution of the own revenue to state finance is quite low and its growth is diminishing although positive. Thus, the state is far away from becoming self-dependent and is highly dependent on central transfer. While power sector is a major contributor of the state revenue, the expansion of this sector is very slow. In this regard, development of basic infrastructure for rapid expansion of power sector and identifying the potential power sources and extracting them can be suggested to improve the revenue collection of the government. Another potential contributor to the state revenue is tourism sector which is yet to develop fully. While undeveloped transport and communication is hindering the expansion of this sector, factor like restricted area permit is also limiting the number of tourist arrivals from abroad to the state. Therefore, improvement of infrastructure along with steps to get the permission of visit the place by foreigner as easily as possible and also in a very short period of time can help to grow the tourism sector at a faster rate. Further necessary action has to be taken to improve the efficiency of tax collection as inefficient tax management is one of the factors limiting tax revenue collection by the state.

Stressing on the social sector expenditure, the overall per capita expenditure on the sector has increased over the last decade. As a percentage of GSDP and aggregate expenditure, there are fluctuations in the expenditure and the growth of expenditure during 2004-05 to 2009-10 was higher than the period 2010-11 to 2014-15. After the significant dip 2010-11 due to new FRBM targets, there has been a considerable improvement in the social sector expenditure in the last few years. However, the growth of capital expenditure has not matched with the growth of the revenue expenditure even after being one of the major beneficiaries of 14th Finance Commission Grants. Given the composition statistics, the focus has been shifted from rural development to promote education among the people in the last few years. Promotion of elementary education has been given the top priority followed by water and sanitation. Within the rural development, the state government has gradually cushioned the expenditure on water and sanitation in the recent years and giving more focus on housing and urban development.

Notes

1. The FRBM Act had been implemented in Arunachal Pradesh since 2006-07.
2. Average of revenue surplus of 2001-02 to 2003-04 is INR 96 crore as per *A Study on Finances of Arunachal Pradesh*, 14th Finance Commission, GOI.

References

Ahluwalia, M.S. (2000). "Economic performance of states in post-reform period", *Economic and Political Weekly,* 35 (19), 1637-1648.

Bhattacharjee, G. (2014). "The reality of special category states", *Economic and Political Weekly, 49*(40): 48-56.

Dev, S.M. and Mooij, J. (2002). "Social sector expenditures in the 1990s: Analysis of central and state budgets", *Economic and Political Weekly, 37*(9): 853-866.

Goswami, B. and Bezbaruah, M.P. (2011). "Social sector expenditures and their impact on human development: The Indian experience", *Indian Journal of Human Development, 5*(2).

Government of India (2016). *A Study on Finances of Arunachal Pradesh. 14th Finance Commission.* Accessed on October 12, 2016 from http://fincomindia.nic.in/writereaddata%5Chtml_en_files%5Cfincom14/others/2.pdf

Kurian, N.J. (2000). "Widening regional disparities in India: Some indicators", *Economic and Political Weekly, 35*(7): 538-550.

Mooij, J. and Dev, S.M. (2004). "Social sector priorities: An analysis of budgets and expenditures in India in the 1990s", *Development Policy Review, 22*(1): 97-120.

Prabhu, K.S. (2001). *Economic Reform and Social Sector Development.* New Delhi: Sage Publications.

Prabhu, K.S. (2005). "Social sectors and economic development", In: R.K. Sen (ed.), *Social Sector Development in India* (pp. 3-25). New Delhi: Deep and Deep Publications.

RBI (2016). Database on Indian Economy. Reserve Bank of India. Accessed from https://dbie.rbi.org.in/DBIE/dbie.rbi?site=statistics

Nayak, S.K.; Roy, N.C.; Mitra, A.; Nochi, L. and Lama, M. (2013). *A Study on Finances of Arunachal Pradesh.* Study report prepared for and submitted to 14th Finance Commission, Government of India. Accessed on October 01, 2016 from http://fincomindia.nic.in/ShowContentOne.aspx?id=27&Section=1

18
Digital Literacy and Entrepreneurship Development

A Case of Arunachal Pradesh

Mudang Tagiya, S. Sinha and *Gebi Basar*

Introduction

Today digital technology is moving at such a breakneck pace that it is difficult to keep up. In certain sectors, like the gaming and ICT industry, they cannot afford not to keep up. But other sectors may not appreciate this and could be missing out on opportunities.

Disruptive business models and technology will definitely create new opportunities. In the past, the Internet was one of the biggest disruptive technologies, and although it shook business models from top to bottom, it created so many global opportunities that today most successful companies cannot survive without it. But a technology trend does not have to be something large to be disruptive. It can be something that starts small but its use brings a radical change to the business, increased success in the market, and a better place for business and investment.

Information and communications technologies (ICT) have become pervasive in modern societies as tools for transforming education systems, supporting economic development through the creation of new products and services, providing access to information and expertise to support improvements in agriculture, health and education, and connecting communities, teachers and students. ICT provides teachers and students with the resources to collect and analyse data, create multimedia presentations and acquire a greater depth of knowledge.

However, one of the conditions for using the potential of ICT is to have access to the technology and the internet, and it is evident that there are wide disparities in the extent to which those technologies are available to people, both between and within countries (Anderson & Ainley, 2010). A second condition for employing the whole range of prospects offered by ICT is the development of expertise to use ICT in effective ways. The European Commission suggested that digital literacy is "increasingly becoming an essential life competence and the inability to access or use ICT has effectively become a barrier to social integration and personal development" (European Commission, 2008: 4). There are also many national statements of goals that include similar statements (MCEETYA, 2008; QCA, 2009; Office of Educational Technology, US Department of Education, 2010).

As the value of proficiency in using and managing digital technologies has become increasingly evident, its assessment has become an important component of monitoring the extent to which students develop "skills and knowledge for tomorrow's world" (OECD, 2014). Various forms of assessment of ICT literacy, either as part of large assessment programmes or as tools for teachers, are evident in countries such as Australia (ACARA, 2015), Chile (Claro *et al.*, 2012), Norway (Hatlevik, 2009) and the United States (Institute of Education Sciences, National Center for Education Statistics, 2012). International projects such as *Preparing for Life in a Digital Age* (Fraillon, Ainley, Schulz, Friedman & Gebhardt, 2014) and the *Assessment and Teaching of 21st Century Skills* (Griffin, McGaw & Care, 2012) are indicative of the increased interest at the international level in defining appropriate capabilities for the emerging age and exploring how those competencies can be assessed. With regard to adult skills in working with ICT, the Programme for the International Assessment of Adult Competencies (PIAAC) has examined the capacities of adults to solve problems in rich technological environments (OECD, 2013).

ICT literacy and digital literacy are conceptualized in a variety of ways. In general, the term digital literacy has been used in relation to a wider range of technologies than ICT literacy but the terms overlap to a considerable extent and are often used interchangeably. Neither has had a focus on technical aspects of the field such as programming and computer operations. Rather, they (and ICT literacy in particular) have had a focus on using ICT in various ways. The emphasis has been on computer applications because computers (and similar devices) have been regarded as an important element of ICT. Understandings of ICT literacy over the past 15 years have been much influenced by definition developed by the International ICT Literacy Panel in 2002 (International ICT Literacy Panel, 2002).

This definition stated that:

> ICT literacy is using digital technology, communications tools, and/or networks to access, manage, integrate, evaluate, and create information in order to function in a knowledge society.
> (*International ICT Literacy Panel*, 2002, p. 2)

An important feature of this definition is that it lists a set of cognitive processes associated with ICT literacy. Moreover, those processes were argued to represent a sequence of "increasing cognitive complexity".

Objectives of the Study

1. To study the status of digital literacy among the local women entrepreneurs of Arunachal Pradesh.
2. To study the level usage of the various digital platform in the business by the women entrepreneurs.

Review of Literature

Tailone Taylor Chiyangwa (2017) stated that digital skills will greatly reduce the operating costs and that improves the chances of success for an entrepreneur. Digital skills will make it possible for entrepreneur's to compete with larger business and improve the efficiency of the business. One does not have digital skills then it will be short changing oneself as an entrepreneur.

Patrice Braun (2008) from the study give the insight that today's business climate, women require meta competencies that range from technology skills to problem solving, initiative and enterprise skills, to teamwork, learning and self-management as well as communication and digital economy skills such as understanding the use of technology, new business models, interactive communication and social networking.

Patrick Barwise, Anita Elberse and Kathy Hammond (2002) review the research to-date on how the Internet is impacting marketing. It covers internet adoption and usage; online purchasing behaviour; internet advertising; internet economics and pricing; channels and intermediaries and online marketing strategy.

National Lifelong Learning Strategy (2020), Alex Grech (2014), "Having the knowledge and ability to effectively and critically navigate, evaluate and create information using a range of digital technologies. A digitally literate person can use technology strategically to find and evaluate information, connect and collaborate with others, produce and share original content, and use the Internet and technology tools to achieve many academic, professional and personal goals."

Erstad (2007) quoted "Digital skills include the ability to exploit the opportunities offered by ICT, and use them critically and innovatively in education and work. Digital skills also include the ability to be critical to sources and assess content. Use of digital tools is a skill the individual must acquire, maintain and continually develop, if he or she is to be a digitally skilled and critical citizen."

Ferrari (2012) stated that "Digital Competence is both a requirement and a right of citizens, if they are to be functional in today's society."

Canada Business Network (2017) in its publication mentioned that "It's important to look at the risks and benefits of using different information and communications technologies to improve business processes before investing in them. Streamlining your business systems with tools to manage your documents, your human resources, and your customer relationships works only if they can be implemented successfully and are beneficial to everyone involved."

Suzy Jackson (2017) in the article quotes that "Digital technology has vastly changed the work place for all types of business, not just those in IT or the tech sector. Ensuring that all members of your team at all levels have the right digital skills is vital on your route to growth."

Research Methodology

The present study was conducted in Itanagar the capital city of Arunachal Pradesh. The study conceived to be empirical in nature where both primary and secondary sources of information were used. The primary focus of the study concentrates on Digital Literacy aspects, the data were collected from diversified sets of the population representing different sections of the business. This may include Hospitality, Grocery, Garments and Textiles, Hardware and Electricals, and Beauty Parlor etc. The detailed Sampling frame is mentioned below:

Sample Frame

Study Region	*Sample Units*	*Size of the Universe*	*Total Sample*
Capital Complex, Arunachal Pradesh	Women (Local) Entrepreneurs	150 (Development Commissioner Govt. of India report)	40 (26.67%)

Types of Business	*Frequency*	*Percentage*	*Sampling Technique*
Hospitality	6	15%	
Garments	12	30%	
Grocery	7	17.5%	
Beauty Parlor	9	22.5%	Convenient
Hardware and Electricals	2	5%	
Browsing Centre	2	5%	
Any Other	2	5%	
Total	**40**	**100%**	

Tools and Techniques

The collected information was tabulated using statistical software SPSS version 21. Descriptive statistics have been performed to understand and interpret.

Analysis of the Data

The analysis of the data is done by considering research objectives of the study and hence landed into the following results.

Analysis I

The primary data was collected with the aim to study digital literacy among the women entrepreneurs of the local economy especially the local women who are the domicile of the state. The various digital platforms have been considered for the study which is mentioned in the official website of Ministry of Skills Development and Entrepreneurship. Those platforms were Internet banking, Mobile banking, Point of Sale, Unified Payment Interface (UPI), Mobile Wallet, Adhaar Enabled Payment System (AEPS), Unstructured Supplementary Service Data (USSD), Banking Cards etc.

It is found that different levels of response have collected for all the mentioned platforms. From the data set it is observed that the digital platforms like Adhaar Enabled Payment System, Unstructured Supplementary Service Data and Unified Payment Interface are not at all familiar by the respondents (0% of the total respondents) followed by POS which is 17.5 per cent of the total respondents. On the other hand, it is clearly seen that 100 per cent respondents familiar about banking cards like ATMs, credit cards etc. and 55 per cent respondents (n = 22) are aware of internet banking followed by 50 per cent respondents about Mobile Banking (n = 20).

Knowledge of Digital Platform

	Internet Banking	*Mobile Banking*	*POS*	*UPI*	*Mobile Wallet*	*AEPS*	*USSD*	*Banking Cards*
YES	22	20	7	0	11	0	0	40
NO	18	20	33	40	29	40	40	0

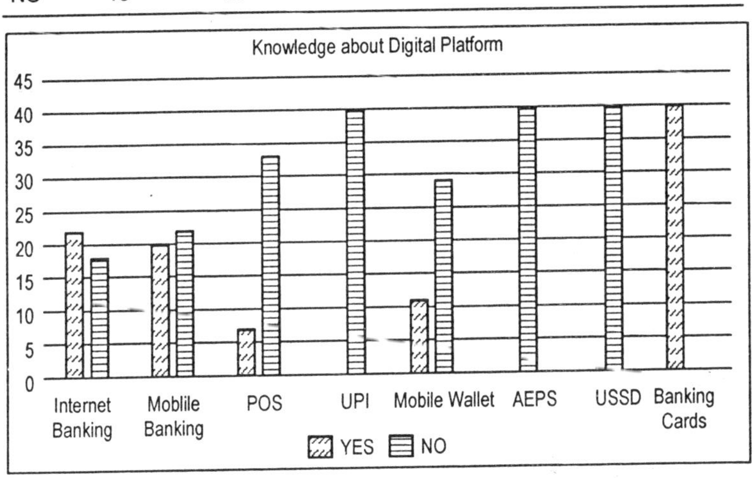

Analysis II

In the study, the attempts were made to understand the mode of level usage of the various digital platform in the business activities by the women entrepreneurs. For this, the researcher developed the scale using 5 points Likert scale to measure the objectives. The respondents were asked the question regarding the level of frequency in terms of usages and rate them in 1-5 scale where *1= Never, 2= Rarely, 3= Sometimes, 4 = Almost every time, 5= Every Time.* The following data set comes up.

Level of Uses of Digital Platforms

	Internet Banking via PC	*Mobile Banking*	*POS*	*UPI*	*Mobile Wallets (Paytm, Mobikwik etc.)*	*AEPS (Adhaar Enabled Payment System)*	*USSD*	*Banking Cards (ATMs, Credit Cards etc.)*
Mean	2.25	2.2	1.35	1	1.53	1	1	3.53
Median	2	1.5	1	1	1	1	1	4
Mode	1	1	1	1	1	1	1	4
Std. Deviation	1.37	1.45	.89	0.0	1.01	0	0	1.15
Variance	1.89	2.113	.797	0.0	1.03	0	0	1.33

From the data set it is clearly observed that Banking Cards (ATMs, Credit Cards etc.) has got the highest rate of usage in their business activities with the values of mean = 3.53, median = 4 and Mode = 4. However, Internet Banking stands in the second position with the mean value of 2.25, Median-2 and Mode =1 followed by Mobile banking with the mean value of 2.2, Median = 1.5 and Mode = 1. From the above discussion, there is no doubt that Banking Cards are the most used for the business activities by the entrepreneurs which may be due to fewer requirements of electronic platforms like computers, laptops, Mobile phone or any communication medium.

Limitations of the Study

The present study was conducted to understand the present status of digital literacy in the local economy of the study region of the state of Arunachal Pradesh. The outcome results of the study cannot be generalized to the state as a whole as well as for the region since the study was conducted in the capital complex of the state. Since sample size was 40 so the possibilities of sample adequacy would likely to be possible.

The concept of digital literacy is not popular in the study region and the idea of the digital mode of transactions is a very new initiative after demonetization, so there was a very little possibility of non-sampling errors. However, efforts were taken to minimize such non-sampling error.

Conclusion

This research paper essentially focuses on digital literacy among women entrepreneurs in Arunachal Pradesh. The research outcomes are indeed quite interesting. The study found that the local women entrepreneurs in the organized market are very less as compared to the outlanders doing business in the state especially the entrepreneur's domicile from Manipur, Nagaland, Nepal, Tibet and Mainland India. The reason could be that the respective respondent women entrepreneurs were the first generation entrepreneurs of the state.

The result has also revealed that there is a knowledge gap between various digital platforms since many respondents have not even heard about the certain digital mode of transaction platforms like USSD, UPI and AEPS for their business. However, it is found that banking cards are very much popular and in the practices in the business activities, the reason could be it exists decade back compare to other transactions mediums. Now, it is a high time to fill up these gaps by the concern authorities by providing adequate educations in terms of training, seminars, and workshops so as to build their digital competency in the age of cashless economy. The vision of Government of India to make digitalize to rural India by 2019 will take a longer time to achieve unless the segment, as well as the region, is not literate or competent enough in the area of digitization. This study may be taken as a foundation work in this respective dimension.

References

Anderson, R. and J. Ainley (2010). *Technology and learning: Access in schools around the world*, 21-33.

Australian Curriculum and Reporting Authority (ACARA) (2015). *National Assessment Programme—ICT Literacy Years 6 and 10 2014 Report*. Sydney: ACARA. http://www.nap.edu.au/verve/_resources/D15_8761__NAPICT_2014_Public_Report_Final.pdf

Barwise, Patrick, Anita Elberse and Kathy Hammond (2002). *Marketing and the Internet: a Research Review*. London, UK: London Business School.

Beetham, Helen, Lou McGill and Allison Littlejohn (2009). "Thriving in the 21st century: Learning Literacies for the digital age (LLiDA project): Executive Summary, Conclusions and recommendations."

Buckingham, David (2009). *The future of media literacy in the digital age: some challenges for policy and practice*. na.

Canada Business Network (2017). What is digital literacy and how can it help in your business? https://canadabusiness.ca/blog/what-is-digital-literacy-and-how-can-it-help-your-business/

Chinien, Chris and France Boutin (2011). *Defining essential digital skills in the Canadian workplace*. Human Resources and Skills Development Canada.

Claro, Magdalena, David D. Preiss, Ernesto San Martín, Ignacio Jara, J. Enrique Hinostroza, Susana Valenzuela, Flavio Cortes and Miguel Nussbaum (2012). "Assessment of 21st century ICT skills in Chile: Test design and results from high school level students", *Computers and Education* 59, No. 3: 1042-1053.

Chung, JiEun and Stuart Elliott (2015). *Adults, Computers and Problem Solving: " What's the Problem?" OECD Skills Studies*. OECD Publishing. 2, rue Andre Pascal, F-75775 Paris Cedex 16, France.

Fraillon, J., Schulz, W., Friedman, T., Ainley, J. and Gebhardt, E. (Eds.) (2015). *International Computer and Literacy Information Study 2013 Technical Report*. Amsterdam, The Netherlands: InternationalAssociation for the Evaluation of Educational Achievement (IEA).

Erstad, Ola (2007). "Conceiving digital literacies in schools-norwegian experiences," *Digital Literacy* 310.

Europea, Commissione (2008). "Digital Literacy European Commission working paper and Recommendations from Digital Literacy High-Level Expert Group. e-Inclusion Ministerial Conference & Expo. 30 novembre-2 dicembre 2008." *URL:< http://ec. europa. Eu/information_society/eeurope/i2010/docs/ digital_literacy/digital_literacy_review. pdf>.(ultimaconsult azione 30.05. 2011).*

Ferrari, Anusca (2012). "Digital competence in practice: An analysis of frameworks." *Sevilla: JRC IPTS. (DOI: 10.2791/82116)*

Ferrari, Anusca, Yves Punie and Christine Redecker (2012). "Understanding digital competence in the 21st century: An analysis of current frameworks." In: *European Conference on Technology Enhanced Learning*, pp. 79-92. Springer, Berlin, Heidelberg.

Force, Gender Equity Task (1997). "Ministerial Council on Education, Employment, Training and Youth Affairs." *Gender equity: A framework for Australian Schools*.

Griffin, P. and Care, E. (Eds.) (2015). *Assessment and teaching of 21st-century skills: Methods and approach*. Dordrecht: Springer.

Grimes, Seamus (2003). "The digital economy challenge facing peripheral rural areas." *Progress in Human Geography*, 27(2): 174-193.

Hartley, John (2010). *The uses of digital literacy*. Transaction Publishers.

Hartley, John, Kelly McWilliams, Jean Burgess and John Banks (2008). "The uses of multimedia: Three digital literacy case studies." *Media International Australia* 128(1): 59-72.

Hatlevik, O.E. (2009). "How to identify and understand digital literacy among 9th-grade Norwegian students: Examining the influences from school and home on student's digital literacy", *Nordic Journal of Digital Literacy*, (03/04), 159-173.

Hobbs, Renee (2010). *Digital and media literacy: A plan of action*, Washington, DC: The Aspen Institute.

Institute of Education Sciences, National Center for Education Statistics. (2012).

National Assessment of Educational Progress (NAEP) Technology and Engineering Literacy (TEL) Assessment. Washington, DC: Retrieved from http://nces.ed.gov/nationsreportcard/tel/

Panel, ITC Literacy. "Digital Transformation (2002). A Framework for ICT Literacy. A Report of the International ICT Literacy Panel, Educational Testing Service."

Johansson, Börje, Charlie Karlsson and Roger R. Stough (2006). "Entrepreneurship, clusters and policy in the emerging digital economy." *The emerging digital economy*: 1-19.

Johansson, Börje, Charlie Karlsson and Roger Stough (eds.) (2006). *The Emerging Digital Economy: Entrepreneurship, Clusters and Policy.* Springer Science and Business Media.

John Ainley, Wolfman Schulz and Julian Fraillon (2016). "A global measure of digitgal and ICT literacy skills". *Australian Council for Educational Research.* 2-5

Jones, Barbara and Suzanne L. Flannigan (2006). "Connecting the digital dots: Literacy of the 21st century", *Educause Quarterly* 29(2): 8-10.

Kollmann, Tobias (2006). "What is E-Entrepreneurship?—Fundamentals of Company Founding in the Net Economy", *International Journal of Technology Management*, 33(4): 322-340.

Koltay, Tibor (2011). "The media and the illiteracies: Media literacy, information literacy, digital literacy", *Media, Culture and Society*, 33(2): 211-221.

Malecki, Edward J. and Bruno Moriset (2007). *The digital economy: Business organization, production processes and regional developments.* Routledge.

Martin, Allan (2008). "Digital literacy and the 'digital society'", *Digital Illiteracies: Concepts, Policies and Practices*, 30: 151-176.

McAuley, Alexander, Bonnie Stewart, George Siemens and Dave Cormier (2010). "The MOOC Model for Digital Practice."

Media Smarts, (2016). *Digital literacy fundamentals.* Retrieved from http://mediasmarts.ca/digital-media-literacy-fundamentals/digital-literacy-fundamentals

Mutula, Stephen M. and Pieter Van Brakel (2007). "ICT skills readiness for the emerging global digital economy among small businesses in developing countries: a Case study of Botswana." *Library Hi Tech* 25, no. 2: 231-245.

OECD (2012). Literacy, numeracy and problem-solving in technology-rich environments: Framework for the OECD survey of adult skills.

OECD (2013). *OECD Skills Outlook 2013: First Results from the Survey of Adult Skills.* OECD Publishing. http://dx.doi.org/10.1787/9789264204256-en

OECD (2014). Technical Report of the Survey of Adult Skills (PIAAC). OECD Publishing.

Office of Educational Technology US Department of Education (2010). *Transforming American education: Learning powered by technology (US National Education Technology Plan 2010).*

Patrice Braun (2008). WOMEN ENTREPRENEURS IN THE DIGITAL ECONOMY: WHAT SKILLS DO THEY REALLY NEED? *AGSE*

Prensky, Marc (2001). "Digital natives, digital immigrant's part 1." *On the horizon*, 9(5): 1-6.

Pandey, Ms. Vandana Soni Dr. Mrs. BB (2016). "Impact of Digitalization in E-Marketing."

Qualifications and Curriculum Authority (2007). *About information and communication technology: Assessment guidance*. London, UK

Suzy Jackson (2017). "*Developing digital literacy to grow your business*". North east growth hub, 20th September, https://www.North Eastgrowthhub.co.uk/index.php/insights/developing-digital-literacy-grow-your-business.

The European e-Skills Forum. (2004). E-Skills for Europe: Towards 2010 and beyond.

Tailone Taylor Chiyangwa (2017). Why Digital Skills are key to successful entrepreneurs. https://www.linkedin.com/pulse/why-digital-skills-key-successful-entrepreneurship-chiyangwa. Retrived on 12.01.2018

Tyner Kathleen (2014). Literacy *in a digital world: Teaching and learning in the age of information*. Routledge.

Visser, Marijke (2013). "Digital Literacy and Public Policy through the Library Lens", *Maine Policy Review* 22(1): 104-113.

Vuorikari, Riina, Yves Punie, Stephanie Carretero Gomez and Godelieve Van Den Brande (2016). *DigComp 2.0: The Digital Competence Framework for Citizens. Update Phase 1: The Conceptual Reference Model*. No. JRC101254. Joint Research Centre (Seville site), 2016.

Warnick, Barbara (2001). *Critical literacy in a digital era: Technology, rhetoric and the public interest*. Routledge.

Warschauer, Mark (2004). *Technology and social inclusion: Rethinking the digital divide*. MIT press.

Websites accessed on 15 January, 2018

https://www.North Eastgrowthhub.co.uk/index.php/insights/developing-digital-literacy-grow-your-business

https://www.clickz.com/how-can-digital-literacy-help-you-understand-your-customers/108894/

https://www.mashandco.tv/en/the-importance-of-digital-literacy/

https://landing.adobe.com/content/dam/offermanager/en/na/marketing/Education/5_Benefits_of_Digital_Literacy.pdf?trackingid=Q3FWPYK8&mv=email

https://theaccountant.org.mt/the-importance-of-e-leadership-in-the-digital-economy/

http://afrodigital.org/digital-skills-key-successful-entrepreneurship/
http://www.oecd.org/skills/piaac/PIAAC%20Framework%202012—20Revised%2028oct2013_ebook.pdf
http://www.ecompetences.eu
http://afrodigital.org/digital-skills-key-successful-entrepreneurship/
https://www.linkedin.com/pulse/why-digital-skills-key-successful-entrepreneurship-chiyangwa

19
Working and Perceptions of Beneficiaries towards MGNREGA in Arunachal Pradesh

Dol Bahadur Thapa

Introduction

Poverty is the root cause of all social evils. A country cannot excel unless its people come out from acute poverty and hunger. An inclusive approach is the only way for bringing those economically unprivileged sections of the society into the mainstream of the country. In order to eradicate the problem of unemployment and poverty, in particular, Government of India enacted the National Rural Employment Guarantee Act (NREGA), 2005 (*renamed as Mahatma Gandhi National Rural Employment Guarantee Act, MGNREGA*). As a safety net for the poor MGNREGA aims at creating a demand-driven village infrastructure, including durable assets to increase the opportunities for sustained employment. It is a biggest poverty and unemployment alleviation programme in the world. The Act provides a legal guarantee for 100 days of employment in every financial year to adult members of every rural household. Adult members of a rural household, willing to do unskilled manual work, may apply for registration in writing or orally to the local Gram Panchayat. The Gram Panchayat after due verification will issue a Job Card within 15 days of application. The Job Card will bear the photograph of all adult members of the household willing to work under MGNREGA and is free of cost. A Job Card holder may submit a written application for employment to the Gram Panchayat, stating the time and duration for which work is sought. The Gram Panchayat will issue a dated receipt of the written application for employment, against which the guarantee of providing employment within

15 days operates. Employment will be given within 15 days of application for work, if it is not then daily unemployment allowance as per the Act, has to be paid. Liability of payment of unemployment allowance is of the States. Work should ordinarily be provided within 5 km radius of the village. In case work is provided beyond 5 km, extra wages of 10 per cent are payable to meet additional transportation and living expenses. Wages are to be paid according to the Minimum Wages Act, 1948 for agricultural labourers in the State unless the Centre notifies a wage rate which will not be less than Rs. 60/per day. Equal wages will be provided to both men and women. Wages are to be paid according to piece rate or daily rate. Disbursement of wages has to be done on weekly basis and not beyond a fortnight in any case.

In the context of Arunachal Pradesh, a tribal dominated state, MGNREGA is seen as a very powerful instrument responsible for driving rural transformation processes and economic empowerment. However, due to low literacy and capabilities to negotiate with the systems, these tribal communities are often at a receiving end although the Act has given enormous importance to the communities as an entitlement. Coupled with a low level of functional literacy on NREGS on one hand and the low performance of Panchayats in dealing with the multitudinal processes as provided under the Act, the anticipated level of development in tribal villages is not happening properly. The Act has given special status to tribal communities in terms of prioritizing their land development and production needs but in the absence of enough facilitation and linkages the tribal communities are failing from accessing or properly utilizing the provisions of the Act.

The performance of MGNREGA in the Arunachal Pradesh with regard to providing employment to the household is declining very rapidly as compared with the other states like Assam, Tripura, Madhya Pradesh, Gujarat, Rajasthan, Himachal Pradesh, Karnataka, Maharashtra and other states. The statistical figures collected from Ministry of Rural Development, Government of India unfold that Arunachal Pradesh stands in the first position among the low performing States in providing employment (Table 19.1).

Hence there is every reason to investigate as to why MGNREGA in Arunachal Pradesh appears to be on the relatively slower side of progress. There is also the existence of misplaced priorities between the objective of the act and actual ground level implementation of the programme. Work on water conservation and harvesting hold ranks first in state priority list, however, work mostly undertaken is towards rural connectivity which is ranked 8th on the basis of state priority.

Table 19.1: Household Employment Provided: Low-Performing States

State	Overall Decline (%)
Arunachal Pradesh	**71**
Karnataka	33
Gujarat	32
Maharashtra	25
Assam	17
Himachal Pradesh	10
Rajasthan	10
Madhya Pradesh	7
Tripura	4

Source: Ministry of Rural Development, Government of India, 2011.

The experience of MGNREGA implementation has also thrown up some issues in terms of the inadequate spread of awareness regarding the Act, low demand for work, delays in initiation of work and wage disbursements due to Panchayat's dependencies on already overworked technical staff. Further, the sectoral allocation under MGNREGS is not proportionate and also does not follow a logic. As per the Acts, Land Development and Flood Control get the least priority and hence get the lowest sanction. The mechanism of payment through Post offices also raised many questions in terms of timely payment and required cash availability at the branch post offices. The one aspect that is starkly evident in the villages is that there is an urgent need for support to Gram Panchayats. Assigned with the task of implementing a project of a magnitude as the MGNREGS, many Panchayats find themselves unprepared to shoulder the responsibility with inadequate human resource skilled in technical projects. Many members are also relatively inexperienced in the processes of systematic problem solving, planning and analysis etc. Besides, many Panchayats are also wrought with problems from within, with much left to be desired especially in terms of transparency and public accountability. Further, as per Ministry of Rural Development, Government of India reported that the work completion rate of MGNREGA in Arunachal Pradesh was found to be only 9 per cent.

Under this backdrop the current study intends to unfold the performance of MGNREGA with suggestive measures in Arunachal Pradesh, viewing that MGNREGS is the largest public investment in developing sustainable assets and rural infrastructure; as the largest employment generation programme in the Nation; as a social safety net; as an entitlement empowering rural people; apart from the fact that it contributes to the economic empowerment alongside better management of natural resource base.

Review of Literature

MGNREGA is considered as a "Silver Bullet" for the eradication of rural poverty and unemployment, by way of generating demand for productive labour force in villages (Jena & Ghosh, 2014). MGNREGA was implemented in the year 2006 with the main objective to eradicate poverty by providing 100 days of work per year to all rural households whose adults are ready to do unskilled physical labour at the minimum wage. Every year, on an average, 2320 crore person days are generated, 5 crore rural households and 9 crore adults are given guaranteed employment with about half of them being women and another half coming from Scheduled Tribe categories thereby constituting massive exercise at social inclusion (Goyal, 2014).

Borah & Bordoloi (2014) conducted their study in 14 blocks of Sonitpur district of Assam. They have studied the impact of MGNREGA on women empowerment in the district. They concluded that the performance of MGNREGA is not fully satisfactory. The scheme could not ensure the 100 days job guarantee to the majority of job card holders in the studied district. Further, they have attempted to identify the various obstacles that lies in the implementation of the scheme.

Kumar (2014) in his study conducted in Sirsa, Ambala and Hissar districts of Haryana attempted to explain the importance of social audit in developmental schemes like MGNREGA. The study found out that most of the Gram Panchayats had conducted social audit twice in a year. But very few issues were raised by the people in those Gram Panchayats.

Sharma (2014) explained the reasons for migration in urban and rural areas and how MGNREGA can be an effective tool for reducing such migration. She conducted a study in Anantapur, Andhra Pradesh and observed that MGNREGA had brought down the migration level substantially due to the availability of work. Her study in Gujarat, Maharashtra, Rajasthan, and Madhya Pradesh found out that the intensity of migration had come down to the families of the respondents and also children's education was positively benefited.

Hazarika (2014) examined the impact of MGNREGA on income and migration of people of Lakhimpur District, Assam. The study found that scheme has a positive impact on eradicating poverty by increasing income of people and decreasing the rate of rural migration.

Data and Approach

The present study has made an attempt to understand the working and perceptions of beneficiaries towards MGNREGA in the state of Arunachal Pradesh.

The study is based on both primary and secondary data. Primary data were collected from the well-structured questionnaire, discussions with PRI members, workers, the general public, block and district officials and Cardholders. The analysis is based on the primary data collected from 450 households from the three districts in Arunachal Pradesh. Further, three blocks from each district and one village from each block has been selected on the basis of its remoteness from the urban centres. For secondary data, various books, journals, handbooks, government reports etc. related to the study has been duly referred. The collected data have been analyzed and interpreted with the help of simple percentage method.

Basic Profile of the Surveyed Households

The presence of physical capital and the way it is managed and maintained is a key determinant of the quality of life in any given community. The physical resources like schools, hospitals, post offices, banks etc. provide requisite services to the public at large (*see* Table 19.2).

The infrastructure and services are most important in offering direct benefits and support to rural households. However, the above-surveyed villages did not have post office branch, bank, primary health centres or even schools beyond middle level. These significantly undermined livelihood outcomes. The Anganwadi Centres and Fair Price Shops/PDS depots are functioning in all the villages but people have reported dissatisfaction (*see* Table 19.3).

Table 19.3 presents the basic characteristics of the households covered in field survey across in East Siang district of Arunachal Pradesh. Among the selected households, 93.3 per cent belong to the Scheduled Tribe social group; 6.4 per cent belong to the 'Other Backward Caste' (OBC) and remaining. As regard to whether the surveyed households had a ration card, it was found that 62.9 per cent had the Below Poverty Line (BPL) card, while 29.6 had the Above Poverty Line (APL) card, 2.0 per cent had the AAY card and 5.6 per cent did not possess any ration card. As regard to the Mahatma Gandhi National Rural Employment Guarantee Act (MGNREGA) job card, it was found that 91.3 per cent of

Table 19.2: Selected Characteristics of the Surveyed Villages

Sl. No.	*Characteristics*	*Districts*								
		East Siang			*Changlang*			*West Kameng*		
1.	Name of the Circle	Mebo	Pasighat	Ruksin	Changlang	Khimiyong	Nampong	Bomdila	Dirang	Kalaktang
2.	Name of the Village	Mebo	Niglok	Berung	Khengku	Bobang	Manchum	Sera	Yewang	Morshing
3.	Major Tribe	Adi	Galo	Adi	Thangsa	Thangsa	Thangsa	Monpa	Monpa	Monpa
	Availability of Infrastructural facilities									
4.	Pucca Road	Yes	Yes	Yes	Yes	No	No	No	Yes	Yes
5.	Fair Weather Road	Yes	Yes	Yes	Yes	No	Yes	No	Yes	Yes
6.	Primary school	Yes	Yes	Yes	Yes	Yes	Yes	Yes	Yes	Yes
7.	Middle school	Yes	No	Yes	Yes	Yes	No	Yes	Yes	Yes
8.	Higher secondary school	No	No	No	No	No	No	No	No	No
9.	Primary Health centres	No	Yes	Yes	No	No	Yes	No	No	Yes
10.	Doctors	No	No	No	No	No	Yes	No	No	No
11.	Community Health Worker	Yes	Yes	Yes	Yes	Yes	Yes	Yes	Yes	Yes
12	Fair Price Shop	Yes	Yes	Yes	No	No	No	No	No	Yes
13	Market	No	Yes	No	Yes	Yes	No	Yes	No	Yes
14	Post Office	No	No	No	No	No	No	No	No	No
15	Banks	No	No	No	No	No	No	No	No	No
16	Public Transport	Yes	No	Yes	No	No	No	No	No	Yes

Source: Field Survey 2017.

Table 19.3: Socio-Economic Profile of the Surveyed Households

Characteristics	*Classification*	*Percentage (%)*
Social Group	SC	1(0.2)
	ST	420(93.3)
	OBC	29(6.4)
Household having MGNREGA job card	Yes	411(91.3)
	No	39(8.7)
Type of Ration Card held	APL	133(29.6)
	BPL	283(62.9)
	AAY	9(2.0)
	None	25(5.6)
Ownership of House	Own	433(96.2)
	Rented	17(3.8)
Type of house	Pucca	90(20.0)
	Semi-Pucca	181(40.2)
	Kutcha	179(39.8)
Household with access to electricity	Yes	442(98.2)
	No	8(1.8)
Household with access to toilet facilities	Yes	394(87.6)
	No	56(12.4)
Major source of drinking water	Hand Pump (own)	4(0.9)
	Tap Water (own)	197(43.8)
	Hand borewell (public)	6(1.3)
	Water tap (public)	234(52.0)
	Tank/pond/stream	9(2.0)

Source: Field Survey 2017.

the surveyed households did possess a job card while 8.7 per cent of the households did not have the job card. As regard to the ownership of the house in which they were staying it was found that 96.2 per cent of the respondents surveyed stayed in their own house and only 3.8 per cent stayed in accommodations provided by their landlords. Further with regard to the type of house in which they were staying, 39.8 per cent had Kutcha houses, while 40.2 had semi-pucca houses and only 20.0 per cent had pucca houses. When enquired as to how did they acquire the house then the majority of the respondents (83.3%) said that they had built the house themselves. When enquired if their dwellings had electricity connection, then as high as 98.2 per cent of them replied in affirmative. But everyone complained about the supply of electricity. As regard to availability of toilet in the houses around 87.6 per cent households had toilet facilities at home, whereas 12.4 per cent did not have that facility. With regard to the major source of drinking water, it was observed that 52.0 per cent of the households had a public water tap nearby, while around 43.8 per cent had tap water system in their homes.

Perceptions of Beneficiaries Towards MGNREGA

The perceptions of the beneficiaries towards MGNREGA was assessed in terms of obtaining of job card, use of job card, number of job card and number of days of employment, work undertaken etc. in a year.

Table 19.4: Responses of the MGNREGA beneficiaries on Job Card

Sl. No.	*Responses on*	*Options*	*Beneficiaries (N = 411)*	*Percentage (%)*
1.	Place of getting job card	Panchayat Office	402	97.7
		BDO	9	2.3
2.	Use of job card	Know	353	86.0
		Don't know	58	14.0
3.	Problem in getting job card	Faced	93	22.6
		Not faced	318	77.4
4.	Number of job card in the family	1	332	80.8
		More than 01	79	19.2

Source: Field Survey 2017.

It is found from Table 19.4 that 97.7 per cent of beneficiaries had received job card from Panchayat Office whereas rest 2.3 per cent beneficiaries got job card from block development office. Interestingly it was found that only 14.0 per cent of the beneficiaries do know about the use of job card and its various benefits whereas the rest 86.0 per cent of cardholders had no idea about its use. Further, it was also found that only 22.6 per cent of the cardholders faced difficulties to obtain the job card, while the rest 77.4 per cent of beneficiaries did not face any kind of problem to obtain the job card. Around 19.2 per cent of beneficiaries had more than one job card in their family, whereas as high as 80.8 per cent beneficiaries had only one job cardholder in their family.

As a whole, it was found that the beneficiaries had very little knowledge about the MGNREGA. It was found that 78.4 per cent of cardholders did not have any knowledge about the various schemes under the act, whereas only 21.6 per cent of cardholders were aware of the schemes under MGNREGA like sanitation, flood control, rural connectivity, canals, horticulture, land development etc. Further, when asked about the existing wage rate under the scheme, it was found that there was no fixed wage rate in all the surveyed villages. Till now only 79.4 per cent cardholders had opened a bank account, whereas rest 20.6 per cent cardholders did not have any bank account, they used to receive

Table 19.5: Awareness among the Beneficiaries about MGNREGA

Sl. No.	*Responses on*	*Options*	*Beneficiaries (N = 411)*	*Percentage (%)*
1.	About Various schemes	Do	89	21.6
		Don't	322	78.4
2.	About Wages per day	Yes	333	81.0
		Can't say	78	19.0
3.	About Opening bank account	Yes	326	79.4
		No	85	20.6
4.	About funding	Yes	49	11.9
		No	362	88.1
5.	About activities undertaken	Do	404	98.2
		Don't	7	1.8
6.	About social audit	Do	78	18.9
		Don't	333	81.1

Source: Field Survey 2017.

their wages in cash. Whereas, the act says that all cardholder should have an account and the entitled remuneration are to be credited to their account. Among the surveyed beneficiaries only 18.9 per cent beneficiaries had some knowledge about the social audit System. Surprisingly, 81.1 per cent of the cardholders did not have any idea about the social audit system.

Table 19.6 shows that 65.8 per cent of the beneficiaries were not satisfied with the average days of employment generated annually. Further 77.0 per cent of the surveyed household were not satisfied with the quality and the work that was being undertaken. In total 67.1 per cent of the beneficiaries felt that their livelihoods had improved because of MGNREGA. As those beneficiaries believed that the act has increased the daily income for the household which in turn has led to increase in their household savings. But, the remaining 32.9 per cent of the

Table 19.6: Perceptions of the Beneficiaries of MGNREGA

Sl. No.	*Responses on*	*Options*	*Beneficiaries (N = 411)*	*Percentage (%)*
1.	Average days of employment provided per household	Satisfied	141	34.2
		Not satisfied	270	65.8
2.	Work undertaken	Satisfied	316	77.0
		Not satisfied	95	23.0
3.	Improves livelihood	Yes	276	67.1
		No	135	32.9
4.	Successful	Yes	241	58.7
		No	170	41.3

Source: Field Survey 2017.

beneficiaries felt that MGNREGA had no impact on their livelihoods. It was also found that the in some cases they were not paid the total amount entitled to them.

It is found from Table 19.6 that 58.7 per cent of the respondents felt that MGNREGA had succeeded in their areas as they were successful in constructing assets like retaining wall, roads, CC drain in their villages. This employment scheme was also helpful in increasing the savings of households. The remaining 41.3 per cent of respondents felt that MGNREGA was a failure programme in their circle as the scheme was not providing 100 days of work and because of the corrupt practices of ill-distribution of pay to the workers.

Conclusion

From the above discussion and findings, it may be concluded that most of the beneficiaries of Arunachal Pradesh did not have proper knowledge about the MGNREGA programme. The job cardholders did not get actual wage amount as per MGNREGA. Most of the respondents did not have proper knowledge about the schemes, benefits available etc. under MGNREGA. Some of the beneficiaries did not have a bank account and their wages were not being credited to a bank account. From the personal interview, it was found that a system of favouritism prevailed in terms of allocation of the card and receiving wages. A job card is usually distributed as per the will of Panchayat leaders. Hence, it is a big question that whether MGNREGA is successful in the studied district or not, as mixed responses from beneficiaries has been observed in the present study. If government actively monitors all the activities under MGNREGA, there is a greater possibility that knowledge and perceptions of beneficiaries will change in future towards MGNREGA.

References

Sharma, A. (2014). "MGNREGA: An alternative to migration," *Kurukshetra*, 62(11): 26-28.

Kumar, G. Ravi and Sandhya, S. (2014). "Mahatma Gandhi National Rural Employment Guarantee Programme and its impact on the livelihood opportunity's in village Economy", Acharya Nagarjuna University, *Social Science Journal*, p. 10.

Borah, K. and R. Bordoloi (2014). "MGNREGA and its impact on daily waged women workers: A case study of Sonitpur district of Assam," *IOSR Journal of Economics and Finance,* 4(4): 40-44.

Tripathy, K.K. (2013). "Rural wage guarantee: Implementation and challenges", *Kurukshetra*, February 2013, 61(IV): 12-15.

Prasad, K.V.S. (2012). "Performance of Mahatma Gandhi National Rural Employment Guarantee Act (MGNREGA): An overview," *International Journal of Management and Business Studies*, 2(4): 99-103.

Goyal, L.C. (2014). "Removal of rural poverty," *Yojana*, 58 (May issue): 58-60.

Pal, M. (2013). "Impact of rural development programme on the quality of life of rural people," *Kurukshetra,* 6(12): 20-23.

Hazarika, S. (2014). "MGNREGA and its impact on migration in Lakhimpur district of Assam," *Vision NE,* 1(2): 116-126.

Jena, S.K. and K. Ghosh (2013). MGNREGA "Silver Bullet" for Sustainable Poverty Eradication: A Case Study of Koraput District of Odisha," Proceedings on Rural Development in India: Issues, Progress and Programme Effectiveness. RGU, *Archers and Elevators*, Bangalore, pp. 18-33.

Kumar, V. (2014). "Social audit in MGNREGA: A case study of three districts of Haryana," *Shiv Shakti International Journal in Multidisciplinary and Academic Research*, 3(3): 177-181.

http://nrega.nic.in

http://arunachalpradesh.gov.in

20
Women's Work and Time Utilisation Pattern in Rural Arunachal Pradesh

A View from the Field

Dil Bahadur Gurung

Introduction

Women continue to do majority of the household work, whether employed or not, which is the most striking characteristics of household labour (Shelton and Daphne, 1996). In the traditional societies, domestic work is the main input for household production and consumption. Household economic activities consist of both market production and non-market production; and non-market production is meant for household consumption (Shimray, 2004). In rural areas, the basic nature of women work falls in the non-market activity. Women perform seasonal work, raising children, cattle work (milking, feeding and cleaning cow sheds), fetching water, fuel wood and fodder etc. "In poor agrarian economies with significant component of non-market activities the range of what constitutes housework is different from those of the advanced market economies. Boundaries of household work and economically gainful work are difficult to draw in such economies where non-market activities predominate" (Kalpagam, 1999).

Apart from domestic house work duties, women are involved in rural activities at varying level in different farming system across the globe. The most influential school of thought in explaining women's participation in agriculture is the one which views women's participation rates in agriculture by the nature of farming system (Boserup, 1970). There are the "female farming system" present in Africa, where 'hoe cultivation' is practiced and there are the "male farming system" prevalent in Asia, where plough cultivation is practiced. In the 'female farming system', most of the work related to food production is done by women. The sedentary farming communities in Asia are 'male farming system' where men, plough or do some other hard work, while women associate with the men in harvesting, weeding, and other allied activities (Acharaya, 1987). Boserup, was of the view that in shifting cultivation it is the women folk who enjoy a prominent position precisely because of their higher participation in work as well as other productive activities and hence an enhanced social status. In the plough-based, male centric cultivation, women are totally exempted from working in the fields and hence men occupy a prominent place. Thus by linking Boserups argument to ownership of land, we find that female labour participation is higher in the tribal regions because of the prevalence of Jhum cultivation compared to the settled cultivation, where there is private ownership of land and hence a lower status of women.

The north-eastern region is predominantly inhabited by large numbers of tribal community in general and Arunachal in particular. The North-Eastern Region of India, comprising the states of Arunachal Pradesh, Assam, Manipur, Meghalaya, Mizoram, Nagaland, Sikkim and Tripura, lies between 21.5°N to 29.5° N latitude and 85.5° E to 97.5° E longitude. Majority of the population in the region is mainly dependent on agriculture and land-based activities. The tribal population of the country, as per 2011 Census, is 10.43 crore, constituting 8.6 per cent of the total population. 89.97 per cent of them live in rural areas and 10.03 per cent in urban areas. The decadal population growth of the tribal's from Census 2001 to 2011 has been 23.66 per cent against the 17.69 per cent of the entire population (Statistical Profile of Scheduled Tribes in India, 2013).

In the tribal regions of North East India, more specifically in Arunachal Pradesh women are engaged in agriculture, cooking, housekeeping, child care, fetching fuel wood and water, care of livestock, storing grains etc. They also play an important role in gathering forest products for domestic consumption as well as for commercial use. Much of the work which is of importance for the maintenance for families is largely done by women. According to anthropologists and some historians, women were the major producers of food, textiles and handicraft throughout human history and continue to provide a major labour input, in production and in the small scale subsistence sectors. Mostly women's work is not visible or partially accounted for in the data on workforce participation. Beneria in a study has observed that there is often underestimation of women's work in four areas of activity, namely: (a) Subsistence production, (b) Informal paid work, (c) Domestic production and related task, and (d) Volunteer work (Beneria, 1992). Women's work also differs according to age, gender, income, occupational group, location, size and structure of family. As women's work is mostly for self-consumption, much of the work they do is not recognized as 'work' in national income statistics. Women's low level participation in paid work does not imply that they have less work burden. They disproportionately have higher share in reproductive responsibility, including rearing and caring of children and also other types of domestic work. In addition to it women perform most of the onerous and tedious task and also spent considerable time and energy in doing unpaid domestic work along with host of 'productive' and income generating activities, but their contribution remains undervalued and unrecognized.

In Arunachal Pradesh, underestimation of female work is far more serious given the relative importance of subsistence production and low level of commercialization of economy. As per the 2011 census, female work participation rate in the state of Arunachal Pradesh was 35.4 per cent as compared to 25.5 per cent at the national level. Rao, has thrown some light on women's work, distribution of work load and decision making in Arunachal Pradesh. The author reveals that majority of the women, work on an average for 8-12 hours a day. Women attend to activities like cooking, fetching water, washing clothes, upkeep of houses, collecting firewood, collection of vegetables and fruits from forest, caring of children, agriculture, feeding animals, preparation of rice beer and social visits. Average work load (hour/day) of respondents hovered around 12 hours a day. Minor variation in workload was also observed across the districts. On 'exchange of labour', majority of the respondent reported that there was a need for it. On an average, 4.5 days of advance notice was required for getting such labour. Factors like number of *jhum* plots, numbers of animals, years of schooling, and index of awareness were found to be positive and significant. Decision-making regarding important activities were decided by husbands, while decisions associated with responsibilities and duties of use value were left to women. Thus, it was observed that there was a positive change among younger generation and they were actively participating in making variety of decisions (Rao, 2003).

Data Source and Methods

The study is based on the primary and secondary sources. Primary data are collected through time use survey in four district of Arunachal Pradesh, namely East Siang, Lohit, West Kameng and Lower Subansiri. Through time use survey, the chapter tries to highlight the time spent by women on different activities in rural areas and also the women's work burden across the districts. The Secondary data are mainly from the various reports of the Census, as well as reports from Statistical Profile on Women Labour and Labour Bureau Ministry of Labour and Employment, Government of India. The chapter is organised in the following way, Section I deals with Introduction, followed by the data source, Section III deals with the female work participation in the North East region, followed by the work participation rate in Arunachal Pradesh, Section IV deals with women's contribution of their time in various activities in rural Arunachal and finally conclusion has been placed in the last section.

Trends in Female Work Participation in North East India

The data of various census years in the table highlights the female WPR in North East India. The female WPR in North East Region (NER) is high compared to rest of India. The region is predominantly inhabited by tribal population and many scholars in their studies have pointed out that in general tribal women do more physical work in forests and in agricultural fields than the tribal men (Gummadi, 2014; Upadhyay, 2013). Though the general trend in the WPR for female shows a declining trend, but in the NER, some States like Nagaland, Tripura and Sikkim show an increasing trend over the last three decade as shown in Figure 20.1.

Table 20.1: Female Work Participation Rate in North East India

Sl. No.	*State/Union Territories*	*Female Work Participation Rate*		
		1991	*2001*	*2011*
1	2	3	4	5
1	Arunachal Pradesh	37.5	36.5	35.4
2	Assam	21.6	20.7	22.5
3	Manipur	39.0	39.0	38.6
4	Meghalaya	34.9	35.1	32.7
5	Mizoram	43.5	47.5	36.2
6	Nagaland	38.0	38.1	44.1
7	Sikkim	30.4	38.6	39.6
8	Tripura	13.8	21.1	23.6
9	**All India**	**22.27**	**25.63**	**25.5**

Source: Statistical Profile on Women Labour of various years, Labour Bureau, Ministry of Labour and Employment, Government of India, Chandigarh/Shimla.

The state-wise comparison of FWPR shows that except for Assam and Tripura, all other States in NER have higher FWPR compared to that of all India average during the year 1991. The State of Mizoram has the highest FWPR with 43.5 per cent, followed by Manipur (39.0%), Nagaland (38.0%), and Arunachal Pradesh (37.5%). Tripura has the lowest FWPR (13.8%) during the same year. Even during 2001, Mizoram recorded the highest FWPR of 47.5 per cent which is four percentage point higher compared to previous census period, followed by Manipur (39.0%), Sikkim (38.6%), Nagaland (38.1%), and Arunachal Pradesh (36.5%). It is to be noted that during 2001, only Assam and Tripura recorded the lowest FWPR compared to that of all India average. Though the figure of Tripura shows 8 percentage point increase over the last census of 1991 but in case of Assam it shows a fall of 1 percentage point in the FWPR during the same time period.

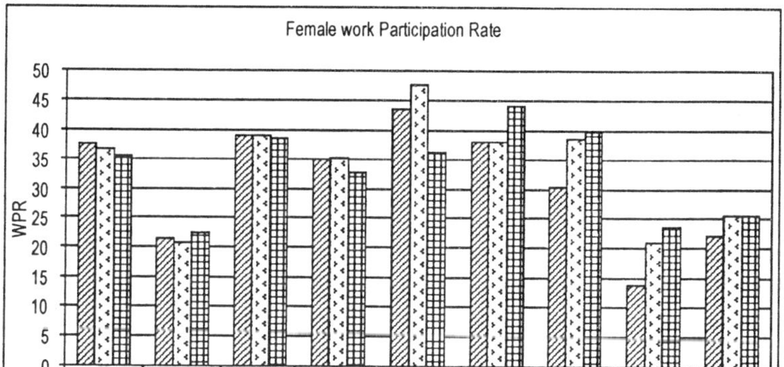

	Arunachal Pradesh	Assam	Manipur	Meghalaya	Mizoram	Nagaland	Sikkim	Tripura	All India
1991	37.5	21.6	39	34.9	43.5	38	30.4	13.8	22.27
2001	36.5	20.7	39	35.1	47.5	38.1	38.6	21.1	25.63
2011	35.4	22.5	38.6	32.7	36.2	44.1	39.6	23.6	25.5

Fig. 20.1: Female Work Participation Rate in North East Region

Source: Statistical Profile on Women Labour of various years, Labour Bureau. Ministry of Labour and Employment, Government of India, Chandigarh/Shimla.

The Census of 2011 shows some what a different picture compared to 1991 and 2001 data. Nagaland recorded the highest FWPR (44.1%) among all the North Eastern states and registered an increase in 6 percentage point over the last census year; while on the other hand, the state of Sikkim recorded the second highest FWPR with 39.6 per cent followed by Manipur with 38.6 per cent. Further, the State of Mizoram registered a fall by 11 percentage points in its FWPR, though the state of Assam showed an improvement of 2 percentage point increase over the last census year. During 2011, the FWPR of Assam and Tripura were below the national average of 25.5 per cent.

Figure 20.2 clearly reflects that the State of Arunachal Pradesh and Manipur have a declining trend in FWPR, whereas Assam, Meghalaya and Mizoram show a fluctuating trend during the same time period.

Work Participation Rate in Arunachal Pradesh: A District Level Analysis

Arunachal Pradesh is predominately a hilly state. Agriculture and animal husbandry is the main occupation in the rural areas. Women in the rural areas contribute immensely to agriculture especially in "Jhum" cultivation. The system of Jhum cultivation or shifting cultivation is widely prevalent in the State and it is one of the important means of livelihood. In fact the system of Jhumming is closely associated with the culture and tradition of the tribes of Arunachal Pradesh (Murtem *et. al., 2008*). Though the prevalence of the Jhumming system in State is reduced to some extent due to government intervention and environment concerns but still in remote part, it is still practiced by the tribal population of Arunachal Pradesh.

The district level work participation rate (WPR) of Arunachal Pradesh for various years is shown in Table 20.2. In 1991, the total WPR in Arunachal Pradesh stood at 46.24 per cent. At a disaggregate level, the district of Tawang has the highest WPR both in case of male (61.71%) and female (48.38%). The second highest WPR is observed in Upper Siang (52.41%), followed by Tirap (51.79%), and East Kameng (50.77%). The district of Papumpare has the lowest WPR with 40.22 per cent during the same time period. As far as the male WPR is concerned, after Tawang (61.71%) the district of Upper Siang has the second highest male WPR, followed by Dibang Valley (56.11%) and West Kameng (55.88%). For female WPR, Tawang has the highest participation rate with 48.38 per cent followed by East Kameng (47.43%), Tirap (47.08%) and Lower Subansiri (42.78%). The lowest male WPR is observed in the East Siang (49.94%) and in case of female WPR it is Papumpare district which has the lowest with 26.31 per cent during 1991.

In the year 2001, the total WPR in Arunachal Pradesh stood at 43.97 per cent, which was 2 percentage point lower compared to 1991 data. The districts level analysis shows that Tawang has the highest WPR (56.3%) followed by Upper Siang (51.3%) and Tirap (48.84%), while on the other hand the district of Papumpare (36.32%) has the lowest WPR in the State. In case of male WPR, Tawang has the highest (64.55%), followed by West Kameng (58.4%) and Upper Siang (57.34%). For female also, it is observed that the district of Tawang has the highest FWPR (45.71%), followed by Tirap (43.23%) and Lower Subansiri (44.5%). So far as the State level figure for male and female WPR is concerned it is 50.69 and 36.45 per cent respectively during 2011.

Table 20.2: District Level Work Participation Rate (Rural + Urban) of Arunachal Pradesh: 1991-2011

Districts	*1991*			*2001*			*2011*		
	Total	*Male*	*Female*	*Total*	*Male*	*Female*	*Total*	*Male*	*Female*
Tawang	55.61	61.71	48.38	56.31	64.55	45.71	57.15	67.08	43.25
West Kameng	44.08	55.88	29.72	46.09	58.40	29.69	50.62	61.34	37.52
East Kameng	50.77	53.98	47.43	45.42	48.63	42.76	40.30	42.36	38.30
Papum Pare	40.22	51.78	26.31	36.32	46.71	24.79	37.25	46.27	28.05
Upper Subansiri	47.38	51.37	42.78	40.22	44.17	36.12	39.99	42.86	37.11
West Siang	43.14	50.20	35.05	41.30	47.07	34.95	43.80	50.12	37.00
East Siang	41.24	49.94	31.31	38.45	45.41	31.01	40.54	47.07	33.87
Upper Siang	52.41	58.64	44.83	51.30	57.34	44.17	49.95	53.31	46.18
Changlang	45.53	53.15	36.70	47.88	52.82	42.43	42.48	51.11	33.16
Tirap	51.79	55.85	47.08	48.84	52.13	45.23	44.80	47.82	41.61
Lower Subansiri	50.12	53.21	46.88	46.08	47.63	44.50	36.37	41.44	31.23
Kurung Kumey	NA	NA	NA	NA	NA	NA	41.32	40.67	41.95
Dibang Valley	45.77	56.11	32.65	44.31	52.53	34.51	44.42	50.48	36.96
L/Dibang Valley	NA	NA	NA	NA	NA	NA	41.28	50.27	31.60
Lohit	44.12	55.31	30.09	42.04	51.38	31.16	41.82	51.05	31.70
Anjaw							49.61	54.09	44.28
Arunachal Pradesh	**46.24**	**53.76**	**37.49**	**43.97**	**50.69**	**36.45**	**42.47**	**49.06**	**35.44**

Note: NA (Not available).

Source: Upadhyay and Mishra (2005), Arunachal Pradesh HDR (2005) and for 2011 WPR: Author's own calculation from Census 2011 data.

In 2011, the total work participation in Arunachal Pradesh was 42.47 per cent, and the male WPR was 49.06 per cent which was much higher than the female WPR (35.44%). The disaggregate district level data show that Tawang has the highest WPR with 57.15 per cent followed by West Kameng (50.62%) and Upper Siang (49.95%), while, the district of Lower

Subansiri has the lowest WPR with 36.37 per cent. In case of male WPR, Tawang has the highest participation rate with 67.08 per cent, followed by West Kameng (61.34%) and Anjaw (54.09%), while the lowest male WPR is observed in Kurung Kumey district (40.67%). Female WPR figure shows that Upper Siang has the highest participation rate with 46.18 per cent, followed by Anjaw with 44.28 per cent, and Tawang with 43.25 per cent. The lowest participation rate for female is observed in Papumpare district (28.05%).

Time Use Pattern of Women in Rural Arunachal Pradesh

Women constitute 48 per cent of total population in India and 47 per cent in Arunachal Pradesh according to the Census of 2011. The hard working women of rural areas of the State are still relegated in different studies due to geographical isolation in general and lack of data set in particular. However, most of the women's works are not assessed in the traditional framework of national statistics. In such a situation, women's contribution to Gross State Domestic Product (GSDP) are hidden both in the National and the State economy. Work that does not receive direct remuneration falls under the purview of unpaid work and its size is higher in developing countries as compared to developed countries. This is because of significant prevalence of both SNA and non-SNA work in these economies. Some of the characteristics of developing countries like poverty, unemployment, prevalence of large informal sector, lack of human development, gender disparities can be well defined only if unpaid work is well analysed. Non-SNA unpaid work which is also known as care economy plays a vital role in those developing countries where infrastructure and public services are very weak (**Hirway, 2015**). Indian economy is not an exception to it. Thus, collection of statistics for unpaid work for policy formulation is the need of the hour.

Time Use Statistics (TUS) is an instrument to capture the comprehensive information of unpaid work. It provides detail information on human activities and how individuals spend their time on SNA and Non-SNA activities. The allocation of time for each activity over 24 hours of a day or seven days of a week are quantitatively summarised in TUS. In early years of twentieth century, TUS was used to understand lifestyle and social life of people where no information was available in conventional statistics. Later on, especially in the last few decades, need was felt to measure invisible unpaid work done by both men and women and their contribution to human welfare. Unpaid activities are primarily of two types, those which need to be included in economic activities (as per the SNA 1993) and those which fall outside the Production Boundary of the SNA, but fall within the General Production Boundary. The activities include household management, care activities, production of goods for self-consumption, collection of fuel, fodder, water, fruits, other services like transporting children, repairing household durables, social work etc. These activities certainly lead to human welfare and more women than men are involved in these activities. Sometimes, these activities are also called Gross Household Product (GHP). Therefore, TUS can be a novel approach for understanding the contribution of those activities in human welfare. It includes non-market activities too which are always under-measured in the conventional statistics.

Weekly Average Time Spent on Different Activities

In rural part of Arunachal Pradesh time utilisation pattern of men and women in different activities to a great extent is influenced by its geographical location and also agricultural season. Since, agricultural and allied activities are common practice in the rural part of the State, their time allocations in various activities also varies from hills to plain. Thus the present chapter deals with the time spent by gender in SNA, ESNA and Non-SNA activities in all the four districts which comprise four villages in the two hill districts and four villages in the plain districts.

On an average, weekly time spent on different activities are shown in Table 20.3 at an aggregate level. The figures at district level in general reveal that females both in the hills and plains are spending much of their time in SNA primary activities, except in case of district Lower Subansiri, where the difference in time spent by both male and female is very negligible in this district. Thus, women are still an integral part or may be considered as the backbone in the agricultural sector in rural areas. It is also to be noted that in the figures of the combine village total, women spent 31 hours in SNA primary activity whereas; in case of their male counterparts it is 28 hours on an average in a week. A comparative analysis of the hill and plain district figures shows that in both plain districts women spent much of their time in these activities compared to men. In case of hill districts, in Dumkho-Morsing and Michi-Bamin village men spent around 4 hours and 1 hour more than women respectively, but rest of the villages in the hills follows the same pattern as that of the plains.

In case of SNA secondary and SNA Tertiary activities, which is considered as male dominated activities, the figures from the sample villages reveals the same. Also the figures of the combined total shows that males spend 6 and 19.5 hours a week on an average and that of the women is much less. Irrespective of male and female in all the sample villages, the total time spent both on secondary and tertiary SNA activity is 3 and 13 hours respectively. On the other hand the figures of total SNA activity show that males spend much of their time than females in all villages, irrespective of hill and plain districts. Thus, the combined total figure shows that men and women spend 54 and 39.5 hours in a week on an average.

In case of extended SNA (ESNA) activities which include household maintenance, management, caring for children, sick and elderly members of the household etc., is always the responsibility of women. In rural areas apart from working in the agricultural field, women have a compulsion to do these activities too. The figures reveal that if women devote 100 per cent of their time in these activities, male on the other hand are contributing less than 50 per cent of their time. For example see Table 20.3.

The figures of combine total shows that woman spends around 44 hours on an average in a week on ESNA, while men contribute only 18 hours. Further, this pattern is followed in all the districts as well as the villages of the sample. In non-SNA activities also women spend less time compared to that of men.

Percentage of Weekly Average Time Spent by Gender in Sample Village: Activity-wise Classification

The percentage of weekly average time spent on different activities is shown in Table 20.4 combined total figures show that in SNA primary activities women and men spent 18.7 and 17 hours respectively. Whereas in SNA secondary and tertiary activities, it is found that men spend 3.5 per cent and 11.6 per cent and for women it is 0.4 per cent and 4.4 per cent in the sample villages. Thus, the percentage of time spent under SNA primary activities for both men and women was found to be 32.1 and 23.5 per cent in combined total. Around 28 per cent of the total time is spent by both men and women in SNA total category in the sample villages. In case of ESNA and Non-SNA activities, the figures from the combined total in the sample villages shows that, women spend more percentage of their time in ESNA activities that is around 26 per cent. On

Table 20.3: Weekly Average Time Spent on Different Activity (District level)

Activity	*Village*	*Gender*	*SNA Pry*	*SNA Sec*	*SNA Ter*	*SNA Total*	*ESNA*	*Non-SNA*
(1)	(2)	(3)	(4)	(5)	(6)	(7)	(8)	(9)
East Siang	I	M	24.6	3.7	19.5	47.8	15.9	104.2
		F	30.1	0.1	3.2	33.5	46.0	88.5
		T	27.5	1.8	10.9	40.2	31.9	95.8
	II	M	24.4	3.4	23.0	50.8	15.8	101.4
		F	30.7	0.0	3.3	34.1	49.8	84.1
		T	27.5	1.7	13.4	42.6	32.4	93.0
	Total	M	24.5	3.5	21.3	49.4	15.8	102.8
		F	30.4	0.1	3.3	33.8	47.8	86.4
		T	27.5	1.8	12.1	41.4	32.2	94.4
Lohit	III	M	27.8	5.0	12.6	45.4	19.1	103.5
		F	31.9	0.1	2.5	34.5	46.9	86.5
		T	29.9	2.5	7.3	39.7	33.6	94.7
	IV	M	24.6	2.6	28.7	55.9	12.6	99.5
		F	32.4	0.1	5.8	38.4	42.2	87.3
		T	28.6	1.4	17.0	46.9	27.7	93.2
	Total	M	26.2	3.8	20.6	50.6	15.9	101.5
		F	32.1	0.1	4.1	36.4	44.7	86.9
		T	29.3	1.9	12.1	43.3	30.7	94.0
West Kameng	V	M	36.4	5.3	18.0	59.6	21.4	86.9
		F	32.8	1.3	15.3	49.4	40.1	78.6
		T	34.5	3.3	16.7	54.4	30.8	82.7
	VI	M	31.7	11.0	14.3	57.0	18.5	92.5
		F	37.5	0.6	4.9	43.0	40.4	84.6
		T	34.7	5.7	9.5	49.8	29.8	88.4
	Total	M	34.1	8.1	16.2	58.4	20.0	89.7
		F	35.1	0.9	10.1	46.2	40.2	81.6
		T	34.6	4.4	13.1	52.1	30.3	85.5
Lower Subansiri	VII	M	24.1	0.8	22.5	55.4	23.5	89.1
		F	26.6	0.8	13.7	41.0	42.4	84.6
		T	25.3	4.8	18.1	48.2	32.9	86.9
	VIII	M	34.2	7.3	17.5	58.9	18.6	90.4
		F	29.9	2.5	9.7	42.1	42.8	83.0
		T	32.0	4.9	13.6	50.5	30.7	86.7
	Total	M	29.1	8.1	20.0	57.2	21.0	89.8
		F	28.2	1.6	11.7	41.5	42.6	83.8
		T	28.7	4.8	15.8	49.4	31.8	86.8
Combine Total		M	28.5	6.0	19.5	54.0	18.3	95.7
		F	31.5	0.7	7.3	39.5	43.8	84.6
		T	30.0	3.3	13.3	46.6	31.3	90.1

Note: 1. M = Male; F = female and T = Total

2. Village I is Mongku, Village II is Yagrung, Village III is Loiliang, Village IV is Danglat, Village V is Dumkho-Morsing, Village VI is Kalaktang Village, Village VII is Hari-I and Village VIII is Bamin-Michi

Source: Field Survey, 2015-16.

Table 20.4: Percentage of Weekly Average Time Spent on Different Activities (District Level)

District	*Village*	*Gender*	*SNA Pry*	*SNA Sec*	*SNA Ter*	*SNA Total*	*ESNA*	*Non-SNA*
East Siang	I	M	14.6	2.2	2.2	28.5	9.5	62
		F	17.9	0.1	0.1	19.9	27.4	52.7
		T	16.4	1.1	1.1	23.9	19	57.1
	II	M	14.5	2.0	2.0	30.3	9.4	60.4
		F	18.3	0.0	0.0	20.3	29.6	50.1
		T	16.4	1.0	1.0	25.4	19.3	55.3
	Total	M	14.6	2.1	2.1	29.4	9.4	61.2
		F	18.1	0.0	0.0	20.1	28.5	51.4
		T	16.4	1.1	1.1	24.6	19.2	56.2
Lohit	I	M	16.5	3.0	3.0	27.0	11.4	61.6
		F	19	0.1	0.1	20.5	27.9	51.5
		T	17.8	1.5	1.5	23.7	20.0	56.3
	II	M	14.6	1.6	1.6	33.3	7.5	59.2
		F	19.3	0.1	0.1	22.8	25.1	52.0
		T	17.0	0.8	0.8	27.9	16.5	55.5
	Total	M	8.7	0.9	0.9	19.8	4.5	35.2
		F	11.5	0.1	0.1	13.6	15.0	30.9
		T	10.1	0.5	0.5	16.6	9.8	33.0
West Kameng	I	M	21.6	3.1	3.1	35.5	12.8	51.7
		F	19.5	0.8	0.8	29.4	23.9	46.8
		T	20.6	1.9	1.9	32.4	18.4	49.2
	II	M	18.9	6.6	6.6	34	11.0	55.1
		F	22.3	0.4	0.4	25.6	24.0	50.4
		T	20.6	3.4	3.4	29.6	17.7	52.6
	Total	M	20.3	4.8	4.8	34.7	11.9	53.4
		F	20.9	0.6	0.6	27.5	24.0	48.6
		T	20.6	2.6	2.6	31	18.0	50.9
Lower Subansiri	I	M	14.3	5.3	5.3	33	14.0	53.0
		F	15.8	0.5	0.5	24.4	25.2	50.4
		T	15.1	2.9	2.9	28.7	19.6	51.7
	II	M	20.3	4.3	4.3	35.1	11.1	53.8
		F	17.8	1.5	1.5	25	25.5	49.4
		T	19.1	2.9	2.9	30.1	18.3	51.6
	Total	M	17.3	4.8	4.8	34	12.5	53.4
		F	16.8	1.0	1.0	24.7	25.3	49.9
		T	17.1	2.9	2.9	29.4	18.9	51.7
All Combine Total		M	17.0	3.5	3.5	3.5	10.9	57.0
		F	18.7	0.4	0.4	0.4	26.1	50.4
		T	17.9	2.0	2.0	2.0	18.6	53.6

Note: 1. M = Male, F = Female and T = Total.

2. Village I is Mongku, Village II is Yagrung, Village III is Loiliang, Village IV is Danglat, Village V is Dumkho-Morsing, Village VI is Kalaktang Village, Village VII is Hari-I and Village VIII is Bamin-Michi.

Source: Field Survey, 2015-16.

the other hand, men spend around 11 per cent. And in Non-SNA activities, it is 50.4 per cent for women and 57 per cent for men. Thus, women generally spend most of their time in agriculture and household activities.

At disaggregated level the district figures shows that women in hills and plains spend most of their time in SNA primary activities. The total figures of plain districts show that in East Siang around 18 per cent of their time is spent by women in these activities and that for Lohit it is 11.5 per cent. And in case of hill districts, women in West Kameng and Lower Subansiri spend around 21 per cent and 17 per cent respectively. In case of male, their contribution to SNA primary activity is low compared to that of women in the three districts of East Siang, Lohit and West Kameng. Exception is Lower Subansiri, where mens contribution is high compared to women by 1 percentage point.

In SNA secondary and tertiary activity, it is found that men spend more percentage of their total time to that of women in both plains and hill districts. Figures of the plain districts show that in East Siang men spend around 2 per cent of their time in SNA secondary and women spend only 1 per cent. In Lohit, figures for men and women in same activity are 0.9 per cent and 0.1 per cent respectively. On the other hand, in hill district of West Kameng, men spend 4.8 per cent and that for women is 0.6 per cent.

Lower Subansiri figure shows that men spend around 5 per cent of their total time in SNA secondary and that for women it is 1 per cent only. Further, in case of SNA tertiary activity which includes trade, business and services; figures reveals a vast disparity among men and women in their percentage of total time contribution. In East Siang, men spend around 13 per cent of their average time and that of women it is only 2 per cent. In the same way, figures of Lohit show that men spend around 10 per cent and that for women it is 2 per cent. However, in hill districts, the figure shows that both men and women more or less equally contribute their time in SNA tertiary activity. In West Kameng, where men spend around 10 per cent women spend 6 per cent of their total time in the same activity. The figure for Lower Subansiri shows that men spend around 12 per cent and women spend 7 per cent of their time on weekly average basis. Finally, the total SNA figures shows that in all the four district, men spend more of their time in these category than female.

From Table 20.4, the figure of ESNA shows that in all the villages of the sample districts, women spend almost more than double of their time in these activities. Thus, the figure in the plain district shows that women in East Siang spend around 29 per cent whereas men spend around 9 per cent at the same time. Women in Lohit used to spend 15 per cent of their time in ESNA activities, whereas men spend only 4.5 per cent. In case of the hill district, the figure of West Kameng shows that around 24 per cent of total time is spent by women in the same activity. On the other hand, it is around 12 per cent for men. Likewise in Lower Subansiri, it is around 25 per cent for women and for men it is 12.5 per cent. As far as Non-SNA activity is concerned women in all the sample villages spend less time as compared to that of men.

Proportionate Share of Time Spent by Gender and Work Burden on Different Activities

Table 20.5 shows the proportionate time spent on different activities by gender and the work burden on women. The proportionate share of time spent by women to that of men is calculated to see the work burden among women in the sampled districts and villages. The table reveals that work burden for women is high in SNA primary and ESNA activities. It is to be noted that, men are generally engaged in paid job, therefore, their contribution in SNA secondary and tertiary activities are found to be high in the sampled villages. Further, the total combined figures reveal that women's proportionate shares of time in SNA primary activities are high and their overall work burden is also high. In case of ESNA activities too, the work burden for women was found to be high.

At a disaggregate level, the figures reveal that irrespective of hill and plain districts, women's over all work burden in SNA primary activities are found to be high. A comparative analysis of hill and plain areas shows that women in plains have more work burden compared to women in the hills in SNA primary activities. This is mainly because of the fact that in plains, agriculture and farming activities continue throughout the year while in the hills the same activities are done on seasonal basis. However, it is to be noted that in one village each in the two hill districts, men were found to be working more compared to women in SNA primary activities, i.e. in Dumkho-Morsing in West Kameng and Bamin-Michi in Lower Subansiri districts. In the same manner work burden for women is high in ESNA activities both in hill and plain districts.

Conclusion

Women in Arunachal Pradesh in particular and India in general have been doing different unpaid works which are generally designated under

Table 20.5: Proportionate Time spent by Gender and Work Burden (District Level)

Districts	*Village*	*Gender*	*SNA Pry*	*SNA Sec*	*SNA Ter*	*SNA Total*	*ESNA*	*Non-SNA*
East Siang	I	Male	44.9	96.5	85.8	58.8	25.7	54.1
		Female	55.1	3.5	14.2	41.2	74.3	45.9
		Work Burden	10.1	-92.9	-71.6	-17.6	48.6	-8.2
	II	Male	44.3	100	87.3	59.9	24	54.7
		Female	55.7	0	12.7	40.1	76	45.3
		Work Burden	11.4	-100	-74.6	-19.7	51.9	-9.3
Lohit	III	Male	46.5	97.3	83.8	56.8	28.9	54.5
		Female	53.5	2.7	16.2	43.2	71.1	45.5
		Work Burden	6.9	-94.6	-67.5	-13.7	42.2	-8.9
	IV	Male	43.1	94.7	83.2	59.3	23	53.3
		Female	56.9	5.3	16.8	40.7	77	46.7
		Work Burden	13.7	-89.3	-66.3	-18.6	54	-6.5
West Kameng	V	Male	52.6	80.8	54	54.7	34.8	52.5
		Female	47.4	19.2	46	45.3	65.2	47.5
		Work Burden	-5.2	-61.5	-8	-9.4	30.3	-5.1
	VI	Male	45.9	94.6	74.5	57	31.4	52.2
		Female	54.1	5.4	25.5	43	68.6	47.8
		Work Burden	8.3	-89.2	-49	-14.1	37.2	-4.4
Lower Subansiri	VII	Male	47.5	92	62.3	57.5	35.6	51.3
		Female	52.5	8	37.7	42.5	64.4	48.7
		Work Burden	5.0	-83.9	-24.6	-14.9	28.7	-2.6
	VIII	Male	53.3	74.3	64.4	58.3	30.3	52.2
		Female	46.7	25.7	35.6	41.7	69.7	47.8
		Work Burden	-6.7	-48.6	-28.9	-16.7	39.4	-4.3
All Combine Total		Male	47.6	89.3	72.7	57.7	29.4	53.1
		Female	52.4	10.7	27.3	42.3	70.6	46.9
		Work Burden	4.9	-78.7	-45.3	-15.5	41.1	-6.1

Note: Village I is Mongku, Village II is Yagrung, Village III is Loiliang, Village IV is Danglat, Village V is Dumkho-Morsing, Village VI is Kalaktang Village, Village VII is Hari-I and Village VIII is Bamin-Michi.

Source: Field Survey, 2015-16.

extended SNA activities. Unpaid extended work basically includes (a) cooking, cleaning, washing etc., (b) taking care of children, elderly people and disabled etc., (c) production of goods for self-consumption, and (d) transporting of children to school and other voluntary social works.

Thus, it is seen that most of these extended SNA activities are performed by women. It is, therefore, rational for the policy makers, statistician and researchers to enumerate women activities under time use statistics in order to get the real picture of development. The present chapter highlighted that women are working more than man in the unpaid care work and hardly get any time for self-maintenance.

Some of the non-economic activities which essentially generate both goods and services are produced by households without undergoing monetary transactions. These kind of non-economic activities come under extended System of National Accounts (SNA). Secondly, there are some personal activities which cannot be delegated to others and is known as non-SNA activities. However, all human activities contribute to human well-being. But all such activities whether it is SNA, extended SNA or Non-SNA are not enumerated completely in the conventional statistics. Under such circumstances the conventional national statistics exclude a large part of unpaid activities performed by the people. In this regard the worst sufferers are women since most of their works are unpaid in nature.

References

Acharaya, Sarthi (1987). "Women participation in agricultural and rural activity", *Women and Rural Development in Third World*, Bombay: Tata Institute of Social Science.

Beneria, L. (1992). "Accounting for women's work: The progress of two decades", *World Development*, 20(11): 1547-1560.

Boserup, E. (1970). "*Women's Role in Economic Development*", George Lodon: Allen and Unwin.

Government of India (Various Years). *Statistical Profile on Women Labour*, Labour Bureau, Ministry of Labour and Employment, Government of India Chandigarh/Shimla.

Gummadi, Naresh (2014). "Work participation of tribal women in India: A development perspective", *IOSR Journal of Humanities and Social Science (IOSR-JHSS)*, Volume 19, Issue 12, Ver. II, pp. 35-38.

Hirway, Indira (2015). "Unpaid Work and the Economy, Linkages and their implications", Working Paper 838, Levy Economics Institute of Bard College, New York.

Kalpagam, U. (1999). "Women, work and domestic duties: Income planning for housewives", *Indian Journal of Labour Economics*, 42(4): 567-580.

Ministry of Tribal Affairs Statistical Division (2013). Statistical Profile of Schedule Tribal in India

Murtem, G., G.N. Sinha and J. Dopum (2008). "Jhumias view on shifting cultivation in Arunachal Pradesh", *Bulletin of Arunachal Forest Research,* 24(1&2): 35-40.

Rao, V.M. (2003). *Tribal Women of Arunachal Pradesh Socio-economic Status*, New Delhi: Mittal Publication.

Shelton, B.A. and John Daphne (1966). "The division of household labour", *Annual Review of Sociology*, 22: 299-322.

Shimray, U.A. (2004). "Women's work in naga society: Household work, workforce participation and division of labour", *Economic and Political Weekly*, 39(17): 1698-1711.

Upadhyay, Vandana (2013). "Patterns of Employment in Arunachal Pradesh: Implications for Inclusive Development", In: *Perspectives on North East India: Tradition and Modernity in Arunachal Pradesh,* edited by Sanjay Pulipaka, Rakhee Bhattacharjee and Saritk Chaudhuri. New Delhi: Anshah Publishing House, pp. 168-176.

Upadhyay, Vandana and Deepak K. Mishra (2005). *A Situational Analysis of Women and Girls in Arunachal Pradesh,* National Commission for Women, New Delhi.

21
Children in Drudgery
A Study of Arunachal Pradesh

Apilang Apum

Introduction

The problem of Child Labour is a complex phenomenon and it is not easy to identify and categorised the activities which can be included in Child Labour. Moreover, there is no universally accepted definition of child labour[1]. The activities in which children are engaged are very diverse; there are paid or unpaid works, work within one's own households or outside and some of them may work part-time and few may work full time. Therefore, different scholars have different views over the definition of Child Labour. At the most basic level, every researcher accepts the view that all children should be provided with basic education. However, in terms of non-schooling activities, there is a wide range of differing positions prevailing among the researchers as to what kind of activities should be identified as Child Labour. At one extreme, some take the view that all non-school and non-leisure activities of children constitute child labour. According to this view, child labour would include light work in household enterprises after school, or even help with domestic chores such as home cleaning or looking after younger siblings. Other observers maintain that child labour should include only those economic activities that deny a child the possibility of normal development into a responsible adult. This perspective reserves the term "Child Labour" for strenuous or hazardous employment in economic activities by younger children, as well as children in the worst form of child labour sectors (Child labour Manual). Census of India defines child labour as the participation of a child less than 17 years of age in any economically productive activity with or without compensation, wages or profit. Broadly we can define child labour as any activities that are harmful to the child not only physically but also mentally, emotionally, and socially, thereby affecting their education and spiritual development.

There have been a number of studies on Child Labour in the world and in India but only a few studies have been done in North East India, particularly in Arunachal Pradesh. Many researchers have studied the causes and the determinants of Child Labour, where they observed that Education plays a vital role in the elimination of child labour. Subhash Barman (2011) in his study found that a negative relationship exists between the level of education of the child and their parents with the participation of children in the workforce. Hence, as the level of education of parents improves the participation of children in the workforce declines. Gender discrimination exists among child labour. The nature of the job of boys and girls differs by industry and country. It is found that boys are more economically active than girls in Latin American countries like Bolivia and Colombia, but in African countries such as Cote d'Ivoire and Ghana, girls are more involved in economic activities. Further boys are found to be more employed in manufacturing, restaurants, trade, hotels, and transport, while girls are more employed in domestic work and in agriculture (World Bank: 2005). The employers prefer a child to an adult worker as they are cheap, productive and obedient. The other reason why there exists a demand for children is that children are supposed to be better than adults at tedious, mechanical jobs that require manual dexterity and nimbleness, rather than training and skills. As a result, they are considered more adept at labour-intensive work that categorises the method of production in small-scale units (Kiran Bhatty, 1996). Apart from these reasons, employers prefer children due to their sympathy for children's families, on such considerations that they can easily be removed, create little industrial relations problems and no need to pay retirement benefits (K. Rao and M. Rao, 1998).

Poverty is also one of the factors which force families to send their children to work. In a study of government-aided school in Delhi (2017), Farooq (2017) revealed that school children are compelled to work and shoulder the economic burden of their families and labour in *karkhanas*. Also a great deal of work, namely household work, child care etc. remain unnoticed, unappreciated and most importantly unpaid. Therefore, there is a need to revisit and treat children's work on par with adult labour, such that children enjoy better social and economic status (Gayathri, 2002). Neera Burra (2001) also argued that there is a need for widening the definition of Child Labour beyond wage employment, otherwise much of the economic contributions given by young girls are ignored and unnoticed. Particularly in rural areas, the children contribute a lot in the economic welfare of the family by engaging in different activities so that the adult would be free to work. This study is an attempt to highlight the various kinds of activities that children are engaged in the rural areas.

Objectives of the Study

The aim of this chapter is basically to identify the various kinds of activities where the children are engaged in the selected villages of Arunachal Pradesh.

Methodology

The study is descriptive and analytical in nature and is based on primary data. The sample has been selected purposively. It was conducted in two villages of Upper Siang district, namely Pasi and Damro village. An attempt was made to interview at least 15 per cent of the total households of the selected villages. Altogether 60 households were interviewed from both the villages. Only those households where there were children in the age group between 5-14 years were interviewed.

Results and Discussions

The sex composition of the children shows that out of a total of 60 children, 61.7 per cent were female and of the rest 38.3 per cent were males. Therefore, Result reveals that the number of female workers is much more than that of the male. The age group division of child worker shows that 38.3 per cent were in the age group of 5-9 years and as high as 61.7 per cent in the age group of 10-14 years.

Table 21.1: The Age Group Division of Child Worker

Sex	*Percentage*	*Age Group*	*Percentage*
Male	25.9	5-9	38.3
Female	74.1	10-14	61.7

Source: The primary field study data, conducted in January 2018.

In order to know their participation in work, they were asked if they had worked at least one hour during the past week, it was observed that majority of them, i.e. 72.2 per cent replied in affirmative, while 27.8 per cent said no.

Table 21.2: Percentage Distribution of Children on the Basis of Engagement in Work

Did you engage in any work at least one hour during the past week?	*Percentage*
Yes	72.2
No	27.8

Source: The primary field study data conducted in January 2018.

Children Activities

There were various activities in which the children were found to be engaged. As our first Prime Minister, Pt. Jawaharlal Nehru, had rightly said "Today's children are tomorrow's citizen", therefore, it is important to invest in children so that they would serve the country, society and home tomorrow. Children have the right to get compulsory education up to 14 years of age according to Art. 14(1) of the Constitution of India and they also have the right to enjoy leisure. However, many times they are deprived of their basic needs and leisure hours especially children belonging to the low-income families and in the rural areas. Therefore, in this section, an attempt has been made to identify a different kind of activities performed by the children.

Table 21.3: Percentage Distribution of Children on the Basis of Activities

Activities	*Yes (%)*	*No (%)*
Shopping	6.7	93.3
Cooking	11.7	88.3
Cleaning utensil	86.7	13.3
Washing clothes	23.3	76.7
Caring for siblings/Old	81.7	18.3
Poultry	22.2	
Husking	44.4	
Collect firewood for household use	90	10
During the past week when did you usually carry out these activities? Time		
Weekend	2	
Both before and after school	98	

Source: The primary field study data, conducted in January 2018.

The above table shows that 93.3 per cent of the children were not engaged in shopping. This may be because the study villages were situated in the rural areas and there was an only countable number of petty shops in the villages. In addition to this only 11.7 per cent of the children are found to be engaged in cooking which was quite obvious because the children hardly know how to cook. Further out of all the activities listed above, the three most important works where children were found to be engaged were, namely collecting firewood (90%), cleaning utensil (86.7%) and caring for siblings/old (81.7%). Most of the girls were also found to be engaged significantly in husking of grains (44.4%). Further, in order to know, during which time of the day the children would perform these activities, they were asked about the usual timing of their work, and it was found that as high as 98 per cent of the children said that they would do it both before and after they returned from the school. Before going to the school, they would do activities like husking and cleaning of utensils and after they returned from school, then they go for collecting firewood and go to the agricultural field to help their parents and also take care of their siblings. In some cases, it was found that when there is no one to take care of the younger siblings the parents would wait for their children to return from the school so that they can go for work. The life is challenging and the ambiance is not good for study at home. In such environment, it is a huge challenge for the children to excel in their studies. Simply teaching and getting admissions in the school is not sufficient for the growth and development of the children. A good and conducive study environment at home is very much required.

School Attendance

It was also felt important to know whether the children are attending school or not. As regard to their attendance it was found that 95 per cent of the children surveyed were studying in the school. However, 47.5 per cent of them had missed the school at least once in a week. On an average, they miss 2.11 days of school in a week. There were many reasons as to why they missed their classes. They missed their school because they had to help their parents in the agricultural field (50%), take care of siblings (39.3%), and help in household tasks (3.6%) (see Table 21.4).

Further, the male-female breakup shows that the female child misses school much more than that of a male child. This may be mainly because the female children have more engagement at home and they are better than male in terms of taking care of their siblings, helping in the

Table 21.4: Percentage Distribution of Children on the Basis of School Attendance

Are you attending school or pre-school during the current school year?	*Percentage*
Yes	**95**
No	**5**
Did you miss any school day during the past week	
Yes	**47.5**
No	**52.5**
Why did you miss school day(s) during the past week?	
Taking care of siblings	**39.3**
Helping parents in the agricultural field	**50**
Helping in household tasks	**3.6**
Others	**7.1**

Source: The primary field study data, conducted in January 2018.

agricultural field etc. In fact, the boys are not taught to do these activities. Also, the age group division shows that those who are in the age group of 5-9 years (52.2%) are missing school more than those in the age group 10-14 (55.6%) years. This may be because the parents take them to the agricultural field to carry their younger siblings (see Table 21.5).

Table 21.5: Percentage Distribution of Children on the Basis of Missing School Day

Did you miss any school day during the past week?	Sex		Age of the Children	
	Male	*Female*	*5-9*	*10-14*
Yes	43.8	48.8	52.2%	44.4%
No	56.3	51.2	47.8%	55.6%

Source: The primary field study data, conducted in January 2018.

Conclusion

The basic aim of this chapter was to identify a different kind of activities that the children are engaged in rural areas of Arunachal Pradesh. The children were found to engage in many activities and almost all of them were related to household activities. Since both, the study villages were situated in the backward region, so there were no hazardous industries, and hence no children were found to be working in hazardous activities as defined in the Child Labour Prohibition and Regulation Act (1986). However, even if they are not engaged in such activities, they were living a very difficult and challenging life. They had to carry firewood from the hilly jungles. Even though they have adapted to this kind of environment, also it is not free from risk i.e. risk, from falling down the dense hilly jungles, which can be a threat to their life. They also have to work before and after the school and therefore, they are overburdened and hence no time to study at home. No doubt more than 95 per cent of the children are attending school but simply attendance is not sufficient. One needs a conducive study environment at home for their healthy growth. Otherwise, such adverse environment at home leads to many dropouts, and the children end up doing the same activities that their parents do. In all these activities the female child is victimised. Therefore, there is a dire need of the uplift of the villages. The parents need to be taught not only about the importance of children education at school but also at home. There is also a need of continuous spending from the government through various schemes to uplift the socio-economic status of the poor. The present study also reinforces the findings of Neera Burra (2001) where she argued that there is a need of widening the definition of Child Labour beyond wage employment otherwise much of the economic contributions given by girls are ignored and unnoticed.

Note

1. Child labour statistics manual on methodologies for data collection through surveys, 2014, page no. 17.

References

Barman, S. (2011). "Socio-economic and demographic impact on child labour in India", *Journal of Alternative Perspectives in the Social Sciences*, *3*(2): 376-403.

Bhatty, K. (1996). "Child labour: Breaking the vicious cycle", *Economic and Political Weekly*, *31*(7): 384-386.

Burra, N. (2001). "Cultural stereotypes and household behaviour girl child labour in India", *Economic and Polical Weekly*, (February 3-10), pp. 481-488.

Gayathri, V. (2002). "Labour of children", *Economic and Polical Weekly*, (January 5), pp. 43-44.

Farooqi, F. (2017). "Silenced and marginalised voices from a Sarkari-aided school of Delhi", *Economic and Polical Weekly*, *III* (No. 38), 76-81.

Rao, K.H.R. and Rao, M.M. (1998). "Employer's view of child labour", *Indian Journal of Industrial Relations*, *34*(1): 15-38.

Ramachandran N. and Massun L. (2002). *Coming to Grips with Rural Child Work: A food Security Approach.* Insititute for Human Development.

Statistical Information and Monitoring Programme on Child Labour (SIMPO) Geneva, 2014.

22
Influence of Folklores on the Farm Culture in the Naga Hills
A Study of the Sumi Tribes of Nagaland

Lilika K. Zhimomi and *Papiya Dutta*

Introduction

Nagaland is the 16th state of the Indian Union. It came into existence on 1st December, 1963. It is located in the North-Eastern part of India. It lies between 25°12′N and 27°2′N latitude and between the longitudes 93°20′ E and 95°15′ E. It has an area of 16,579 sq. km. Nagaland is bounded by Myanmar to the east, Manipur to the south, Arunachal Pradesh to the north and Assam to the west. The precise account of the origin of the Nagas is shrouded in obscurity and is encapsulated in folklores and legends. After examining various sources Sanyu (1996:35) concluded that the Nagas belong to the Mongoloid racial stock and that their place of origin is Central China. The exact number of tribes is not known because they are not only confined to Nagaland but are scattered in the adjoining Indian states of Manipur, Assam, Arunachal Pradesh and also in Myanmar (Burma). Thus, the Naga inhabited area sometimes called Greater Nagaland is divided by state and national boundaries.

The Sumi tribe popularly known as the "Warrior Tribe" is one of the 16 recognised tribes of Nagaland inhabited dominantly in the district of Zunheboto and scattered in almost all the other districts in small number as well. Like all the other Naga tribes, agriculture is the main occupation of the Sumis. Land is the common property of a family and every member of the household has a customary ownership of the agricultural land. *Jhumming* is the most common agricultural practice of the Sumis which has significance on their culture till today. In the Sumi practice of cultivation, the arable lands are segregated in patches dividing them into a minimum of 7 and a maximum of 20 *Aluche* (groups) depending on the availability and fertility of the soil which in turn determines the fallow period, i.e. the cycle at which the land is cultivated. The fallow period over the years have shortened due to increase in the population that are dependent on the constant rather decreasing land. The land to be cultivated during a single season is decided by the *Akukau* (chief) or the *Awowu* (the priest). One patch of land is cultivated mostly only for a single season but it can sometimes be cultivated for successive seasons depending on the fertility of the soil. The farming operations begin by felling of trees which is used as firewood, construction purposes and for sale as well. Multiple crops are grown in the *Jhum* field; however, rice, millets and Job's tears are grown at the most along with many other secondary crops. The *Jhum* cycles starts in November. As the women folk engage themselves in clearing the old *Jhum* field, the men folks clear the new field simultaneously. This is followed by digging of little hollows by the men using *akuphu* (digging hoe) for the women to sowing the seeds which is then followed by the women crushing the earth and then filling up the hollows using a hoe made of bamboo or iron (*akuivo*). Harvest is done in the late September or early November depending on the climatic condition which calls for a celebration of a festival known as *Ahuna* with which the agriculture operation of that season concludes, after which they begin to organise for the next season and the cycle goes on.

Materials and Methods

The aim of the research is basically centred on the agrarian aspect followed by the folklores associated to it. The study was conducted among the Sumi tribes of Nagaland occupying the hill district of Zunheboto. The respondents of the study include purposively selected individuals belonging to various categories, such as member of cultural organisations, social sciences researchers, religious persons (priest) and elderly persons. The data were collected using unstructured interview schedule, recording an oral history tradition and consultation from expert in the field.

Influence of Folklores on Farming

The Nagas have always had an intimate relation with the nature; they perceive themselves as a part of the nature. They consider the mountains, hills, forests and rivers to be sacred and respected, for they are the source of all the good things which is said to have the power to affect crop and fertility—all believed to be controlled by supernatural forces. The continuous acquaintances with the nature have created a huge sense of attachment towards it. Their love and appreciation for the nature is profusely expressed in different forms of art and crafts, dress, ornaments, stories, songs of rich oral tradition. Agriculture is the main occupation of the people which is dominated by two types of cultivation, namely *Jhum* or Shifting or Slash and burn and Terrace rice cultivation. *Jhum* is however the popular farming system practiced by majority of the hill dwellers. The practice is mostly guided by indigenous knowledge which people embraces relentlessly. Farming in the Naga Hills is mostly imbedded in their cultural and religious beliefs.

It is said that in the field of agriculture, there can be no better technique than that what the hill dwellers have developed over the years. Without having to depend on the external forces, a simple farmer knows how to overcome the obstacles that come along the process of his strive for survival. Farming has been in practice in the hills of Nagaland as earliest as the arrival of the habitants and its obstacles are no alien to them. Trials and errors over the years of experimentation with the surroundings have paved ways for developing coping mechanisms utilizing the available resources. A farmer possesses an ample knowledge of his environment, he even knows the periods at which various activities must be undertaken. In case of farming, he knows exactly when to sow a particular kind of seeds, when it ripens and when it is time to be harvested. Characterised by various chain of events the farmer somehow find ways to accurately indicate different agricultural seasons.

Folk Tales/Folk Stories

The Sumi tribal farmers believe that the birds have innate ability to behave or react in accordance with the nature. They know when to start sowing of the paddy just by listening to the sound of the Cuckoo bird. There is a folktale associated to this bird that has a huge influence on their farm culture and has made them remember the seasons precisely. The villagers can as well predict the monsoon by observing the environment and correspondingly advances or delay the agricultural operations. As narrated by the natives, it is said that in one village of the Sumi tribes, there lived a son named Kasho with his father. As Kasho grew older he turned out to be a handsome young man who acquired the skills of hunting from his father and excelled in it. One day his father decided to check the credibility of his son's strength and courage by analysing how he would react when he's faced with certain circumstances. He quietly hid among the bushes in the forest where Kasho was out hunting. He then shook the bushes where he was in, to see if his son would flee in fear, but to his utter dismay Kasho pulled out his spear and threw right in the bushes where he was hiding killing him as the spear pierced through his heart. On realising what he had done, Kasho feeling guilty and remorseful quickly ran to his father's aid asking for forgiveness but the father told him not to feel guilty for killing him rather he expressed his pride for his son's bravery and courage. Now since he won't be around for cultivation, he told his son to always look out for the sound of a bird that would come as a reminder to indicate the time of sowing the seeds in the field. Saying this he succumbed to his injuries and passed away. The following season while Kasho waited for his father's signal, the villagers had already sown seeds which made Kasho impatient and disheartened. He started to organise the materials for farming thinking his father won't come. As he headed towards the field he heard the sound of a bird (Cuckoo) that sounded '*Kashopappu*' (Kasho's father). That was when he realised that it is indeed his father indicating him to go ahead with the farming operation. That year while all the crops of the villagers dried off as a result of sowing too early, Kasho's crop on the other hand yielded bountifully. To this day the farmers of the hills wait for the sound of Cuckoo to begin their operation.

Here is another folktale that has its significance till date. Once there was a farmer whose crop did not grow well, hence he began to worry that there won't be any harvest to feed his family. His grief was noticed by the earthworm, on enquiring about his sadness, the farmer told the earthworm that his soil has become very dry and the crops are not growing properly. The earthworm then came forward to help the farmer but on the condition that if it did, the man must not hate or despise them. The man was also asked not to crush them and in return they would make the land fertile for the crops to grow well. The man agreed to the conditions and declared that the curse will be upon him if he or his children despises or hurt the earthworm. From that time onwards the man yielded good harvest as the earthworm made the soil fertile.

Folk Songs (*Lejole*)

Lejole is a native term for Folk song. It is an art of expressing untold emotions and feelings. Folksongs play a significant role in the lives of the Sumi Nagas. It can be of many forms depending upon the situation on which it was sung. In the early days prior to the introduction of writing, the messages were carried on through songs and the stories were stored in the form of lyrics. Most importantly, Folksongs played a vital role during farming operations. It acted as an instrument of motivation to the farmers while labouring in the field. The farmers would sing together in harmony during the farming process. And sometimes womenfolk would sing to motivate the male labourer which enhances their ability to work efficiently. Today, with the invention of many modern types of gadgets, the farmers seldom need the folksongs to enhance their work. However, they are not completely out of practice. Now the folksongs have become a crucial part of every tribal festivals celebrated today though it has undergone a series of changes over the years. Nevertheless, the songs are still in practice and serves as a store house of the age old traditions. It is through these songs that the forgotten practices are revived. The song tell stories of the past and portray the life of the people through its melodies and lyrics.

Ayekuzule (Cotton Yarning/Spinning)

The Sumi Nagas cultivate variety of crops among which cotton used to be one of the prominent crops. *Ayekuzule* is a work folksong that is simultaneously and rhythmically sung in perfect coordination with action during the entire process of cotton yarning/spinning. This folksong is performed by the females; it helps them to carry out their work infused with fun and energy. After the harvest, the cotton is stored in the granary. On the day of the practice the women is supposed to keep her family members warm and fit. At a tender age a girl is trained well by her mother and the elders at *Iliki* (Morung). This is how a Sumi woman gets into the traditional structure of professional textile work and lives an independent life. Cotton spinning and manufacturing is done in two ways, at home and at *Iliki*. Working at home does not necessitate the folksong to be sung. While at *Iliki* folksong is a complementary and without which no activities are undertaken. Today the folksong is hardly performed at its true sense. It is now performed only in festivals and culture related events in composed contextual lyrics.

Rationality

Drawing a conclusion from the above folklores, it can be said that the

Sumi Nagas maintained a close relation with the nature. Due to which they have managed to coexist well, until the recent onslaught of the western elements. However, the practices have survived the transition partly due to the people's attachment to folk culture and mainly due to the applicability of the practices even today. The Cuckoo is a seasonal bird which immigrates to the Naga Hills during spring season, a season which is favourable for sowing seeds in the field. So, there may not be any evidences of the actual occurrence of these folktales like any other Naga tribal myths and legends, nevertheless the lesson it bears is still applicable today. In fact in the earlier days when there was barely any means to identify the months and dates for undertaking certain livelihood operations, these folktales reminded them of the seasons precisely. The fact that the sound of the Cuckoo bird is heard only in the spring season has been backed by a researcher Mahmood (2016) who says, "The breeding season of these Cuckoo species is from May to July in Indian Subcontinent" and the fact that the earthworms do fertile the soil is backed by the findings of a researcher Levelle (1988) who says, "Earthworms are important decomposers contributing to nutrient cycling processes" which has further been validated by Fredric (2013) who says, "Earthworm is a potential indicator of sustainability of agriculture practices that farmer could use thereby optimizing different farming system." Regarding the folksongs, researchers have proven that music is an art that can be of many forms, an element of motivation that has been acknowledged since long (Thomas Schafer, 2013). Different forms of music have different impact on the listeners depending on the intention on which it is made. Folksongs like any other music form, is a medium of disseminating a message to a target group which is now regarded as a source of many native legends that depicts the life and culture of the people during which it was made. It serves as a way of expressing one's emotion in a way more influencing than that expressed simply with words of mouth. Not only does it soothes the ear of the listeners but it also serves as a motivator when performed during work hours which is evident from the practice of the hill dwellers of the Naga Hills. Though the way in which it is performed varies from one tribe to another, nonetheless it always has a purpose and carries a message for a target group for whom it has been made. There are many other folklores which are the outcome of various chain of mysterious events which people still remembers, that may or may not have a physical trace but the message that it bears and the information it carries are still being applied by the farmers today.

Conclusion

Agriculture and Folklores are interlinked and both influence one another. Agriculture forms certain attributes of folklores while, folklores act as a guiding principle in agricultural operations. The foiklores which have been passed on from generation to generation portray the lifestyle and the social scenario of that particular period and give the sense of what the societies were like in the past. It reveals a lot about the people and their way of life. The Nagas in general have a strong sense of regard for the folklores due to the fact of their origin being basically shrouded in these folklores. The Nagas have always been a nature lover. In fact the early dwellers had a profound affection for the nature more than today, it is evident from the few unforgotten folklores preserved somehow in an oral form. All the attributes with which they are identified are in one way or the other influenced by the nature. The influences are evident in the way they dress, the food they eat, their agricultural operation and many other dimensions. The many forms of folktales and folksongs associated with different walks of life are the true gospel of how closely acquainted they were with their surrounding environment. They are known to have a good sense of relation and interaction the nature that includes birds, animals, forests, water etc. They realise that the sustenance of one depends on the wellbeing of the other and therefore have always found ways to maintain equilibrium with the nature. However, this noble intension is now hardly observed. With the fast pacing social, political and most importantly economic aspects, people are merely concerned about the conventional way. The primitive agrarian society is diminishing at an alarming rate. In fact in some areas the people have completely abandoned farm culture. They have been captured by the sizzling modern element that promises short term gains. With rapid increase in urban migration, it has become more difficult for the few surviving practitioners to pass on the traditional knowledge to the younger ones who like any other wishes to live the life comfortably with less hardship. Therefore, with almost all the practitioners gone and the possible successors showing less or no interest in learning them, let alone practice; it has become a necessity to codify these folklores and preserve it, so that the following generation could enjoy its benefit as well, or they would at least have the glimpse of their origin and safeguard their identity.

References

Chishi, D.H. (2009). *Introduction to Sutsah.* Dimapur, Indigenous Cultural Society.

Fredric, (2013). *Impacts of earthworm on soil components and dynamics, Areview,* Biotechnology, Agronomy, Society and Environment.

Hutton, J.H. (1921b). *The Sema Nagas.* London, Macmillan and Co. Limited.

K.M. Sreekumar, C.T. (2006). *Indigenous Knowledge of Farming in North Malabar.* New Delhi: Foundation Books Pvt. Ltd.

Khala, K. (2012). *Women and Agriculture in Nagaland: A Study of Sumi Customary Law and Customs.* Dimapur: Shikhu Scholastic Press.

Lavelle, P. (1988). "Earthworm activities and the soil system", *Biol. Fertil/Siols.* 6(3): 237-251.

Mahmood (2016). *Indian Cuckoo,* Birds of India, Bird World, http://indian birds.thedynamicsnature.com/2016/12/indiancuckoo-cuculuc-micropertus. html?m=1

M.P. Jayashree, F.M. (2005). "Influence of farming culture in rituals of north Malabar region of Kerala state", *An International Journal of Ethnobotanical Research, 2005*(1).

Nekha, K.N. (2015). *The Nagas, Culture and Tradiiton.* Dimapur: Heritage Publishing House.

NIENU, V. (2015). *Naga Cultural Milieu, An adaptaiton to mountain cosystem,* San Francisco: Dorylus Publishing Group (DGP).

Sanyu, V. (1996). *A History of Nagas and Nagaland,* New Delhi: Commonwealth Publishers.

Siddharth Edake, D.J. (2015). *A People's Biodiversity Registrar of Village Sukhai, Zunheboto, Nagaland,* New Delhi: The Energy and Resources Institute.

Souza, A.D. (2001). *Traditional System of Forest Conservation in the North East India, The Angami Tribe of Nagaland.* Guwahati: North East Social Research Centre.

Thomas Schafer, P.S. (2013, July 18). *Frontiers in Psychology,* Retrieved from Frontiers in Psychology Web site: http://www.frontiersin.org/articles/10.3389/fpsyg2013.00511/full

Index